Therapeutic Uses of Rap and Hip-Hop

Therapeutic Uses of Rap and Hip-Hop

Edited by
Susan Hadley and George Yancy

Routledge
Taylor & Francis Group
New York   London

Routledge
Taylor & Francis Group
711 Third Avenue
New York, NY 10017, USA

Routledge
Taylor & Francis Group
27 Church Road
Hove, East Sussex BN3 2FA

International Standard Book Number: 978-0-415-88473-0 (Hardback) 978-0-415-88474-7 (Paperback)

Library of Congress Cataloging-in-Publication Data

Therapeutic uses of rap and hip hop / edited by Susan Hadley and George Yancy.
    p. cm.
    Includes bibliographical references and index.
    ISBN 978-0-415-88473-0 (hardback : alk. paper) -- ISBN 978-0-415-88474-7 (pbk. : alk. paper)
    1. Music therapy. 2. Rap (Music)--Psychological aspects. 3. Hip-hop--Psychological aspects. I. Hadley, Susan (Susan Joan), 1967- II. Yancy, George.

ML3920.T54 2011
615.8'5154--dc22   2011011252

Visit the Taylor & Francis Web site at
http://www.taylorandfrancis.com

and the Routledge Web site at
http://www.routledgementalhealth.com

We dedicate this book to those whose voices long to be heard.

Contents

CONTENTS

CONTENTS

Acknowledgments

We would like to thank all of the therapists who made indispensable contributions to this very important text, a text that helps to fill a lacuna regarding the vital significance of rap and Hip-Hop in terms of their therapeutic aims of providing healing, growth, self-expression, individual and collective catharsis, positive alternative ways of expressing emotions and feelings, creative improvisation, self-discovery, and a sense of positive self-regard. We would also like to thank these therapists for their insights into, and affirmations of, the value of rap and Hip-Hop to young people who find themselves silenced and marginalized. By giving each person one mic, we see this as affirming the unconditional worth of each individual voice to speak beyond barriers (internal and external) in ways that create spaces for growth and freedom. We also want to acknowledge all those clients who have helped to shape the therapists in this book in terms of their understandings of and appreciation for the value of rap and Hip-Hop.

We would also like to thank Dr. George P. Zimmar, our editor at Routledge, for his immediate recognition regarding the importance of publishing a book that explores and uses rap and Hip-Hop as significant therapeutic media for reaching youth and adults. His support was crucial. Thanks also to Marta Moldvai, senior editorial assistant at Routledge, for her support, professionalism, and handling of the logistics involved in seeing this book through the publishing process.

Of course, without the musical and oral creative genius of rap artists and the larger cultural force of Hip-Hop, this project would not exist. Therefore, we give a collective shout-out to all of those rap artists and

Hip-Hop heads who have engaged rap and Hip-Hop, dared to be original, dared to be true to their inner voice and vision, and dared to express a critical consciousness *and* conscience in a world that often stifles and occludes creativity. These artists shake up calcified and myopic ways of seeing and ordering the world, ways that militate against the growth and flourishing of the human spirit. We thank all of you for your global efforts to create a more humane world. We send out a special thanks to rap and Hip-Hop scholars for the work that they have done to capture the complex creative cultural productions that continue to evolve out of rap and Hip-Hop. Mentor and colleague James G. Spady is to be thanked in particular, especially given his incredible body of work exploring, articulating, and theorizing rap and Hip-Hop. His work goes to the source by capturing rap artists and Hip-Hop progenitors within their own *lived* context.

We would also like to thank our students and our mentors alike for the myriad ways they continue to extend us into new spaces. There are too many to name, but you know who you are.

Finally, we thank our families and especially our children for helping to "keep us real" when we start to drift into the abyss of academia. Their love, support, guidance, patience, and understanding are always felt and greatly appreciated.

Contributors

Mandana Ahmadi graduated from the University of Pretoria with her master's degree in music therapy in 2005. She has since been working for the Music Therapy Community Clinic in Cape Town as a music therapist and recently also as project manager of the Heideveld (Trauma) Project (2009). She has worked with children, youth, and adults in diverse settings, from schools to hospitals to children's homes, with a variety of different diagnoses. These include issues related to trauma such as death of a close family member, parent in jail, abuse, exposure to violence, and illness (tuberculosis and HIV/AIDS). Mandana has also been involved with mentoring music therapy assistants and community musicians with whom she works.

T. Tomás Alvarez III, ACSW, received his master's degree in social work from Smith College School for Social Work, Northampton, Massachusetts, and his bachelor's degree in social work from San Francisco State University. He is the founder and executive director of Beats, Rhymes, and Life (BRL), a clinically based community organization that aims to promote mental health and wellness among youth and young adults by utilizing Hip-Hop and other forms of popular culture. Tomás lives and practices social work in Oakland, California, where he specializes in culturally responsive strength-based therapeutic group work with adolescents of color. In 2009, his performance-based Rap Therapy group became the focus of a feature film titled *Beats, Rhymes and Life Film Project,* set to premier in 2011. In addition to his work with BRL, Tomás serves as a transitional age youth advocate and consultant for Alameda County. In 2010, he was selected to serve as an advisory committee member for the California Institute for Mental Health Center for Multicultural Development (CMD), an entity designed to promote the cultural competence of publicly funded behavioral health systems.

Felicity A. Baker, PhD, is associate professor, director of music therapy training, and director of research in the School of Music at the University of Queensland, Brisbane, Australia. She has over 50 publications including coediting (with Tony Wigram) the text *Songwriting: Methods, Techniques and Clinical Applications for Music Therapy Clinicians, Educators and Students* (London: Jessica Kingsley, 2005) and coauthor (with Jeanette Tamplin) of *Music Therapy in Neurorehabilitation: A Clinician's Manual* (Jessica Kingsley, 2006). She is editor of *The Australian Journal of Music Therapy* and serves on the review boards of the *Nordic Journal of Music Therapy* and *Canadian Journal of Music Therapy*. In 2008, Felicity was awarded the University of Queensland Research Excellence Award for her outstanding and sustained contributions to research. From 2011 to 2015, Felicity will hold an Australia Research Council Future Fellowship to research therapeutic songwriting and develop a multidimensional model of therapeutic songwriting.

Alissa Carver earned her bachelor's degree in music therapy and her dual master's in music therapy and counseling and development from Texas Woman's University, Denton, in 2006. She has been working as a board-certified music therapist since 2006 and as a licensed professional counselor intern since 2010. Her experience includes working with clients diagnosed with autism spectrum disorder, clients in the chronic and acute psychiatric mental health setting, clients receiving hospice care, and clients in the juvenile correctional setting. She has professional interest in working with clients with sexual disorders and gender identity issues and an interest in family therapy, and is receiving training in guided imagery and music. She is currently working as a full-time therapist in the acute mental health setting and is accruing hours toward the title Licensed Professional Counselor.

Stella Compton Dickinson is a health professions registered (HPC) music therapist employed by Nottinghamshire Health Care NHS Trust as clinical research lead in arts therapies at Rampton High Secure Hospital, one of the three UK national high-secure hospitals for the treatment of people who have committed serious and dangerous offenses. Stella has an MSc in mental health studies and accreditation in Cognitive Analytic Therapy (known as CAT) from the medical school of Guys and St. Thomas's Hospitals in London (King's College London). She trained in music therapy at the Guildhall School of Music and Drama. Stella has developed and is implementing a practice-based doctoral research mixed methods study at Rampton Hospital, a purpose of which is to test the clinical effectiveness of group cognitive analytic therapy for patients in forensic treatment. As well as working in the secure hospital setting, Stella works psychotherapeutically in private practice with a wide range of clients including those with profound anxiety, depression, eating disorders, life crises, major bereavement, trauma, and physical and sexual abuse. Her work has been recognized in the NHS as notable for in-depth understanding and focus on the cultural and creative therapeutic needs of ethnic and other minority groups. She has presented on music therapy at national and international conferences on four continents.

Konstantin Detchkov obtained his BA in psychology from Hunter College, New York, and is currently in the process of obtaining his MSW from Fordham University, Bronx, New York. Upon completion of his education, Konstantin hopes to work directly with the youth population, particularly in disenfranchised communities, as well as work on developing new methods of delivering effective services to that population. His past experience includes volunteer work at The Door—a support center for NYC youth.

Genevieve A. Dingle, PhD, is a lecturer in the School of Psychology, University of Queensland, Australia. She has published in the areas of adult mental health, group therapy, and substance abuse treatment, including a chapter (coauthored with Tian Oei) in the *Encyclopedia of Psychotherapy* (San Diego: Academic Press, 2002) and a chapter (coauthored with Sharon Dawe and Natalie Loxton) in the forthcoming *Encyclopedia of Addictive Behaviours* (Elsevier). Her current research is focused on music and emotion in healthy adults and in adults experiencing a range of mental health and substance use problems. Genevieve has worked as a clinical psychologist for over 13 years, including a period as the manager of the drug and alcohol treatment program at Belmont Private Hospital, and a period as a clinical psychologist in the Veterans Alcohol Treatment program at Toowong Private Hospital in Brisbane, Australia.

Amy M. Donnenwerth received her BA in music therapy and MA in music from the University of Missouri–Kansas City. She also received a BSE in music education from the University of Arkansas, Fayetteville. She has worked clinically with people diagnosed with cancer, adults with developmental disabilities, and most recently male and female adolescents with emotional and behavioral problems. She has presented at regional and national music therapy conferences.

Erin Eastwood obtained a BA in Latin American studies and Spanish literature and a BS in business administration from the University of Kansas in 2004. She is currently in the process of obtaining her MSW from Fordham University. Upon completion of her MSW degree, Erin aims to work in direct practice with underserved youth in New York City, while preparing to take the LCSW licensing exam. Erin's ultimate goal is to obtain her PhD in social work and conduct research on youth interventions.

Don Elligan, PhD, received his degree in clinical psychology from Fairleigh Dickinson University, Teaneck, New Jersey. He is a tenured, full-time assistant professor at Harold Washington College, Chicago, Illinois, in the Department of Social Sciences and is a licensed clinical psychologist in private practice. He specializes in culturally sensitive supportive and solution-focused psychotherapy. He has published in journals such as *Diversity and Ethnic Minority Psychology, Cultural Diversity and Mental Health, Psych Discourse*, and *Journal of African American Men*. He is the author of *Rap Therapy: A Practical Guide for Communication With Youth and Young Adults Through Rap Music* (2004).

Andrea Frisch Hara is a board-certified music therapist and a licensed creative arts therapist who received her master's degree in music therapy from New York University. She holds a certificate from the advanced Intensive Psychoanalytic Psychotherapy Program at the William Alanson White Institute in New York and has maintained a private practice in music therapy, psychotherapy, and music psychotherapy in New York City since 1997. She was the program field director of the *9.11 New York City Music Therapy Relief Project*, sponsored by the Recording Academy, the producers of the Grammys, and the American Music Therapy Association. Andrea began her career in adolescent psychiatry 25 years ago and holds this population very close to her heart. A director of the Music Therapy Institute of the Music Conservatory of Westchester for 13 years, Andrea has also been a music therapy consultant to the Jewish Board of Family and Children's Services and a variety of other treatment programs, including therapeutic nurseries, senior facilities, and special education settings. Andrea was formerly on the faculty of the New York University Graduate Music Therapy program, where she served as an adjunct clinical assistant professor and has supervised numerous graduate music therapy interns. A former vice president of the American Association for Music Therapy, she was an editor of the AAMT newsletter *Tuning In*. Andrea has presented workshops on her clinical work at regional and national conferences, authored articles, edited music therapy publications, and served on the editorial review board of the journal *Music Therapy Perspectives*. In 2002, the AMTA awarded her the Presidential Award for exemplary service for the program direction of the *9.11 NYC Music Therapy Relief Project.*

Libby M. Gleadhill completed her master's degree in music therapy at the University of Queensland, Australia, and since has been working predominately in the field of psychiatry. Her clinical work and research has largely focused on the use of cognitive behavioral music therapy within specific subspecialties including drug and alcohol, postnatal depression, trauma and dissociation, and general psychiatry. Libby's work in mental health was featured on national television in 2007 in relation to a large-scale songwriting and recording project she led; the CD was an originally written and recorded work in which consumers told their story of living life with a mental illness. Libby is currently residing in Japan and completing her PhD at the University of Queensland. She is exploring the ways in which music therapy for bereaved parents, specifically song parody technique, shapes clients' engagement with music in their lives.

Susan Hadley, PhD, MT-BC, is professor of music therapy at Slippery Rock University, Pennsylvania. Her previous edited works are *Psychodynamic Music Therapy: Case Studies* (Barcelona), *Feminist Perspectives in Music Therapy* (Barcelona), (with George Yancy) *Narrative Identities: Psychologists Engaged in Self-Construction* (Jessica Kingsley), and *Qualitative Inquiries in Music Therapy, Vol. 4* and *Vol. 5* (Barcelona). Hadley has also published numerous articles in peer-reviewed journals and presented at regional, national, and international music therapy conferences.

Florence Ierardi, MM, MT-BC, LPC, is the director of field education and music therapy faculty member in the Department of Creative Arts Therapies at Drexel University, Philadelphia, Pennsylvania. She received bachelor's and master's degrees in percussion performance from Temple University, Philadelphia, Pennsylvania, where she later studied music therapy. She has worked with various populations in clinical settings and has facilitated drumming events in clinical and community settings. She coauthored a chapter on clinical musical improvisation in adult psychiatric settings in the AMTA publication *Music Therapy for Children, Adolescents and Adults With Mental Disorders.* She was the lead author on a chapter describing creative arts therapies with at-risk youth in Camilleri's *Healing the Inner City Child: Creative Arts Therapies With At-Risk Youth,* where she described her music therapy work in a mandated after-school prevention program. Flossie is currently the chair of the International Relations Committee of the American Music Therapy Association.

Nicole Jenkins, MT-BC, is completing a Master of Arts degree in Creative Arts in Therapy-Music Therapy at Drexel University, Philadelphia, Pennsylvania. Prior to her music therapy education, she worked as a vocal and general music teacher at the middle and high school levels in Prince George's County Public Schools in Maryland. She has studied classical voice and is a neo-soul singer with a commercially released CD. She completed her music therapy internship in a short-term juvenile detention facility and her practicum training included an adolescent inpatient psychiatry unit, a program for families affected by domestic violence, and a long-term care facility for adults who are ventilator dependent.

Stephen "Buddha" Leafloor, BA, MSW, is the founder of BluePrintForLife.ca (Outreach through Hip-Hop in Canada's remote Arctic). Stephen has a MSW degree and over 25 years of experience as a social worker in the areas of probation, wilderness programs, street work with youth at risk, residential group homes, child protection, and community outreach. Stephen has also been an active participant in the Hip-Hop culture as a dancer since 1982 and completed his master's thesis on this culture and its importance for educators and social workers in 1986. Stephen has been a guest lecturer at many universities and is often a keynote speaker at conferences, including a number of international United Nations youth conferences. He has also spoken on behalf of Justice Canada at conferences, and at international conferences on outreach through Hip-Hop. Other keynote presentations include the National Aboriginal Health Conference, International Crime prevention, and school board presentations on alternative education and bullying. He has also trained Cirque Du Soleil's cast members, consulted for new show creation, and trained its social outreach workers. On the performance side of things, Stephen (Buddha) Leafloor is the founder of the Canadian Floor Masters (Canada's oldest bboy crew celebrating 27 years of Canadian history). He has performed for James Brown, rapper Ice-T, Grandmaster Flash, Black Eyed Peas, and George Clinton. His dancing has been featured on Much Music, in assorted music videos, and in a number of documentaries. He has also performed privately for the Kirov Ballet of Russia and opened for La La La Human Steps.

Aaron J. Lightstone, MMT, MTA, graduated in 2004 from the Master of Music Therapy program at Wilfrid Laurier University, Waterloo, Ontario, Canada, where his research on the use of Hip-Hop aesthetics and rap lyrics in music therapy won a number of academic awards. He is currently a music therapist at the Sunnybrook Veterans' Centre, in Toronto, Ontario, where he specializes in the care of aging war veterans and palliative care. Aaron has practiced music therapy since 1997 with trauma/abuse survivors, homeless populations, people with autism, people in addictions recovery programs, children with a range of learning disabilities, and psychiatric patients and has assisted in the training of music therapy students. He has presented often about various aspects of his clinical work at national music therapy conferences in Canada. In addition to his work as a music therapist, he is the founder of and a performer (oud, guitar) in the award-winning world music band Jaffa Road (http://www.jaffaroad.com).

Scott MacDonald, MMT, MT-BC, is a music therapist at the Belmont Center for Comprehensive Treatment, Philadelphia, Pennsylvania, and with the Arts and Quality of Life Research Center (Temple University) for the Hear Our Voices project. He received his master's degree from Temple University in 2008, completing a thesis on a phenomenological analysis of group music therapy experiences for adult psychiatric inpatients.

Katrina McFerran, PhD, is a music therapist and senior lecturer at the Faculty of the VCA and Music, University of Melbourne, Australia. She completed her PhD in 2002 on the topic of group music therapy with bereaved adolescents and has continued to focus her research and clinical work on adolescents across a range of settings using qualitative and quantitative methods of inquiry. She has published in a range of international refereed journals and has recently released her first book *Adolescents, Music and Music Therapy: Methods and Techniques for Clinicians, Educators and Students* with Jessica Kingsley Publishers (2010).

Emma O'Brien, MMus, RMT, and PhD candidate at the University of Melbourne, Australia, is the manager and senior clinician in music therapy at the Royal Melbourne Hospital and the recipient of the Victorian Cancer Agency Scholarship for Research into Supportive Care. Emma was the founder of the music therapy program at the Royal Melbourne Hospital (1997), where she specializes in supportive care for cancer patients across all treatment streams and stages of their illness. The RMH music therapy team has three therapists on staff providing services to oncology, hematology, bone marrow transplant service, the eating disorders unit, and rehabilitation for severe traumatic brain injury. Emma has published her research in major peer-reviewed journals and has presented at national and international conferences in music therapy and psycho-oncology. Emma has also worked extensively on special music therapy projects linking the arts community with the hospital such as the release of a triple CD, *Living Soul*, of songs written with people with cancer; she also led the inaugural Opera Therapy Project (February to June 2004) and created a new opera with four people living with cancer which resulted in a 52-minute documentary screening, which has subsequently won many major international documentary film awards. Emma also works with community support groups. She lectured at the University of Melbourne from 1999 to 2007 in music therapy in cancer care, music medicine, music and the brain, and the application of specialized techniques for the voice and songwriting in music therapy.

Helen Oosthuizen completed her master's degree in music therapy at the University of Pretoria in 2005. Since that time, she has held various clinical posts in Gauteng (Johannesburg, Soweto, Pretoria, and Krugersdorp) and Cape Town (working with the Music Therapy Community Clinic in Nyanga, Khayelitsha, Heideveld, and Brooklyn). Her work has included community work with children affected by poverty, trauma, and HIV/AIDS and with young offenders; work in the health care sector including a psychiatric hospital and tuberculosis hospital; and work in schools and in private practice. She is currently involved in developing a music therapy program for young sexual offenders in Gauteng. Helen also serves as one of the African editors for the international online music therapy journal *Voices* and works as a part-time supervisor for music therapy students at the University of Pretoria.

Amanda Sehr, MS, received her master's degree in counseling and development from Texas Woman's University, Denton. She is currently completing her music therapy internship pursuant to the requirements for her master's degree in music therapy from Texas Woman's University. While pursuing degrees in music therapy and counseling, she has obtained clinical training with juvenile offenders in a residential treatment facility and with adults and adolescents in a psychiatric facility. She has also presented at regional and national music therapy conferences on her work with adolescents in the juvenile correctional setting.

Pauline Souflas, MD, is a consultant forensic psychiatrist at Rampton High Secure Hospital (UK), with dual training in child and adolescent and forensic psychiatry specialties. She has the diploma in forensic psychotherapy from the Portman Clinic, London. She finds the creative arts therapies extremely useful in helping patients to develop a therapeutic relationship and to identify unconscious motivation for offending. She has a particular interest in young offenders who end up in high-security treatment, where the developmental aspects of their offending can mature and resolve over time, despite their label of "dangerousness."

Nicole Steele, MT-BC, is a music therapist at the Children's Hospital of Pittsburgh of UPMC, Pittsburgh, Pennsylvania. She received her undergraduate degree in music therapy from Slippery Rock University,

Pennsylvania. She has presented at national and regional music therapy conferences as well as medical conferences including the International Transplant Nursing Society Conference. She is currently participating in interdisciplinary research with pediatric transplant patients.

Edgar H. Tyson, PhD, is an assistant professor at Fordham University, Bronx, New York. He received his BS and MSW from Barry University, Miami, Florida, and his PhD from the University of Tennessee. Although his expertise lies in the area of social work and social welfare, his formal training and development has been grounded in a multidisciplinary perspective (statistics, religion, philosophy, economics, law, political science, cultural and intercultural studies, musicology, sociology, and psychology). The convergence of these diverse and rich disciplinary fields/subject areas has forged his scholarly interests and research program in three main focus areas: cultural competence in assessment of child mental health and behavioral outcomes; applying contemporary, urban youth culture (e.g., Hip-Hop) in prevention and intervention research; and developing and strengthening Hip-Hop-based delinquency prevention and civic engagement models for youth, from a holistic, family-centered, and community-centered approach. He has published numerous articles in a wide variety of scholarly journals. His academic training is complemented by 16 years of social work practice experience in community-based, psychiatric, child welfare, and juvenile justice settings.

Vanessa Veltre, MSW, MT-BC, is a licensed social worker and music therapist in Pittsburgh, Pennsylvania. She works as a researcher at Carnegie Mellon University, focusing on the issue of teen pregnancy prevention. Vanessa is passionate about youth and works toward improving the environments in which they live and grow. Vanessa's research interests are in gender-related issues, community violence, and education systems. She has presented at several conferences, including the Pennsylvania Governor's Conference for Women. Vanessa received her Master of Social Work from the University of Pittsburgh and her Bachelor of Music Therapy from Slippery Rock University.

Michael Viega, MMT, MT-BC, is currently a PhD candidate in music therapy at Temple University, Philadelphia, Pennsylvania. His primary clinical and research focus has been working with children and adolescents in various settings, with a focus on therapeutic songwriting techniques and clinical uses of popular music genres. He is an advanced trainee in the Bonny Method of Guided Imagery and Music. He is currently special projects coordinator and adjunct faculty member at Molloy College, Rockville Center, New York.

CONTRIBUTORS

George Yancy, PhD, is associate professor of philosophy at Duquesne University, Pittsburgh, Pennsylvania. He is the author of *Black Bodies White Gazes: The Continuing Significance of Race* (2008), which received an Honorable Mention from the Gustavus Myers Center for the Study of Bigotry and Human Rights. He is the editor of over 10 books, three of which have received CHOICE Outstanding Title Awards. Yancy has also published in numerous scholarly journals. In 2008, Yancy was nominated for Duquesne University's Presidential Award for Faculty Excellence in Scholarship.

Introduction

Give 'em Just One Mic: The Therapeutic Agency of Rap and Hip-Hop

George Yancy and Susan Hadley

[Rap has] always been a form of therapy.

Doug E. Fresh

If people are to recover a sense of identity that is both usable
and relevant . . . they must also gain the license to forge
cultural links and empowering narratives.

Russell A. Potter

[Personal Reflections from George]

Everywhere I looked, there were Black youth engaging Hip-Hop culture
and the highly demanding art of rap music. In the early 1990s, in North
Philly, I vividly recall looking out the back window of my house and seeing
young Black men rapping. Trying to listen through other urban sounds
that were distracting (dogs barking, police car sirens), I could, at times,

make out what was a moving syncopated voiced rhythm. This could go on for most of the night. Seen through a conceptual framework that portrays young Black males as loitering and engaging in acts of vagrancy, who are deemed "lazy," wasting time and perhaps wasting away, a conceptual framework that perpetuates a pathological view of Black youth within post-industrial urban spaces, I would have missed the social and existential agency and urgency that was taking place before my eyes. I would have missed the dynamic way in which space was being claimed and reconfigured. What I witnessed was the exercise of brilliant verbal skill and virtuosity, physical endurance, a powerful work ethic, high aesthetic values and expectations, forms of social bonding and cohesiveness, mutual affirmation, acts of agency and self-definition, and vigorous competition. I was observing a site of rich and dynamic autopoiesis, that is, self-creation.

On those corners, I had the opportunity to witness a powerful dialectic where each individual encouraged the other within the cipha to reach higher, to strive for greater verbal dexterity and self-creativity. The cipha is a value-laden configured space, though not fixed, where one has to prove oneself; it is a dialogical and dialectical site of exchange that encourages mastery, expertise, and self-confidence. It can also be said to function as a space of verbal battle. "Battlin' in the cipha can be compared to the competition among choirs in Gospel music, 'exchanges' in Doo Wop music, jam sessions in Jazz music, and streetdancing (breakdancing) battles. The criteria in each one of these artistic endeavors are very high" (Alim et al., 2006, p. 6). Yet, like playing the dozens or a ring shout, there is respect, cohesiveness, a collective group sense of mutuality, intersubjectivity, and meaning-making. The individual is important, his/her imprimatur is essential, but the collective synergy is equally important.

What was so fascinating is that the manifestation of these lyrical expressions and self-creative efforts were not restricted to physical corners. I would see this kind of creativity on subway trains, outside schools, from youth walking down the street alone or together. This speaks to the vitality of rap and Hip-Hop culture to take root anywhere and to flourish, to reconfigure space and to be reconfigured by specific spaces. Rap and Hip-Hop culture constitute both a concrete particularity and an expansive universality. "Localization forces us to contend with the 'on-the-ground' realities, the specific ethnographic contexts, and the sociopolitical arrangement of the relations between language use, identity, and power" (Alim et al., 2006, p. 9). Yet, rap and Hip-Hop culture transcend their specific concrete expressive locations. The cross-cultural and adaptive dynamism of rap and Hip-Hop speaks to a wide audience. Alim, Meghelli, and Spady demonstrate the existence and importance of a global cipha. They write:

Since its inception in the 1970s, members of this "nation without borders" have recognized the desirability of change based in human self and group emancipation. Members of this vast body can be found in Philly, East Palo Alto, San Juan, Brooklyn, Chicago, the Bronx, Miami, Mexico City, Cairo, Johannesburg, Algiers, Marseille, Dakar, Bordeaux, Berlin, Oakland, Sao Paulo, Ramallah, Newark, Havana, Miami, Milan, New Orleans, Los Angeles, Toronto, Kingston, New Haven, Auckland, Shaolin, Tokyo, London, Washington DC, Memphis, Atlanta, Nairobi, Dar Es Salaam, Sydney, Harlem and Paris. (Alim et al., 2006, p. 8)

Rap's mobility speaks to its multi-spatial sites of creation and its capacity to transcend its communicative emergence within a particular context. In short, then, within the context of North Philly, I witnessed Black youth creatively appropriating audible space. They were being heard. I came to realize that more than aesthetic choice, engaging in rap music became a way in which Black youth created a vitally shared linguistic community, a sense of belonging, a sense of collective catharsis. More accurately, rap aesthetics, from a specific style of dress to a preferred beat and linguistic choice, was inextricably linked to their sense of belonging. Rap functioned as a modus vivendi or way of life. Spittin' lyrics became a way of telling their shared and unique local stories, their narratives, and modes of being. Speaking both to the shared experiences communicated in rap music and the importance of community, James Spady (1995) writes, "It is the agency of actual lived experiences in the corrugated spaces that one finds reflected in the lyrical content of rap songs. To speak of a community of rap artists is to speak of a community of people" (p. 1). Through such dynamic communicative acts, I witnessed that Black youth voiced what it meant for them to be alive; they expressed their pain and joy, sorrow and ecstasy. The power of voicing sustained them. The music was engaged and their street reputations were being established; they rapped 24-7, or so it seemed. I would argue that rap music functioned as an important vehicle through which a sense of sanity was maintained within urban spaces that were typically high in unemployment and poverty. Rap became a medium through which these youth described and interpreted the existential density of lived urban spaces and thereby were able to achieve an important level of transcendence, though without denial.

The youth that I witnessed, to my knowledge, never went on to become professional rap artists. However, whether rapping the lyrics of some well-known rap artist or creating one's own raps, performing rap and creating raps provided them with a "metaphoric mic,"* a way of seizing the moment, stepping into the cipha and being heard, speaking out,

---

* Stephen Leafloor also utilizes this theme of "one mic" (see Chapter 8).

stepping up, representing, engaging in communicative agency/praxis, and dropping science/knowledge. It didn't matter whether there was a literal mic. In other words, the "mic" signified an open space to be listened to, an opportunity to be heard, a chance to be recognized, and a moment of validation. As Nas says, "All I need is one mic to spread my voice to the whole world." Nas's minimalist requirement has important implications for self-empowerment. His minimalism valorizes the importance of simply being able to speak and the sheer power and transformative possibilities inherent in lyrically or rhythmically expressed speech. His minimalism also points to the singular importance of self-expression and its cathartic possibilities for oneself and others.

Giving a person "one mic" signifies an ethical movement toward others, of demonstrating a profound respect for the interiority of the lives of others. Giving "one mic" is an invitation that suggests the power of a single voice. Using "one mic" involves risk. Having "one mic" is a call to the other. Yet, it does not presume that the person with the "mic" can speak for all those who have been marginalized or deemed the subaltern. In fact, "one mic" says that *you* can speak for *yourself.* The metaphor of "one mic" is a source of empowerment. Through this "one mic," rap— through its aesthetics of freestyle—provides a venue through which one is able to free associate, improvise, and thereby maximize the potential to unblock repressed pain and existential angst, the opportunity to address levels of anguish previously unrecognized, to bring to the surface feelings previously denied. The "mic" encourages a person to find his/her voice and to articulate issues that are important in order to flourish and to promote self-awareness. Finding one's own voice, especially within communicative spaces where people are seeking their own voices and trying to combat issues that occlude self-growth, may also have implications for others. Others may be encouraged to open up, to overcome fear of expression, and to begin to recognize their problems in the words of those with the "mic." This is why rap music is indispensable within the context of doing therapy. Rap music's valorization and encouragement of oral facility and storytelling provide a powerful impetus for finding one's voice, making sense of one's own narrative. And within the larger space of Hip-Hop culture, there are important norms (aesthetic and otherwise) that provide a sense of mutual recognition, a space of we-affirmation. Within our contemporary moment where youth feel rejected, isolated, unheard, and misunderstood, where their views on life are sometimes deemed immature or even nugatory, rap and Hip-Hop provide healthy ways of shared (and sharing) vernacular expression, and healthy ways of affirmed (and affirming) modes of being (ontology) and complex ways of knowing (epistemology) that are important for youth identity and survival. Indeed, rap and Hip-Hop provide structure within which youth can achieve a sense of themselves as creators. Focusing on rap's form, Andrea Frisch Hara argues that "RAP music's form is about as close to perfection as one can get to a therapeutic medium! Its structure provides structure. Simultaneously, it allows freedom of expression and myriad ways to improvise" (see Chapter 1).

While we acknowledge rap and Hip-Hop in all its complexity, it is not our aim here to tackle the ongoing claims regarding the glorification of violence, misogyny, homophobia, and commercialization in rap and Hip-Hop. Despite its powerful and global ongoing success, rap is still characterized by many as an inferior form of music (or not music at all), as lewd, as saturated with infectious beats and lyrics that breed aggression, and as a questionable art form that is at best an instance of moral dereliction. Our aim is not to sidestep the issue. Rather, we understand that the realities of violence, misogyny, homophobia, and commodificationism form part of the larger American landscape, which, of course, does not excuse the presence of such elements within rap or Hip-Hop culture. Rap and Hip-Hop are not insular cultural formations and as such imbibe values from the larger American ethos. Yet, part of the very structure of rap—indeed, what makes rap so incredibly powerful in a society filled with denial and simulacra—is its attentiveness to social reality, its deep (in-your-face) existential urban chronicalization of pain, drug use, murder, poverty, anger, disappointment, feelings of rage, and narratives of loss and regret. There is also the often explicit exploration of and narrating of sexual exploits (by male and female artists). However, rap narratives are also filled with themes regarding the importance of family, positive role models, perseverance/resiliency, warnings/cautionary tales, positive self-image, healthy choices, change, and planning for the future. It is also important to note that there are complex *expressive techniques* that inform the musical genre: complex themes of signification, double entendre, playfulness, braggadocio, and exaggeration. Hence, given this caveat, we argue that *context* is important when it comes to the ways in which rap and Hip-Hop are used and engaged within therapeutic settings. In short, we argue that therapists have a professional and ethical obligation *to know* when and to what extent rap and Hip-Hop would be *contraindicative* within specific therapeutic milieus, that is, therapists must be cognizant of factors that would rule out the use of rap and Hip-Hop.

[Personal Reflections from Susan]

I remember my first encounter with rap in a therapy session. It was in my first couple of years of clinical practice (back around 1990) and I was working with adolescents in the psychiatric ward of a children's hospital in Western Australia. I had asked the adolescents to bring in a song to share with the group. One young White adolescent boy brought in a rap by NWA. It was one of the first times I had heard rap, and I had trouble understanding the narrative, although I had no trouble hearing that some of the language was rather explicit. He was obviously finding this aspect amusing. There was a reactive impulse in me to turn off the music, but I resisted it. I felt that he was testing me and if I turned off the music I would fail the test. So, we sat and listened to it and gave it the same serious attention that we gave to each selection. When the rap came to an end I said, "I had some trouble following what the rap was about. Could you explain it to me?" In some ways I was testing him. I thought he had just brought it in for shock value. What followed was one of the most valuable lessons for me as a developing therapist. He proceeded to tell me that the rap was about how because of the way society is structured it favors those in the majority (White people and people who are above the poverty line) and unfairly discriminates against minority groups, particularly Black people. He went on to say that the police tend to target minorities and mistreat them. I was impressed with how well he articulated the ideas expressed in the rap and it led to an interesting discussion about how different people in the group felt that they got unfairly discriminated against for various reasons. The group was made up of males and females and some of the females expressed that they did not like listening to the rap because they felt that the language used was offensive to them. This led to a very fruitful discussion about respect, respect for others in the group in terms of what they feel comfortable listening to and respect for the different musical choices of members of the group.

Moving forward in my career, I remember when I began teaching in my current university position (in the late 1990s) and I was supervising students in their clinical work with adolescent males in a residential treatment community for youth with histories of moderate to severe emotional disturbances, delinquency, aggression, truancy, abuse, neglect, or other behavioral problems. The majority of the music therapy students were Caucasian females from rural or suburban areas and the clients were Caucasian, Hispanic, or African American and mostly from large urban settings and from low socioeconomic contexts. At one of my first orientation meetings between the students and the cottage supervisor, the supervisor stipulated that the therapy students could bring in any music except for rap. I asked him what the rationale for that was and he said that rap was about violence, drugs, and sex, and it was full of cursing/swearing. He also commented that the strong beats sometimes make the boys hyper-stimulated. I remember talking to him about music being part of the identity of these boys and to reject their music was in essence to reject a part of them. I felt strongly that if rap was their music of preference we needed to honor that, even if they put some restrictions on the rap that was brought into the sessions. Since then, I have often found that facilities place limits on the use of rap music. I have not found this with any other genre of music. This brings up important questions for therapists who use music in their work. In the documentary video *Dreamworlds 3: Desire, Sex, and Power in Music Video,* Sut Jhally masterfully illustrates that misogyny and objectification are not limited to rap, but are endemic across music video genres. And violence and drug use are sung about in many genres, including but not limited to heavy metal, rock, death metal, rap, gansta rap, industrial, hardcore, and alternative music. So, why is it that rap is being singled out?

I have had interesting conversations with music therapists about the use of rap in therapy. There are, of course, a variety of views about it. Some feel that in order to best serve any client we must follow their lead toward the musical language that they feel best expresses their culture and inner dialogue. Therapists who hold this view obviously would value the use of rap and Hip-Hop in therapy. Others feel that if facilities prevent the use of rap, then therapists who work in those facilities should abide by the rules that the agency has regarding the use of rap. Taking these two positions seriously sets up a dilemma for therapists. On the one hand, as therapists we should honor the musical preferences of our clients, while on the other hand, agencies have the right to ban an entire genre of music. This particular genre of music is one of the major players in the contemporary music industry. Obviously, both positions cannot be accepted without contradiction or at least some inconsistency. In my opinion, rap music should not be banned from therapeutic facilities, certainly not the entire genre. Therapists have a responsibility to help to advocate for clients who are not being treated fairly. There are many subgenres of rap. To characterize all rap, or even all rap by certain rap artists, as negative or inappropriate discounts its diversity and complexity. I believe that it is the ethical responsibility of therapists to educate those who have a blanket ban on the use of rap in certain settings.

Rap music has been maligned as a site of misogyny, violence, and drugs, a site that has little if anything to do with personal and social uplift. However, for many of the people with whom therapists work, rap music is an integral part of their identity—it both speaks to their experiences and allows them to locate their identities within particular narrative constructions. Questions of identity and rap music speak to an intimate and dynamic relationship, a relationship that is symbiotic. Identity impacts lyrical content and lyrical content helps to crystalize aspects of identity that might otherwise remain hidden. In this sense, rap music functions as a medium through which various feelings and impulses get expressed. And given the relationship between identity and various complex life-worlds that individuals inhabit, rap music functions as a powerful form of storytelling that allows others entry into various complex environmental spaces that rappers call home. Given this, rap music speaks to the hearts and minds—indeed, the *lived* experiences—of those whose lives and experiences resonate with various narratives found in rap compositions. And while rap does grow out of a specific social context, it is not limited to that context. The multiple existential and deep socio-psychological themes that rappers engage have global meaning and resonance. Hence, to reject a client's preferred music—in this case rap music—is to reject a part of who they are. To dismiss their musical preferences as worthless or inappropriate is to dismiss, for all intents and purposes, how they conceptualize themselves. Within this context, musical choice functions as an important index that speaks to aspects of their identity that are held dear and bespeak aspects of a worldview. Many people who work with youth and young adults have seen the therapeutic effects of rap music and Hip-Hop culture and how potential feelings of alienation might result from privileging other musical genres that may not resonate with their life experiences.

As stated above, rap and Hip-Hop have been very significant in terms of providing an important avenue for expression in a world of pain and suffering. In the early 1990s, for example, New York rap group Gravediggaz saw themselves as tarrying beneath the surface of "sanity," that space of lived terror and madness that is a function of the nightmarish lives of Black people living under conditions of existential duress. When rapper Frukwan explains the name of the rap group, he discusses not only how the group functioned as social gadflies but also how they functioned to provide psychological well-being. He says, "It means digging graves of the mentally dead, and it stood [for] resurrecting the mentally dead from their state of unawareness and ignorance."* Like the blues genre, the objective, of course, is *not* to remain in the grips of depression, anger, and angst, to be static and imprisoned by debilitating psychological and socio-psychological problems. As Poetic says, "That's the whole revolving door with 'Gravediggaz.' We're using darkness to bring light. You know what I'm saying? And you have to actually become a gravedigga to listen to a 'Gravedigga'" (Spady et al., 1995, p. 67). Poetic's point is that one must be willing and prepared to explore the deeper levels of one's experiences.

By using darkness to bring light, Poetic speaks to the importance of becoming aware (and making others aware) of the often complex disheartening aspects of life, and the "darker" aspects of the self. The metaphor of archaeology signifies the necessity to engage the deeper regions of one's unconscious, to unflinchingly look at the self in all of its psychological complexity, with its ruptures and imperfections. Poetic is also suggesting that to be able to listen to the pain and suffering of another, one must be personally invested in, and willing to engage in, introspection and

---

* See http://www.wu-international.com/misc_albums/Interviews/Frukwan%20Interview.htm.

self-disclosure. Poetic is speaking to how important it is to be in the company of others (co-sufferers) who are willing and able to self-explore and who are willing to share hurtful and painful personal experiences without fear of guidance or correction. He is suggesting that one must be part of a discursive community, a communicative space where others are willing to be vulnerable and to go the distance of facing and talking about their own experiences. Speaking directly to the ways in which the Gravediggaz have created a space within which to discharge their anger in creative and safe ways, Poetic says, "I can go out and shoot somebody or I can put it on wax.... We have an outlet for our stress and anger. We use it. You know what I'm saying?" (Spady et al., 1995, p. 67). Poetic speaks to the power of choice and how engaging in rap provides an alternative mode of expression, an alternative way of dealing with one's potentially destructive emotions.

That rap provides this important alternative, functioning as a site of emotional release, speaks to the deeper ways in which rap functions as a site of counter-nihilism and counter-destructiveness. Rap does give voice to feelings of meaninglessness and dread, but the power of giving voice to such feelings creates an important psychological distance from such feelings. Rapper Prince Paul, describing a low period in his life, says, "So, instead of going out and pulling guns on brothers and trying to assassinate them, I figure I'd take out vengeance on wax" (Spady et al., 1995, p. 56). This is Prince Paul's way of appropriating "one mic." As the title of this introduction suggests, to give 'em just one mic creates conditions for providing youth with "a mic" (literal or metaphoric)—a chance and a safe space, indeed, a safe and inviting cipha, to speak, to voice, to narrate their lived experiences.

It is not by accident that rap is centered on the activity of voicing. Rap is rooted in a long and dynamic history of orality. The concept of Nommo has been used to point out the cultural and metaphysical importance of the use of words for people of African descent. Nommo implies the power of the spoken word to change and reconfigure reality. The importance of orality within African American culture is pervasive. Rapping, then, as a manifestation of Nommo, is a form of *creating*. As Geneva Smitherman (1999) writes, "The oral tradition, then is part of the cultural baggage the African brought to America. The pre-slavery background was one in which the concept of Nommo, the magic power of the Word, was believed necessary to actualize life and give [persons] mastery over things" (p. 203). Rap artists are contemporary griots; they have assumed the important role of telling and retelling collective and individual stories. The stories are both informed by reality and form and shape reality. Furthermore, the stories are embedded within a resistance discourse that is itself complex and hypertextual. Within the context of rap and Hip-Hop culture, Potter (1995) refers to such discourse as *"resistance vernaculars,* since even to speak these vernaculars is in a crucial sense to make inroads against the established power-lines of

INTRODUCTION

speech" (pp. 57–58). In short, then, rap music has its roots in a long tradition of a people striving for linguistic agency, self-definition, and a positive sense of themselves.

It is important to note, however, that rap music isn't simply about rhyming and oral mastery. As Prince Paul says, "The beats got to be as fly as the rhymes" (Spady et al., 1995, p. 69). As one of the progenitors of Hip-Hop, Grandmaster Caz observes that Hip-Hop began before rap. He says, "Actual rap didn't start until later. It was deejaying and breakdancing at first. Not everybody even had a mic. It was about the beats. Who had the baddest beats. Me too, I was deejaying" (Eure & Spady, 1991, p. xvii). And while everyone didn't have a mic, the DJs provided a rich and infectious invitational beat to which people danced and moved in liberating/cathartic body articulations. The beat itself functioned as an instigator of *movement*. Even if the manifest function of the DJ was to produce the most aesthetically demanding and rewarding beat, the reality of dancing bodies in motion, whether in parks, in the street, or at clubs, no doubt had a profound latent therapeutic impact on the lives of those inhabiting urban spaces that often constrict movement and are heavy-laden with disproportionate economic burdens.

"Movement" is an important therapeutic value; it implies progress and open spaces—as when one says, "She no longer occupies that *debilitating space*; she has *moved* on with her life." Murray Forman (2002) argues that from the beginning Hip-Hop culture was driven by *spatial* logics. We agree with Forman that these spatial logics point to modes of expressive freedom, ways of reconfiguring space, reconfiguring perception, and reconfiguring *lived* reality. Indeed, Hip-Hop provides a context, driven by spatial logics, among other elements, that encourages movement, modes of liberation, and ways of deconstructing collective and individual stasis. Forman (2002) writes, "The culture of Hip-Hop embodies a range of activities that not only display but consciously foreground spatial characteristics, whether through the sonic appropriation of aural space, the appropriation of street corners (where, at an earlier stage in Hip-Hop's development, rap improvisation and breakdancing were common), or appropriation of the city's architecture through the ubiquitous display of spray painted graffiti tags, burners, and pieces" (p. 42). The point here is that rap evolved out of an elaborate matrix of *expressive* cultural formations that functioned as social forces of movement. As Spady and Eure (1991) write, "The Bronx. Locus of the Hip Hop World. Breakdancers. DJ's. Graffiti Artists. Rappers. Locators of the next generation of black *nomadic forces*" (p. xiii).

It is important to note that the context out of which rap and Hip-Hop developed was heterogeneous and multivalent. "The Bronx is a vast cityscape of multiple realities" (Spady & Eure, 1991, p. xi), a culturally confluent context involving African American and Afro-Caribbean influences.

Grandmaster Caz narrates, "[Hip-Hop] began in the Bronx. It began in a club atmosphere with Kool Herc, who is the Godfather of Hip Hop in my and everybody else's opinion. Kool Herc is West Indian and rap as we know it today originated from other forms of rap, that just wasn't called rap, like The Last Poets and like toasting from Black Americans and Jamaicans. Rap was just talking. That's what rap is. Now it's just syncopated" (Spady & Eure, 1991, p. xiii).

We believe that this multifaceted form of "syncopated talking" and the larger Hip-Hop culture out of which it evolved are indispensible in terms of their therapeutic value to speak to young people, to address them within the context of their complex and complicated psychosocial lives, their struggles, their plights, their challenges, their disappointments, their failures at empowerment, their sense of being misunderstood and discarded. In short, rap and Hip-Hop are powerful contemporary cultural forms that have within them expressive modalities that invite and encourage exploration of the inner self, its weaknesses and strengths. Rap and Hip-Hop provide spaces that free up ways of expressing the self and of acquiring new, positive, and effective ways of being empowered.

In keeping with the heterogeneous nature of rap and Hip-Hop in terms of its origins and its genres, we have brought together therapists from a variety of backgrounds. While many of the contributors to this book are music therapists, we also have social workers, psychologists, psychiatrists, and psychotherapists, all of whom are doing groundbreaking work in the area of using rap and Hip-Hop in therapy. Furthermore, we have contributors from various countries: the United States, Canada, the UK, South Africa, and Australia. The work they describe is with people of a variety of ages, from a variety of cultural, ethnic, and racial groups, with a variety of therapeutic/health needs.

There are multiple ways that rap and Hip-Hop can be used in therapy—by listening and discussing, performing, creating, or improvising. Each of these techniques addresses different therapeutic needs and is described below:

> Listening as a Therapeutic Technique—Sometimes the therapeutic effects of rap music are seen as a result of listening to certain rap selections. What results is an in-depth discussion about the clients' life experiences, attitudes about various subjects significant to their lives, their relationships, their understandings of themselves, their circumstances, their future possibilities, how they are perceived by the dominant society, and so on. Indeed, listening to rap music can trigger a profound response that stimulates a powerful and insightful discussion about their personal narratives—stories filled with pain, loss, grief, and joy. This speaks to the powerful

force of rap music to speak to/reflect the storied lives of others. Of course, this happens with music more generally and is a salient theme within music therapy. Rap music, however, has been under-theorized in terms of its potential to instigate in a fruitful and exploratory fashion particular insights, emotions, forms of suffering, and so on. Rap music, then, can be used as a cognitive and emotive vehicle to elicit and reshape aspects of the self. Moreover, through the use of vernacular forms of expression, those specific to rap music, rap musicians speak to those whose vernacular styles often reflect the speech-choices of the rappers themselves. Within a therapeutic context, this can function as a powerful personal invitation for individuals to speak. In this sense, rap music might be said to function as a surrogate voice for those who have been told, explicitly or implicitly, that their use of language is "broken" or "inferior." Hesitant to speak within certain linguistic communities, listening to a rap selection might lead someone who was generally silent to bellow, "That's what I'm talking about!" In this way, rap music can function as a cathartic release of emotions that have been calcified after years of refusing to face them. The function of rap music as a surrogate voice speaks to the reality of the social interconnectedness of voices and how particular lyrical content and forms of voicing/rapping speak to shared pain, angst, and joy.

Performing as a Therapeutic Technique—Sometimes the therapeutic effects of rap music are seen as a result of performing rap music or breakdancing, perhaps altering the lyrics or movements slightly from the original to fit the clients' own life stories. In this way, those performing the rap music and dance can integrate their own experiences into a particular rap, marking it as their own, augmenting the rap in ways that are reflective of their own life experiences. This allows for a greater sense of "ownership" of the rap, a co-creative act. This also speaks to ways in which rap music can be used in an invitational fashion and how it functions as a powerful vehicle in which clients get to perform their identities through rapping, breakdancing, or graf art. In its communal beckoning, rap music engages the individual in a co-creative act of listening, creating, and meaning making. This is not simply a case of performing something that pre-exists, but incorporating one's own story, one's own identity; it is a powerful form of co-performance that allows for levels of suspension that are freeing, spontaneous, and creative. Viewing rap music as a communal beckoning presupposes the self as socially transversal, as part a social network of shared cultural assumptions, values, and shared narrative intelligibility. Within this framework, individuals are able to articulate their lives in both literal and symbolic forms that are therapeutically rich. One form of performance is seen in the practice of battling (as described by Leafloor in Chapter 8 and Lightstone in Chapter 13). In a battle, two or more people engage in verbal sparring or in a kind of dance challenge. The more creative and spontaneous, the wittier a person is, the more esteem s/he receives. It requires great verbal/physical skill, rhythmic complexity, precision, confidence, and imagination.

Creating as a Therapeutic Technique—Sometimes the therapeutic effects of rap and Hip-Hop are seen as a result of clients creating their own lyrics, beats, dance steps, or graf art. The creation of original lyrics, beats, dance, or art can be empowering and can encourage greater levels of introspection. This particular approach is significant not only in terms of the manifest and latent content that gets expressed, but the very act itself is a site of creation. Individuals are able to take pride in an act of creative autonomy, something that they may have been denied in their lives. Moreover, being allowed to be creative through a mode of communication that they value communicates respect for their identity and their choices. In effect, the therapist is saying, "This is about you, not me." Hence, the act of creating becomes a vehicle for trust between client and therapist. Through what appears to be a simple act of creating lyrics, beats, dance, or art, the individual or group is affirmed on multiple levels and a foundation is established for future acts of risk taking and mutual trust.

Improvising (Freestyling) as a Therapeutic Technique—Sometimes the therapeutic effects of rap and Hip-Hop are seen as a result of clients improvising, whether it is lyrics, beats, or dance. Improvising or freestyling in rap and Hip-Hop involves extemporaneously creating rhythmically complex lyrics, beats, or dance moves. Therapeutically, according to Bruscia (1991), improvisation helps to develop "spontaneity, creativity, freedom of expression, playfulness, a sense of identity, or interpersonal skills—as these are basic characteristics of the improvising experience" (p. 7). He goes on to say that it "provides a safe means of experimenting with new behaviors, roles, or interactional patterns, while also developing the ability to make choices and decisions within established limits" (p. 7). The act of improvising is an act of what Christopher Small (1998) terms musicking. McFerran (2010) interprets this act as a "potentially authentic self-representation" (p. 142). Lightstone (Chapter 3) warns that for some clients, "the opportunity to engage in wordplay can provide a convenient cover for them to continue avoiding themselves, their issues, or otherwise manifest therapeutic resistance." To be successful when freestyling, a person must be spontaneous and be able to deal with the unexpected; he/she must be able to cope with not following a set script. Improvising requires actively listening and creatively utilizing all the resources that one has available. One must learn to actively and openly receive what is at hand. Improvising involves risk. It involves making choices on the spot and living with those choices. Battles, as described above, are most often improvisational and require linguistic skill and diversity.

Each of these techniques of using rap and Hip-Hop in therapy—listening and discussing, performing, creating, and/or improvising—meets the needs of clients in very important ways. In this unprecedented book, *Therapeutic Uses of Rap and Hip-Hop*, we explore each of these techniques within the therapy setting. By doing so, our project not only fills a significant gap in therapeutic practices but also speaks to the problematic ways in which rap and Hip-Hop have been dismissed as expressive of meaningless violence and of little social value.

Therapeutic Uses of Rap and Hip-Hop is divided into three sections. In the first section, the contributors explore historical and theoretical perspectives of the use of rap and Hip-Hop in therapy. In the first chapter, music therapist Andrea Frisch Hara provides a brief history of rap. She examines the genre in depth, from its historical roots and evolution into its modern strains. She breaks down its form into essential musical elements, enabling therapists to comprehend it. Frisch Hara emphasizes that it is rap's *form* that makes it an ideal tool for creative and successful therapy work. She examines the reasons that rap speaks to so many adolescents, and particularly, adolescents with severe emotional and learning issues.

In the second chapter, Don Elligan, the clinical psychologist who first coined the term *rap therapy*, explores the use of rap music as a receptive technique in verbal psychotherapy with people with emotional, behavioral, or cognitive challenges. He provides definitions for the various subgenres of rap. He describes the phases of his rap therapy approach and shows how rap music can be used to help clients gain insight and as an expressive tool for cathartic release, cognitive restructuring, and behavioral modification. Furthermore, he explores and discusses challenges of incorporating rap music into psychotherapy practice. He believes that using a culturally sensitive approach to psychotherapy allows the client's cultural environment to be acknowledged in the therapeutic process, and demonstrates that as the language of Hip-Hop culture, rap music can be used as a therapeutic tool with inner-city youth. As such, the use of rap music in this setting helps establish a trusting and nonjudgmental relationship between therapist and client. He shows that by focusing on the lyrics of respected rap artists, the therapist can influence values and provide insight into more positive behaviors and beliefs.

In Chapter 3, music therapist Aaron Lightstone explores the potential importance of Hip-Hop for the field of music therapy. Having a music-centered improvisational music therapy background, Lightstone emphasizes the importance and primacy of cooperative music-making in the therapeutic process within the context of a client-centered therapeutic relationship. He provides a critique of music therapy in terms of the almost nonexistent exploration of rap and Hip-Hop to date. Lightstone goes on to explore the aesthetics of Hip-Hop and how these relate to music therapy, specifically to a groove-based music therapy as articulated by Ken Aigen. Lightstone then explores Hip-Hop music therapy as being the middle ground between music-centered music therapy (in which musicing is primary) and music psychotherapy (in which music is used as a catalyst to initiate therapeutic verbal exchange).

In the fourth chapter, music therapist Michael Viega describes ways in which the Hero's Journey myth and its associated Jungian archetypes have been used in therapy in general and in music therapy in particular. He then provides a brief history of Hip-Hop and shows how it can be seen in terms of the Hero's Journey, with certain archetypes appearing to be active during each portion of the journey: the Preparation, the Journey, and the Return. Viega describes music therapy's role in the journey. He examines ways that the development of rap and Hip-Hop mirrors the individual myths of the people who live within Hip-Hop culture. To illustrate this, he discusses his work with a young African American male in terms of the myths and archetypes that were active in his preferred music, his lived experiences, and in his therapeutic journey.

In Chapter 5, music therapist and social worker Vanessa Veltre and music therapist Susan Hadley explore a Hip-Hop feminist approach to music therapy with adolescent females, particularly adolescent females of color. Veltre and Hadley provide a historical context out of which Hip-Hop feminism evolved and delineate some of its main aims. Drawing from these and from feminist therapy, they explore an approach to feminist therapy in which rap and Hip-Hop are central. They explore ways in which the use of rap and Hip-Hop promotes collaboration and helps to build strong female communities, helps adolescent females to explore identity formation and gender-role socialization, can empower young women to develop and honor their voices as females, and helps to promote social transformation. They provide excerpts of lyrics from specific rap selections to illustrate the presence of these themes.

In the final chapter in this first section, social workers Edgar Tyson, Konstantin Detchkov, and Erin Eastwood and music therapists Alissa Carver and Amanda Sehr present a study in which they identify and discuss socially, spiritually, politically, educationally, economically, and/or culturally relevant themes found in a fairly large sample of some of the more popular Hip-Hop and rap songs to date. These songs are presented by themes and subthemes in tables that identify the artist and album, and the song that was found to have a specific message or meaning (i.e., theme). This chapter, along with the one preceding it, provides a wonderful resource for therapists who want to use rap and Hip-Hop in their work and for those who already do.

In the second section, the contributors share their work using rap and Hip-Hop with at-risk youth. Social worker Tomás Alvarez, in Chapter 7, describes his work using rap therapy to provide strength-based, culturally responsive therapeutic services to at-risk youth of color in Oakland, California. In his chapter, he describes the unique challenges that many young men of color in the United States face and how innovative models like rap therapy can be utilized as a tool for engagement and to help promote healthier psychological and social outcomes. Through the performance-based rap therapy program he pioneered called Beats, Rhymes, and Life (BRL), he offers a strength-based lens through which mental health providers can more fully comprehend youth behavior in the context in which it occurs, instead of subjecting youth to a system of pathology.

In Chapter 8, social worker Stephen Leafloor, aka Buddha, describes his therapeutic approach with the BluePrintForLife team using breakdancing with Inuit and First Nations youth in the Arctic region of Canada. He describes the work they did incorporating Hip-Hop culture and traditional cultural practices. Buddha describes how the work that they do incorporates mentorship and role modeling, cognitive therapy techniques, group therapy, resiliency training, humor and laughter therapy, anger management training, safety planning, sport, play and art therapy in a cultural context, disclosure and healing path stories, goal setting (daring to dream), self-regulating techniques and self-discipline, leadership training (cooperation skills), positive risk taking, and meditation techniques. Buddha also provides an example of the powerful therapeutic value of what he calls "frost graffiti" for processing loss and grief.

In Chapter 9, music therapists Michael Viega and Scott MacDonald describe an innovative project in which they used therapeutic songwriting to provide "at-risk" youth in the Philadelphia region an opportunity to express their stories, experiences, and concerns about the community and the world. This chapter focuses on one particular songwriting group, the Little Saints, who used the familiar soundscape of rap and Hip-Hop music as a vehicle through which to communicate what was happening in their community from their unique perspective. They describe how the culture of rap and Hip-Hop provided a model for the various roles that each child took in the music-making process: from performer, musician, and lyricist to producer, videographer, and artist. These roles gave opportunities for individuality and allowed them to participate in their vision of pop culture.

In Chapter 10, music therapist Katrina McFerran describes the profound relationship between adolescents and songs. She discusses the role of music as significant in the process of differentiation and the process of identity formation during adolescence. She argues that performance of identity can be fostered by music therapists through the technique of songwriting. She describes the process of songwriting with adolescents and the challenges that can arise when writing in the genre of rap and Hip-Hop. She then examines the lyrics of two young men whose affinity with the genre of Hip-Hop was used as a resource. She provides each young man's unique personal, cultural, and systemic context and then examines the lyrics composed for their raps in terms of their connection to themes regarding relationship dynamics, identity formation, and aspirations.

In Chapter 11, music therapists Mandana Ahmadi and Helen Oosthuizen describe how the violent historical oppression of apartheid in South Africa has had lasting effects in the community of Heideveld in Cape Town, where poverty, inadequate access to medical facilities, underresourced educational services, and neglect of children have resulted in a community plagued by a sense of apathy, disempowerment, and voicelessness. They go on to describe their use of rap to address the needs of young people in this context. This chapter draws on individual and group work where rap was often the preferred mode of self-expression. They examine the use of rap as an intervention by which clients voice their stories and dreams for the future. They show that the process of composing raps enables young people to tell their side of the story and to forge positive identities. They then explore the process of refining words as a means of making sense of one's inner life. Finally, they examine performance as a way of delivering a message to the audience and the implications this has for those who hear it.

In Chapter 12, music therapist Aaron Lightstone shares findings from his master's research on Hip-Hop aesthetics and rap therapy in an urban youth shelter. He explores the therapeutic potential of producing and recording rap music as a clinical technique in music-centered therapy, the meaning contained in the improvised and precomposed rap songs of youth, as recorded during music therapy sessions, and the content and nature of this form of self-expression. Using a grounded theory research method, he shares the various themes that emerged from the clients' lyrics. His research provides support for the powerful therapeutic value of the use of rap and Hip-Hop aesthetics in therapy with urban youth.

In Chapter 13, music therapists Flossie Ierardi and Nicole Jenkins explore the use of rap music in the context of music therapy in a short-term juvenile detention center, a transitional facility where youth await decisions on their placement. The therapists describe their work using African-influenced drumming, blues improvisation, and rap improvisation and composition in a 10-week pilot program. They provide both group and individual case examples with male and female youth. The authors found that successful musical/instrumental risk taking and expression of plans for the future via rap improvisation were part of a therapeutic approach in this short-term environment that encouraged the youth to envision their full potential and a more positive future.

In Chapter 14, music therapist Amy Donnenwerth describes her work using rap in song communication (listening and discussing) with teenagers in a residential treatment center for youth offenders in a large metropolitan area. Coming from a background of classical music training, she describes her journey into the therapeutic use of rap. She provides a mission statement for the therapeutic use of rap and then a protocol for therapists who are unfamiliar with the genre. She describes goals that have been achieved in her groups and positive responses from clients. She concludes with some contraindications for the use of rap in therapy, which she shows are not different from the kinds of contraindications for the use of various types of music in therapy.

In the third section, the contributors discuss the ways in which they have used rap and Hip-Hop with clients with specific diagnoses. In Chapter 15, social worker Edgar Tyson provides a detailed description of a specific intervention that he developed called Hip-Hop Therapy (H²T). He then describes his work with a 16-year-old African American male who presented with school problems that were exacerbated by the death of his father. After providing the background and context of the client, he provides a truncated chronology of the therapeutic relationship and application of H²T. The original rap lyrics of the client are included and discussed. Tyson also provides a 1-year follow-up report showing that the client was able to resolve some of his issues with his father and his father's death, and was also able to improve his school outcomes. Tyson also provides limitations, caveats, and cautions when using H²T and other Hip-Hop-based interventions.

In Chapter 16, music therapist Nicole Steele provides case vignettes of the varying ways that she uses Hip-Hop in her clinical work with adolescents in a pediatric medical setting. In these short vignettes Hip-Hop is used as an icebreaker and in songwriting, song discussion, playing instruments, improvising, recording, musical instruction, and movement. Though these adolescents are often referred to as a "lost population," given their liminal status between childhood and adulthood in an environment designed for young children, and given their teenage developmental issues coupled with their medical complications, Steele observes that the music, their music (Hip-Hop), finds them, and that allows her to find them as well.

In Chapter 17, music therapists Felicity Baker and Libby Gleadhill with psychologist Genevieve Dingle examine the use of rap in drug and alcohol rehabilitation. As a result of survey research that they conducted, they found that rap music is often the music of choice of people with substance use disorder and therefore more likely to engage them in music therapy than other types of music. They suggest that the clients relate to these songs because they typically express many of the issues affecting people with substance use disorders. The authors also suggest that the dichotomy of rap songs' lyrics, which may feature pro- or anti-drug use themes, is an apt vehicle for exploring and reframing within the therapy context. Furthermore, the authors claim that by writing their own lyrics, the clients can tell their story and express difficult emotions within a drug-free context. The authors provide several advantages for using rap over other musical genres for use in therapy with people affected by substance use disorders.

In Chapter 18, music therapist Emma O'Brien presents two very different music therapy case examples of using rap music in songwriting sessions with people with cancer that highlight the surprising diversity of the medium across demographics of age and experience. The first case example is with a 24-year-old woman, who was a long-term patient, undergoing treatment for cancer, which was complicated by her past history of drug use. The second case example is with a group of women with breast cancer attending a community-based creative music therapy program. O'Brien considers the use of rap as an appropriate and effective genre for setting prewritten lyrics; as a tool for stimulating further creation of lyrics; and in terms of its role in performance.

In Chapter 19, music therapist Stella Compton Dickinson and psychiatrist Pauline Souflas explore the use of rap with a British-born, 18-year-old Black Caribbean man who showed problems of aggression and sexualized behavior, as a result of a severe episode of encephalitis at the age of 16. This client was placed in a high-security hospital after having committed an offense of assault causing actual bodily harm. The authors describe 4 years of music therapy treatment, 2 years in individual therapy followed by 2 years in a cognitive analytic music therapy group, in which the main focus of therapy was the creation of original raps. This work enabled him to move directly from hospital into the community.

Reading through these chapters, the reader will note that each contributor takes the use and value of rap and Hip-Hop as therapeutic tools very seriously. The text is designed not only to provide a rationale for the use of rap and Hip-Hop in therapy but also to encourage therapists to validate the experiences for those for whom rap music is a significant mode of expression. A further extension of this aim is to promote a shift away from a negative perspective held by society more generally and many therapists in particular toward a more complex understanding of the ways in which rap and Hip-Hop are attentive to the lived experiences (both positive and negative) of many therapy clients and how this aspect of rap and Hip-Hop is inevitably helpful within the therapeutic context. Hence, the text is designed to create a paradigm shift.

References

Alim, H. S., Meghelli, S., & Spady, J. G. (2006). *The global cipha: Hip Hop culture and consciousness*. Philadelphia, PA: UMUM Press.

Bruscia, K. B. (1991). *Case studies in music therapy*. Phoenixville, PA: Barcelona.

Eure, J. D., & Spady, J. G. (1991). *Nation conscious rap*. New York: PC International Press.

Forman, M. (2002). *The 'hood comes first: Race, space, and place in rap and Hip-Hop*. Middletown, CT: Wesleyan University Press.

McFerran, K. (2010). *Adolescents, music and music therapy: Methods and techniques for clinicians, educators and students*. London: Jessica Kingsley.

Potter, R. A. (1995). *Spectacular vernaculars: Hip-Hop and the politics of postmodernism*. Albany, NY: SUNY Press.

Small, C. (1998). *Musicking: The meanings of performing and listening*. Middletown, CT: Wesleyan University Press.

Smitherman, G. (1999). *Talkin that talk: Language, culture and education in African America*. New York: Routledge.

Spady, J. G., Dupres, S., & Lee, C. G. (1995). *Twisted tales in the Hip Hop streets of Philly*. Philadelphia, PA: UMUM Press.

Part 1

HISTORICAL AND THEORETICAL PERSPECTIVES

Chapter 1

RAP (Requisite, Ally, Protector) and the Desperate Contemporary Adolescent

Andrea Frisch Hara[*]

Introduction

During a substantial time period of my professional life, I worked as a music therapist with adolescents in a variety of settings. Beginning in the late 1980s, a common request was for RAP music,[†] a genre that was definitely not my personal cup of tea! But was I really listening? Teen after teen would request a "song" that had a driving beat and a machine gun-like oral

---

[*] Acknowledgment: Profound gratitude to my husband, and fellow therapist, Gary M. Hara. Without his love, devotion, and professional expertise, this chapter would never have been written! Feedback and questions are welcome: AFrischMTBC@aol.com.

[†] The term RAP has been capitalized throughout to specify its status as a genre, making it unnecessary to use the term rap *music* and so as not to confuse it with the slang, meaning "to speak."

narrative. I often felt assaulted by the violent words, the dissonant, synco-pated rhythms, and, always, the over-the-top volume that was requested. And sometimes, I felt afraid. The techno timbre and varying intoned beats could be chilling. The music seemed to unleash a basic, "primitive" force within my clients, and within me. It was raw and unformed, and it was deter-mined to find expression.

My passive and depressed clients came alive when this music played. They moved their withdrawn, hidden, clothing-covered bodies to the groove. Their faces, frozen with fear, frustration, despair, sadness, and anger, became animated. They rapped along and displayed their own (out) rage, showed determination to right the wrongs done to them, and vowed to survive and to prevail. My "acting out" clients settled down and became regulated by the beat. Their constant, hyper-motion found its expression through the complex collage of sounds. To chant along, they had to focus and concentrate and I was awed by their ability to memorize and repeat the lyrics of long narrative passages. Even the adolescents who had difficulty reading were able to become a part of this form. I listened. They noticed. And our therapeutic work began.

At music therapy conferences, and in my field's professional publica-tions, I was stunned by the lack of presentations and articles about RAP music. The few that I found focused on the lyrics. And of course, society, mainstream society, was consistently disparaging RAP as violent, fringe, not "real" music, dangerous, and so on. I felt that my colleagues were missing the point. What about the *music,* I wondered, the *music* of RAP? And from where did this music come? What were its origins? Why was it so popular? And most importantly to me, why was it captivating my clients and how could I facilitate their growth by harnessing its power and meaning?!

This chapter will provide a brief history of RAP music and introduce its different types. The genre will be examined in depth, from its historical roots and evolution into its modern strains. Its form will be broken down into essential musical elements, enabling music therapists to comprehend and reproduce it. An attempt will be made to go beyond the "obvious" regarding RAP, that is, that it often reflects the listener's environment and expresses experiences of rage, frustration, discontent, and disenfranchisement and sometimes advocates a life of antisocial behavior and violence. The chapter will emphasize that it is RAP's *form* that makes it a perfectly ideal tool for creative and successful therapy work.*

Theoretical constructs regarding RAP's popularity, purpose, and func-tion will be presented. Attention will be paid to how and why adolescents

---

* In this chapter, it is the audio experience of RAP music that is explored. It is important to note that RAP videos are also important and another artistic form that can affect the listener.

use RAP music in their lives. A major focus will look at the reasons it speaks to so many adolescents, and particularly, adolescents with the most severe emotional and learning issues. The chapter will analyze the phenomenon of adolescents struggling with major issues of emotional and physical survival, and why they demonstrate an urgent, sometimes consuming, need for RAP music. This will be viewed within the context of "typical" adolescent development. Details and descriptions of how and why music therapists can constructively utilize this music within treatment will be suggested.

The clinical topics of therapeutic value, acting out versus expression and sublimation, clinical effectiveness, aesthetic meaning, transitional object, identity crisis, ego formation, countertransference, interfacing with clinicians, and reactions from society will be addressed. Guidelines for synthesizing RAP music will be offered and will include the use of acoustic and electric instruments, vocal techniques, and electronic and recording devices. The international appeal and lasting power of RAP music, and therefore some critical implications for contemporary society, will be touched upon.

History

From Africa

RAP music traces its origins to the rich body of music that comes from Africa. The great oral and vocal tradition that gave the United States gospel, blues, jazz, R&B, soul, and rock'n'roll is also responsible for RAP. The earliest examples of the form are in the chanting of the griot, the African keeper of ancestral history. (The word *griot* is French in origin and the term *jelli*, of Manding origin, means "musicianhood.") RAP contains African and African diasporic antecedents and influences.

> RAP's forebears stretch back through disco, street funk, radio DJs, Bo Diddley, the bibop singers, Cab Calloway, Pigmeat Markham, the dancers and comics, the Last Poets, Gil Scott-Heron, Mohammed Ali, acappella and doo-wop groups, ring games, skip-rope rhymes, prison and army songs, toasts, signifying and the dozens, all the way to the griots of Nigeria and Gambia. (Toop, 1991, p. 16)

The griot's function is to keep an oral history of a tribe or village. The griot also sings praises and can be a wandering musician, like the troubadour. He can entertain with stories, poems, songs, and dances. In this expanded role, he must also have the expertise to improvise about current issues and events. He can use wit, humor, and satire to comment about local

Table 1.1 Audio Examples

Griot, Griot and String/Kora	
Togo Griot 00	http://www.youtube.com/watch?v=PVSsHc9RenQ
Togo Griot 01	http://www.youtube.com/watch?v=jsW4sdOVDLM
Kora Music from West African Griot Lankandia Cissoko	http://www.youtube.com/watch?v=JNl8klwj1_k
Djele Lankandia-Kora Music	http://www.youtube.com/watch?v=KMp_El9ltAs
Vocal, Polyrhythmic, Polyphonic	
Griot Dagara (go to 3.15 time for hand-clapping rhythms and vocals)	http://www.youtube.com/watch?v=H8uOBLqKQ5s
Kora Playing by Toumani Diabate and the Symmetric Orchestra (go to 1.17 time regarding Kora's bass, melodic, and improvisational elements)	http://www.youtube.com/watch?v=UfRUH2fKUgA

Note: All audio examples are from http://www.youtube.com, except as noted, "Hambone," from http://www.rhapsody.com.

and world politics. I think it is quite striking that modern RAP artists are often serving a similar function within our society. In many ways, the functions of RAP music, and its musical predecessors, and the music of music therapy are similar; they are process-oriented, improvisational, and social in nature (see Table 1.1).

Another common African root is the ancient singing tradition of the *gawlla*, a poem of gossip or abuse, sung by Yoruba women. (Yoruba people are a large ethnic group of West Africa.) It was used when two women argued and they needed to vent to each other in public. The galla would be sung in a public place where other women would hear it. Sometimes it could be used for social pressure, and to get a woman to conform to public opinion.

Continuity through the Diaspora

As the African American community survived through enslavement and beyond in the United States, there are several other noteworthy musical forms that contain the roots of modern RAP. These may be unfamiliar to many and yet they lend credence to RAP as an evolved form of the music of the griot. Two audio examples follow: Mississippi blues, with percussive

Table 1.2 Audio Examples

Booker White—Aberdeen Mississippi Blues HIFI	http://www.youtube.com/watch?v=bsMpHHSLSlc
Negro Prison Songs/"Black Woman-Murder's Home-Jumpin' Judy"	http://www.youtube.com/watch?v=FZs45oL_n8k&feature=PlayList&p=5EF49DD405701E0C&playnext=1&playnext_from=PL&index=3

Table 1.3 Audio Examples

Hambone with Bessie Jones and children	http://www.rhapsody.com/bessie-jones/put-your-hand-on-your-hip-let-your-backbone-slip
Hand Bone Basics	http://www.youtube.com/watch?v=fQRALdJCOh4&NR=1
Hambone Knee slap	http://www.youtube.com/watch?v=YMJeaZtgwng&feature=related

elements in addition to the guitar and voice, and blues from imprisoned women in the United States during the 1930s, a time when Jim Crow laws were prevalent and, therefore, African American women could easily be unjustly imprisoned (see Table 1.2).

Next is an example of a type of children's clapping and rhyming song. Some may be familiar with this African American musical tradition of which Miss Mary Mack is an example. (Miss Mary Mack is of Scots-English derivation and was sung by American enslaved children.) The first sample is of Bessie Jones, who was a Georgia Sea Island Native, singing with children. The granddaughter of an enslaved man, she learned many songs like these from her grandfather. The others demonstrate the use of the body as a percussion instrument. The use of hand and body percussion combined with chanting and singing shares much in common with modern RAP (see Table 1.3).

Continued Historical/Musical Roots and Influences

There are several African American oral traditions that are important because of their influence on RAP music. The following are some that have shaped RAP's many different types or forms:

> *Toasts*—Long, rhyming stories that can be violent, obscene, or misogynistic in nature. A well-known example is the *Signifying Monkey*.

Table 1.4 Audio Examples

The Signifying Monkey by Doug Hammond	http://www.youtube.com/ watch?v=hJAusfEalfo
Rudy Ray Moore Is . . . Dolemite—Signifying Monkey	http://www.youtube.com/ watch?v=Xkp_v1zldxE&feature=related

Early versions are based on an African tale in which a monkey and lion try to outsmart and outwit each other. It takes tremendous verbal acumen to recite a toast. Two examples are shown in Table 1.4. The first is traditional; the second, more modern with a generous use of profanity.

The Dozens (also known as *ranking*)—Rhyming couplets and a driving 7/8 meter, these improvised word competitions often begin with "your mother" ("Yo Mama") or "your father." A common one is, "Yo Mama so stupid it takes her 2 hours to watch *60 Minutes*." The two participants take turns insulting and disparaging each other, or a family member, using clever put-downs to describe their adversary. (The term has many possible origins, but one is from disabled slaves, often made so from oppressive violence, being sold by the dozen.) Table 1.5 shows a contemporary example that features profanity and some base, potentially offensive commentary.

1950s Jive Talk—Also known as *hepcat* jive, it is the type of talking that Wolfman Jack, the DJ, was known for (see Table 1.6).

Civil Rights Leaders' Speeches—Prominent during the 1960s, orators such as the Reverend Dr. Martin Luther King, Jr., and Malcolm X exemplified the power of the spoken word. *Message RAP* has its antecedents in these speeches and delivers a social message via the RAP. I believe that sermons by preachers, in the African American tradition, may also be a primary source of this subgenre.

Table 1.5 Audio Example

Tracy Morgan vs. Carlos Mencia Yo Mama Battle	http://www.youtube.com/ watch?v=W8fcsaPRLRA&feature=related

Table 1.6 Audio Example

Segment of the Wolfman Jack Show	http://www.youtube.com/ watch?v=34rU-TXcVtg&feature=related

Ballad, Soul, and R&B music—These genres are utilized within RAP to create soft-spoken phrasing in between, or over, rhythmic beating. In more recent RAPs, the rapper often collaborates with an R&B artist to create a contrast of staccato RAP lyrics and smoothly sung sections.

The rich tradition of storytelling to teach life lessons or morals—From *Anansi the Spider,* an example of West African Folklore, to *Uncle Remus,* African American stories gathered during the late 19th century, there is a tradition that uses the oral word to tell a story. Storytelling is a prominent feature in RAP songs.

There are also social, political, racial, and economic influences upon the development of RAP music. In addition, developments in the music world have contributed to the creation and evolution of RAP. It is beyond the scope of this chapter to focus on all of these areas in-depth except for the musical developments, which are concrete and important. They will be discussed further in the next section.

The Evolution of RAP Music

In the early 1980s RAP, originally referred to as *MCing,* emerged on the musical scene. Many believe it was a reaction against the genre of disco. In these early days, the break within the record, or between records, in which drumbeats were prominent, began to be extended into an instrumental section by using two turntables.

Hip-Hop was a term that Kool Herc—sometimes considered the first RAP artist—introduced to describe his Jamaican-style scatting. A style of dancing originated and was facilitated by his scatting. In between records at block parties in the South Bronx in New York City, his scatting was danced to by *break dancers* (see Table 1.7).

One reason that RAP may have so quickly replicated and become accessible to so many is due to advances in technology. Reasonably priced drum machines, mixers, electronic keyboards, and multi-track recorders for in-home use began to proliferate during this period of time. And, of course, turntables with records were already in use and available for creating original RAP.

Table 1.7 Audio Example

Viva Freestyle Kool DJ Herc Live	http://www.youtube.com/watch?v=CjmXMvLU1ps&feature=related

Historically, RAP music is the first genre originated by African Americans* that has gone beyond their community, has simultaneously been created and performed by them, and remains primarily attached to them. While other racial and ethnic groups create, perform, and listen to RAP, I believe that RAP is universally known to have originated within the African American community. In the past, in the United States, when other African American art forms crossed over into the mainstream, they were taken over and popularized by non–African American artists. (Al Jolson, Elvis Presley, and DJ Wolfman Jack are examples.) Otherwise, the art form remained segregated, available only to the African American community in which it was created. The influences discussed above, such as toasting, are prime examples.

This is an important phenomenon, for both societal and therapeutic reasons. I believe that one reason RAP music is so popular and controversial within our culture is because of the empowerment it represents. An example of genuine empowerment of a nondominant group, derived from creating a unique art form and receiving public recognition for that form, RAP is (now) a part of mainstream culture and known throughout the world.

This speaks to the evolution of society. More importantly, and for the purpose of this chapter, it speaks to the inherent strength and pride that RAP lends to the desperate contemporary adolescent; it can signify the triumph of the *underdog* and the righting of the wronged.

Various Forms

Since I first began researching RAP in the 1990s, the genre has expanded to include more subtypes. RAP has gone from being unconventional and fringe to mainstream and popular. It can be found in every region of the world, in many countries—Japan, Korea, Pakistan, the Dominican Republic, Haiti, France, the UK, Australia, Brazil, Mexico, Poland, Germany, Israel, Palestine, the Czech Republic, Kenya, and South Africa, to name a few—and

---

* In our culture, the term *African American* is all too commonly used to describe a very specific subgroup of a widely diverse community. Frequently the descriptor is often referencing poor, urban, under-formally-educated, disenfranchised people of African American ancestry. In reality, and like any other racial or ethnic group in America, the African American community is diverse economically, geographically, and socially and possesses a wide range of educational achievement.

RAP music is, indeed, *derived* from African American roots. This assertion is correct. However, to declare that it is reflective of the African American community is not necessarily completely accurate. It is reflective of some members of the African American community and perhaps other Americans as well.

is listened to by a wide variety of people. People of different ages, races, ethnicities, socioeconomic classes, geographic locations, and so on, may all listen to RAP.

Table 1.8 lists some of its forms. These categories do not consistently refer to the same characteristics. Old School primarily refers to a *time period* during which the earliest RAP of the 1970s and 1980s was composed. Sometimes it refers to a particular style that was prevalent during this time. Gangsta or Christian refer to the *themes* within the song. East Coast and Southern refer to the *geographical region/location* in which the particular style originated. Crunk and Snap mainly refer to the *specific musical elements* that the style employs. (The name *crunk* is derived from a combination of the words *crazy* and *drunk*. It is RAP that is fast, with many easily imitative sounds or phrases. It is mostly played in clubs as dance music and is used in a responsorial way with the attendees. *Snap* refers to the snapping of fingers that is predominant in its composition.) However, the basic musical elements that are arranged to make the RAP collage remain the same.

Musical Elements

The following are several very specific traits that are synthesized to create a RAP:

> *Repetitive and grounding rhythm*—The meter is organized and the beat patterns repeat to create a predictable expectation for the listener.
>
> *Layering*—The basic musical elements are present and happen concurrently. Rhythmic, melodic, and harmonic essentials are all used. Record scratches, a vocal line spoken, a vocal line sung, a drum or percussion beat, precomposed music from another song (*sampling*, see below), sound effects, sirens, screams, finger snapping, hand clapping, whistling, an instrumental melodic line—all are arranged and rearranged; the elements are sculpted into a simultaneously occurring body of sound.
>
> *Syncopation*—Each separate track—vocal line, percussion, harmonic passage—may be syncopated throughout. This unexpected shift in rhythmic accent may create a feeling of temporary disorientation until the predominant beat reemerges. Conversely, the consistent use of syncopation can actually lead to a strongly experienced downbeat for the listener. (A good example of this is Latin dance music in which the dancer moves within the downbeat spaces left by the musical syncopations.)

Table 1.8 Audio Examples

Old School

Sugar Hill Gang, "Rapper's Delight" (1979)	http://www.youtube.com/ watch?v=diiL9bqvalo&NR=1	A comprehensive example of sophisticated lyrics
Grandmaster Flash & the Furious Five, "The Message" (1982)	Audio version: http://www.youtube.com/ watch?v=dShcXDacNXM Live version: http://www.youtube.com/ watch?v=BN9-K0aZXRg	The first RAP that was a social commentary

Gangsta/West Coast

N.W.A. (Niggaz with Attitude), "Fuck the Police" (1988)	Unedited version: http://www.youtube.com/ watch?v=ro08blLEvqc	The first RAP to create major societal controversy, including demands for artistic censorship. The FBI was accused of intimidating the record company that produced the song (Arnold, 1989).
2Pac, "Dear Mama" (1995)	http://www.youtube.com/ watch?v=JncloTmvTeA	Tupac Amaru Shakur was one of the most famous rappers of all time and was murdered in 1996. He, with Notorious B.I.G., were the main rivals in the East Coast–West Coast RAP rivalry.

Hardcore/East Coast

Public Enemy, "Fight the Power" (1989)		Known for its provocative political commentary
Public Enemy, "Get the Fuck Outta Dodge" (1991)	Unedited version: http://www.youtube.com/ watch?v=4lmh4kCNlWo	Known for its provocative political commentary

Table 1.8 (continued) Audio Examples

New School

L.L. Cool J, "Stand by Your Man" (1993)	http://www.youtube.com/watch?v=nRrzNlsPg5g	An example of more commercially ready RAP

Southern

Outkast, "Rosa Parks" (1999)	http://www.youtube.com/watch?v=7Z3niFJugp8	One of the most famous Southern school's groups

Crunk/Snap

Lil Jon, "Snap Yo Fingers" (2006)	http://www.youtube.com/watch?v=AoA-Byjlf2M	Mesmerizing club composition

Christian

Tedashii, "I'm a Believer" (2009)	http://www.youtube.com/watch?v=Ac80JEvwjEw	Lyrics related to a Christian lifestyle

Table 1.9 Audio Example

Lil Wayne, "A Milli" (2008) (original version)	http://www.youtube.com/watch?v=JgjJndOlbUs&feature=related

Table 1.10 Audio Example

Beyoncé and Jay Z, "03 Bonnie and Clyde" (2002)	http://www.youtube.com/watch?v=UGhRhaKmD8s	The loop is a Spanish melodic phrase, played on guitar and heard mostly in the beginning and at the end.

Popping—Technique that leaves gaps in between phrases in unobvious places. Usually this is done with a spoken vocal line. It takes skill and practice to accomplish this (see Table 1.9).

The loop—A line that is repeated throughout and usually refers to an instrumental melodic line. It can apply to a beat pattern as well. This facet is probably employed by all RAP forms! (See Table 1.10.)

Table 1.11 Audio Example

RAP version: Marky Mark and the Funky Bunch, "Wildside" (1991)	http://www.youtube.com/ watch?v=oHUDlXJ5Wfc
From the original song, "Walk on the Wild Side" by Lou Reed (1972)	http://www.youtube.com/ watch?v=4FKts1JoaJc
RAP version: Coolio "I'll C U When U Get There" (1997)	http://www.youtube.com/ watch?v=tP1PXRiVoJw&feature=related
From the original Pachelbel Canon in D	http://www.youtube.com/ watch?v=JvNQU1_HQ0

    Sampling—This refers to taking sounds (i.e., samples) from a piece of prerecorded music and using it within the RAP song. (Interestingly, a *remix* is a later version of a RAP, in which major portions are samples; see Table 1.11.)

    Lyrics—The words in RAP songs are powerful because they are positioned carefully to stand out amid the other musical elements. No other recent musical form has stirred so much controversy as have the lyrics of RAP music. They are often slang, profane, explicitly sexual, and graphically violent and advocate an antisocial lifestyle. Because of this, they have offended, frightened, marginalized, and also appealed to, the public. RAP's slang lyrics can create a "private language" within a community. This code can support the feeling of an underground, subculture, or secret society. It is important to note that sometimes RAP songs also offer honest and hopeful messages. Some also offer religious commentary.

What makes RAP unique is the uncommon usage of these elements. The listener's predominant experience may be to hear all of these elements as foreground or background *rhythms*. The voice, or vocal sounds, can be used percussively. The same is true for melodic phrases and for harmonies. Harmonic moments can be used in chunks, like chords, to create short beat patterns. However, sometimes, the repeated and complex sub-rhythms can feel hypnotic and almost melodic, a melody of rhythm.

Adolescent Development, Identity Crisis, and Ego Formation

Adolescence is a time of massive and rapid change. There is an increase in physical, psychic, and sexual energies, and creative drive. It is also a time of transition between childhood and adulthood. Inherent in this period is the normal and necessary identity crisis, "a crucial moment when development must move one way or another, marshaling resources of growth, recovery and further differentiation" (Erikson, 1968, p. 26).

During the adolescent years, the individual's identity, or sense of self, coalesces and "there's no feeling of being alive without a sense of identity" (Erikson, 1968, p. 130). It is ego strength that allows the adolescent to successfully go into, and through, the identity crisis. The ego is solidified during the identity crisis and a new sense of self is born. While it is beyond the scope of this chapter to delve into "normal" adolescent development in depth, two psychic structures—ego strength and ego formation—are quite pertinent. This is because a deficit in ego strength and an immature ego formation are most often what music therapists must address when working with adolescents with emotional and learning difficulties.

When development has been arrested it means that the adolescent has not had enough (prior) practice with a myriad of nurturing experiences. This, in turn, means that the teenager arrives at the identity crisis without the necessary skills to undergo it. The adolescent has neither internalized sufficient structure, nor has become proficient in the manipulation of symbols. Without remediation (of the consciousness), there is little hope for mastering the adolescent milestones and, consequently, having the chance for a meaningful or productive life. Music therapy, in general, is a highly effective means to increase ego strength and to improve ego formation (Frisch, 1990).

The therapeutic use of RAP is able to prepare the adolescent with emotional or learning difficulties for the identity crisis; experience in music therapy with RAP music can ameliorate maturational shortfalls, especially ego strength. The form of RAP music is perfectly suited to move adolescents into and through the identity crisis. I believe that this accounts for RAP music's popularity with the world's youth! It gratifies basic maturational needs and provides an expression that facilitates development.

RAP: The Perfect Form for Music Therapy

The structural and thematic aspects of RAP organize the adolescent's struggles of development into an aesthetic form. As a genre, RAP music is profoundly rich. Its scores can have as many parts as symphonies, with many aural and rhythmic lines occurring through time. It has always been striking to me that so many music therapy clinicians' negative reactions to RAP have prevented them from using it in therapy. RAP music's form is about as close to perfection as one can get to a therapeutic medium! Its structure provides structure. Simultaneously, it allows freedom of expression and a myriad of ways to improvise. Its components are simple enough so that one needs no musical skill or competence to participate in, or master, it.* It combines vocal and instrumental music. It can be easily created. It is an integration of process and product. It can serve as a gratifying transitional object. It provides consistent practice with (musical) transitions. It allows acting-out impulses to be channeled (or sublimated) into gratifying aesthetic expressions.

The manner in which RAP music is formed parallels the way music should be utilized in music therapy with adolescents needing treatment. So, in studying its form, one can learn about how to utilize and maximize the benefits of music therapy for adolescents in need. Many people, clinicians included, believe that RAP music is an extreme art form. Perhaps, but so, too, are the life circumstances of many of the teens who rely upon us to help them to grow. Consider the following quote and ask yourself if it could also be speaking about the motive for composing RAP music, that is, a situation that many RAP artists would be able to understand: "Should a young person feel that the environment tries to deprive him[her] too radically of all the forms of expression which permits him[her] to develop and to integrate the next step, he[she] may resist with the wild strength encountered in animals who are sufficiently forced to defend their lives" (Winnicott, 1965, p. 187).

"RAP is an angry voice of . . . a nation that cannot secede and may not assimilate and thus is driven still deeper inside" (Costello and Wallace, 1990, p. 40). The (sub)culture that originated RAP was urban, poor, marginalized, and discriminated against for multiple generations. Finding a means of expression was a way out of problematic circumstances, and for many, it worked. So, too, can RAP provide a pathway to maturity and health for the adolescent with emotional and learning difficulties. Like any musical form well suited to music therapy, RAP simultaneously speaks to and for others (Costello & Wallace, 1990). It raps a message to which the listener is able to relate and gives a voice to the listener with which he/she can connect to other people in his/her life and community.

The Therapeutic Value of RAP's Form

The most effective music therapy for adolescents is engaging, active-oriented, and structured to provide a holding environment, with as much freedom as possible for improvisation and creativity. How lucky, as therapists, for us to have a form that has already been created that gives our clients

---

* This does not mean that everyone can be a skilled or brilliant rapper, but this is not a prerequisite for therapeutic efficacy.

what they need to grow. We do not have to create a form or search for ideas. We need, instead, to familiarize ourselves with the genre and then offer it. The challenge, typically, is to give enough structure so that the health-giving experience of creation is facilitated. Without the structure, some level of bedlam will occur and creativity will be too hard to achieve. Without the chance for improvisation and creativity, some level of bedlam will occur because therapeutic engagement will be too boring. RAP music enables us to offer this dual experience.

It is organized yet has unpredictable components. It is structured, yet has space for improvisation. It can be created in the moment, yet its sampled excerpts need to be manipulated to create its multilayered form. It balances between words and beats, song and instrumental, allowing the composer, DJ, and rapper to each take what he/she needs to create the art. As the teen is able to create, take risks, create some more, he/she is manipulating symbols—musical elements—and repeatedly strengthening his/her ego. It is necessary, it is gratifying, it is growth-enhancing. It is clinically effective. Using RAP's form can help our clients to heal and to grow.

Like all participation in music therapy, this is metaphoric—that is, picking and choosing musical samples, lyrics, and so on, can symbolize what he/she did not get emotionally in the past, but simultaneously, he/she *is* getting it in the music. I believe that we use the music of music therapy as a concrete metaphor. Anyone with an early traumatic injury needs concrete experience in creating to develop and their deprivations need to be gratified within the creative process. RAP's clinical effectiveness is, in large part, due to the opportunities it offers in creating and manipulating its lyrical and musical symbols. The adolescent, in general, and the ones we see in treatment, specifically, can receive necessary fundamentals within the experience of creating RAP. For example, supportive mirroring, the basic, earliest, interaction between caregiver and infant, is experienced during the responsorial element within RAP. The *loop* can repeatedly mirror and *sampling* can certainly reflect.

RAP exerts a motivational force over our adolescent clients that assists us with their initial engagement. The urge to be a star, the need to be noticed and to gain (positive) attention drives these clients to RAP. It motivates them to master RAP's form. They gain competency during this learning and their ego, sense of self, develops. While mastery, especially cognitive mastery, is a normal challenge of adolescent development, the adolescent with emotional or learning difficulties often has impaired cognitive ability. Their early stages of ego deprivation may have affected cognitive intactness negatively. (Cognitive deficits typically manifest in reading difficulty, reticence to attempt even simple music-making, and laborious efforts to master simple RAP patterns.)

These teens exhibit low frustration tolerance, making the prospect of music improvisation daunting. Yet, even with this attribute and shaky self-esteem, these teens sooner than later find RAP to be accessible. Due to its varied components, there is always a way to pick one of its musical elements and to use it to begin creating, simultaneously making an inroad into the therapy they need.

RAP as a Transitional Object

One of music's most helpful functions is its ability to serve as a transitional object. This is true for any type of music and across all populations. RAP music is no exception and I believe that teenagers use it to help them with the little, as well as the big, transitions in their lives. Not unlike the toddler who sings throughout the day, and oftentimes before sleep, the adolescent singing or chanting RAP as they make their way around is quite a familiar sight! Furthermore, we can hear it blasting loudly from cars or through iPOD headphones. It may be RAP's vocal aspect that makes it particularly useful as a transitional object. The individual can sing it to themselves and can soothe or nurture themselves in the process.

We do not question a young child's need for a security blanket and so we must accept an adolescent's desire, and need, for a musical transitional object. This is critically important for adolescents in crisis. These teenagers may have *no* permanent safe place; their external environment may be unsteady, even dangerous, and they may not have been able to internalize a safe space within themselves. Transitional objects help them to feel safe so that they can take on the tasks of maturation and growth. This is why RAP music may be so successful in terms of engaging teens. At first, RAP functions as a transitional object, and then it continues to facilitate their development.

The Elements of RAP as Therapeutic Tools

The DJ hovers ever nearby . . . . His responsibility is the song behind and around the RAP—the backbeat, krush groove and the "sound carpet," i.e., a kind of electric aural environment, a chaos behind the rapper's rhymed order, a digitalized blend of snippets, squeaks, screams, sirens, snatches from pop media, all mixed and splattered so that the listener cannot really listen but only *feel* the mash of "samples" that results. (Costello & Wallace, 1990, p. 25)

Sampling can enable the adolescent to get or take what he needs to develop. Of course, sampling is also an acute way for the therapist to observe what the teen might be saying to us. Why is a scream chosen, or a birdsong or a video game sound? What are we being shown? Why would a contemporary song phrase be used or an older one? Whose voice(s) are we hearing? In addition, the adolescent can create an ideal representation of what he/she would like his/her environment to be and to sound like.

RAP music is a thick collage. It can offer the experience of integrating all of these elements to create a whole form. This is another real metaphor; it symbolizes, and really is, an experience of self-integration. The multi-tracked characteristic allows for a wonderful juxtaposition of order and chaos, control and out-of-control, so in sync with the turmoil of adolescence! The musical parts can be manipulated over and over and over again, not solely as practice, but within the actual finished product. The recurring loop is a good example of this. Therapeutically, this allows multiple attempts at (re)mastery, until the teen's ego gets it just right and can move on to the next developmental challenge.

Aesthetic Meaning, Countertransference, and Sublimation

What does it mean that so much of RAP is violent, graphically sexual, and antisocial in nature? What does it mean to each member of the therapy dyad, to the client and to the therapist? I am not sure what percentage of RAP music does embody these characteristics, but they are what is often conjured up when people hear or think about RAP music. On a societal level, RAP can reflect the community in which it originated, and its major issues. We may not like to hear about violence, trauma, injustice, poverty, oppression, discrimination, and rebellion, but we cannot deny their existence.

Sometimes clouding this issue is the reality of the subculture that surrounds some RAP—that is, that some rappers have been or are currently involved in violence and/or advocate it. This needs to be discussed with clients if necessary, but the advocation of violence is not a function of RAP's *form*! The form remains a therapeutic tool with the potential to profoundly help adolescents in need. I have found that many adolescents who admire violent and Gangsta RAP (though certainly not all) have been exposed to the most extreme life circumstances.

When I can demonstrate to them that I want to know more, that I can tolerate hearing the cursing, the violence, the desperation, and the fury, often the intensity of what they need to express dies down and they are able to work in therapy with less extreme lyrics or sounds. It is not my role as a therapist to edit my client's expression, only to listen, to point out how it makes me feel, and sometimes, to tell them what I think they might be trying to tell me. With adolescents in crisis, I can also offer alternate strategies for expression, at least outside of the treatment space.

On a therapeutic level, when violent or Gangsta RAP is requested or referred to, we need to ask why. Is it autobiographical for a client? Literally? (Did our client lose a parent or a sibling or a friend to violence? Is the brutality of poverty part of his everyday life?) Or, figuratively? (Is a wealthy, member of a dominant race, suburban teen wanting to play or compose Gangsta RAP? If so, were neglect, emotional deprivation, and parental oppression part of his childhood?) If rage is present, it needs to have an avenue for expression. That will lead to constructive development. If, instead, a clinician's countertransference impedes its reception, and suppression occurs, there is no outlet for expression and growth is frustrated.

If we are unable to tolerate a specific form of expression, we need to question, explore, and understand it. Why are we offended by this RAP? Does it scare us? Why? Does it tap into our own rage? That can be scary. Do we feel threatened by the *underdog*, taking over and dominating us? Is that what the *in-your-face* quality feels like? Does it imply a shift in power? Something we are not used to? Are there gender, class, and race issues that the music raises for us? How fortunate we are to have a form that can bring these dynamics into consciousness so that we can explore them. They need to be personally explored and then we need to guide our clients' explorations as well.

Sometimes it is the profanity or graphic sexual imagery and descriptions that clinicians worry about. My thoughts about the use of explicit sexual activities are specific. For an adolescent, sex is a fairly new territory. Sexuality blossoms during adolescence and the lure and excitement of becoming an active sexual human being is strong. It is a bridge that takes us from childhood into adulthood. Sex is powerful and can make an individual feel alive. Sex is connection. Sex creates life. Sex is creative; it can serve the function that play once did for a child. Ideally, it teaches us how to share and take turns, about give-and-take, how to collaborate and deepen friendship. It shows us how to love and be loved. It asks that we take our prior nurturing experiences and use them with a peer.

For the adolescent in crisis, there is often a distortion in the area of sexuality for the straightforward reason that their previous nurturing experiences were less than ideal. Regardless of their debilitating issues, teenagers with emotional issues are still teenagers; they may be developmentally stuck in childhood, but they also are chronologically aged adolescents. Their bodies are going through puberty and, perhaps more than their "normally" developing counterparts, they possess a desperate need to feel alive! The sexual lyrics of RAP are a profound way to grapple with these issues with our adolescent clients.

All adolescents are relieved when they discover that a respected adult recognizes, accepts, and understands that they are sexual human beings. Therapy is clearly a place where the nitty-gritty of the teen's sexual wishes, hopes, fears, fantasies, and actions need to be processed. If the lyrics are violent or speak of abuse, and a teen is drawn to them, they need to be discussed so that the resonant issues can be worked through. During adolescence, the teen may sometimes be too guarded, sensitive, or uncomfortable to verbally discuss sexual issues. That is why our tool of musical form is a gift. The music says it and then we engage in a musical dialogue about it. RAP facilitates this process if we allow sexual lyrics to be played, sung, composed, and heard.

Please note one of my least favorite clinical terms is *acting out* because it is not usually used in a clinically observant or neutral way and typically has a negative connotation. Of course many adolescents in need of therapy *act out!* It demonstrates their minimal ability to manipulate symbols, to express or sublimate. Creating RAP offers vast possibilities in terms of expression. Gradually, the teen becomes more agile in manipulating the musical elements and creating RAP. Each creation, in turn, becomes a building block in ego development and strength. Over time, the ego, the sense of self, becomes stronger and expressing (versus acting out) is less of a challenge.

Countertransference and Our Role as Clinicians

Regardless of what population or what genre we are working with, we must always question our observations and reactions. When I offer supervision to clinicians, I find the following questions to be the most thorough way to figuring out how we can best use ourselves to serve our clientele. Why do we think our clients are attracted to RAP music? What do they like about it? How do we feel about it? How does their musical taste make us feel about them? Why are we attracted to or repelled by it? What kind of music do we like? Why? What did we listen to as adolescents? Why? What purpose did it serve? What did the music say to us? What does RAP music say to us? Usually a clinician can discover some common ground between their own musical tastes and those of their clients, thereby accelerating the initial bonds between them.

There are times when we interface with other clinicians and they question our use of RAP music. We need to educate our colleagues as to why RAP is so effective. We may need to share personal experiences or session excerpts to convince them of why it is OK to use within therapy. Sometimes an institution we work in does not permit it. I believe that we need to have our own clinical autonomy and that our judgments need to be respected. I would encourage advocating for RAP just like one would for any other clinical necessity! Sometimes compromises can be reached that do not jeopardize the effective use of RAP.

For example, in residential treatment, there may be different rules for the teens' therapy, education, or living environments. These rules may be appropriate. If we use RAP in therapy, that does not mean it needs to be allowed in other areas of an institution.

We might suggest that a facility require that the teens listen to edited (i.e., non-profane) versions outside of therapy. Again, as clinicians, we need to exemplify that we need access to RAP's *form* because it is such a therapeutic asset. With adolescents, it is hard to offer a form without partaking of its manifestations, as is the case in precomposed RAP. As *music* therapists, we offer a unique expertise that qualifies us to promote RAP music. Perhaps this book will be a good resource for clinicians making the case to use RAP to achieve clinical efficacy!

Clinical Use and Creation

I believe that *creating* RAP, or any music, offers the most potential healing. As I stated earlier, it is the act and the process of creation that ameliorates deficits and promotes growth. It is fine to analyze RAP's lyrics and to share opinions and feelings about precomposed RAP songs. Sometimes this is the only way to begin in therapy. A gradual bridge from working like this to composition is to ask clients to improvise some parts within a precomposed RAP. This is so easy because of RAP's form. It is as simple as the use of a fill-in phrase with young children. Teens can use the music-minus-one (karaoke) style to fill in their own lyrics. They can also play along with a particular beat pattern. They can add another musical line, a rhythm, a melody, a sound effect, and so on. As they become comfortable, we can suggest that they make up their own RAPs.

Some adolescents will start with their own RAPs. They will probably need help in cultivating some patience to finish a song or to add another layer or to collaborate with a peer, or two, to perform it for their therapy group. These clients can be helped to facilitate the clients who are more reticent to create. They can all experience cooperating and the mutual joy of co-creation. In our role as therapist, we need to have a large repertoire of musical elements and ideas that they can pick from to create their own compositions. There are many materials available to us to accomplish this.

Synthesizing RAP

Because RAP music is like a sound collage, we can draw upon many types of aural representations in its creation. Here I offer some practical guidelines and ideas for composing RAP music with clients. Acoustic and electric instruments, vocal techniques, and electronic and recording devices can all be instrumental in producing RAP. While we each have different levels of strength in each of these areas and can always learn more about others, I have always found the best resource for finding elemental materials to be my clients. Because mastery is such an intrinsic part of their developmental stage, teenagers are usually very familiar with the different facets of RAP. They may need our assistance to produce a sound or style that they desire, but they can tell and show us what they want and need!

Many may already know how to use an electronic keyboard or a 4-track recorder, or if not, they may be motivated to learn very quickly. Recently, I used a keyboard with a young client. He had never been exposed to one with as many functions before. Momentarily, I could not remember how to program each key to sound like a percussive instrument. In the few seconds that I hesitated, he shouted, "Like this?!" By quick trial and error, he had figured it out. And in no time, we were on our way to creating a simple percussive RAP line.

It is usually helpful to begin with a repetitive, rhythmic line composed of beats and then to layer other lines on top. Listening to already-composed, popular RAPs is a great way to generate ideas. Clients and clinicians, alike, will gain knowledge by repetition and some may have a greater aptitude for the layering process than others.

When I was a young professional, I worried about not being the *expert,* until I learned instead that being a therapist meant being a source of expertise for my clients. When our clients experience that they, too, can literally be equal partners in creating and that we rely upon *their* expertise as well, they may feel a mutual trust that they have never known. This experience can be one of the most valuable and therapeutic for their growth and development. It is a main reason that I prefer improvisation and creation whenever possible. It is a concrete experience in the supported manipulation of symbols. This process-oriented way of working strengthens the ego and advances ego formation.

In my experience, when clinicians come to me and state that they want to do RAP music with their clients but they do not know how to do it, that is not exactly the case. Usually, they have given up because of their own personal reaction to the genre or because of their clients' difficult behavior. It is my hope that this chapter will assist clinicians to listen to RAP and to hear its separate elements. Simultaneously, I have made an effort to offer fellow therapists some explanations for why adolescents may behave as they do. Mostly, I hope to have demonstrated a viable connection between the population and the form that will enable music therapists to utilize RAP to foster health and productivity among the desperate contemporary adolescent.

Table 1.12 Audio Examples

Kenny Arkana, La Rage (2006)	http://www.youtube.com/watch?v=z8txhtB2e5M	Refers to the 2005 riots in Paris ghettos and the outcry regarding global politics
Statik Selektah, "So Close So Far" (2010)	http://www.youtube.com/watch?v=hf0Jgl5xM4A	Deals with recent U.S. issues, especially the economic crisis

Societal Ramifications

RAP has spread to many corners of American society and the world. It is a successful vehicle for transporting contemporary issues into the public's awareness. The youth population of any culture is typically the truest messenger of society. They see reality and are not afraid to expose the truth. Perhaps, like therapists, listening, without judging, can teach us all what our societal needs are, and what we need to do to meet them (see Table 1.12).

Conclusion

RAP music is a requisite for adolescents who need to survive and to work in therapy to live more healthfully. It is their ally as they learn to listen, to share, to create, and to trust. It is a protector, until they become stronger and do not need so much protecting. Its form can teach us how to help them. RAP demonstrates a way to make music in an efficient and meaningful way. Like all art forms, RAP is a reflection of its time. It is a desperate time. In music therapy, RAP can offer help to the contemporary adolescent. Its rich compositional elements can allow a teen to find some relief, and to begin to experience a less desperate existence, to express anger and to feel whole.

Postlude

As I was researching relevant online audio examples for this chapter, I came across rich musical excerpts of traditional African American music. I have been privileged to be familiar with many of these genres and artists, and yet there were many that I had never heard or seen, simply because they have never been a part of dominant American culture. I had been denied what felt like a right, as an American citizen, a right to access cultural art forms that enrich and inform my existence and teach me about my fellow citizens.

Throughout history, African American art forms, including poetry and music, were able to function as a social *weapon*, sometimes private, to express what could not be otherwise expressed. The arts often serve this function, to allow the inexpressible to be expressed, and sometimes known, in an intrapersonal, interpersonal, and societal manner. RAP music is no exception. It is used in society and in therapy to cathart, to sublimate (i.e., it is *not* the action, it is dramatic expression), and to say what needs to be said. "It's kids to a great extent—mixed up and confused—reaching out to express themselves. They were forcefully trying to express and they made up in fantasy what they missed in reality" (Bobby Robinson, in Toop, 1991, p. 5).

RAP artists as criminals represent the increasing criminalization of public figures—sports stars and athletes, CEOs, politicians and elected officials. This is a disturbing trend and yet a familiar contemporary reality. I think that RAP's role in modern society can be viewed through an artistic as well as a clinical lens. We internalize its lyrics without even trying. We move to its rhythms without even noticing. It affects us. It is a social force to be dealt with. Many styles of RAP tell us what is wrong, what is yearned for, and concretely, how it *feels* to be a *have-not*. RAP is such a great form for delivering the message, positive or negative, pessimistic or optimistic, the reality of our times. Society needs to listen.

References

Arnold, J. (1989, September 30). FBI accused of intimidating company over rap-music lyrics. *The Philadelphia Inquirer*, p. 4D.

Costello, M., & Wallace, D. F. (1990). *Signifying rappers*. New York: Ecco Press.

Dines, G. (Ed.). (1995). *Gender, race and class in media*. Thousand Oaks, CA: Sage.

Erikson, E. (1968). *Identity youth and crisis*. New York: W. W. Norton.

Frisch, A. (1990). Symbol and structure: Music therapy for the adolescent psychiatric inpatient. *Music Therapy, 9*(1), 16–34.

Jones, B. (1987). *Step it down: Games, plays, songs, and stories from the Afro-American heritage*. Athens, GA: University of Georgia Press.

Sexton, A. (Ed.). (1995). *Rap on rap*. New York: Delta.

Small, M. (1992). *Break it down*. New York: Citadel.

Stancell, S. (1996). *Rap whoz who*. New York: Schirmer.

Stavsky, L. (1995). *A2Z: The book of rap and hip hop slang*. New York: Boulevard.

Toop, D. (1991). *Rap attack 2*. London: Serpent's Tail.

Winnicott, D. W. (1965). The maturational processes and the facilitating environment: Studies in the theory of emotional development. *The International Psycho-Analytical Library, 64*, 1–276.

Chapter 2

Contextualizing Rap Music as a Means of Incorporating into Psychotherapy

Don Elligan

Introduction

Though controversial for many, rap music as a psychotherapeutic tool has been found to be very curative. As a receptive tool, rap music can be used to deconstruct and gain insight, and as an expressive tool, rap can be used for cathartic release, cognitive restructuring, and behavioral modification. However, for therapists unfamiliar with rap music, its use in therapy may be uncomfortable and challenging. The use and challenges of incorporating rap music into psychotherapy will be explored and discussed.

The use of music as a therapeutic tool has been utilized for years (De Mers et al., 2009). Therapists have found the use of music to be beneficial for a variety of reasons ranging from its ability to help facilitate relaxation to exploring and expressing emotional conflict (Matzo, 2009). Rap music, however, has been a bit more challenging to introduce into therapeutic settings (Elligan, 2004). These challenges may include unfamiliarity on the part of the therapist with rap, the word choices of certain rap artists, the sexism, misogynist lyrics, or any other commentary that is foreign and indigestible for the provider. Regardless of the difficulty, often the challenge can be summarized as one in which the therapist's comfort and sense of control are stretched to difficult and unfamiliar limits. Although many of the concerns may be legitimate, they should not prevent one from taking advantage of this therapeutic tool if it can be utilized in the interest of treatment for clients who are influenced by rap music.

Rap music has been present as an influential part of American culture since the early 1980s (Elligan, 2004; George, 1998). Rap music's growth continued through the 1980s and 1990s into the new millennium. However, many have argued that rap music's golden age may have taken place during the mid-1990s due to the greater appreciation of the heterogeneity of the music. In the mid-1990s there was an appreciation for each of the genres of rap, ranging from "gangsta rap" to pro-social rap, including religious rap. Each of the different genres received "air play" on the radio, at dance clubs, and at parties. Although the music has always had its critics and has promoted controversy, during this golden age there were internal checks and balances due to the diversity inherent in the music. However, as rap became progressively more commercial, its development and direction were more influenced by record labels and music executives who promoted "gangsta rap" and all of its angry and violent content. The latter led Nas (2006) to pronounce, "Hip-Hop is dead." Rap music lives on. However, the culture of Hip-Hop is dying because so many of the voices and perspectives have been silenced. It is the death of Hip-Hop that makes incorporating rap music into therapy more challenging and awkward for therapists who are unfamiliar with the history of rap music and have only been exposed to the current diluted version of the genre. With this in mind it is necessary to review the history of rap music and the different categories that rap music can be classified into.

Rap Music

Rap music is different from Hip-Hop (Asante, 2008; Watkins, 2005). Rap is the music, the beats, and the rhyme of a culture known as Hip-Hop. Rap music is said to have its genesis in the early 1970s in the Bronx. Since then it has grown into a billion-dollar global industry that has taken on the identity of a cultural movement.

Rap music grew out of the interaction of poverty, music, dance, graffiti, and fun. Historical icons that contributed to the birth of rap music include DJ Kool Herc, Afrika Bambaataa, Grandmaster Flash, Soul Sonic Force, the Cold Crush Brothers, and the Sugar Hill Gang. The Sugar Hill Gang's smash hit "Rapper's Delight" was the first rap song to climb the

Billboard R&B charts to #4 in the fall of 1979. In 1982, the release of "The Message" by Grandmaster Flash and the Furious Five marked the beginning of another major milestone in the growth and development of rap music. "The Message" marked a turn in rap music from simply being music about fun and dance to presenting a commentary on the anger, politics, issues, and challenges confronting Black adolescents and young adults. In the early to mid-1980s, rap music took another step forward in its evolution with the introduction of new artists such as Kurtis Blow, Whodini, Run-DMC, the Fat Boys, LL Cool J, and Eric B and Rakim, to name a few. New record labels such as Def Jam, Death Row, Profile, and Tommy Boy also began to spawn. The mid-1980s also marked the beginning of rap music's significant national influence on music, art, media, and the social development of youth.

Some religious leaders have recognized the potential utility of rap music to convey positive messages to youth. Rap music has recently been incorporated into gospel music and sermons to convey a religious message to those who may otherwise not listen to spiritual messages. Rap music has become such a large industry that it is now the subject of national summit meetings, multiple award shows, and international magazines. Fortune 500 companies, public health organizations, sports teams, and the media who market products to youth and those influenced by the Hip-Hop culture have also recently used rap music. Rap music's influence on people and society is undeniably significant. Rap music can be classified into one or more of six broad categories. The categories include (1) gangsta rap, (2) materialistic rap, (3) political/protest rap, (4) positive rap, (5) spiritual rap, and (6) rap not otherwise specified (NOS), which includes music with rap fusion. Before I say more about rap music and therapy, the following is a review of the several different categories of rap music.

Gangsta Rap

I argue that gangsta rap promotes an antisocial message of violence, crime, and sexism. The origins of gangsta rap come primarily from resource-poor communities that are confronted with a number of issues that are not endured by economically stable communities. Most notably, poor communities are plagued by higher rates of violence and crime and higher mortality rates. These higher rates of violence contribute to reduced life expectancies, which create a very different meaning of adolescence for many of those rappers who come from these poor communities. As a consequence of living in these community settings, many young rappers perceive adolescence as a shortened period and are driven to enter adulthood at a faster rate. For many, there is a sense of urgency to engage in what they consider to be grown-up activities because of the higher incidence of deaths and incarceration seen within their communities. With this in mind, it is not surprising that many of the gangsta rappers sing of these themes and glorify these images in their rap videos. This is the very argument that many of the gangsta rap artists use when they suggest that their music simply reflects the reality of the circumstances they have witnessed growing up or continue to witness in their communities. Furthermore, they argue that their music is a broadcast to the world of the misery and inhumane circumstances that many people living in urban poor ghetto communities must confront on a daily basis. They suggest that they are simply the reporters of the atrocities of the inner city and that their commentaries share the psychology and orientation of many of the people who live the lifestyle that they rap about.

In the 1990s, gangsta rap garnered greater mainstream attention with Ice T's song "Cop Killer." Not only did "Cop Killer" get widespread attention due to the content of the song, but it also bridged gangsta rap lyrics with rock music, which generated a broad cross section of attention. As "Cop Killer" glorified violence against police, other factors took place in the 1990s that increased the general paranoia of many American police departments. The Rodney King beating in Los Angeles generated greater national concern about police brutality, which in turn converted many more sympathetic ears to the mantras of the gangsta rap movement.

During the 1990s, several "hard" and gangsta East Coast rappers began to rap about guns, violence, and antisocial behavior as well. The late Notorious B.I.G., Mobb Deep, the Lost Boyz, and other East Coast rappers began rapping about being gangstas. The glorification of gangsta rap content has become the norm for many rap artists. As rappers such as the late 2 Pac and 50 Cent glorify the fact that they have been shot several times and survived to sing about it, they convey a message to young impressionable listeners that living the thug life will not necessarily lead to death. Unfortunately, many youth believe these messages and begin to glorify and value these "rites of passage" into becoming a thug or gangsta. They begin to believe that they are not hard, tough, or worthy of respect if they have not been the victims of a shooting, drive-by, or stickup. Others have suggested that by glorifying the lifestyle of the inner-city gangstas, gangsta rap not only reinforces their behavior but also encourages and promotes this lifestyle to the millions of impressionable children and young adults who listen to the lyrics of gangsta music. In doing so, the music is said to reinforce and generalize racist stereotypes that contribute to the difficulties these communities have had in overcoming the obstacles of poor education, unemployment, and violence that have plagued them for years. Rap therapy (Elligan, 2004) attempts to challenge and restructure what I would call delusional masochistic beliefs. In fact, these themes can be discussed with many youth to help them begin to realize the dangers of living the gangsta rapper lifestyle or the so-called thug life.

Materialistic Rap

Materialistic rap, unlike gangsta rap, focuses on promoting messages of the value of wealth, sex, possessions, and the trappings of affluence. The music videos and lyrics of these songs often make reference to expensive jewelry, clothing, food, spirits, extravagant parties, vacations or travels to exotic locations, exclusive automobiles and homes, cruising on yachts, and flying in private jets. In many ways, materialistic rap, in my view, can be conceptualized as the soap operas of rap music. Materialistic rap and gangsta rap together are what have given rise to the concept of "ghetto fabulous." While gangsta rap glorifies certain aspects of the thug mentality of the ghetto, materialistic rap has made certain aspects of the ghetto lifestyle exclusive, desirable, and associated with wealth. The "bling bling" of rap music is reinforced by the celebrity status of rap stars.

Materialistic rap is a perfect fit for the orientation of American capitalism, and America has capitalized on the presence of rap music. Rap music has become one of the most influential tools for marketing products to American youth and urban adults. Rap artists are seen and heard daily on a variety of commercials singing jingles and promoting the materialism of their image. Rap music's commercial influence is even seen in its presence in video games marketed to a large cross section of society. As rap music progressively became mainstream and its popularity began to cross socioeconomic and cultural barriers, its appeal and importance to record executives became more apparent. Rappers were not just singing about making money; they were actually being paid big money by top recording labels. Rap music had entered its adulthood when it began being mass marketed through different mediums. The materialism of rap music was seen not only in the clothing, jewelry, and cars driven by rap superstars but also through the mass marketing in movies, videos, and new clothing lines. The progressive development of materialistic rap coincided with rap music's enormous commercial and economic contribution to the American economy. Rap music has become a billion-dollar industry, and as such it has developed into its own cultural identity. Terms such as *ghetto fabulous* personified and demonstrated Hip-Hop's insatiable appetite and consumption of Prada, Armani, and Dolce & Gabbana, expensive real estate, and cars.

Most if not all of the rappers that have become successful have worked very hard for their success. They have tirelessly sacrificed for their art. These messages need to be conveyed to those that learned from their lyrics. Some of the newer shows on MTV that give a glimpse into the hard work of becoming a rap performer are beneficial in that they educate youth about the perseverance and sacrifice that contribute to success. It is believed that these lessons could be generalized to other areas of growth and development that require patience, perseverance, commitment, and practice for success, such as education, entrepreneurship, or promotion within one's place of employment.

Political/Protest Rap

Political/protest rap developed out of the music of Gil Scott Haron and the Last Poets. It is rap music that has a political message or takes a political stand. Political rap is known to take on big political issues such as drugs, sexism, racism, the judicial system, poverty, and apartheid, and bring them to public attention during periods of entertainment. Chuck D is reported to have said that the goal of Public Enemy was to "uplift Black youth" to believe that they can make a difference politically. Public Enemy was actively involved in the Rock the Vote campaign promoted by MTV to get youth involved in politics by voicing their political positions through voting.

Political rap was a bit more prevalent in the early days of rap music. It has since gradually declined in popularity. Salt N' Peppa's "Let's Talk About Sex" and the public service announcement they did on their *Very Necessary* CD with We Talk titled "I've Got AIDS" is another example of the use of rap music to promote a political message. Another example of the easily forgotten political history of rap music and rap artists includes *Self Destruction* in which a group of rappers (KRS-1, MC Delight of Stetasonic, Kool Moe Dee, MC Lyte, Just Ice, Doug E Fresh, Heavy D, and Public Enemy) worked on a song together to promote a message of "violence prevention."

Political rap demonstrates the value of rap music as a politico-educational tool, as rap music has educated many people about issues that they may have never been exposed to or thought about in depth. It is not uncommon to hear people who have been listening to rap music speak about how rap music has changed and is not as "political" or "educational" as it once was. Basically, these people are indicating that rap music played a significant role in their lives and that they have learned from the music that they once sang naively. The same argument holds true for the negative impact that gangsta rap can have on influencing how one views life or one's interactions with others. This subliminal influence of music must be considered as a relevant sociological tool for teaching positive messages about life.

Political rap, unlike gangsta rap and materialistic rap, is not as popular to audiences or producers unless it is making a political commentary about itself. It is unfortunate that political and protest rap has declined in popularity given that political rap has a significant place in the history, growth, and development of rap music. Furthermore, political rap has been found to have a significant positive influence on many youth who listened to the lyrics. The latter was seen by the "Stop the Violence" movement that took place in the 1980s following the release of Boogie Down Productions *By All Means Necessary* CD. The Stop the Violence movement was spearheaded by KRS-1, who did a 40-city college tour and reportedly raised over $400,000 to help the Urban League fight violence in the inner city. The theme song for the movement was "Self Destruction" in which an all-star cast of rappers such as Chuck D, Kool Moe Dee, MC Lyte, and others promoted the values of putting an end to the senseless killings taking place in many inner-city settings. Political rap, like positive rap and spiritual rap, is limited in its commercial distribution in comparison to gangsta and materialistic rap.

Positive Rap

Positive rap, like political rap, is generally not as commercial as gangsta or materialistic rap. Positive rap promotes the values of education, responsibility, and ethnic pride. Often there is some overlap between rappers who are considered to be "positive" or "political" depending on the specific song. Positive rap can be considered to be pro-social and/or promoting messages that can contribute to the good of the individual listener or humanity. However, unlike political rap, positive rap may not have a political message or agenda. Positive rap tends to be value oriented.

Positive rap is the benchmark for rap therapy. An interesting aspect about positive rap is that it is not necessarily a constant for specific rappers. Rather, positive rap manifests in a variety of different formats and on different songs. The best way to illustrate the educational and inspirational aspect of positive rap is to listen to or read the lyrics of selected positive rap songs. Rappers in this category often have eclectic jazz grooves playing with their music and may rap about seemingly abstract and irrelevant content. However, their music rarely crosses over to such a degree that it would be classified as gangsta rap. It may at times be political, but it is usually not defined as political rap. In contrast, it is usually referred to as positive or "conscious" rap. The bridge of political and positive rap is also well illustrated by the music of the Native Tongues, which *Vibe* describes as good music about family, fun, and tolerance.

Spiritual Rap

Spiritual rap by artists such as Kirk Franklin incorporates rap music with traditional gospel music to appeal to many youth who would otherwise not listen to gospel music. Franklin's enlightened approach of incorporating rap into gospel to spread a religious message to urban youth influenced by rap music and the culture of Hip-Hop is in many ways similar to rap therapy's use of rap music to make traditional therapy and work with youth more accessible to those influenced by rap music.

The spread of rap music to the pulpits of preachers and gospel music is a good example of the infectiousness of rap music. However, many have suggested that rap music, preaching, and orating all grow out of the same heritage. In fact, the church has become the home for several retired rappers who have become preachers. From the materialistic rap background as a P Diddy protégée, MASE has retired from rap to become a preacher. Likewise, Run, of Run-DMC, has transitioned from the rap game to become a preacher in New York and M.C. Hammer has become a reverend in California. The similarity between rapping and preaching is undeniable. As mentioned earlier, many rappers are promoting messages that many in the church would consider to be blasphemy. However, their methods of sharing their words are similar. The relationship between rap music, preaching, and the church in general is also seen by the large number of rappers who make spiritual references in their rap songs.

Although I have discussed five distinct categories of rap music, it is unlikely that any one rapper fits exclusively in one category. Their music often spans a couple of categories. Even gospel rappers can be heard making political statements, as is the case with many sermons.

Rap Not Otherwise Specified

The sixth category, which I call rap not otherwise specified (rap NOS), is basically reserved for rap music that does not fit into one of the five categories described above. This includes music that may simply add a rap hook or sample but is basically classified as R&B, rock, alternative, pop, jazz, or some other form of music.

These different forms of rap music are the very reason why rap music has such a large appeal to a broad cross section of youth and adults. With this in mind, rap music has become the common ground for dialogue and conversation between youth and adults that may otherwise be separated by generation gaps that make communication and dialogue difficult.

Rap music's appeal to youth and young adults is very idiosyncratic. Many people like rap for the way its lyrical expression represents the realities of their lives and struggles. Some people are attracted to the messages promoted by rap music and others simply listen to the melodic beats initially and eventually take note of the lyrics or message. Regardless of the specific reasons for rap music's appeal, the important issue for those trying to communicate with youth or young adults such as parents, teachers, and social service workers is the realization of rap music's influence on a large cross section of society. Furthermore, rap music's appeal is not only consumed by youth. Rap music's appeal has grown to become intergenerational and cross-cultural. Rap music is consumed through direct purchase, radio, Internet, graffiti images, posters, television, and video. Rap videos are available on a range of cable television stations throughout any given day. Rap artists have become household names for many people. Rap music's appeal to youth and young adults has been acknowledged and integrated into a variety of agendas. Parents, teachers, and others interested in bridging the communication gap with those influenced by rap music would be wise to follow the lead of many major marketing companies, though without the often self-serving economic motive. Marketers for clothing, beverages, and public service announcements about public health issues frequently utilize rap in their commercials to appeal to urban youth of color because they realize that rap is the language of those people who are members of the Hip-Hop culture. Furthermore, as mentioned earlier, gospel music producers such as Kirk Franklin have created a new genre of gospel music, which incorporates rap and Hip-Hop to appeal to youth and young adults. Each of the latter developments has culminated into what has now become known as the culture of Hip-Hop. Rap music is simply the language of the culture of Hip-Hop.

Why Incorporate Rap into Therapy?

Despite the difficulties of Hip-Hop as a culture, rap music continues to be very influential and informative for many of today's youth (Kobin & Tyson, 2005). Rap music and its videos continue to define for many such critical issues as masculinity, values, ethics, relationships, honor, code of conduct, dress, language, finance, education, drug use, parenting, and responsibility. Considering the far-reaching cognitive influence rap music has on the development of youth, it is imperative that therapists utilize rap music in therapy when working with clients influenced by rap music. Utilizing rap music in therapy when indicated is a culturally sensitive approach to treatment. Culturally sensitive therapy recognizes, values, and respects the cultural aspects of clients. If clients' cognitions, affects, or behaviors are influenced by rap music, it is a culturally sensitive approach to incorporate rap music into the therapeutic process.

How Can One Incorporate Rap Music?

If therapists find that the clients they are working with enjoy listening to rap music, they should be encouraged to inquire into the depths of the interest. If the client has a fleeting or mild interest in rap music, it may not be appropriate to incorporate rap music into the therapeutic relationship. However, if the client's interest is found to be substantial, rap therapy may be indicated. Substantial interest would include clients who listen to rap music exclusively or clients who primarily listen to rap music in comparison to other music genres.

The first step simply involves asking clients which rap artists are their favorite and why. This simple question often opens a dynamic exchange between client and therapist. After a session or two of exploring each of the rap artists the client enjoys listening to, the therapist can begin to explore why the client enjoys listening to the particular artist/artists. If the client enjoys several artists, the therapist can inquire into the similarities and differences of the artists. The purpose of this stage of dialogue is educational for the therapist and helps facilitate and develop a therapeutic alliance between the client and therapist. It is important for the client's interest in rap music to be validated and accepted during this stage of dialogue. The latter will allow for an easier transition to the next stage of therapy in which the client is challenged to deconstruct and become a bit more critical of the lyrics they are listening to. As the client begins to listen to the music with a more critical ear, they are able to begin to gain insight into how the music may have influenced their thoughts and feelings about certain topics or those of their peers. Likewise, the client may begin to find some factors in the music that have contributed at an unconscious level to the presenting issues that prompted the visit to the therapist. As the client becomes more critical of the music and gains greater insight into its influence on his/her cognitions, affect, and behavior, his/her appreciation of the music may or may not be altered. Changing one's appreciation of rap music is not the goal of rap therapy. The goal is to use rap music to help the client gain insight, restructure thoughts or behavior, and eventually use rap music to give a voice to the changes they would like to pursue in their life. Furthermore, as the client begins to deconstruct some of the lyrics, they often begin to gain a greater appreciation of the complexity of the music and of themselves. Recognizing that they can disagree with certain aspects of a song or artist but continue to enjoy the music can be transformative for a person who once thought they had to agree with all of the lyrics of an artist to whom they enjoy listening. It is transformative because it becomes a lesson in cognitive dissonance, which is often an element in many close interpersonal relationships. By learning about the complexities of interpersonal relationships, clients begin to learn that relationships are not simply all-or-nothing, but have complex subtleties that must be worked through to avoid abandoning the relationship.

After deconstructing the music and gaining a greater sense of insight, some clients may benefit from composing their own rap to help work through the presenting issue. For example, a sixth-grade boy having difficulties with behavior management may be encouraged to write a rap about how he can better manage his behavior in the classroom. Upon completion of the rap, the student can share his writing with the therapist and have further discussion about the proposed solution. Regardless of the solution proposed by the student, the therapist should try to be supportive and affirming of the effort invested. If the solution is maladaptive, the therapist may encourage the client to consider other strategies for solving the problem in the format of a rap. If the client is unable to come up with any new ideas, the therapist may give an example or ask the client to come up with another example. The client can then incorporate these examples into a new rap. If the proposed solution is adaptive, the therapist may push the limits by asking the client to solve the difficulty if an unexpected challenge were to present itself in the classroom. The client may be asked how best to manage his behavior if another student did something to irritate or frustrate him. If behavior management is the presenting issue for the client, the therapist may also challenge the client by developing other hypothetical scenarios for the client to solve in the form of a rap. This process can become an empowering experience for clients as they come up with their own functional and adaptive solutions to hypothetical obstacles to managing their behavior in the classroom.

If the client is unable to express themselves in the form of a rap or poem they may be encouraged to find a rap song in which the rap describes how to best manage the hypothetical challenge. The client is then encouraged to bring their findings to the next session to be further discussed. During the following session, the client and therapist listen to the rap and analyze and process the lyrics together. The therapist can begin to help the client recognize the appropriateness of their solution or discuss why the rap may not be the best solution to the presenting issue. Likewise, the therapist may help the client recognize that the solution he/she found may be one of many solutions. Within the therapeutic context, the therapist and client can then begin to explore other potential solutions to the presenting issue. Once clients have begun to understand how they may be able to use rap music as a therapeutic tool, it becomes a resource that they can utilize after the therapeutic relationship with the provider has concluded. Clients who are able to conclude psychotherapy with concrete tools that can be utilized in the future are well served.

Incorporating rap music into therapy is a creative process that utilizes many of the inherent strengths of the client. Furthermore, it encourages clients to take an active role in their treatment and helps them explore solutions from within. The latter has been found to be one of the most therapeutic and enduring aspects of change for clients in psychotherapy (Buckner, 2009). Rap therapy can be difficult for therapists who are unfamiliar or uncomfortable with rap music. If therapists are able to overcome the barriers presented by their discomfort, rap therapy can be very therapeutic.

Contraindications of Rap Therapy

Rap therapy can be utilized with a wide range of clients as has been discussed in this chapter and further discussed in this book. However, rap therapy may not be the therapy of choice for some individuals. Rap therapy is contraindicative for individuals who are not influenced by Hip-Hop culture and do not enjoy listening to rap music. Additionally, rap therapists should be cautious and understand that rap therapy may not be appropriate for individuals who have difficulty with understanding and utilizing metaphoric language. These individuals tend to be very literal and their strict interpretation of rap lyrics may not allow them to comprehend the multiple meanings of the lyrics and the creative artistic intention of the music. Furthermore, in cases in which individuals who are in rap therapy are having difficulty changing their cognitive style of interpreting their presenting issue, and the therapist finds that the use of rap music is maintaining or exacerbating the presenting issue, rap therapy should be discontinued.

References

Assante, M. (2008). *It's bigger than Hip Hop: The rise of the post-Hip-Hop generation*. New York: St. Martin's Press.

Buckner, J. (2009). Motivation enhancement therapy can increase utilization of cognitive-behavioral therapy: The case of social anxiety disorder. *Journal of Clinical Psychology, 65*, 1195–1206.

Elligan, D. (2004). *Rap therapy: A practical guide for communicating with youth and young adults through rap music*. New York: Kensington.

George, N. (1998). *Hip Hop America*. New York: Penguin.

Kobin, C., & Tyson, E. (2005). Thematic analysis of Hip-Hop music: Can Hip-Hop in therapy facilitate empathic connections when working with clients in urban settings? *The Arts in Psychotherapy, 2006*, 343–356.

Matzo, M. (2009). Music and stress reduction. *The American Journal of Nursing, 109*, 40.

Mers, C., Tenace, M., Van Norman, R., & Higgins, K. (2009). Effects of music therapy on young children's challenging behaviors: A case study. *Music Therapy Perspectives, 27*, 88–97.

Nas. (2006). *Hip hop is dead*. New York: Def Jam Recordings.

Salt and Pepper. (1991). *Let's talk about sex*. New York: Next Plateau Records.

Watkins, C. (2005). *Hip hop matters: Politics, pop culture and the struggle for the soul of a movement*. Boston: Beacon Press.

Chapter 3

The Importance of Hip-Hop for Music Therapists

Aaron J. Lightstone

In 2003–2004, I was a student in the Master of Music Therapy program at Wilfrid Laurier University. While studying there, I was continuing to work in private practice as a music therapist. I had a contract working with homeless youth on a drop-in basis in a residential youth shelter. The experience acquired by working in the residential youth shelter became the basis of the research I conducted as a Master of Music Therapy student (Lightstone, 2004). The more I learned about Hip-Hop culture and the history of rap music, and the more I engaged with these youth through the medium of rap music, the more amazing and unconscionable it became to me that this popular, powerful, and transformative musical form was barely even mentioned during my music therapy training and was rarely mentioned or discussed in professional music therapy circles; I was shocked that I had never met a music therapist who actively developed specific skills related to the production or facilitation of rap and Hip-Hop. This chapter explores the potential importance of Hip-Hop for the field of music therapy.

As a music therapy clinician, I believe in the importance of facilitating the creative act of music-making with my clients. My training in and approach to clinical work is reflective of a music-centered approach. Music-centered approaches to music therapy emphasize the importance and primacy of cooperative music-making in the therapeutic process within the context of a client-centered therapeutic relationship. My clinical approach relies on improvisational music and is influenced by the theories of Aesthetic Music Therapy (AeMT) as formulated and described by Colin Lee (2003), Creative Music Therapy (CMT) as formulated by Nordoff and Robbins (1977) and Ansdell (1995), and the diversity of musicians and music cultures that I have studied.

With the exception of Aigen (2002) and Wigram (2004), significant texts on improvisation in music-centered music therapy (Ansdell, 1995; Lee, 1997, 2003; Nordoff & Robbins, 1977; Robbins & Robbins, 1998) make little mention of the potential importance of contextualizing clinical improvisation in popular music forms. None discuss rap music as a clinical resource for collaborative clinical music-making. This may be due to the fact that creating Hip-Hop music requires the use of technological devices with which most music therapists may not be familiar. Those who do have the skill and technical facility generally gain the requisite knowledge in their lives as musicians outside of their music therapy training courses.

Also, the musicological thinking behind rap operates under musical paradigms that are inherently non-Western. Rap is rooted in and informed by African musical worldviews that are drastically different from the European musicology in which most (Western) music therapists are raised and trained.* Music therapy that is culturally sensitive to the needs of clients involved in contemporary youth culture should use the musical vernacular of the clients. Engaging in music therapy that is culturally sensitive to the needs of youth culture requires knowledge of popular music styles. As such, there is no way that Hip-Hop can be ignored or neglected by music therapists. In the last two and a half decades, the culture of Hip-Hop, and its musical expression of rap music, has made an indelible mark on global culture. As a music therapist, I am all too familiar with the cliché that music is a universal language. When it comes to youth culture, Hip-Hop *is* the universal language. My personal travels have taken me from the shores of the Arctic Ocean in Canada's far North to the Jungles of Cambodia, and to the deserts of the Middle East. Everywhere I have been I have heard Hip-Hop in the local languages.

While Hip-Hop has been examined by a very wide diversity of academic disciplines, references to Hip-Hop in the music therapy literature are noticeably and shamefully scarce. Music therapy theorists such as

---

* A complete discussion on the differences between the musical paradigms of European and African music is beyond the scope of this chapter. One significant example is that in many music cultures from Africa there is an absence of functional harmony as it is understood in European-based music. This absence of harmony and the primacy of what are often complex polyrhythms require flexibility and adjusted thinking on the part of musicians who are trained in a European worldview. For a more complete discussion on Afro-centric musicology see Perkins (1998), Rose (1994), and Keyes (1996).

Ruud (1998) and Stige (2002) have eloquently argued that music therapy is inseparable from music and culture. Music therapists must keep themselves up to date not only on the recent developments in psychotherapy and its related disciplines but also on the latest developments in contemporary music and popular culture. As powerful forces in contemporary culture and music, Hip-Hop and rap music have an important place in the music therapy literature. Furthermore, I believe that rap is not just relevant to music therapy because of its popularity, but also precisely because of its social power. Music therapists are interested in the transformational power of music. From the earliest days of rap music, important subgenres have acknowledged the ability of music to facilitate group experiences and to catalyze personal and social transformation.

Note on Terminology

Rap and Hip-Hop

We can say what makes it hip-hop is this black, urban experience da-da-da. But no! Hip-hop is no longer that. I mean, hip-hop has existed in ... Japan for at least 10 years—has existed where there are no African American experiences. So what is hip-hop?

Saul Williams (2001)*

There is often confusion over the terms *rap music* and *Hip-Hop*. The general trend in the academic literature defines Hip-Hop as a specific cultural group or youth arts movement, while rap is the musical expression of that social group. In terms of its genesis in the 1970s, the original creators and members of Hip-Hop culture were young, urban, African Americans (Keyes, 2002). As the popularity of Hip-Hop culture grew, more and more youth from other ethnic and socioeconomic groups began to identify with the message, style, and culture of Hip-Hop, which could also be described as a countercultural movement. The disenfranchised Inuit youth that I encountered in extremely remote communities in Canada's Eastern Arctic (Nunavut) could not be more remote from the urban origins of the movement. Yet many of these youth identify very strongly with the message and culture of Hip-Hop. Hip-Hop culture expresses itself artistically in four main modes: music, dance, visual art, and fashion (Rose, 1994). The musical expression of Hip-Hop culture is primarily rap music and DJing.†

---

* Quoted in Chang (2001, p. 2).
† Sometimes spelled deejaying. Referring to the musical activity and contribution of the turntablist.

Hip-Hop culture is expressed through the body in a dance style known as break dancing. Visually, the culture is expressed through urban graffiti art and its own rules of fashion, which tend to favor oversized clothing, accessories originally designed for outdoor/wilderness activities, and prominent displays of large jewelry.

Keyes (1996) prefers to define Hip-Hop as a youth arts movement that engages in "'cultural revisioning'—the foregrounding (both consciously and unconsciously) of African-centered concepts in response to cultural takeovers, ruptures, and appropriations" (p. 224). She further explains that as a youth arts movement, Hip-Hop is an "expression that embodies those attitudes, language, dress, and gestures affiliated with street culture" (Keyes, 1996, p. 231). Because many regard it as a culture, I will use capital letters when referring to Hip-Hop.

To the extent that rap music is the music of Hip-Hop culture (or the Hip-Hop youth arts movement), the terms *rap music* and *Hip-Hop music* can be used interchangeably. It is worth noting, however, that some aficionados use the term *rap* music to refer to music that has been co-opted and commercialized by the big record companies. These individuals reserve the term *Hip-Hop* for music that they consider to be the authentic expression of Hip-Hop culture and not tampered with by record company executives.

Aesthetics of Hip-Hop

> First of all, let me tell you that the music (beats) that makes up Hip-Hop, comes from different nationalities and races, especially from black people.... It comes from many categories in music, for example: Hip-hop music is made up from other forms of music like funk, soul, rhythm & blues, jazz, rock, heavy metal, salsa, soca (calypso), TV shows, kiddie shows, horror movies, techno, pop, disco, african, arabic, reggae -etc.... you will see that the music is made by people from different races or nationalities from all over the planet, but its roots start with black people.
>
> Afrika Baambatta (1995)

As a music therapist trained in music-centered music therapy and particularly in Aesthetic Music Therapy as described by Colin Lee (2003), it is important to me to understand as best as possible the aesthetic qualities of any musical form I am attempting to use in music therapy. A deep understanding of the aesthetics of a form might mean that while I may not achieve mastery of the form (something that could take years of dedication and practice to achieve), I certainly need to acquire the skills to approximate or to be competent in that form, and be able to conduct therapeutically meaningful/valuable work.

As an American art form with Afro-diasporic roots, rap deviates sharply from musical aesthetic conventions that listeners and musicians from European-rooted traditions take for granted. In its purest form, rap consists of a programmed rhythm (sampled turntabling, or drum machine and bass line generator) and a syncopated rhyming chant. Melody and functional harmony (as they are understood in Western music) are de-emphasized (or nonexistent). The text is usually in a vernacular or slang that can be difficult for listeners from outside Hip-Hop culture to decipher (Salaam, 1995). Rap performances highlight black language, rhetorical style, and music-making practices. The lyrical content is often the most English misunderstood and controversial aspect of the genre (Keyes, 1996). Most rap music is based on "black street speech" (Baugh, 1983, in Keyes, 1996). In this vernacular, words can have a double meaning or an altered meaning depending on the tone or inflection of the speaker.

Rose (1994) identifies three defining characteristics of artistic expression in Hip-Hop culture. These characteristics are all found in rap music, break dancing, and graffiti art. The three characteristics are flow, layering, and rupture in line. "In Hip Hop, visual, physical, musical, and lyrical lines are set in motion, broken abruptly with sharp angular breaks, yet they sustain motion and energy through fluidity and flow. . . . Rappers speak of flow explicitly in the lyrics, referring to an ability to move easily and powerfully through complex lyrics as well as of the flow of the music. The flow and motion of the initial bass or drum line in rap music is abruptly ruptured by scratching" (Rose, 1994, p. 39). Layering is an aesthetic feature that takes place mostly in the instrumental parts where different rhythms and textures are layered to create a polyrhythmic texture. Some scholars (Rose, 1994; Keyes, 2000) trace this aesthetic feature back to the polyrhyth-mic drumming of West Africa that is at the root of many African American forms of musical expression.

Salaam (1995) adds to the discussion of Hip-Hop aesthetics by identi-fying four key aesthetic features: lyrics, style, flow, and sound. *Lyrics* refer to the words used in the song and to the subject matter and construction of the song. *Style* refers to the tonal quality of the rapper's voice and the delivery of the lyrics. For example, some rappers have a style that could be described as a seamless monotone, while others are very emotional and dynamic.

Keyes (1996) adds the concept *time* to the discussion of rap music aes-thetics. She considers the construct of time to be one of many *Africanisms* that remain in rap music. According to Keyes, the Western concept of lin-ear time is not useful in understanding African music. She references a number of ethnomusicologists who have shown that the concept of time in African and African-derived musics is a network of layered structures. One of the most important distinctions to be made between Afro-centric and Euro-centric conceptions of time is the importance, role, and meaning of repetition. Keyes compares her studies of rap music to Chernoff's (1979, in Keyes, 1996) study of Ghanaian drumming where

> the repetition of a well chosen rhythm continually reaffirms the power of music by locking that rhythm, and the people listening or dancing to it, into a dynamic and open structure. The power of music is not only captured by repetition, it is magnified. Similarly, rap DJs are revered for their sustaining prowess on the turntables; however they do not sustain their music by repeating the same record, but rather by selecting a danceable tempo with the pitch control, then spinning a succession of records for a long period of time. (Keyes, 1996, p. 236)

Sampling is perhaps the most controversial aspect of Hip-Hop aesthetics as it stands in opposition to Western music's notions of copyright laws and ownership of intellectual property. According to Porcello (1991), sampling is not coincidental in that rap musicians intentionally use the sampler in a way that is oppositional and countercultural as it challenges capitalist ideals by using tabooed modes of quotation. Fricke and Aheren (2002) describe the origins of Hip-Hop in the impoverished urban ghettos of America. Few had the economic means to afford music lessons. Many of the original Hip-Hop artists were electronics repair technicians. They were able to modify and manipulate the conventional record player into a musical instrument of quotation and reinterpretation. Turning the conventional record player into a musical instrument of reinterpretation made the music-making experience accessible. The turntable is still an important instrument in Hip-Hop performances, but the sampler is perhaps the most important instrument in creating the sound track for rap music. During production the sampler allows the musician to create many complex levels of flow, layering, and rupture in line.

In recent years, therapists trained in different disciplines have come to realize the importance of culturally sensitive and culturally appropriate therapy techniques. Contemporary thinking considers multiculturalism the "fourth force" in therapy, following the forces of psychodynamic, behavioral, and humanistic movements in psychotherapy and counseling (Pedersen, 1991, in Bula, 2000). "Street youth" in a multicultural environment, such as Toronto, represent a wide variety of ethnic backgrounds. Cultural identity is made up of more than ethnicity. For most youth it includes gender, level of education, musical tastes, and a variety of group affiliations. While the youth involved in my clinical work came from a variety of ethnic groups, they are united by varying degrees of identification with contemporary youth culture. They are further united by varying degrees of affiliation to the subculture of street-involved youth. Moreno

(1988) discusses the common practice of music therapists who use the ethnic music of clients to establish trust and relationship. I argue that for many individuals who identify with contemporary youth culture, Hip-Hop music functions as their "ethnic music," often irrespective of their national, racial, ethnic, or religious backgrounds.

Though rap music began as the specific musical expression of young African Americans in the Bronx (Keyes, 2002), it is well documented that the genre's popularity quickly spread to most other African American communities in North America, then became popular with youth in many diverse parts of the globe (Shabtay, 2003; Osumare, 2001; Lusane, 1993).

According to Elligan (2000), rap's appeal to young Black men is partially due to the fact that the "lyrical expression represents the realities of their lives and struggles" (p. 30). However, he does not discuss its wide appeal beyond this group. Though I have worked with many Black youth, none were African American. My clients were Canadians of varied ethnic backgrounds. It is important to note that my many clients of African heritage are of a different demographic than their African American counterparts. Most of my Black Canadian clients are recent immigrants (second or first generation) from the West Indies or Africa. Their families have not been in North America for multiple generations. Furthermore, rap music was a useful therapeutic modality for many clients who were not of African heritage or ethnicity. An example is First Nations[*] youth. Many First Nations youth in Canada identify with the culture and message of Hip-Hop (Leafloor, 2011).[†]

Hip-Hop and Music Therapy

Oppressed people across the world were like, "Wait, we're gonna speak up through this art form, because it's fucking powerful. In this way, we can just deliver speeches over beats." And since we nod our heads to beats, that's instant affirmation.

Saul Williams (2001)[‡]

It is remarkable that the most commercially successful genre of popular music of the previous two decades (Rose, 1994; Tyson, 2002) is scarcely

---

[*] The term *First Nations* refers to the indigenous peoples of Canada, except for the Arctic-situated Inuit, and peoples of mixed European–First Nations ancestry called Métis. First Nations peoples used to be referred to as *Indians*, a term that is now reserved for people from the Indian subcontinent.

[†] For examples of this, see Stephen Leafloor's chapter and my other chapter in this book.

[‡] Quoted in Chang (2001, p. 1).

mentioned in the music therapy literature. The existing literature on rap music in therapy focuses on receptive rather than active techniques (Elligan, 2000; Tyson, 2002; Wyatt, 2002; Tenny, 2002).

The idea that musical expression or exposure can initiate personal or social transformation is alluded to in the literature on rap and Hip-Hop. A number of writers (Sylvan, 2002; Keyes, 2000; Pinn, 1999; Lusane, 1993) discuss the transformative power of rap music and other related African American genres. Tyson (2002) uses the widespread popularity of rap music as a rationale for its inclusion in therapy. He cites the "social, cultural, and political lyrical content and underlying themes" as useful therapeutic tools (Tyson, p. 132). His findings demonstrate that by utilizing the clients' strengths and interests, he was able to engage a challenging client population in a therapeutic process. Although I do not dispute his findings, it should be noted that he studied clinical techniques based on lyric analysis of existing material and not the *creation* of rap songs.

An important component of therapy with oppressed and marginalized people is working toward feelings and realities of empowerment and learning to use the sense of empowerment to overcome the oppression they suffer (Bishop, 2002). Forty-seven percent of street youth report a background of physical or sexual abuse (Delivering Health Care to the Homeless, 2003). Achieving mastery and learning to trust others are the pillars of recovery from trauma (Buchele, 2000). Engagement in group music experiences can be one means of learning to trust others and coming to feel a sense of mastery, particularly when this occurs within a genre to which the participant feels a connection. Furthermore, rap music can act as an empowering transformative agent by offering challenges to the politics and ideology of the dominant culture (Stephens & Wright, 2000; Pinn, 1998).

Groove-Based Music Therapy

It don't mean a thing, if it ain't got that swing.

Irving Mills

Aigen's (2002) work, *Playin' in the Band,* provides a qualitative look at the use of popular music in clinical improvisation. He documents a single case study with a nonverbal, severely disabled client, working with two music therapists. Despite the important and obvious differences[*] in our clinical

---

[*] Aigen's study examined his work with a mentally disabled, nonverbal individual using acoustic popular music intervention facilitated by two music therapists. I am working with groups of highly articulate street youth using electronic instruments, recording equipment, and Hip-Hop aesthetics.

work, many of his conclusions apply to the clinical recording of popular music styles with highly verbal clients including youth in urban shelters. In his conclusions, Aigen touches upon some key ideas that are particularly relevant to work with popular music styles and street involved youth.

> These observations on the function of style point to the value of music therapy processes occurring within popular music styles. They also provide insight into the role that relating in these styles can have in creating identity, or more accurately, in engaging participants actively in the ongoing, never-ending process of identity formation and evolution. . . . A form of expression that might be a consequence of motor regularity has taken on stylistic significance and all of its implications regarding participation in social life and individual identity. One can imagine Lloyd's [the client] internal sense of self as articulated by thoughts such as, *I am someone who plays rock and roll, who enjoys its boldness, vitality, rebellion, bodily and sexual energy, and life affirmation* [italics in original]. (Aigen, 2002, p. 111)

Aigen further suggests that different human attitudes are manifested by different popular music styles. "Cool jazz expresses sophisticated restraint and subtle sexuality" (Aigen, 2002, p. 111). I suggest that Hip-Hop expresses rebellion, overt sexuality, confidence, and outsiderness. "These are gratifying and self-affirming experiences for all those who participate in these forms of music, *but particularly so for clients in music therapy for whom this may be the only connection to these essential, foundational experiences* [emphasis mine]" (Aigen, 2002, p. 111).

Groove-Based Music Therapy, Rap Music, Hip-Hop Aesthetics, and Musicing

Rap is a musical style that is highly groove-oriented. Groove*-based musical styles have properties that make them particularly well suited to therapeutic applications. Feld (1994) notes the comfort that is often felt by members of a music community when people are "in the groove." Aigen (2002) notes that the rhythms of groove-based music invite movement, dancing, and other forms of participation that have therapeutic relevance:

> One becomes more comfortable within one's own body as control over it becomes a source of enjoyment; this comfort extends to social acceptance as one becomes a valuable member of one's peer group; and one also

---

* According to Feld and Keil, groove is what defines style. It is the subtle rhythmic discrepancies between the various parts that create the groove and invite participation.

becomes comfortable within the larger culture as one becomes accultur-
ated through participation in the groove. (Aigen, 2002, p. 35)

Aigen (2002) writes about the inability of drum machines to groove
because they do not texture their expression. I argue that drum machines
can be part of a groove experience, especially when they are capable of
creating *participatory discrepancies (PDs)** by also playing bass lines, or
when they can be *part* of a groove that invites participation. It has been
my experience in doing clinical improvisations with street youth that the
presence of a drum machine can facilitate the musical process. Although
the drum machine can be limiting because it locks in the tempo and rhythmic patterns, the familiar musical framework and timbres it provides are
potentially liberating, because the comfort and familiarity it provides
allows the participants to engage in rhythmically intense, life-affirming,
and expressive musicing that invites movement. The data collection in
my research was carried out almost entirely to the accompaniment of
a drum machine or loop sampler. The data analysis demonstrated that a
high degree of musical and lyrical creativity and self-expression occurred
within the Hip-Hop aesthetic, which is by definition technologically mediated and groove based. Instruments such as the drum machine played a
crucial role in the creation and collection of the data. In recent years, I have
witnessed performances of groups such as the Balkan Beat Box and others who integrate drum machines, samples, and live drumming into their
performance. These experiences show me that drum machines can very
certainly be part of the creation of a very compelling groove. The strong
rhythmic nature of rap makes it a potentially important groove-based music
therapy intervention. However, clinicians need to use these powerful musical forms with care. This point is illustrated by two interesting and related
processes that occurred in the sessions that I studied. The participants generally attempted to express some important stories, ideas, or emotions. At
times, this became difficult because of the technical demands of the strong
rhythmic and rhyming structure of rap music. In improvised rap music, it

---

* Participatory discrepancies (PDs) is a term used by ethnomusicologists (Feld &
Kiel, 1994) to describe the rhythmic characteristics of music that invite participation through the very subtle variations in performance, and micro-rhythmic and tonal
inconsistency between complementary parts. PDs give music its social power and
the power to move people. It involves both process and texture. The textural aspect
involves musical concepts such as "'inflection', 'articulation', 'creative tension', 'relaxed
dynamism', or 'semiconscious or unconscious slightly out of syncness'" (Keil, 1994,
p. 96). The process aspect of PDs is reflected in the vernacular of various music styles.
They are commonly referred to as *swing, groove,* or the *beat, vital drive, pulse,* or *push.*
As music technology becomes more sophisticated, computer musicians are able to
humanize their music by programming PDs into the music (Progler, 1995).

is particularly challenging to stay in this structure. Participants often and temporarily lost their ability to both conform to the structure *and* produce meaning. As a result, sometimes content was very meaningful but it fell outside the rigid structures of conventional rap music. At other times words were strung together only because they rhymed or were loosely associated, or nonsense words were made up to keep the rhythmic scheme going. When this happened during the early stages of this work, I was concerned that the lack of representational meaning might make these experiences un-valuable or not therapeutic. On reflection, I realized that taking such a position was contrary to the music-centered values that I was developing as a practicing music therapist.

Music-centered therapy finds inherent value in musicing (Elliot, 1995; Aigen, 2002; Aasgaard, 2002; Stige, 2002). Therapists working in a music-centered theoretical framework frequently engage clients in instrumental improvisations, acknowledging that these experiences can be therapeutic when there is representational meaning behind the music *and when there is not.* The participants in this study did not use instruments but rather they used words, a medium that creates an *expectation* of representational meaning. Yet I realized in the course of this work that the concept of musicing can apply also to words, and that participants can *music* with words and vocal sounds in a nonrepresentational and potentially therapeutic way. When music therapy clients engage in rap music improvisations, their voices and the microphones are the instruments. Thus, the experience can be therapeutic both when the words have representational meaning and when they do not. Even when the clients are engaged in wordplay* and not intentionally "meaning" anything with their words, they are still using engagement in the musical experience to foster communication and group cohesion, and to bring joy into a difficult environment. They are also using music involvement to elevate mood, and their acts of musicing are part of a process that keeps the music going.

Despite this exciting finding, I suspect that sometimes a purely improvisational approach to rap music production in music therapy may not always be the most appropriate choice. For some clients who are resistant to self-expression, the opportunity to engage in wordplay can provide a convenient cover for them to continue avoiding themselves and their issues or otherwise manifest therapeutic resistance. Some clients may want to

---

* I am tempted to write here "even when the clients are *just* engaged in wordplay," but like Aigen (2002, p. 9) I recognize that the word *just* implies that there is something missing or inadequate about the experience, when, in fact, the experience of *just musicing* can be an extremely socializing, life-affirming, uplifting, and mood-enhancing experience even when there are no other therapeutic objectives attached to it. For an important and complete discussion of the role of musicing with nonverbal clients refer to Aigen (2002).

express ideas, thoughts, or stories but feel unable to do so within the rigid structural confines of rap music. Clients such as these may benefit from improvised singing in related genres. Because of the greater possibility for lyric repetition, melisma, and other singing devices, musical structure may be less restrictive in other popular genres. Alternatively, some participants were very willing and able to precompose rap but were less able in the improvisation of rap music. A number of clients kept journals and wrote down their original rap songs. These clients tended to be more musically able when working with precomposed material. An allusion to this occurred in one of the improvisations:

> I don't have my book with me
> I'm all outa saliva*
> Yo, it's not getting that brighter

—Bill: Group Improvisation #1

Music therapists working with youth populations need to be alert to the importance of an individualized approach, just as music therapists working with any other population do. The data suggests that even for some clients who may want to do their musicing through the genre of rap, the genre may be too structured to allow for truly free self-expression. This point becomes more complicated when I examine the pieces that could be labeled *spoken word*. These are pieces where the individual is speaking with rhythmic cadence over a musical accompaniment. In these examples, the individual is not as concerned with adhering to the strict rhythmic and rhyming structure that the aesthetic of the background music suggests. Perhaps these examples imply a higher level of cognitive maturity because the individual tacitly realizes that they can be more creative and step outside of the structure. These examples do not fit in the *wordplay* category as there is clear meaning in the words.

The analysis of lyrics in my research did not include any attempt to determine the originality of the participants' lyrical expression. Although the phenomenon of cover songs does not exist in Hip-Hop, and rappers are generally expected to create their own lyrics, singing familiar songs is a useful technique in music therapy (Amir, 1997). I was not particularly interested in whether the lyrics were original or if they were quotations from the Hip-Hop canon, because the singing of familiar songs can be a nonthreatening way to express emotions, as it offers the singer symbolic distance from his/her thoughts or emotions. When people sing cover songs they can

---

* *Spittin'* or *spittin' on the mic* is a frequently heard expression for rapping. So when he says that he is *"outa saliva,"* he is suggesting that without the aid of his journal, he does not have much more to say.

still channel their emotions through the lyrics, especially if the content is meaningful to them.

Having the opportunity to conduct my master's research allowed me to understand and to become more comfortable with my emerging clinical techniques. I found myself moving toward a clinical approach where, as a musical facilitator, I listened deeply to the clients' music to match their expression to appropriate grooves. Aigen (2002) writes:

> The creation of vital, alive, quality music does not derive from the ability of musicians to link with each other around perfect tunings and precise co-temporal musical events, merging their identities into some perfect unity. Instead, music is created by an ability to connect with others in unique ways that preserve their separateness. (Aigen, 2002, p. 54)

Linking Music-Centered Music Therapy and Music Psychotherapy

Music-centered approaches to therapy are occasionally at odds with the music *in* therapy* approaches that emphasize using music as a tool or catalyst to initiate therapeutic verbal exchanges. Hip-Hop music therapy provides insight into a middle ground. For the therapy clients, there is generally more creative improvisation and expression in the words than the music. This seems to resemble a music *in* therapy approach, but the verbal expression all occurs in a musical context and so I conceptualize the work in a music *as* therapy framework. Music-centered thinkers such as Lee (1997) often advocate that at times the music can speak for itself and may not need verbal processing. In my work with rap music and "street youth," I often felt that they had said what they needed to in the song, and to process it further would diminish the experience. At other times, I felt that there may be a need for verbal processing and discussion of the lyrics and experience. This was sometimes welcomed and sometimes resisted. Because of the need to build trust in such a short and unpredictable amount of time, and my belief in the music-centered approach, I developed the personal policy of generally not initiating further verbal processing following a musical experience.

In music psychotherapy (Ahonen-Eerikainen, 2002), the therapist is much less directive in the music, and words play a much more important

---

* Bruscia (1998) broadly classifies music therapy systems by an orientation toward music *as* therapy or music *in* therapy. When music is used *as* therapy the musical experiences and interactions may be a sole or dominant focus of the therapy. When music is used *in* therapy the musical experiences are used to facilitate other therapeutic processes.

role. These two approaches sometimes seem mutually exclusive or at least opposite points on a theoretical continuum. The data suggests that the clinical recording and analysis of rap songs may begin to provide a theoretical bridge between these two approaches. I believe that Hip-Hop aesthetics in the music created the conditions for the creativity of this specific client group to flourish. Unlike most other music-centered models of music therapy, most of the clients' creativity took place through words. Yet the words of the clients are not regularly spoken words; they are spoken in the context of a musical experience.

This is why music therapists working with rap as a clinical resource have the responsibility to create music that comes as close as possible to the Hip-Hop aesthetic. I suggest that when we do so, we will engage our clients in what is for them a richer and more engaging therapeutic experience. When a client from this culture-sharing group hears the heavy rhythms of a drum machine with samples of record scratching, the deep bass lines, and they are holding a handheld microphone, they are absorbing a Hip-Hop aesthetic. This kind of approach to therapy communicates acceptance and tacitly creates an expectation that it is the time to engage in authentic self-expression.

In Creative Music Therapy (Nordoff & Robbins, 1997; Ansdell, 1995; Robbins & Robbins, 1998) and Aesthetic Music Therapy (Lee, 2003), music therapists are trained to listen to the music of their clients and use various improvisational techniques to meet them in their music. Lee (2003) emphasizes the importance of giving form and structure to the client's music. From my own experiences as a performer and listener, and as a reader of Feld and Keil (1994), I realized that what is generally inviting about music is "the groove." I also realized that groove is a microstructure that can give clients' music shape and meaning and invite further participation. Whether creating composed or improvised songs, or playing music therapy improvisations, the youth residents/clients seem to engage in longer, more frequent and involved improvisations when the structure was a clear groove provided by the drum machine, and/or by the guitar and bass through a loop sampler.

Clinical Applications

For many years, music therapists have used a variety of related disciplines to inform clinical practice. For most of the history of music therapy, our attention has been on psychology, social work, medicine, and other clinical disciplines. I do not downplay the importance of knowledge of these disciplines to our clinical practice. I agree with the growing body of academics (Lee, 1997, 2002; Ansdell, 1995; Aigen, 2002; Nordoff & Robbins, 1977;

Stige, 2002) that suggests that more attention needs to be paid to music and musicology in music therapy. As the field of musicology expands its scope to consider the role of music in culture (Stige, 2002), music therapists must also increase their cultural fluency, particularly as it pertains to the musical manifestations of the cultures we work with.

Rap music and Hip-Hop aesthetics must become relevant to music therapists, not only because of the popularity that rap artists enjoy (and have been enjoying for the last 30 years) but also because rap is a social form that "voices many of the class, gender, and race related forms of cultural and political alienation" (Rose, 1994, p. 184). I would add that the data demonstrates that the alienation expressed in rap music is not just limited to the types mentioned by Rose. Rap, particularly in the context of group therapy, can be used to express any form of alienation. Alienation has always been an important theme in existential psychotherapy approaches (Yalom, 1980). Yalom wrote 30 years ago that problems with meaninglessness are an increasingly common cause of psychopathology and emotional crisis, and that as society gets increasingly fast paced, technologically dependent/ sophisticated people lose touch with that which previously gave purpose or meaning to life. For youth in therapy, Hip-Hop is a natural way to confront, express, and begin working through those frustrations, because it has always served that purpose for its creators.

> Black music has always been a primary means of cultural expression for African-Americans, particularly during especially difficult social periods and transitions. In this way, rap is no exception; it articulates many of the facets of life in urban America for African-Americans situated at the bottom of a highly technological capitalist society. . . . As more and more of the disenfranchised and alienated find themselves facing conditions of accelerating deterioration, rap's urgent, edgy, and yet life-affirming resonances will become a more important and more contested social force in the world. (Rose, 1994, p. 184)

Lee (2003) has lamented a general lack of skill and knowledge of important trends in contemporary music among music therapists. One of the central aims of this chapter and this book as a whole is to begin to add an important form of contemporary popular expression to the music therapy dialogue. The nature of Hip-Hop as a clinical intervention is full of potential benefits and potential difficulties. By sharing thoughts about my work, I hope to add missing voices to the new and exciting dialogue that has been initiated by Aigen (2002), Lee (2002), Stige (2002), and Keil (1994).

The flexibility of rap as a mode of expression, and the universal themes that are expressed in both commercial rap music and the data that I collected, suggest that the findings of my original study (Lightstone, 2004) may have a high degree of *transferability* (Smejsters, 1997) to other clinical contexts. Every clinical context is different, but I would expect that other music therapists using similar techniques with verbally articulate youth would come to similar findings. The power of groove-oriented aesthetics to invite listeners into participation is powerful. This is demonstrated by how much transferability there was from Aigen's (2002) study on groove in clinical improvisation to my research study, despite the vast differences in our clinical context and client population.

The time for music therapists to pay serious attention to the study of Hip-Hop culture, rap music, and other forms of groove-based popular music genres is long overdue. Hip-Hop began its life as a countercultural movement around 35 years ago and has long since become part of mainstream popular culture. I have spoken to a number of young, novice, classically trained music therapists who have endeavored to work with youth populations. They generally feel ill-prepared to confront the musical and clinical challenges of this work. I hope this book will go a long way toward giving music therapists and music therapy students more tools for doing this valuable and powerful work.

References

Aasgaard, T. (2002). *Song creations by children with cancer: Process and meaning.* Unpublished PhD dissertation, Aalborg University.

Ahonen-Eerikainen, H. (2002). Group-analytic music therapy. *Nordic Journal of Music Therapy, 11*(1), 48–54.

Aigen, K. (2002). *Playing in the band: A qualitative study of popular music styles as clinical improvisation.* New York: Nordoff-Robbins Center for Music Therapy, Steinhardt School of Education New York University.

Amir, D. (1997). Understanding the role of folk songs in Jewish-Israeli culture: Implications for music therapy. *The World of Music, 39*(1), 111–127.

Ansdell, G. (1995). *Music for life: Aspects of Creative Music Therapy with adult clients.* London: Jessica Kingsley.

Bambaataa, A. (1995). The true meaning of Hip-Hop culture. *The Bomb Hip-Hop Magazine, 38*(3). Retrieved June 5, 2004, from http://www.bombhiphop.com/bam.htm

Bishop, A. (2002). *Becoming an ally: Breaking the cycle of oppression in people* (2nd ed.). Halifax: Fernwood.

Buchele, B. (2000). Group psychotherapy for survivors of sexual abuse and physical abuse. In R. Klein & V. Schermer (Eds.), *Group psychotherapy for psychological trauma.* New York: Guilford.

Bula, J. (2000). Use of the multicultural self for effective practice. In J. Bula (Ed.), *The use of self in practice* (2nd ed.). New York: Haworth Press.

Chang, J. (2001). Interview: Saul Williams slamming Hip-Hop. *Motherjones.* Retrieved June 5, 2004, from http://www.motherjones.com/arts/qa/2001/07/saul_williams.html

Delivering Health Care to the Homeless. (2003). Retrieved June 6, 2004, from http //www.deliveringhealthcaretothehomeless-youth–factsheet.mht

Eliot, D. (1995). *Music matters.* New York: Oxford University Press.

Elligan, D. (2000). Rap therapy: A culturally sensitive approach to psycho-therapy with young African American men. *Journal of African American Men, 5*(3), 27–37.

Feld, S. (1994). Aesthetics as iconicity of style (uptown title); or, (downtown title) "Liftup-over-sounding." Getting into the Kaluli groove. In C. Kiel & S. Feld (Eds.), *Music grooves* (pp. 109–150). Chicago: University of Chicago Press.

Fricke, J., & Ahearn C. (2002). *Yes Yes Y'all: The Experience Music Project, oral history of Hip-Hop's first decade.* Cambridge MA: Perseus.

Kelly, R. D. (1996). Message rap. In W. P. Perkins (Ed.), *Droppin' science: Critical essays on rap music and hip hop culture.* Philadelphia: Temple University Press.

Keyes, C. (1996). At the crossroads: Rap music and its African nexus. *Ethnomusicology, 40*(2), 110–125.

Keyes, C. (2000). Empowering self, making choices, creating spaces: Black female identity via rap music performance. *Journal of American Folklore, 113*(449), 225–269.

Keyes, C. L. (2002). *Rap music and street consciousness.* Chicago: University of Illinois Press.

Kiel, C., & Feld, S. (1994). *Music grooves.* Chicago: University of Chicago Press.

Lee, C. A. (1997). *Music at the edge: The music therapy experiences of a musi-cian with AIDS.* New York: Routledge.

Lee, C. A. (2003). *The architecture of aesthetic music therapy.* Gilsum, NH: Barcelona.

Lightstone, A. (2004). *Yo! Can ya flow?: A qualitative study of hip hop aesthet-ics and original rap lyrics created in group music therapy in an urban youth shelter.* Unpublished master's research. Available at http://www.wlu.ca/soundeffects/researchlibrary/Aaron.pdf

Lusane, C. (1993). Rap, race and politics. *Race and Class, 35*(1), 42–56.

Nordoff, P., & Robbins, C. (1977). *Creative music therapy.* New York: The Nordoff-Robbins Centre for Music Therapy.

Osumare, M. (2001). Beat streets in the global hood: Connective marginali-ties of the hip hop globe. *Journal of American and Comparative Cultures, 11*(2), 171–183.

Perkins, W. P. (1996). *Droppin' science: Critical essays on rap music and hip hop culture.* Philadelphia: Temple University Press.

Pinn, A. B. (1999). "How ya livin'?" Notes on rap music and social transforma-tion. *Western Journal of Black Studies, 23*(1), 10–21.

Porcello, T. (1991). The ethics of digital audio sampling: Engineers discourse. *Popular Music, 10*(1), 69–84.

Robbins, C., & Robbins, C. (1998). *The healing heritage: Paul Nordoff exploring the tonal language of music.* Gilsum, NH: Barcelona.

Rose, T. (1994). *Black noise: Rap music and Black culture in contemporary America.* London: Wesleyan University Press.

Ruud, E. (1998). *Music therapy: Improvisation, communication, and culture.* Gilsum, NH: Barcelona.

Salaam, M. (1995). The aesthetics of rap. *African American Review, 29*(2), 89–97.

Shabtay, M. (2003). RaGap: Music and identity among young Ethiopians in Israel. *Critical Arts, 17*(1,2), 93–105.

Smeijjsters, H. (1997). *Multiple perspectives: A guide to qualitative research in music therapy.* Gilsum, NH: Barcelona.

Stephens, R. J., & Wright, E. (2000). Beyond bitches, niggers, and ho's: Some suggestions for including rap music as a qualitative data source. *Race and Society, 3,* 23–40.

Stige, B. (2002). *Culture-centered music therapy.* Gilsum, NH: Barcelona.

Sylvan, R. (2002). *Traces of the spirit: The religious dimensions of popular music.* New York: New York University Press.

Tenny, S. (2002). Music therapy for juvenile offenders in residential treatment. *Music Therapy Perspectives, 20*(2).

Tyson, E. (2002). Hip hop therapy: An exploratory study of a rap music intervention with at-risk and delinquent youth. *Journal of Poetry Therapy, 15*(3), 131–144.

Wayatt, J. (2002). Clinical resources for music therapy with juvenile offenders. *Music Therapy Perspectives, 20*(2).

Wigram, T. (2004). *Improvisation: Methods and techniques for music therapy clinicians, educators, and students.* London: Jessica Kingsley.

Yalom, I. (1980). *Existential psychotherapy.* New York: Basic.

Chapter 4

The Hero's Journey in Hip-Hop and Its Applications in Music Therapy

Michael Viega

The "Hero's Journey" and Archetypes

> All these different mythologies give us the same essential quest. You leave the world that you're in and go into a depth or into a distance or up to a height. There you come to what was missing in your consciousness in the world you formerly inhabited. Then comes the problem of either staying with that, and letting the world drop off, or returning with that boon and trying to hold on to it as you move back into your world again. That's not an easy thing to do. (Campbell, 1988, p. 157)

Think about the last movie that moved you emotionally, where the hero or heroine's story resonated deeply within you. Chances are the narrative arc that propels the protagonist's adventures follows the same outline that is shared in most myths passed down throughout human history. Joseph Campbell, renowned anthropologist and mythologist, identified this mythological pattern as the Hero's Journey. For Campbell, each hero cycles through the stages of separation, initiation, and return. The ultimate goal of this journey is transformation of consciousness, bringing the boon received on the journey back into the world for others to benefit from (Campbell, 1949/2008).

As a music therapist, I work primarily with adolescents in diverse clinical settings and the teenagers I have worked with have all had a range of musical tastes. However, one of the primary genres of music that I have worked with in music therapy in an urban setting has been Hip-Hop. My own love for all popular music genres, including Hip-Hop, has informed my own journey, as I have always felt that my preferred music speaks to me and for me on metaphorical levels, a mythic soundtrack to my life. Campbell's Hero's Journey has provided me with the language and context for understanding my own experience with my own preferred music. I have used this understanding to conceptualize my adolescent clients' journey in therapy as well.

Though the narrative cycle of Campbell's Hero's Journey is replicated and reflected in the various myths across cultures and traced back to the earliest myths created by human beings, it is important to note that the Heroine's Journey, as written about by Maureen Murdock (1990), reflects a feminine version of the cycle that addresses such topics and challenges as the rejection of the feminine and the mother daughter split, a cycle that Joseph Campbell does not address. It should also be noted that the themes and cycles of the Hero's Journey may not reflect universal cultural themes. Therefore, this chapter is an attempt to share how Joseph Campbell's writings have influenced me as a music therapy clinician in how I conceptualize both the journey of my clients and the journey of the music as well, in this case looking at the journey of Hip-Hop culture, the transformation of adolescence, and the implication of these sagas in music therapy.

In his landmark book *The Hero With a Thousand Faces*, Campbell (1949/2008) describes and names each stage of a hero's journey. These stages include (1) the call to adventure; (2) supernatural aid; (3) crossing the threshold of adventure; (4) trials and tasks; (5) reaching the nadir; (6) receiving the boon; (7) the return; and (8) the crossing of the return threshold. Along each stage of the journey, the hero must discover new strengths and powers within him/herself to face certain trials and tasks. The hero also meets new characters that aid him/her in times of need or provide him/her with new weapons and tools for the journey.

Many of the hero's internal struggles are similar, such as when the hero/heroine is pulled from comfortable surroundings and thrown into adventure, having to overcome fear of the unknown to help save others. Also, each hero/heroine encounters similar character types in his/her adventures, such as the meeting with a wise old man or something or someone with supernatural powers that helps the hero on his/her quest (think of

Obi-Wan Kenobi, from *Star Wars*, and Glinda the Witch, from *The Wizard of Oz*). These basic character outlines are also known as archetypes.

Archetypes, a term coined by Carl Jung, are representational mental forms, which both Freud and Jung surmised are remnants from our most primitive unconscious psyche. However, Jung thought that archetypes are manifested through the biological powers of our bodily organs, rather than emerging from unconscious repressed traumatic experiences. Jung referred to archetypes as "primordial images" that can "reproduce themselves in fantasies and often reveal their presence only by symbolic images" and universal mythological motifs (1964, p. 58). Though these motifs may change depending on the dream or the story in which the archetype is revealed, the basic archetypal pattern for the symbol remains the same (Jung, 1964). Authors Faber and Mayer (2009) define an archetype as "an internal mental model of a typical, generic story character to which an observer might resonate emotionally" (p. 307). Therefore, archetypes also serve as internal guides to our own individual Hero's Journey as well.*

Carol Pearson (1991), author of *Awakening the Heroes Within: Twelve Archetypes to Help Us Find Ourselves and Transform Our World*, likens the ritualistic transformation within the Hero's Journey to the psychological goal of fully realizing the *Self*. For Pearson, the task within the first stage of the Hero's Journey is to strengthen one's *Ego* to *prepare for the journey*.[†] In the next stage, one's task is to *become real* by discovering the depths of the *Soul* through exploration of the unconscious. Finally, the task is to *return* back home within ourselves with a stronger sense of our true identity or *Self*, and to take on the responsibility of our lives. For each of these three stages, Pearson notes the archetypes that are likely to be activated within us, acting as our guides through this psychological development. It is important to note that each archetype has a shadow side that represents the fear held within that archetype. Therefore, the archetype that is most strongly present for us can either help us achieve our needs along our journey or hinder our personal development if caught in its shadow. For instance, the archetype of the Destroyer may help us to let go of old patterns and accept our mortality, or we can be pulled down by unconscious self-destructive behaviors out of the fear of our own death. (See Table 4.1.)

---

* The archetypes described throughout this chapter once again reflect primarily Western approaches to understanding these concepts. It is recognized that these archetypal titles may not reflect certain cultures. This chapter is a reflection of the author's own understanding of the concepts and does not suggest universality of these concepts.

† The italics are to denote the stages of the hero's journey according to Pearson (1991) as well as the major task toward wholeness within each stage: (1) Build and contain ego; (2) discover depth of one's soul or unconscious; and (3) return with a sense of an integrated whole self.

Table 4.1 The 12 Archetypes and the Hero's Journey

Separation Preparation for the Journey	Initiation The Journey— Becoming Real	Return The Return— Becoming Free
The Innocent	The Seeker	The Ruler
The Orphan	The Lover	The Magician
The Warrior	The Destroyer	The Sage
The Caregiver	The Creator	The Fool

Note: From Pearson, C. S. (1991). Awakening the heroes within: Twelve archetypes to help us find ourselves and transform our world. New York: HarperCollins.

The ritualistic path of the Hero's Journey and the archetypes that guide that journey provide a way to view psychological, social-cultural, environmental, and musical processes as mythological formations. These processes occur simultaneously on a micro and macro level in our lives. On an individual level, we each wake up to the dawn of a new day, experience the sun's cycle peak at midday, and fall into the mysterious world of sleep and dream, only to wake up new and refreshed again. Thus, on a micro level we live our own myths within our own daily experience in life, while simultaneously on a macro level, the planets cycle through a similar voyage daily. Campbell (1988) summarizes this process eloquently, stating, "The myths that link you to your social group, the tribal myths, affirm that you are an organ of the larger organism. Society itself is an organ of a larger organism, which is the landscape, the world in which the tribe moves" (p. 90).

The Mythic Journey of Hip-Hop

Prelude to Adventure

Clark (1995) argues that "music itself is an archetype. It is indigenous to every culture and can transcend cultural associations to address collective experiences. It speaks to and about each person's experience as he lives through the trials and tasks of his life" (p. 51). Jeff Chang (2005) writes about the cultural influence of Hip-Hop in similar terms. In the prelude to his publication, Chang argues that Hip-Hop transcends academic labels such as *postmodernism* and tells a greater story, especially that of a period of African American history between the passage of the Civil Rights Act of 1964 and the rise of Hip-Hop's global influence during the presidencies of Ronald Regan and George H. W. Bush in the late 1980s and early 1990s.

My own feeling is that the idea of the Hip-Hop Generation brings together time and race, place and polyculturalism, hot beats and hybridity. It describes the turn from politics to culture, the process of entropy and reconstruction. It captures the collective hopes and nightmares, ambitions and failure of those who would otherwise be described as "post-this" or "post-that." (Chang, 2005, p. 2)

Theologian and researcher Robin Sylvan (2002) goes even further back to trace the hero's journey of modern popular music forms, including that of Hip-Hop, starting with its roots in West African possession rituals. Sylvan puts the voyage of Hip-Hop culture into the larger context of the greater human story. The story Sylvan (2002) tells begins with the uprooting of West Africans, particularly the Fon and Yoruba tribes, in the transatlantic slave trade to the Americas. Families, religion, culture, and musical traditions were scattered, fragmented, and suppressed. The music began to reappear in the form of African American spirituals, and later blues and jazz, and served as a connection for many African Americans back to their cultural and religious roots. By the 1950s, the rhythm and blues and gospel music of African Americans began to integrate with the country and western traditions of many rural White Americans, and rock'n'roll was born. It is like the music had gone on its own Hero's Journey, leaving Africa, getting "submerged" during the time of slavery, and reemerging to the world through blues, jazz, and rock'n'roll.

Sylvan (2002) believes that the beat-driven possession rituals of West Africa resurfaced in the forms of modern popular music and thus the religious components of the music are still present. The music carries this religious message in the driving rhythms of popular music, a groove that is prevalent throughout popular culture today. Sylvan describes his research participants' experiences in the music as transcendent encounters with the numinous, the feeling of being connected to something greater than oneself. Through immersing themselves in their favorite bands and sharing the live concert experience with other like-minded listeners, fans of popular music are able to embark on their own unique psychological and spiritual hero's journey, which is reflected back to them in their favorite bands and/or favorite songs (Sylvan, 2002). Though Sylvan's story of popular music's voyage can be seen as a hero's journey in and of itself, Hip-Hop's rise from the decayed urban landscape of the South Bronx in 1972 to the global and generational force that it is today has taken on mythic proportions of its own.

In the following section, a brief history of Hip-Hop will be given, using Pearson's (1991) segments of the Hero's Journey and the possible archetypes that appear to be active during each portion of the journey.

Preparation for the Journey

The music and culture of Hip-Hop rose like a phoenix out of the ashes of two neighborhoods that represented the social, political, and economical dystopia of the early 1970s, Trenchtown in Jamaica and the New York City borough of the Bronx. It is as if the music has its own mythic origins, from the destruction of these neighborhoods came the rebirth of a new musical identity, Hip-Hop. In the 1970s, both areas were forgotten about by their local and federal governments and saw a rise of youth gangs. These youth gangs did not appear to be interested in the Black power politics of their parents; they were more interested in surviving (Chang, 2005).

In many ways, Hip-Hop's journey begins through the activation of the archetype of the Orphan.* On a literal level, the orphan is a child who has been abandoned, victimized, and neglected by his/her parent(s). Many orphans do not feel emotionally or physically safe. When dealing with the psychological effects of being orphaned, Pearson (1991) discusses that the Orphan's path tends to move from being banished from being an Innocent to becoming a Rebel or Outlaw, an archetype that is prevalent within the personas that many rappers have adopted. Other characteristics of the Orphan include resisting rescue, feeling betrayed, and pushing away help. This may lead to the Orphan's shadow, characterized by masochism or sadism, which could be said to be characteristics often found in the misogynistic and violent lyrical imagery of subgenres of Hip-Hop such as so-called gangsta rap.

In preparing for the journey, one's task is to build an ego container through the creation of a safe space so that the hero may begin to connect with others and retain a sense of safety (McKinney & Clark, 2009). Chang (2005) describes a pivotal moment in 1971 when Black and Hispanic gangs came together in the Bronx to sign a peace treaty to quell tensions among rival gangs. This was in response to the murder of a member of the Ghetto Brothers gang, a gang that began to turn from violence and became active in helping the community. They were also well known in the South Bronx for the music they made, a beat-oriented Latin-funk fusion fashioned after their hero, James Brown. Though the peace treaty did not last, it made a lasting impression on many in the audience, including a soon-to-be pioneer of Hip-Hop, Afrika Bambaataa, who was a member of a gang, the Black Spades, but later formed his own collective based upon social awareness, cultural awareness, and self-awareness, the Zulu Nation.

Often in the preparation of the journey, the hero is met with supernatural aid and given the gift or a weapon to assist him/her on his/her quest. For many in the Bronx, three particular DJs—DJ Kool Herc, Afrika

---

* Orphan is capitalized when using it as the title of the archetype and not its literal meaning. The same will occur for the other archetypes discussed throughout this chapter.

Bambaataa, and Grandmaster Flash—possessed supernatural powers to take an everyday item such as a turntable and turn it into a powerful tool to create their own music. Taking just the drum break or instrumental portion of popular rock'n'roll, funk, and R&B songs, these DJs transformed the turntable and record from their everyday use as transmitters of music into a musical instrument all of its own. Along with the DJ's development of *break beats*, the combination of dance (*break dancing*), the style of *b'boying* (the attire and attitude of those who were in the know about this new music and dance), and *graffiti* laid the basic blueprint of Hip-Hop; the music was born and its journey was on its way (Chang, 2005).

The Journey—Becoming Real

In 1982, Hip-Hop began to move from the boroughs of New York City and found cross-cultural success. For over a decade, Hip-Hop entered into a period where trials and tasks were faced. These tasks included facing early discrimination from media sources like MTV that initially excluded Black artists, as well as increased religious, government, and political scrutiny, with attempts to censor rap lyrics from artists such as Public Enemy, N.W.A., and Ice-T (Chang, 2005). In this stage of the Hero's Journey, the hero faces crises and dangerous situations, tries out new behaviors, expands horizons, and ultimately receives the boon for completing these tasks (McKinney & Clark, 2009; Clark, 1995). It could be argued that the emergence of new Hip-Hop global multimedia conglomerations such as Jay-Z's Roc-A-Fella Records or Sean Comb's Bad Boy Entertainment are the result of such a boon: a new, truly American Hip-Hop culture that rose from economic despair of urban decay to a global economic and cultural force.

During Hip-Hop's journey to becoming real, the archetype of the Creator stands out. Pearson (1991) describes the task of the Creator as one to accept the Self fully and realize it in the world through creativity. Another mission of the Creator is to be involved in self-creation and self-acceptance, which can often be seen in vocational choices made by those whose Creator archetype is triggered. The Creator often fears inauthenticity, and not being able to realize his or her own imagination fully.

This message of authenticity in Hip-Hop is most prevalently expressed by the MC. The message was delivered through rapping, an art form that is equal parts improvisation and storytelling. Sylvan (2002) traces the art form of rap back to the oral traditions of West Africa, where "spoken word was seen as potent and sacred, having the power to evoke that which was being spoken about" (p. 184). The potency and authenticity of rapping can be seen within one of the first major crossovers for Hip-Hop, "The Message" by Grandmaster Flash and the Furious 5. The song describes the grim realities of many socioeconomically oppressed persons living in the ghettos of American cities. The narrator of the song describes his environmental surroundings of broken glass, rats, roaches, and junkies in the alley vividly to the listener.

This message could also be deeply personal and reflective, as seen in the lyrics of Tupac Shakur, aka 2Pac. His 1995 song "Dear Mama" is a tribute to his mother Afeni Shakur, whose own journey mirrored the transformation from the political Black Power movement of the 1960s (Afeni Shakur was a prominent member of the Black Panther Party) to the rise of the Hip-Hop generation, of which her son is a highly regarded sage. In the lyrics to "Dear Mama," we witness the artist's profound feelings and appreciation of the struggles his mother went through. Tupac describes how difficult it must have been for her as a single mother with a drug habit and on welfare, raising a son who was breaking the rules, running the streets, and not doing well in school. He goes on to say that despite these conditions, she always provided both love and discipline, and managed to keep them clothed, fed, and with a roof over their heads. In this song he pays tribute to her, letting her know how much he appreciates all that she went through and all that she did for him. Such emotional deepening of feelings is common in the transition of becoming real to becoming free (McKinney & Clark, 2009).

The Return—Becoming Free

The main task for the hero who is returning back from his journey is to consolidate gains from the voyage and bring back one's truth into the world where it can be received and bring light to others. Today, the message of Hip-Hop has certainly spread globally, with Hip-Hop being one of the most chosen art forms for voices of socially, economically, and politically suppressed and oppressed people around the world.* Hip-Hop appears to be the voice of peoples everywhere that have been physically or emotionally orphaned by their country, their communities, and/or their families. One does not have to be literally orphaned to take this journey. Pearson (1991) describes the process of self-orphaning, which will be discussed later as a natural developmental phase in adolescence.

Within the meta-narrative of Hip-Hop that I have presented, the archetypal journey has appeared to be Orphan → Creator → Ruler/Sage. The task of the Ruler in the last phase of the journey is to use all internal

---

* For instance, a Hip-Hop artist like K'naan, who was raised within the civil war in Somalia in the 1990s, brings a modern global voice that integrates reggae, world beat rhythms, and Hip-Hop into his music.

and external resources for the good of society and the planet. Today, Hip-Hop music appears to be as politically, socially, and spiritually conscious as ever, with everyday people who grew up within the Hip-Hop generation attempting to bring the message into social and global concerns of the day. Chang (2005) comments on this new movement of Hip-Hop activism:

> [The activists] were dealing with a unique paradox—a generation that had greater access to the media and culture than any other in history remained as politically scapegoated and marginalized as any in history. They called themselves "hip-hop activists" because it spoke to the way culture and politics came together because it was a way to reclaim and define their generational identity. (p. 454)

These modern-day sages "teach us that we can never be free until we are willing to completely let go of our illusion and attachments and seek to align our own wills with truth itself" (Pearson, 1991, p. 215). The search for authenticity of the Creator is ultimately finding the way to speak one's truth, to find one's voice, and therefore help others to do the same.

Another archetype that is certainly important in Hip-Hop imagery is that of the Outlaw. Faber and Mayer (2009) define the Outlaw as "represented in the rebellious iconoclast; the survivor and the misfit. Often vengeful, a disruptive rule-breaker, possibly stemming from hidden anger. Can be wild, destructive and provoking from a long time spent struggling or injured" (p. 309). When used positively, this archetype can be helpful in questioning and challenging unjust laws (think of Hans Solo's journey in the movie *Star Wars*). In this way, it can aid the Orphan and Creator in becoming a just and fair Ruler. However, as with all archetypes, the shadow side is always present as well.

The Shadow

Faber and Mayer (2009) sum up the Shadow archetype as "represented by the violent, haunted, and the primitive; the darker aspects of humanity. Often seen in a tragic figure, rejected; awkward, desperately emotional. Can be seen to lack morality; a savage nemesis" (p. 309). It is my opinion that this definition of the shadow unfortunately gets projected onto the Hip-Hop artists and their creative output as represented by the negative way that Hip-Hop is often portrayed in popular media, instead of seeing the art as a reflection of the shadowy parts of our society which is often not discussed constructively in mainstream media. Hip-Hop offers an expressive channel to voice the needs and share the lived experiences of marginalized, under-served urban communities that are often neglected and forgotten about in mainstream sociopolitical discourse. For many Hip-Hop artists, the violent, misogynistic, and destructive themes that may emerge in the art of Hip-Hop is a reflection of social ills that mainstream media may not properly represent.* The point is not to hide the shadowy aspects of society, such as poverty, crime, and drug use, but to embrace them authentically, thus offering up a dialogue and providing an insider's viewpoint into the lived experiences of the people in marginalized communities around the world.

Researchers, clinicians, and academic scholars have begun to see Hip-Hop culture as a significant way to gain access to the lived experiences of adolescents, but differ on how they view the lyrics and themes within this culture (Shaffer, 2004; Tyson, 2002). In her 2004 dissertation, titled "The Shady Side of Hip-Hop: A Jungian and Eriksonian Interpretation of Eminem's 'Explicit Content,'" Tani Graham Shaffer argues that "the recognition of our collective shadow and the search for an integrated identity reveal many difficult truths which must be faced and brought to consciousness" (p. 88). Schaffer sees the need for parents, teachers, and all who work with adolescents to "listen to our youth and find a way to understand the meanings of their perceptions and experiences" (p. 88). Examining the shadow is an important part toward a fuller understanding of not only the individual music fan but the collective society as well.

A common archetypal journey of the shadowy side of life in marginalized and impoverished societies that rap lyrics may reflect appears to be Orphan → Warrior/Outlaw → Creator/Destroyer → tyrannical Ruler.† Here, the journey cycle is unable to be completed because it gets stuck on the shadow of the Ruler, who is "prone to either indolence and self-indulgence or spartan rigidity and intolerance" (Pearson, 1991, p. 187).‡ The archetype of the Destroyer is active and harmful when caught

---

* Chuck D of the Hip-Hop group Public Enemy famously stated that "rap was Black America's CNN," a quote that immediately prompted a disclaimer from their record company stating that "the interview with Chuck D in no way reflected the views of Columbia Records" (Chang, 2005, p. 251).
† Rapper 50 Cent's popular media persona appears to play out this Shadow archetypal journey and can be seen in the succession of album titles such as "Get Rich or Die Trying" (2003) [Orphan/Outlaw] and "The Massacre" (2005) [Destroyer]. His media persona appears to stay constantly within these Shadow archetypes; his latest album is interestingly titled "Before I Self-Destruct" (2009).
‡ A common movie character appropriated among many Hip-Hop artists is Al Pacino's character Tony Montana from the 1983 movie *Scarface*. Tony Montana was a Cuban immigrant who flaunted his money and riches he accrued from drug dealing. This is a fitting archetype of the tyrannical Ruler and an image that is prevalent among rap artists.

in the shadow Ruler. The archetype of the Lover can often transform into something more sinister (Pearson, 1991). These destructive archetypes can be said to be displayed in misogynistic, violent, and destructive rap lyrics. The archetypal characters portrayed in certain rap narratives can provide music therapists, social workers, teachers, parents, and others who work closely with adolescents metaphorical insights into the internal developmental tasks and trials they are facing, as well as help these adults gain greater awareness about the external environment in which adolescents live and by which they are affected daily. Therefore, Hip-Hop culture can offer a unique way for the music to be used as a communication device in a way that helps an adolescent express and understand difficult feelings, thoughts, experiences, and emotions that are consistently flooding them as they grow and develop.

The Mythical Transformation of Adolescence

But the structure and something of the spiritual sense of this adventure can be seen already anticipated in the puberty or initiation rituals of early tribal societies through which a child is compelled to give up its childhood and become an adult—to die, you might say, to its infantile personality and psyche and come back as a responsible adult. . . . That's the basic motif of the universal hero's journey—leaving one condition and finding the source of life to bring you forth into a richer or mature condition. (Campbell, 1988, p. 151)

Since Hip-Hop is a common preference for many adolescents, are there similarities between the cycle of separation, initiation, and return within the hero's journey and the transformation from childhood to adolescence to adulthood? If so, can the archetypes and narratives within Hip-Hop culture provide therapists, parents, teachers, and others who work with adolescents with indications about the trials and tasks an adolescent is facing during his or her development? A brief overview of music therapy and adolescent development will be provided in this section to lay the groundwork for the argument that such a perspective can be taken when working with adolescents in music therapy. I will then revisit the story of Braheem, a participant in a qualitative study I conducted in 2008 titled "Conceptualizing the Lived Experience of Three Adolescents Through the Interpretation of the Core Metaphors in Their Preferred Music." In this study, most of the participants' favorite music came from the genre of Hip-Hop. Hip-Hop is not merely a musical preference, but a lifestyle and a culture unto itself (Schaffer, 2004; Chang, 2005) and this was certainly true for my research participants, especially Braheem, a 15-year-old boy submerged in the Hip-Hop culture of North Philadelphia. Though I was unfamiliar with Joseph Campbell's work at the time of my research study, I believe that Braheem's story can be revisited using the Hero's Journey and Pearson's (1991) archetypes to gain new perspectives on Braheem's lived experience and his preferred music.

Adolescence may be seen as the liminal state of transitioning from childhood to adulthood. Suvi Saarikallio (2007) notes that typical developmental tasks and trials that adolescents encounter include physical changes and the heightened awareness of sexuality and body image that come with these changes, emotional-social turmoil that brings peer pressures, anxiety of future occupation, and the increased need for independence while also needing group belongingness. Throughout these tasks, adolescents develop the skills to cope with stress and anxiety internally and learn how to regulate their moods. An adolescent, while needing to feel independent, also relies on friends and mentors to help guide them along their path toward adulthood (Saarikallio, 2007). The ultimate boon for an adolescent after completing the journey from childhood is the "reconstruction of self and establishment of adult identity" (Saarikallio, 2007, p. 18).

Music Therapy's Role in the Journey

Though the Hero's Journey myth has been written about as a way to understand music therapy theory and clinical process,* little has been written on Hip-Hop culture, music therapy, and adolescents within the music therapy literature. Edgar Tyson (2002), a professor in the field of social work and social welfare, reports on the development of what he calls Hip-Hop therapy (HHT), a combination of rap music, Hip-Hop culture, bibliotherapy (a poetry therapy technique that utilizes a client's stories in therapy), and music therapy. Though his initial outcomes from a mixed-method study showed statistical uncertainties about the effectiveness of HHT, primarily due to a small sample size, a qualitative inquiry suggested that participants felt more respected, heard, and motivated while involved in HHT. As mentioned above, HHT was developed by a social worker and the differences, similarities, and connection between HHT and music therapy are unclear. Though to date there has been little written about the impact of Hip-Hop culture on music therapy practice with adolescents, music therapy

---

* For more about the Hero's Journey, archetypes, liminality, and music therapy see Kenny (1982/2006), Rudd (1998), Aigen (1998, 2005), Beer (1990), and Clark (1995).

researchers and clinicians have written about the importance of music's role in the developmental journey of adolescence.

In her doctoral research of music's role in the everyday life of adolescents, Saarikallio (2004, 2007) provides a model that is useful in understanding how adolescents use their preferred music in their personal development and transition into adulthood. Of her model, Saarikallio (2004) states, "The underlying assumption is that engagement in music is a goal-oriented activity of the psyche" (p. 48). This suggests that adolescents, whether consciously or unconsciously, use music to work through trials and tasks that come with the difficulty in transitioning from childhood to adulthood. She labels four categories/functions of music as related to the developmental tasks of adolescents: (1) Emotional Field, (2) Identity, (3) Agency, and (4) Interpersonal Relationships. Saarikallio summarizes that music is a powerful and meaningful tool for adolescents to meet these developmental needs.

Tervo (2005) uses the psychodynamic phenomenon of a *transitional object* to understand music's role in and as therapy for adolescents. The concept of the *transitional object* comes from Winnicott's (1971/1999) observations of the importance an infant places on an object during the developmental shift from symbiotic union with the mother to an autonomous being. The object, such as a soft blanket, "becomes vitally important to the infant for use at the time of going to sleep, and is a defense against anxiety, especially anxiety of [a] depressive type" (Winnicott, 1971/1999, p. 4). In this respect, the *transitional object* is similar to the *supernatural aid* in the Hero's Journey myth, where the hero receives a gift that will aid in the trials and tasks to come. Tervo sees the relationship between the development of an adolescent (which is widely considered a second individuation) and music's ability to provide a *transitional object* for the anxiety of the trials that come with being an adolescent. Therefore, the music is both supernatural aid and a symbolic sage in the fantasies of adolescents, where an object such as an electric guitar or a favorite CD becomes a trusted friend who unconditionally understands and travels with them through their journey into adulthood.

Andrea Frisch (1990) sees song composition as a way for adolescents to access their myths. Within the journey cycle, Frisch sees this music therapy technique as an important tool for the adolescent to move from the *preparation for the journey* stage to the *becoming real* stage, in which the primary goal is containing the ego (Pearson, 1991). "Song composition gives the adolescent the opportunity to make a transition between the expression of musical and verbal symbols; hence it is an activity that can assist in ego development" (Frisch, 1990, p. 28).

Both Tervo (2005) and Frisch (1990) note that the initial phase of music therapy for adolescents is to help them to develop the tools to use music creatively and symbolically. Therefore, one of the goals for adolescents in music therapy is to create a safe therapeutic space where they can prepare for the journey. Within the Hero's Journey, one of the aims for the Orphan is to regain safety. However, an Orphan often resists being rescued and moves dramatically between wanting love and complete rejection of the person offering love (Pearson, 1991). These are common characteristics of adolescents in therapy and often one of the most challenging barriers for a music therapist who is attempting to create a safe musical space for an adolescent to prepare for his or her therapeutic journey.

The connection between the Orphan archetype and adolescent development seems appropriate when considering the nature of adolescence. Goldbeck, Schmitz, Besier, Herschbach, and Henrich (2007) showed that decreased life satisfaction is part of developmental growth, especially in the area of satisfaction with home life, while simultaneously there is an increase in satisfaction with friends and social group. Pearson (1991) describes a similar process with the Orphan,

> Developmentally, the Orphan stage is the time children turn away from reliance on the parents, to reliance on siblings or friends. In a healthy family, they may not be terribly critical of their parents, but they do begin to recognize and chronicle the tendencies of the parents toward dogmatism, rigidity, or clumsiness and ineptitude. (p. 86)

So where childhood may be seen in the archetype of the Innocent where there is bliss with parent and child, the Orphan also believes that anything is possible and is optimistic, yet feels he or she can go at it alone. Adolescent development therefore is akin to what Pearson calls "self-orphaning" (p. 86). This self-orphaning often leads to a wounded sense of self-esteem and self-worth, making it hard for the Orphan to progress at anything (Pearson, 1991). This was certainly one of the primary needs that emerged for Braheem, whose Orphan archetype was present in many of our discussions about the core metaphors in his preferred music.

Case Example of Braheem

As a music therapist working with adolescents, I often consider how my clients' preferred music resonates with the archetypal themes that play out in their lives and how that information can help me understand and aid the developmental growth of my clients. In a qualitative study I conducted on understanding the core metaphors of the preferred music of adolescents, I was able to conceptualize their lived experiences through the relationship built between the participants, their preferred music, and me. One of the important findings that emerged was that the core metaphors were not already in their preferred music waiting to be discovered, but instead came alive through our shared adventures of carefully listening to their music (Viega, 2008). Music therapy literature has suggested that as a clinician one can use the Hero's Journey myth as a frame to view both theory and processes in music therapy (Kenny, 1982/2006; Aigen, 1998, 2005; Rudd, 1998; Clark, 1995). The purpose here in sharing part of Braheem's narrative is to retell the story that emerged from our music listening using the Hero's Journey myth and the archetypes active for Braheem, as a possible way for gaining further insight into his lived experiences that he shared during our time together.

Self-Orphaning

When we first met, Braheem was 15 years old. He is an African American male who proudly resided in North Philly. He reported that he had moved throughout North Philadelphia his whole life. "I just be living all over Philly. My mom, she never liked North Philly but that is where she has been living all her life. My mom does not like being around a lot of violence, like bringing her kids into violence." He was still attached to his mother, but at the same time he was beginning to rely more and more on his older siblings, his friends, and his favorite Hip-Hop artists to provide him with a code to live by. He was resisting positive help in his life such as attending the after-school program, at which this study took place, and had dropped out of a mentoring program. "[The mentor] tried to be like my father or something," Braheem mentioned. Braheem only attended 4 out of the 5 sessions, stating that the music listening sessions he was involved in with me was one of the only reasons he was still coming to the after-school program.* It appeared that Braheem was involved in the process of self-orphaning.

Supernatural Aid

The song "Feel It in the Air" by rapper Beanie Sigel became the chosen piece in which Braheem explored his lived experiences in relation to the metaphors in the song. "Intuition" emerged as a core metaphor for him during our

---

* Other Orphan characteristics for Braheem were the abandonment by his father, and later a stepfather, that he faced as a child, as well as his consistent moving from neighborhood to neighborhood. Therefore, it appears that he had been metaphorically banished from the unification of his parents, as well as the safety of having a consistent community.

music listening experiences. Intuition is internal awareness of something about to happen without being able to perceive it. Braheem discussed developing a sense of intuition as an important part of surviving in his neighborhood. This aid was passed down from the chosen sages in his life, primarily his older brothers, and reinforced within his favorite musical artists.

Intuition could be used as a positive force within Braheem's life, keeping him safe and helping him make good choices in his life. Yet, it became apparent that Braheem did not own his internal intuition. Braheem's intuition was described as an external force that had been controlling him. As a result he reported that he "feels stuck." He likened his situation to the character portrayed in the video for "Feel It in the Air." In the video, the protagonist is teetering between two worlds, being a responsible man who wants to have a normal family life, while having to also sell drugs to deal with the external pressures of his environment. The protagonist makes one last deal to make enough money to escape his environmental pressures and be able to quit the life of a drug dealer. Instead, he sells drugs to an undercover policeman who then catches and arrests the main character.

In the song and the video the protagonist is speaking from the exact moment of realizing that he did not use his intuition in his time of need. Archetypes battle within the narrator. The dreams and aspirations of the Orphan, depicted in terms of being like a shining light and while not in charge, being part of a community, are in competition with the Warrior within, depicted in terms of sitting in his room, ready for battle, decked out in bulletproof vests with guns and ammunition on hand. The song voices the regret of not trusting his intuition when making the deal and the challenges of being caught in a world of opposites, his internal intuition and external forces acting upon him.

Like the narrator of the song, Braheem appeared to be caught in the battle of the opposites. He seemed to both want to do well and make positive choices in his life, yet felt that outside forces and environmental pressures were making choices for him. It appeared to me that the song was a warning that Braheem may be at risk of being manipulated by other people to be involved in dangerous or destructive behaviors.

One of the tasks of the Orphan is to begin developing trust and accepting the need for help. A catchphrase for Braheem was "real recognize real," with the song "Feel It in the Air" being an example of this phenomenon for him. In the song, Sigel describes being hyper-vigilant, sensing that something bad was about to happen. Developing the intuitive sense of who to trust appears to have been an important part of learning how to survive as an Orphan for Braheem. Braheem reached out to me, offering me opportunities to understand his cultural connections to Hip-Hop, such as teaching me about the art and social networking system of the underground Hip-Hop collective in West and North Philadelphia. By understanding Braheem's cultural connection to Hip-Hop, our work in music therapy could provide Braheem the opportunity to face the trials and tasks he is encountering living out an active Orphan archetype—helping him own and internalize his internal gift of intuition.

The Bull and the Snake

Braheem described two types of people that had to be avoided on the streets, the "bulls" and the "snakes." He described a bull as a person who uses physical force as a way of getting what he wants, whereas a snake seems more sneaky, underhanded, and deceiving. He noted that there are bulls and snakes on every corner in his neighborhood and he had to learn where to go and where not to go. "You can't be on a corner Chinese store and just be like I'm going to be alright. You can think it and you can hope it but some stuff just bad."

In many myths, the bull is a symbol of virility, while the snake is seen as representing "the power of life engaged in the field of time, and of death, yet eternally alive. The world is but its shadow—the fallen skin" (Campbell, 1988, p. 53). The snake is also seen as the bearer of knowledge, the guide into awakening in one's own consciousness, moving from innocence (the Garden of Eden) into the world of opposites and the understanding of one's self. These two mythological creatures can be seen as the ultimate battle for Braheem's adolescent development. If he falls prey to the bull or the Orphan's shadow, the dangers are "cynicism, callousness, masochism or sadism; using the victim role to manipulate the environment" (Pearson, 1991, p. 90). On the other hand, the life-affirming qualities of the snake and the vitality of the bull, which appeared to be seen by Braheem as deceiving and dangerous, could hold boons that would help Braheem not to fall prey to powerlessness, not to lose faith in people, institutions, and authority, or not to be a victim; in essence, accepting the snake and bull shadows within himself could be seen as taking control of his life and accepting his intuition as his own.

In our discussion, Braheem brought up the fact that his birth sign was that of a Taurus. "Maybe [bull] means you are strong or something but a lot of Taurus I know, they are not confident. 'Cause when I was younger I used to have low self-esteem. Like I used to look on the ground, when I would walk and stuff. I used to feel down all the time for some reason." Braheem hypothesized the reason why. "I think it came from my weight. That is what I really think it was. Like that is what I was thinking it as at the beginning. I just started eating a lot. And then like the self-esteem went lower."

Figure 4.1 The snake and the bull (Catherine Viega, 2008).

It is interesting that the shadow aspects of the Orphan, low self-esteem and confidence, appeared to reshape his concept of what a bull is meant to be, from something strong and powerful, to an animal that is injured and not confident.*

As part of my data analysis of my 2008 qualitative study, I used images that would emerge while analyzing the music and the participants' narratives. These images allowed me to better conceptualize the connections between the participants' preferred music and lived experience. In the image in Figure 4.1, stemming from imagery in the video "Feel It in the Air" by Beanie Sigel, one can see the battle raging inside Braheem. I am only an observer of this battle, thus the image of me watching this with the barrier of the television.

In describing the self-orphan, Pearson (1991) notes that "it is a self-protectiveness to avoid hurt that leads the Orphan in us to develop a false persona and to betray our deepest natures" (p. 87). She continues, "Ironically, the more we live false, inauthentic lives in order to be safe from hurt, the more Orphaned, hurt, and disillusioned we become. At this point, we have essentially turned against ourselves" (pp. 87–88). It is common that adolescents use their preferred music to try on different personas in

---

* It should be noted that this does not mean that Braheem has to become the literal version of a snake or a bull as depicted in the rap as one who is deceptive and one who is aggressive. Instead, I am using the symbol of the snake and bull that is common in many cultural mythologies as described above.

their adolescent development (Rudd, 1998; Saarikallio, 2004). It could be that Braheem's active Orphan archetype may begin to relate and look for belongingness within the shadow aspects of his preferred music—turning toward the shadow bull or snake, developing an overinflated Outlaw, perhaps leading to the tyrannical Ruler in later adolescence. Therefore, music therapy could offer Braheem a new way to understand his preferred music, allowing new archetypes to feel safe enough to develop, increasing his self-esteem, and helping to guide him safely through the cycle of the Hero's Journey to adulthood.

Braheem appears to be beginning his journey into adulthood relating to and resonating with the Orphan archetype while struggling with developmental tasks of searching for identity and developing healthy interpersonal relationships. Music therapy could have provided Braheem the opportunity to explore conflicting emotions and cultural messages to aid his journey into adulthood, thus providing him with new opportunities to develop the intuition within him, as well as integrating life-affirming qualities of the snake and the vitality of the bull. Unfortunately, with Braheem's sudden departure from the after-school program that we were running and thus losing contact with us and his peers there, we may never know the outcome of his journey.

Conclusion

How much does the development of music within a culture mirror the individual myths of the people who live in that society? Is our preferred music intertwined within a larger human story or does our favorite music simply reflect the times and places in which we have lived? I believe that the mythic journey that unfolds in musical development is interconnected with the individual and collective myths of peoples' lives. Music is the sounding of that myth into the here and now, and whether the music is captured on manuscript or by a recording, people are able to experience that music as if the music is a storyteller telling the tales of the trials and tribulations of the great heroes of our past.

In his detailed account of the rise of the Hip-Hop generation, Chang (2005) states that the story he tells is "a nonfiction history of a fiction—a history, some mystery and certainly no prophecy. It's but one version, this dub history—a gift from those who have illuminated and inspired, all defects of which are my own" (p. 3). The author is telling the reader that by delving into the culture and history of the music, he is sharing his Hero's Journey as well. One of the gifts of rap music is that all stories and myths can be shared using the power of the voice and by doing so one can connect to a deeper oral tradition that is rooted in the most primordial stories of our ancestors. The Hip-Hop generation appears to be using that power to spread the message and to build a positive community, making a global connection in the age of the digital media and the Internet.

Music therapy provides a space where one can sound his or her myth and within the here and now feel a connection back to something greater than oneself. It is a space where our clients' myths come alive, providing music therapists with insight and direction into their therapeutic processes. As music therapists, we need to understand a client's cultural background, as well as the cultural history of his or her preferred music, to gain further access into our clients' myths and the archetypes that may be active for them in their therapeutic journey. Because of Hip-Hop's rootedness within its cultural history, the music becomes a place where people are able to relate the popular culture images, lyrics, and music back into their lived experience. Therefore, it is important for music therapists to develop a Hip-Hop cultural perspective to understand how music is seen and experienced in this culture, especially when working with populations where Hip-Hop is a lifestyle and way of being and not just mere entertainment. Since adolescents use music in such a way to aid in their development into adulthood, and since Hip-Hop is one of the most popular forms of musical expression for young people, it appears natural that the music may be providing music therapists a great deal of information into their adolescent clients' developmental needs along their journey from childhood to adulthood. I have attempted to make this connection by sharing the story of Braheem and his relationship with Hip-Hop. However, reiterating Chang's (2005) request in the prelude of his book, "There are many more versions to be heard. May they all be" (p. 3).

References

Aigen, K. (1998). *Paths of development in Nordoff-Robbins Music Therapy.* Gilsum, NH: Barcelona.
Aigen, K. (2005). *Music-centered music therapy.* Gilsum, NH: Barcelona.
Beer, L. E. (1990). Music therapy: Sounding your myth. *Music Therapy, 9*(1), 35–43.
Bruscia, K., Abbott, E., Cadesky, N., Condron, D., McGraw-Hunt, A., Miller, D., & Thomae, L. (2005). A collaborative heuristic analysis of Imagery-M: A classical music program used in the Bonny Method of Guided Imagery and Music (BMGIM). In A. Meadows (Ed.), *Qualitative inquiries in music therapy: A monograph series* (Vol. 2, pp. 1–35). Gilsum, NH: Barcelona.
Campbell, J., & Moyers, B. (1988). *The power of myth.* New York: Anchor.
Campbell, J. (1948/2008). *The hero with a thousand faces.* Novato, CA: New World Library.

Chang J. (2005). *Can't stop won't stop: A history of the Hip-Hop generation.* New York: St. Martin's Press.

Chase, J., Chase, C., Fletcher, J., Glover, M., Grandmaster Melle Mel, & Robinson, S. (1982). The message. On *Grandmaster Flash & the Furious Five: The Message* [LP]. Italy: Earmark Records.

Clark. M. F. (1995). The hero's myth in GIM therapy. *Journal of the Association for Music and Imagery, 4*, 49–67.

Faber, M. A., & Mayer, J. D. (2009). Resonance to archetypes in media: There's some accounting for taste. *Journal of Research in Personality, 43*, 307–322.

Frisch, A. (1990). Symbol and structure: Music therapy for the adolescent psychiatric inpatient. *Music Therapy, 9*(1), 16–34.

Goldbeck, L., Schmitz, T. G., Besier, T., Herschbach, P., & Henrich, G. (2007). Life satisfaction decrease during adolescence. *Quality of Life Research, 16*, 969–979.

Grant, D. B., Lewis, R. D., & Meyers, D. (2005). Feel it in the air. On *The B. Coming* [CD]. New York: Roc-A-Fella Records.

Jung, C. (1964). Approaching the unconscious. In C. Jung (Ed.), *Man and his symbols* (pp. 1–94). New York: Dell.

Kenny, C. (1982). *The mythic artery: The magic of music therapy.* Atascadero, CA: Ridgeview.

Kenny, C. (2006). *Music & life in the field of play.* Gilsum, NH: Barcelona.

Laiho, S. (2004). The psychological functions of music in adolescence. *Nordic Journal of Music Therapy, 13*(1), 49–65.

McKinney, C., & Clark, M. F. (2009). *Level III training manual for the Bonny Method of Guided Imagery and Music: Myth, archetype, and transpersonal.* June 6–12, 2009, Boone, NC: Appalachian State University.

Murdock, M. (1990). *The heroine's journey.* Boston: Shambhala.

Pearson, C. S. (1991). *Awakening the heroes within: Twelve archetypes to help us find ourselves and transform our world.* New York: HarperCollins.

Pizarro, T., Sample, J., & Shakur, T. (1995). Dear mama. On *Me Against the World* [CD]. Los Angeles: Interscope Records.

Ruud, E. (1998). *Music therapy: Improvisation, communication, and culture.* Gilsum, NH: Barcelona.

Saarikallio, S. (2007). *Music as mood regulation in adolescence.* Unpublished doctoral dissertation, University of Jyväskylä, Finland.

Shaffer, T. G. (2004). *The shady side of Hip-Hop: A Jungian and Eriksonian interpretation of Eminem's "Explicit Content."* Unpublished doctoral dissertation, Pacific Graduate School of Psychology, Palo Alto, CA.

Sylvan, R. (2002). *Traces of the spirit: The religious dimensions of popular music.* New York: New York University Press.

Tervo, J. (2005). Music therapy with adolescents. *Voices: A world forum for music therapy.* Retrieved October 25, 2009, from http://www.voices.no/mainissues/mi40005000169.html

Tyson, E. H. (2002). Hip-Hop therapy: An exploratory study of a rap music intervention with at-risk and delinquent youth. *Journal of Poetry Therapy, 15*(3), 131–144.

Viega, M. (2008). *Conceptualizing the lived experience of three adolescents through the interpretation of the core metaphors in their preferred music.* Final Project Music Therapy, Temple University, Philadelphia, PA.

Winnicott, D. W. (1971/1999). *Playing and reality.* New York: Routledge.

Chapter 5

It's Bigger Than Hip-Hop

A Hip-Hop Feminist Approach to Music Therapy with Adolescent Females

Vanessa J. Veltre and Susan Hadley

In this chapter we explore the benefits and limitations of Hip-Hop in therapy with adolescent females. While a feminist approach is equally valid to use with adolescent males, in this chapter we are focusing on its potential for use in therapy with adolescent females, particularly adolescent females of color. We will specifically focus on the use of Hip-Hop to address four main goals: to promote collaboration and the importance of building a strong female community; to explore identity formation and gender-role socialization; to increase self-esteem of young women through empowering them to develop and honor their voices as females; and to promote social transformation.

Hip-Hop has evolved in many ways over the last 30 years. It grew out of a context in which people were dissatisfied with economic, social, and political conditions that they were being forced to accept, and yet had little to no power to change (Houston, 1994). Over time, Hip-Hop has shifted in style and focus, mostly due to the pressures of the rap music industry and popular culture. In the early days of Hip-Hop, the style was very upbeat and the lyrical content often focused on issues that were current and important to the artist. As Hip-Hop has developed, the style has shifted and branched off in many different directions and has become regionally unique. Today, Hip-Hop has a significant presence throughout the world, specifically with youth and young adult cultures. One thing that has not changed about Hip-Hop is that it remains a representation of the "voices and visions of the culturally, politically, and economically marginal and disenfranchised" (Phillips, Reddick-Morgan, & Stephens, 2005, p. 254).

From the beginnings of Hip-Hop, women have been involved as B-girls, breakers, graffiti artists, deejays, and emcees (Pough, 2007, p. v). In fact, "Grandmaster Flash recalls that, 'back in the day,' there were more female crews than male, though far fewer of them were able to break into the recording side" (Potter, 1995, p. 92). Women in Hip-Hop have worked as writers, producers, and industry executives. In many ways, women have contributed to setting the aesthetic standard for much of what consumers of Hip-Hop value. Although women have played an important role in the evolution of Hip-Hop, their contributions are often not recognized. Despite the integral role that women have played (and continue to play) in Hip-Hop, it is important to consider that women are outnumbered by men in both the artistic and corporate arenas of Hip-Hop; that men are more visible in Hip-Hop, perhaps partly due to sexist practices; and that both men and women alike have participated in Hip-Hop culture in ways that could be viewed as oppressive and liberating (Phillips, Reddick-Morgan, & Stephens, 2005, p. 254).

In addition to the various ways in which women have been involved in the cultural production of Hip-Hop, women have been reflecting critically on Hip-Hop culture. These women are known as Hip-Hop feminists. Hip-Hop feminists aim to "give women in Hip-Hop some recognition, [and] also to provide a critique of Hip-Hop culture that pays attention to issues of race, class, gender and sexuality" (Pough, 2007, p. v).

Gwendolyn Pough (2007) describes Hip-Hop as "a worldview, as an epistemology grounded in the experiences of communities of color under advanced capitalism, as a cultural site for rearticulating identity and sexual politics" (p. vii). She describes the culture of Hip-Hop as being made up of its own types of music, dance, art, dress, film, language, literature, autobiographies, journalism, activism, and knowledge, including its own brand of feminism (p. vi). Hip-Hop, as a worldview, assesses power structures throughout the culture that impact the economy, unemployment rates, the prison system, drug use, social hierarchies, gender relations, and so on (Durham, 2007, p. 306). Through this worldview, artists can understand and critique the existing power structures.

Brief Overview of Feminisms

Joan Morgan (1999), the woman who coined the term *Hip-Hop feminist*, describes her path to embracing feminism. She discovered feminism in college, but she characterizes this feminism as coming in "two flavas—both variations of vanilla" (p. 35). One "flava" she characterizes as those who revile all things male (except their clothing and mannerisms) and who sleep with each other. The other "flava" she characterizes as those who were all in favor of "the liberation of women as long as it did not infringe on their sense of entitlement. They felt their men should *share* the power to oppress" (p. 35).

The early waves of feminism really addressed the concerns of White middle-class women. The first wave of feminism has primarily been associated with access and equal opportunities for women, specifically the drive for women's suffrage. The second-wave of modern feminism in the United States grew out of related emancipation movements in postwar Western societies, including the U.S. civil rights movement, the Black Power movement, student protests, anti–Vietnam War movements, lesbian and gay movements, and the Miss America Pageant protests. White women of the second wave of feminism revived women's political struggles for civil rights. They found that there was still a large gap between what they were told women had achieved and their experiences of their own situations.

Many of the second-wave feminists, however, overlooked the significance of race, class, age, sexual orientation, and ability, in contributing to the intersecting dimensions of oppression, and, thereby, universalized the experiences of oppression had by middle-class White women. Moreover, given the lack of critical attention to the differential ways in which male oppression operates along lines of race, differential class positions, and such considerations, these middle-class White feminists privileged the types of oppression enacted by men who were well educated, White, and occupied a middle-class position.

Although Morgan (1999) was adamantly pro-choice, was against rape and domestic violence, and actively rallied for equal pay for equal work, protecting planned parenthood, legalizing abortion, and quality child care, she states that the feminism that she learned about in college "definitely felt like white women's shit" (p. 36).

Morgan also learned about Black American feminism and womanism while in college. During the second wave of feminism, many feminist groups acknowledged that patriarchal oppression is not experienced in a homogeneous fashion. Various strands of "identity" feminisms began to emerge, including Black American feminism/womanism. The Black feminist agenda didn't always fit the feminist agenda that White women were forming that was meant to encompass "all women." For example, women of color and poor White women were not fighting to work outside the home; many of them had already been doing this by necessity. Audre Lorde (1984) points out that acting as though the White middle-class feminist agenda was the agenda of all women created a space where "only the most narrow perimeters of change [were] possible and allowable" (p. 447).

Black American feminists of the 1960s did not feel well represented by the feminist movement or the civil rights movement. Many Black feminists saw that *Black* was equated with Black men and *woman* was equated with White women. Therefore Black women were an invisible group.

The early Black American feminist movement was

> a socio-cultural, intellectual and political movement grounded in the situated knowledge of women of color from the post-Civil Rights generation who recognize culture as a pivotal site for political intervention to challenge, resist and mobilize collectives to dismantle systems of exploitation. (Durham, 2007, p. 306)

Another term used to describe some African American feminists is *womanist*. *Womanism* is a term coined by Alice Walker. The term *womanist* came from the term *womanish*, a term African American adults used to refer to female children who were being the opposite of *girlish* (frivolous, irresponsible, not serious). *Womanish*, however, referred to someone who was being "outrageous, audacious, courageous or 'willful' .... Acting grown up ... [As in] 'You trying to be grown.' Responsible. In charge. 'Serious'" (Walker, 1967/1983, p. xi).

Many early Black American feminists were aligned with the Black Arts Movement of the 1960s and 1970s with writers such as Sonia Sanchez, Gwendolyn Brooks, and Nikki Giovanni. Some other notable Black American feminists include bell hooks, Toni Morrison, Angela Davis, and Renne Ferguson. Another influential group of Black American feminists is the Combahee River Collective. They produced a comprehensive statement of the issues for Black American feminists in the mid-1970s which acknowledged interlocking oppressions, brought attention to the racism in White feminism, and outlined the importance of Black women's liberation and Black feminism. They described the Black American feminist movement as one that is fighting to reduce racism, sexism, homophobia, and class division.

Morgan (1999) holds great respect for and pays tribute to the Black feminists and womanists who delineated the struggles of and fought for the rights of Black women. Morgan acknowledges:

> We are the daughters of feminist privilege. The gains of the Feminist Movement (the efforts of black, white, Latin, Asian, and Native American women) had a tremendous impact on our lives—so much we often take it for granted. We walk through the world with a sense of entitlement that women of our mother's generation could not begin to fathom. (p. 59)

But as with White women feminists, she felt that many of these women had little to do with her everyday life. She thought of them as intellectuals, academics, historians, and authors. But they were not her contemporaries, "they were not crew" (p. 38).

To explain the ambivalence that many Black women have toward feminism, Morgan points to the historical tendency of Black women to "defend any black man who seems to be under attack from white folks" (p. 58). She states, "Racism and the will to survive it creates a sense of loyalty that makes it impossible for black women to turn our backs on black men—even in their ugliest and most sexist of moments" (p. 36).

In developing a feminism that she could relate to, Morgan felt that it was important to relinquish the illusion that Black women and men were a united front. She also felt that it was important "to explore who we are as women—not victims" (p. 56). She goes on to say that "defining ourselves solely by our oppression denies us the very magic of who we are. My feminism simply refuses to give sexism or racism that much power" (p. 60). What she was searching for was

> a feminism committed to "keeping it real." We need a voice like our music—one that samples and layers many voices, injects its sensibilities into the old and flips it into something new, provocative, and powerful. And one whose occasional hypocrisy, contradictions, and trifeness [*sic*] guarantee us at least a few trips to the terror-dome, forcing us to finally confront what we'd all rather hide from. (Morgan, 1999, p. 62)

Hip-Hop Feminism

Hip-Hop feminism is viewed as an extension of the Black American feminist movement. The following are some of the aims of Hip-Hop feminism:

1. Examine "the ways in which women Hip-Hop artists have made spaces for themselves within the culture" (Pough, 2007, p. viii). Of course, many female Hip-Hop artists are not feminists, but there is certainly a lot that can be gained from an exploration of their work.
2. Examine "the ways in which women have been represented in the culture via the music and the videos" (Pough, 2007, p. ix). Rather than just looking at this in terms of gender, Hip-Hop feminists bring a complexity to the issues by examining the ways in which race, class, gender, and sexuality intersect.
3. To provide a space where women can "talk back" or critique the culture when they see things that are detrimental to women (Pough, 2007, p. ix). An early example is Sistah Souljah, who has been

referred to as "an eloquent feminist critical theorist" (Lightstone, 2004, p. 90).

When early Black feminists explored Hip-Hop, a major focus was on criticizing the misogyny of rap lyrics and videos that didn't allow for exploring other aspects of Hip-Hop culture. Pough (2002) argues that looking at Hip-Hop from a different perspective could actually help create the opportunity for dialogue across the sexes in rap music and Hip-Hop. Pough states, "It is not just about counting the bitches and hoes in each rap song. It is about exploring the nature of Black male and female relationships" (p. 94).

Some scholars believe that the role of the Black woman in Hip-Hop culture got its roots in the time of slavery. Elaine Richardson (2007) links the image of the "video vixen" to the racist characterization of the Black woman as a "wench" or a "jezebel" (p. 790). Richardson (2007) defines a *wench* as a woman who "use[d] her body to produce wealth, labor, and slaves," and a *Jezebel* as "manipulative, using her sexual alluring nature to exploit men" (p. 790). She goes on to compare the stereotypical urban gangsta to the image of the enslaved male as a hypersexual brute who was used to impregnate the "wenches" to create more "slaves." Patricia Hill Collins (2004) describes this early relationship dynamic as very important in truly understanding the systems of social inequality—racism, sexism, classism, and capitalism (p. 10). Whitney Peoples (2008) states that "the images of black male violence and aggression that dominate mainstream rap music are highly marketable in America because of already existing ideologies of racism" (p. 24). And this statement holds true for women as well and the images of sexuality.

Much of the attention that women have gained in Hip-Hop has been around the skimpily dressed women who appear in music videos. These women are commonly referred to as "video vixens" or "video hos." Such representations of women appear to belie the earlier emphasis that Hip-Hop artists placed on the music and message. It is a popular belief that the women in the videos are purely meeting the demands of corporate record companies vying to sell records. Aisha Durham refers to this as the "sexploitation of black women to advance capitalism" (2007, p. 305). There is much controversy surrounding the video vixen. She is often stereotyped and blamed for much of the misogyny in Hip-Hop. In fact, she is blamed just as much as the rappers or writers who wrote the lyrics. Critics make statements such as "she showed up for the video shoot" and accuse her of going too far to get her "big break" or to make money. Providing an alternative perspective, Neal (2007) suggests that perhaps the video vixen is using Hip-Hop as a way to express her sexuality (p. iii).

Feminist Therapy

Feminist therapy, as delineated by Judith Worell and Pamela Remer (2003), advocates for equality in terms of gender, race, ethnicity, culture and nationality, sexuality, socioeconomic status, age, and physical characteristics. Feminist therapists value and advocate gaining greater understanding about the diversity of women's experiences and acknowledge the importance of considering social, political, and economic contexts when working with women. Decision-making processes in feminist therapy should be consensual and must honor all voices, consistent with the feminist principle of mutual respect. Feminist therapists are committed to working for equal justice for all people.

Some of the characteristics of a feminist approach to therapy are to work collaboratively, to foster community, to develop one's identity, to engage in gender-role socialization analyses, to promote equality and empower women, and to work toward social transformation.

The cultural, societal, and health factors affecting the lives of Black women today are countless. Incarceration rates have increased among Black women, as have the number of HIV/AIDS cases. We believe that a very effective way to address these goals is to explore themes that are found in music that adolescent females relate to. For some, this will be rap music. Therapeutically, Hip-Hop is a vehicle for expressing anger, grief, acceptance, coping, and perseverance, and allows its listeners to feel understood and validated.

Hip-Hop in Music Therapy

It is imperative for therapists to use culturally sensitive and culturally appropriate approaches in their work. Lightstone (2004) states that "Rap music is rooted in Hip Hop . . . values [that] reflect a musical world view that sees rap music as a vital, alive, life-affirming sound that is capable of pushing forward personal development and social transformation" (p. 122). He continues, "The deep bass, street sounds, record noise, layers of samples, groove, and aggressive beats that are all part of the Hip Hop aesthetic reflect the world in which [these] clients ... live. This allows those sounds to penetrate and affect them in ways that other sounds and musical aesthetics may not. I believe that this, in and of itself, is a strong justification for the use of rap music as a clinical resource" (p. 126). Thus, for therapists working with adolescents who are part of the Hip-Hop culture, it is essential to incorporate aspects of Hip-Hop. In our opinion, the therapeutic uses of rap music and Hip-Hop may to date have been underrealized. We believe that therapists who refuse to use Hip-Hop when working with youth and young adults who live the culture may render therapy less effective.

Over the last several decades, corporations have used Hip-Hop as a marketing tool to target youth. Hip-Hop's fashion, dance, and music have been incorporated into commercials and print advertisements. The corporate world has taken over this culture for its own gains. Norman Kelley (2002, p. 13) describes the political economy of Black American music as "a structure of stealing" that dates back to American slavery. Now, young White suburban youth represent the largest group of Hip-Hop consumers (Kitwana, 2005). Today, Hip-Hop is America's dominant youth culture and is embraced by youth globally. As such, it is the voice for many youth.

Historically, Hip-Hop has provided a space for disenfranchised youth, including young women, to resist oppression (Rose, 1994). Smitherman (as cited in Oesterreich, 1997, p. 17) argues that Hip-Hop as an art has a job to do—to disturb the peace and break the chains that have bound Blacks in the United States. Although many parents, educators, and much of the general public do not approve of youth listening to rap, it is important to consider the value that it holds in working with youth. When working with young females, in particular, the elements of rap that are controversial are where the opportunities lie, that is, in developing the skills to analyze and think critically about the messages that they are hearing and seeing.

When introducing Hip-Hop into a music therapy session, it is recommended that each music therapist use his or her own judgment when considering the lyrical content. This can be a delicate decision and should take into account the maturity of the client or clients, the setting of therapy (including any agency-wide rules about language use, sexual themes, etc.), and the goals of the therapy. Some people find the use of rap and Hip-Hop in therapy controversial because the content of some rap music is considered to be vulgar, hypersexual, suggestive, disrespectful, and degrading. In fact, the scenes portrayed in some rap music videos would be R-rated in film form, yet are marketed toward youth and popularized by MTV. Much of the media attention regarding Hip-Hop has been around violence, misogyny, drugs, and sex. It is important to note, however, that there is also rap that specifically addresses these issues in a critical fashion. For example, Potter (1995) notes that misogynistic raps were under attack from the outset and often spawned "response raps" from female rappers (p. 91).

There is widespread concern about the potential influence of derogatory sexual themes in Hip-Hop and the impact that these may have on the sexual and psychological development of African American adolescent females (Stokes & Gant, 2002; Cole & Guy-Sheftall, 2003; Wingood et al., 2003; Pough, 2004; Weekes, 2004; Stephens & Phillips, 2005). Rap has introduced a new lexicon of slang for women that has become so commonplace that many young women use it in their everyday conversations, describing another, or even themselves. George (1998) states, "It is one thing to be sexually assertive; it is another to buy into men's negative language about yourself" (p. 186). Jennifer Baumgardner and Amy Richards (2000), however, have criticized sexist language while at the same time discussed the value of the use of mimicry and subversion in terms of exaggerating stereotypes that traditionally have been used against women and the appropriation and resignifying of the meanings of "derogatory" terms for women (such as *girl*, *slut*, *bitch*, and *ho*). This demonstrates the complexity of Hip-Hop in terms of the differential ways in which women and men are positioned within it, at times as empowered and at other times as limited to stereotypical representations.

The beauty is that rap music contains many varied themes, which can address myriad issues for young women. Hip-Hop can adapt to reach an extremely wide variety of therapy goals, from writing a rap about a therapeutic issue to critically analyzing lyrical content. In his groundbreaking research on creating original rap in music therapy, Lightstone (2004) found nine significant themes in the rap of adolescents: authenticity and emotional expression; the rapper as critical theorist; boasting; rap battles/insults; drugs; evidence of group process; spirituality; violence; and musical wordplay. These themes can be found in the larger culture and worldview of Hip-Hop. Of particular importance in this chapter are the themes of authenticity and emotional expression, the rapper as critical theorist, and evidence of group process.

Given the themes in Hip-Hop feminism, coupled with the issues addressed in feminist therapy, as mentioned at the start of this chapter, we will now explore the benefits and limitations of Hip-Hop in therapy with adolescent females. We are focusing on the use of Hip-Hop to address four main goals: to promote collaboration and the importance of building a strong female community; to explore identity formation and gender-role socialization; to increase self-esteem of young women through empowering them to develop and honor their voices as females; and to promote social transformation. In the following section, several rap selections will be referenced.* Because it is difficult to detach lyrical content from the music, readers are urged, when possible, to listen to the selections being discussed.

Hip-Hop Is Collaboration/Community

Hip-Hop is collaborative by nature, as can be seen on multiple levels. One of the most obvious is the collaboration between the DJ and MC, the former

---

* Thanks to Andrea Follmar, Michelle Bonaventura, Nicole Steele, and Adrian Yancy for their suggestions.

Table 5.1 Themes of Collaboration/Community

Artist/s	Song	Themes Addressed in Lyrics
Queen Latifah and Monie Love	Ladies First	Pride in being a woman—emphasizes women's strength in terms of giving birth and raising future leaders. Sense of community and connection—by delineating how we are related to each other.
Salt-n-Pepa	Ain't Nuthin' But a She Thing	Building a strong female community—delineate strengths of women and appeal to listeners to voice their agreement with the sentiments expressed.
Fresh Prince	My Buddy	Honoring collaboration—describes the importance of collaboration between the MC and DJ and that no one could beat this pair.
Sistah Souljah	Umbilical Cord to the Future	The importance of both individuals and the community to raise children responsibly. It also talks about the utter importance of parenting and teaching children or they won't learn what they need to know.

providing the beats and the latter rapping the lyrics. This collaboration is a very close one. An example of its importance is seen in the lyrics of "My Buddy" (see Table 5.1). Another example of collaboration is when one MC joins another and rap together. There are countless instances of this in Hip-Hop with both male and female rappers. One example is "Ladies First" with Queen Latifah and Monie Love, which can be found in Table 5.1. In addition to the above, a singer will often collaborate with a DJ and an MC, singing the vocals that provide the rap's refrain. And sometimes, instead of one MC, there is a crew of individuals who take the mic in a back-and-forth style. The Mercedes Ladies, established in the mid-1970s, is credited as being the first all-female crew. They never had their own record deal and are little remembered, but they paved the way for other female rappers such as Salt-n-Pepa, who hit the rap scene in 1986 and gained huge popularity because of their infectious beats, confrontational lyrics, and fresh Hip-Hop style. Their record, *A Salt With a Deadly Pepa* (1988), sold half a million copies and was the first gold record by a female Hip-Hop group (Phillips, Reddick-Morgan, & Stephens, 2005).

There is a strong sense of community in Hip-Hop. This is seen in terms of fashion, language use, art, and dance. Community is also built through shared lived experiences and shared discontent with social inequality and poor living conditions. Another way in which rap artists build a sense of community is by bridging generations as a result of giving props to those who have gone before. This is most evident in the practice of sampling of songs from the past. This not only honors those who have gone before, but provides a bridge for an older generation to connect with the contemporary music scene and for people of both generations to feel connected through their shared familiarity with these songs.

In a Hip-Hop feminist approach to music therapy, music therapists can use these elements of collaboration and community building therapeutically. Music therapists can bring in raps that specifically deal with issues of collaboration or that build a sense of community among the group members by highlighting their shared experiences and helping to move them from their sense of alienation. Given the precedent of Hip-Hop to give props to those who have gone before, music therapists do not have to feel confined to using contemporary rap, but can also use older rap. By drawing the analogy with sampling, music therapists can help the group members to listen to the messages in these old-school raps and to feel the generational and community connections.

One of the most significant ways of addressing collaboration and community building in a Hip-Hop feminist therapy approach would be to have the young women write their own original raps.

With adolescent female groups, it is important to stress the significance of building a strong female community of like-minded peers. This creates a safe space for exploring creativity through analyzing and writing rap, sharing ideas, giving and receiving encouragement, and learning to honor the female voice. Within a strong and supportive female community, young females can be empowered to achieve, to grow, and to be strong.

Table 5.1 contains a few examples of songs that honor collaboration and/or build strong female communities.

Hip-Hop Is Identity Formation/Gender-Role Socialization

Adolescence is a time of immense change and identity formation. Youth between the ages of 12 and 18 years face many challenges related to a variety of factors, among them further developing their sexuality and gender roles, struggling with issues of body image and peer acceptance, drug and alcohol use, youth violence, educational demands, and gaining employment. Sometimes these challenges lead to poor decision making, which can lead to teen pregnancy, dropping out of high school, gang affiliation, or lack of motivation and unemployment. Social, political, and institutional structures that have given rise to concentrated levels of poverty, institutional racism, and underfunded schools have contributed to young African Americans feeling that there is not much that they can do to be more successful in life (Lipman, 1998).

Many of these issues and challenges find expression in the mass cultural media. Thus, the images that adolescents are continually exposed to have a significant role in shaping their identities. Black women have been associated negatively with sexuality throughout history, with images on display in every aspect of American culture (Collins, 2000; hooks, 1981). African American adolescent females, who are exposed to these images every day, must learn to define themselves and interpret the messages within the framework of a society that repeatedly tells them, in many different forms, that they are no more than a sex object. Sexual scripting theory (Simon & Gagnon, 1986, as cited in Stokes, 2007) identifies three levels of sexual scripts, which provide a framework for understanding how sociocultural and individual factors shape African American females' sexual script development. These levels are cultural scenarios, interpersonal scripts, and intrapsychic scripts. Cultural scenarios are collective beliefs and behaviors of a socially defined group, which can include friends, family, teachers, or the media. Because sex and sexual identity have become such awkward topics of discussion for many families, it is common for adolescent females to turn to the media when developing their sexuality. Interpersonal scripts are developed in relation to the behaviors and beliefs of an in-group acknowledged by the adolescent female. When cultural scenarios are combined with a female's interpersonal scripts, they become intrapsychic scripts.

Developing an identity can be difficult for African American females, because there are many conflicting messages coming from the media, Hip-Hop, peers, and family (Stokes, 2004; Stephens & Phillips, 2005; Brown et al., 2006). In *Hip Hop America*, Nelson George describes a shift beginning in the late 1980s to a view that was "harsh, unsentimental, and anti-woman" (p. 185). He continues, "It was a time when calling a woman a bitch became weirdly respectable" (1998, pp. 185–186).

In music therapy, we can facilitate discussion about the conflicting messages that are presented in Hip-Hop music and videos to explore the healthy and unhealthy ways in which our clients' identities have been shaped. These discussions can lead to a greater awareness about how they, as adolescent females, have been socialized in terms of their gender roles. We can also utilize the same genre of rap to help them to re-narrate their identities in ways that are empowering and that allow their voices and concerns to be heard. For example, this can be in the form of lyric substitution of existing raps or the creation of original raps. (See Table 5.2.)

Table 5.2 Themes of Identity Formation/Gender Role Socialization

Artist	Song	Themes Addressed in Lyrics
Eve	Love Is Blind	Warns women about not being fooled by what they take to be love and to recognize abuse for what it is. Wants women to go beyond how they have come to expect to be treated.
Salt-n-Pepa	I Am the Body Beautiful	Talks about everybody being beautiful and that believing in yourself and carrying yourself with dignity is what matters. They stress that beauty comes from within.
Salt-n-Pepa	Expression	Stresses the importance of being true to yourself, expressing yourself, and not allowing others to determine what you can and can't do.
TLC	Unpretty	Critiques men and women who are so focused on outward appearances and image, and who do not take the time to find out who the person really is inside. Talks about the effect that has on self-esteem in terms of making someone feel unpretty.
Salt-n-Pepa	Independent	Women don't need men to be successful. Women can take care of themselves.
Shanté	The Year of the Independent Woman	Critiques the sexist double standards which allow men to remain uncommitted to the women in their lives.
Yo-Yo	Girl, Don't Be No Fool	Critiques both men and women for falling into sexist stereotypes in terms of what is acceptable regarding the ways men treat women as inferior.

Hip-Hop Is Empowerment/Equality

Many adolescent females, especially those living in low-income households, often feel disempowered due to all the "adult" concerns that they have to face early on. Some concerns that they may face include having little or no money for food or utilities, having inconsistent parental relationships or a lack of parental support, being expected to care for younger siblings, coping with a parent struggling with addiction or in prison, and so on. Often youth are forced into adulthood too quickly and without the coping skills necessary to succeed. All of these challenges that they face can lead to a sense of helplessness and hopelessness.

Hip-Hop was born out of challenges and overcoming obstacles. It provided people with a way to express their feelings and attitudes about the circumstances they were facing. Rap artists use strong driving beats and self-affirming lyrics that result in empowering the rapper, and often the person/people rapped to and sometimes the person/people who are rapped about (unless the rap is demeaning a particular group).

Music therapist Laurie Jones has delineated a number of themes that correspond with messages of empowerment that are essential when thinking about what songs one should use when working to empower women. These include themes of (1) problem solving; (2) self-knowledge/awareness/acceptance; (3) strength/innate power; (4) perseverance; (5) intolerance of "less than"; (6) courage/confidence; (7) growth/risk-taking; and (8) independence (Jones, 2006, pp. 339–340).

On *Hot, Cool, & Vicious*, an early release by Salt-n-Pepa, the group became one of the first in Hip-Hop to bring attention to the way African American women are treated by men, with the song "Tramp" (1986). "Tramp" is an early "dis" song against men. The song was released at a time when women's roles in Hip-Hop were changing and were yet largely undefined. In "Tramp," Salt-n-Pepa demand respect from the men who are chasing them. The themes found in "Tramp" can begin a conversation about appropriate ways that men should treat women.

Tupac Shakur's "Keep Ya Head Up" is a song about working to overcome some of the struggles that African American women may be facing. Many young women find the song very empowering, although some feminists have critiqued Tupac for writing lyrics that in many ways reinforce traditionally practiced gender roles and relationships. The song was released in 1993 on Shakur's *Strictly 4 My N.I.G.G.A.Z.* album. "Keep Ya Head Up" discusses the social institutions of race, class, and gender. Even today, this is a song that adolescents can relate to, whether in terms of a specific issue raised in the rap or just in terms of the feeling or sentiment of wanting to give up.

Queen Latifah's "U.N.I.T.Y." is perhaps the strongest testimony against the treatment of women that exists in Hip-Hop. Queen Latifah released her album *Black Reign* in 1993 and became a well-known female rapper who vocally spoke up against misogyny. "U.N.I.T.Y." is effective in communicating the message that the status quo of how women are treated, both verbally and physically, is unconditionally unacceptable. The last verse

Table 5.3 Themes of Empowerment/Equality

Artist	Song	Themes Addressed in Lyrics
Sistah Souljah	360 Degrees of Power	States that women, specifically Black women, are strong and should be proud of it. Goes on to affirm that it is possible to be feminine and to be strong.
Salt-n-Pepa	Tramp	Describes the way some men treat women as objects and as inferior. Warns women not to think less of themselves when men treat them that way and to know they deserve better. Also warns women not to be the way men see them.
Tupac	Keep Ya Head Up	States that though there are many difficult obstacles in life that you have to deal with and that can make you feel hopeless and helpless, you need to be strong. He assures the listeners that things are going to get easier, and that better times are ahead.
Queen Latifah	U.N.I.T.Y.	Queen Latifah warns young women not to try to act older than they are. She affirms that behaving like a respectable girl is something to be proud of. She encourages women to be proud of who they are.
Monie Love	It's a Shame	This song warns women not to accept being mistreated by any man, that it is unacceptable to put up with less than you deserve. It pays tribute to the importance of protecting one's feelings and sense of self.
Salt-n-Pepa	Ain't Nuthin' But a She Thing	This song stresses women's strength and intelligence. Calls for women to be proud of who they are.
Eve	Heaven Only Knows	Encourages listeners not to let the negative limit them and states that having a positive attitude can help you overcome hard times.
Nas	I Can	Warns girls not to try to look and act older than they are because men will mistreat them in ways that could have irreversible effects. He encourages them to be respectable, to be proud of who they are, to work hard, and make something of their life.

Continued

Table 5.3 (continued)   Themes of Empowerment/Equality

Artist	Song	Themes Addressed in Lyrics
Christina Aguilera feat. Lil' Kim	Can't Hold Us Down	This song encourages young women to be proud, strong, and empowered to be all that they can be. It also tells young women not to let men disrespect their worth.
Eve	As I Grow	Tells listeners that even when people try to bring you down, be strong and committed to doing the right thing.

of this song is targeted to the adolescent female and "calls them out" for taking on the personas that are found in the media, specifically rap videos. It gives a reality check to some who are more concerned with their image on the street than their image in school. This song can be extremely effective in music therapy and can lead to serious discussions about how women are treated by men, the reasons for it, and how we, as a female community, can stop it from continuing. Furthermore, other therapeutic themes may be addressed, like the allure of the "bad girl" image or street life, ways for women to alter the status quo, and how to use Hip-Hop to communicate a powerful and uplifting message. (See Table 5.3.)

Hip-Hop Is Social Transformation

Hip-Hop is a powerful tool when working toward social justice and social transformation. The lyrics of rappers such as Tupac Shakur, Public Enemy, Wu-Tang Clan, Arrested Development, and Eminem, to name a few, have definite subtexts of social transformation. Sistah Souljah, who was known as the "minister of education" for rap group Public Enemy, rapped with a feminist agenda for social transformation and social justice.

Sometimes women have come together as a group to fight against the way they are portrayed in rap and in society more generally. For example, in 2005, a group of Spelman College students and alumnae joined together to protest the "Tip Drill" video by rapper Nelly. According to a CNN News article, the group sought to urge people to think critically about how the images in the video might affect Black women today (2005). The "Tip Drill" video is one of the most controversial pieces of Hip-Hop media. The lyrics of the chorus go: "It must be ya ass, cause it ain't ya face, I need a tip drill." The definition of a "tip drill" varies from an unattractive girl who has sex for money to a stripper who can manipulate men into spending large amounts of money on them (Richardson, 2007). Whatever Nelly's intention, this rap and its accompanying video are not respectful toward women. The video depicts a scene with many women, mostly clothed in bikinis, flaunting their bodies while men throw money at them. In one notorious scene, Nelly himself is shown swiping a credit card between a woman's buttocks. Nelly claims that his video is an expression of art for entertainment. The Spelman College students shared the belief that the "Tip Drill" video was offensive and degrading toward women, so they collaborated and took a stand, not only against that particular video, but about the general portrayal of women in Hip-Hop and rap. This group of college women inspired the national "Take Back the Music" campaign.

In music therapy, Lightstone (2004) found that when youth in therapy created their own original raps, one of the main themes that emerged was that of the rapper as critical theorist (p. 40). He found that similar to their commercial counterparts, clients would engage in critiques of social institutions and structures. This kind of critique is an important first step in the process of social transformation. As in the examples in Lightstone's work, a significant way to work toward social transformation would be to engage clients in the process of creating their own original raps on social issues that are important in their lives.

Some preexisting raps that have a subtext for social transformation can be seen in Table 5.4.

It's Bigger Than Hip-Hop

Hip-Hop is a culture that encompasses so much of youth culture today. For many youth, male and female, Hip-Hop is bigger than the culture. It is a dream, a way out, an emotional outlet, a learning tool, a listening friend, a way of communicating, a political statement, a way to build relationships, and a consistent presence.

Hip-Hop is a powerful force for adolescent females. To really foster meaningful relationships with adolescent females, music therapists, educators, and parents need to acknowledge the role of Hip-Hop in the life of young females. Though females should not be reduced to passive consumers who absorb every media message that they are faced with, it would be beneficial for communities—through their schools, girl-serving organizations, churches, and centers—to work together to provide a safe space for adolescent African American females to come and think critically about the politics of gender and race, while working to develop their identities. This can lead to more secure identities, healthier relationships, and increased confidence.

Hip-Hop feminist Joan Morgan claims that the only way that African American females can really experience empowerment is to first understand

Table 5.4 Themes of Social Transformation

Artist	Song	Themes Addressed in Lyrics
Talib Kweli	Black Girl Pain	Themes of Black pride and female pride. Describes the transformation and growth that has taken place for peoples from Africa and for women. Has a sense that there is still more transformation that is needed.
Common	A Song for Assata	This song speaks to those who have been oppressed, especially those of African descent. It tells a story of power and pride. It shares a vision about what freedom will look like, and that is where oppressed people have the right to blossom/grow.
Talib Kweli	Get By	This rap tells a story of all the self-destructive things that people do just to get by. Then he talks about his own personal transformation and the need to engage in social transformation.
Arrested Development	Tennessee	Talks about appreciating one's history and learning from the lessons of those who came before.
Boogie Down Productions	Why Is That?	Importance of teaching and learning what it means to be Black. Importance of deconstructing stereotypes and reconstructing history in ways that honor Black people.
Queen Latifah	Evil That Men Do	Speaks to an array of social problems and ways in which nothing gets done about them and calls listeners to action for social transformation.

who they are and then to tell the truth about it. Hip-Hop can function as a culturally relevant vehicle to help adolescent females to gain greater understanding in terms of who they are in all of their complexity, to examine and evaluate various ways in which their identities have been formed, and various ways they have been socialized in terms of their gender, sexuality, and race. By doing this and empowering them to develop and honor their voices as females, we can help them gain in self-esteem and to work together collaboratively and build strong communities of young Black women. Thus, a Hip-Hop feminist approach to music therapy with adolescent females leads to social transformation at various levels, at the individual level, the group level, and the community level.

References

Arce, R. (2005, March 4). Hip Hop portrayal of women [protested]. CNN Entertainment. http://articles.cnn.com/2005-03-03/entertainment/hip.hop_1_Hip-Hop-black-women-spelman-college?_s=PM:SHOWBIZ (accessed October 1, 2010).

Baumgardner, J. & Richards, A. (2000). *Manifesta: Young women, feminism, and the future.* New York: Farrar, Straus, and Giroux.

Brown, J., Engle, K., Pardun, C., Guo, G., Kenneavy, K., & Jackson, C. (2006). Sexy media matter: Exposure to sexual content in music, movies, television, and magazines predicts Black and White adolescents' sexual behavior. *Pediatrics, 117.*

Cole, J., & Guy-Sheftall, B. (2003). *Gender talk: The struggle for women's equality in African American communities.* New York: Ballantine.

George, N. (1998). *Hip Hop America.* New York: Viking Penguin.

Hill Collins, P. (2004). *Black sexual politics: African Americans, gender, and the new racism.* New York: Routledge.

hooks, b. (1981). *Ain't I a woman: Black women and feminism.* Boston: South End Press.

Kelley, N. (Ed.). (2002). *Rhythm and business: The political economy of Black music.* New York: Akashic.

Kitwana, B. (2002). *The Hip-Hop generation: Young Blacks and the crisis in American culture.* New York: Basic Civitas.

Lightstone, A. (2004). Yo! Can ya flow?: A qualitative study of Hip Hop aesthetics and original rap lyrics created in group music therapy in an urban youth shelter. Unpublished masters' research. Available at http://www.wlu.ca/soundeffects/researchlibrary/Aaron.pdf

Lipman P. (*1998*). *Race, class, and power in school restructuring.* Albany, NY: State University of New York Press.

Lorde, A. (1984). *Sister outsider.* Freedom, CA: Crossing.

Morgan, J. (1999). *When chickenheads come home to roost: My life as a Hip-Hop feminist.* New York: Simon & Schuster.

Ms. Jade (2002). Why u tell me that? On *Girl Interrupted.*

Nelly. (2003). Tip drill. DaDerrty versions: The re-invention. Audio CD. Universal Records, a Division on UMG Recordings, Inc.

Nelson, M. (1996). Separation vs. connection, the gender controversy: Implications for counseling women. *Journal of Counseling & Development, 74.*

Oesterreich, H. (2007). From "crisis" to "activist": The everyday freedom legacy of Black feminisms. *Race Ethnicity and Education, 10*(1).

Peoples, W. (2008). "Under construction": Identifying foundations of Hip-Hop feminism and exploring bridges between Black second-wave and Hip-Hop feminisms. *Meridians, 8*(1).

Phillips, L., Reddick-Morgan, K., & Stephens, D. (2005). Oppositional consciousness within an oppositional realm: The case of feminism and womanism in rap and Hip Hop, 1976–2004. *Journal of African American History, 90*(3), 253–277.

Potter, R. A. (1995). *Spectacular vernaculars: Hip-Hop and the politics of postmodernism.* Albany, NY: State University of New York Press.

Pough, G. (2002). Love feminism but where's my Hip-Hop? Shaping a Black feminist identity. In D. Hernandez & B. Rehman (Eds.), *Colonize this! Young women of color on today's feminism.* New York: Seal.

Pough, G. (2004). *Check it while I wreck it: Black womanhood, Hip-Hop culture, and the public sphere.* Boston, MA: Northeastern University Press.

Pough, G., Richardson, E., Durham, A., & Raimist, R. (Eds.). (2007). *Home girls make some noise: Hip Hop feminism anthology.* Mira Loma, CA: Parker.

Richardson, E. (2007). She was workin like foreal': Critical literacy and discourse practices of African American females in the age of Hip Hop. *Discourse & Society, 18*(6).

Rose, T. (1994). *Black noise.* Hanover, NH: Wesleyan University Press.

Salt-n-Pepa. (1986). Tramp. On *Hot, cool, & vicious.* Next Plateau Records.

Shakur, T. (1993). Keep ya head up. On Stricly 4 my N.I.G.G.A.Z. Audio CD. Jive Label Group, New York.

Stephens, D., & Phillips, L. (2005). Integrating Black feminist thought into conceptual frameworks of African-American adolescent women's sexual scripting processes. *Sexualities, Evolution, and Gender, 7,* 37–55.

Stokes, C. (2007). Representin' in cyberspace: Sexual scripts, self-definition, and Hip Hop culture in Black American adolescent girls' home pages. *Culture, Health & Sexuality, 9*(2).

Stokes, C., & Gant, L. (2002). Turning the tables on the HIV/AIDS epidemic: Hip Hop as a tool for reaching African-American adolescent girls. *African American Research Perspectives, 8,* 70–81.

Weekes, D. (2004). Where my girls at?: Black girls and the construction of the sexual. In A. Harris (Ed.), *All about the girl: Culture, power, and identity.* New York: Routledge.

Wingood, G., DiClemente, R., Bernhardt, J., Harrington, K., Davies, S., Robillard, A., & Hook, E. (2003). A prospective study of exposure to rap music videos and African American female adolescents' health. *American Journal of Public Health, 93,* 437–439.

Worell, J., & Remer, P. (2003). *Feminist perspectives in therapy: Empowering diverse women.* Hoboken, NJ: John Wiley & Sons.

Chapter 6

Therapeutically and Socially Relevant Themes in Hip-Hop Music

A Comprehensive Analysis of a Selected Sample of Songs

Edgar H. Tyson, Konstantin Detchkov, Erin Eastwood, Alissa Carver, and Amanda Sehr

Introduction

Background and Significance

The authors in this volume have demonstrated the therapeutic use of various components of Hip-Hop culture, particularly the component known as rap music. The work in this volume is consistent with the movement toward cultural competence in the major helping professions, including music and other arts-based therapies, social work, psychology, psychiatry, and the medical profession. In addition to the innovative applications of

Hip-Hop-based techniques found in this volume, there is also a body of previous research on the use of Hip-Hop in therapy (see Kobin & Tyson, 2006, for brief review). Taken together, the significant work in this volume and past research on the therapeutic use of Hip-Hop suggests that these techniques have value with people of all ages and backgrounds, and for a variety of clinical issues. The apparent wide applicability of Hip-Hop in therapy is likely due to the fact that while initially created by urban, Black and Latino youth and young adults (Kitwana, 2002; KRS One, 2009), Hip-Hop and rap music is now a global music format (Chang, 2008), with music artists from a wide range of national, racial, ethnic, and cultural backgrounds.

Format and Structure of This Brief Report

This chapter is a brief research report that identifies positive and constructive themes using a sample (partly random and partly nonrandom) of songs. A brief literature review is presented, followed by a discussion of two important theoretical caveats to this study. Next, the methodology used in this study is explained in detail, followed by the results and a brief discussion of the major findings, the methodological limitations of this work, and a summary of the study's primary implications for practice and research in the area of Hip-Hop or rap therapy.

Brief Literature Review

One of the reasons that Hip-Hop music has been used in therapy is that some lyrics address experiences that many people can relate to (Tyson, 2006). Hip-Hop music often includes a social critique (KRS One, 2009; Pinn, 1999) that also has potential for a variety of intervention and prevention applications (for the remainder of this chapter, *treatment* will be used to refer to all types of prevention and intervention efforts). For example, Ciardiello and colleagues (2003) concluded that Hip-Hop could serve as an outlet for youth because they can identify with the individual, social, and economic struggles represented in some of the lyrics. Moreover, previous research indicates that using lyrics that address certain social problems, such as domestic violence or poverty, has been an effective method for engaging youth in conversations about how they feel about these issues (De Carlo, 2003). Another study suggests that when exposed to socially conscious, positive messages, youth can build a positive sense of self and a more positive sense of their communities (Tyson, 2003a).

There is also some evidence that exists suggesting that rap music can enhance the effectiveness of interventions for "antisocial" youth (Liddle,

Jackson-Gilbert, & Marvel, 2006) and can be useful in attempts to make positive changes in youth behavior in general (Lemieux, Fisher, & Pratto, 2008; Tyson, 2002; Tyson et al., 2008; Williams, 2009). Furthermore, qualitative research suggests that Hip-Hop-based interventions can increase the critical thinking skills of youth (Newman, 2007; Tyson, 2003b) and help youth better understand the complexities of Hip-Hop culture (Lee, 2009; Newman, 2007; Williams, 2009). Finally, KRS One (2009), considered to be one of the pioneer and most popular Hip-Hop artists of record, documents the extensive historical evidence of Hip-Hop as a social, cultural, political, spiritual, and progressive movement. The KRS One document appears to represent one of the most comprehensive analyses of Hip-Hop culture to date and its central thesis is that while Hip-Hop is art (i.e., a musical format or genre), it is also much broader in scope and meaning (e.g., social, cultural, spiritual value) for a very large number of people (KRS-One, 2009).

However, a major weakness of the research in the therapeutic uses of rap and Hip-Hop thus far has been the lack of a comprehensive analysis of rap and Hip-Hop lyrics. This gap has created a void in the identification of lyrics that could be suitable for specific treatment purposes. Ironically, there does seem to be a wealth of research into the negative aspects of rap lyrics (Tyson, 2003b) with most studies focusing on misogynistic images, violence representation, drug and alcohol use, and the negative effects of "gangsta" life (Weitzer, 2009). It seems that there is a need for a greater balance of research on Hip-Hop and rap lyrics, with particular focus on positive lyrics that are potentially useful in treatment (e.g., drug, violence, or AIDS/HIV intervention and prevention). It is equally apparent that in order to utilize Hip-Hop-based therapies that include rap music effectively, it is imperative to develop greater understanding of the lyrical content of this music. This would allow clinicians to select a particular song that would be appropriate for a given issue or set of issues in a specific situation in treatment quickly and easily. While there has been important work describing how specific rap lyrics can be used in treatment (e.g., Elligan, 2004; Kobin & Tyson, 2006; Tyson, 2003a), the previous research is limited to a few selected songs. It appears that no study to date has presented a comprehensive content analysis of constructive Hip-Hop and rap lyrics. As a result, the use of appropriate lyrics in therapy is largely dependent on individual knowledge and understanding of the lyrics and represents a significant limitation in this area of practice.

Theoretical Caveat of This Study

An important issue that must be addressed prior to the presentation of the methodology, findings, and discussion of the present study is that throughout the remainder of this chapter we refer to *Hip-Hop music* as music that has also been labeled and might be considered by many as *rap music* and according to many others might not be considered Hip-Hop music. Similarly, we also use the term *Hip-Hop music* to include songs that might be considered by many as Hip-Hop music and yet by many others would not be considered rap music. The reason for this is these terms have been used interchangeably throughout the scholarly literature and when a distinction has been presented it has been in a confusing and often contradictory manner. Specifically, the primary authors for this chapter could not locate in the currently available scholarly literature a clear, coherent, consistent, and reasonable basis or set of criteria for the distinction between what is commonly referred to as Hip-Hop music and what is also commonly referred to as rap music. When we use the term *Hip-Hop music* we are excluding music that many people would commonly refer to as Hip-Hop music, if it is performed by a popular artist who is primarily a "singer," not a rapper or Hip-Hop artist and if "rapping" (talking and rhyming over instrumental sounds or beats that mimic instrumental sounds) is not the featured music format or is not included at all in the song.

The Present Study

This study aims to fill a critical gap in research on Hip-Hop and rap lyrics. There appears to be a dearth of replicable research on specific rap and Hip-Hop lyrics that may have positive and constructive value. Therefore, the purpose of this study was to identify and discuss socially, spiritually, politically, educationally, economically, and/or culturally relevant themes found in a fairly large, mostly random sample of some of the more popular Hip-Hop and rap songs to date. To aid clinicians in selecting an appropriate song, tables will be presented that identify the artist and album, and the song that was found to have a specific message or meaning (i.e., theme). While this work is extensive, it does not claim to be an exhaustive analysis of these issues and some of the limitations of this study will be addressed in the discussion at the end of the chapter.

Method

Sample Selection Procedures Used to Identify Songs

An initial methodological caveat to this study is that there were two samples of songs generated for these analyses, each with a somewhat different sampling approach. The first sample of songs ($N = 100$), identified as those songs listed in Table 6.1 that are in standard print, were randomly selected for these analyses from a list of 325 songs that were generated as part of a larger study (Tyson, Detchkov, & Eastwood, *forthcoming*). The songs that were part of the larger study were obtained by downloading them on April 9, 2010, from a list labeled "Most Downloaded Songs of All Time" found in the archives of a private Web company that is most appropriately used by only music artists, producers, and DJs (i.e., CICANA.com).

The second sample of songs ($N = 33$), identified as those songs listed in Table 6.1 that are in italics, were provided by two of the authors (Carver and Sehr) who were not part of the study that identified the list of 325 randomly selected songs. The 33 rap selections came from a list of 83 selections; however, 50 of these were replicas of rap selections identified in the first sample. This second sample was borne out of clinical work and the selections were chosen based on therapeutic applicability of the thematic content after examining rap and Hip-Hop music that clients requested as well as rap and Hip-Hop music on rap radio stations and in the therapists' personal collections.* The selections were further narrowed down according to rules set down by the facility that insisted that there were no curse words, no glorification of violence or drug use, and minimized references to misogyny. The therapeutic themes that were identified in these selections were family/role models, social injustice, perseverance/resiliency, warning/cautionary tale, abandonment/isolation, relationships, positive self-image, dependency/addiction, grief and bereavement, choices, change, regret, and planning for the future.

Once the second sample was obtained, the first two authors independently accessed a digital copy of each of the 33 songs and their written lyrics. These raters then completed the same coding process (described below) used to rate the initial 100 randomly selected songs thematically. There was 91.6% ($n = 22$) agreement between the initial two raters in terms of which songs matched the respective subcategories under each of the major themes found in four tables below. A third rater was then used to rate the final two songs and reached 100% agreement with one of the first two authors (i.e., the first two raters for all coding procedures used in this study, which can be found below).

Coding Procedures for Sample of 100 Randomly Selected Songs

To code the qualitative lyrics for the initial sample of 100 songs used in this study, two researchers independently constructed a list of themes. These

---

* This sample was also expanded by selections suggested by others in this text: Michael Viega, Katrina McFerran, and Susan Hadley.

lists were then combined and after eliminating duplications there were a total of 4 major themes and 21 subcategories of these major themes. There was 89% agreement between the initial two raters in terms of which songs matched the respective subcategories under each of the major themes. Using the list of 21 subcategories, a third independent research assistant was then employed to rate each song further and to add any new categories that were deemed appropriate based on her analyses. This third rater had 100% agreement with one of the two original raters in terms of which songs matched the unassigned subcategories, and she found no new categories to include in the analyses. Because each rater was free to interpret a song to express more than one complete thought, idea, or feeling, some songs generated more than one subcategory in each of the major themes.

It is also important to present the approach we took to interpret the themes from the initial sample of songs. The primary author makes the assumption that Hip-Hop music is art and it is part literary art. As such, it incorporates literary techniques that must be "decoded." This is the central thesis of Jay-Z's new book (Jay-Z, 2010). Jay-Z discusses how his music uses poetry to tell the story of "the pain behind" the life of a hustler and that his intentions are to reveal "the interior space of a young kid's [young urban, ghetto, hustlers] head, his psychology" (p. 17). Jay-Z's point is that listeners cannot take everything in his music literally and that his lyrics must be "decoded" to ascertain the underlying message in each song. With this assumption to guide our thinking, we took the following steps: (1) listen and read the entire song; (2) assess the overall message given through the underlying metaphor, analogy, double entendre, allusions, or other literary technique; (3) if a second theme applied, it had to comprise a significant proportion (i.e., 50% or more) of the song.

Results

Overall Thematic Messages

The main findings from these analyses are the lists presented in Table 6.1. It would be difficult to summarize the vast array of themes generated from the lyrics analyzed in this study. The interpretation protocol was flexible enough to capture multiple thematic messages throughout the coding process. The tables show that one of the overall findings was there were four general or broad themes. The themes also generated 21 subcategories, which appeared to reveal deeper or more detailed messages. The four major themes were social criticism, social empowerment, humanistic values, and negative behavior criticism.

Table 6.1 Songs and Therapeutic Themes

Subthemes	Song	Artist	Album
Theme 1: Social Criticism			
Social Oppression	I Wonder if Heaven Got a Ghetto	2Pac	R U Still Down
	Letter to My Unborn	2Pac	Until the End of Time
	A Letter to the President	2Pac	Still I Rise
	The Good Die Young	2Pac	Still I Rise
	Gangsta, Gangsta	Dead Prez	Pulse of the People
	Propaganda	Dead Prez	Let's Get Free
	They Schoolz	Dead Prez	Let's Get Free
	Think Good Thoughts	Drake	So Far Gone Mixtape by Drake
	Why	Jadakiss	Kiss of Death
	Drug Dealin	Kanye West	The College Dropout
	Tie My Hands	Lil Wayne	The Carter III
	Serious New Message	Mobb Deep	The Murda Mixtape Album
	Can't Get It Right	Scarface	Emeritus
	Crack	Scarface	Made
	People Don't Believe	Scarface	The Diary
	All I Know Is Pain	Styles P	Super Gangster (Extraordinary Gentleman)
	Am I in the Right Game	Styles P	Super Gangster (Extraordinary Gentleman)
	I Try	Talib Kweli	The Beautiful Struggle
	My Life	The Game	Lax
	How I Got Over	The Roots	How I Got Over
	Ready for Whateva	TI	Paper Trail
	6 Feet Deep	Ghetto Boys	Till Death Do Us Part

Continued

Table 6.1 (continued)   Songs and Therapeutic Themes

Subthemes	Song	Artist	Album
	Ghetto Gospel	Tupac	Loyal to the Game
	Evening News	Chamillionaire	Ultimate Victory
	99 Problems	Jay Z	The Black Album
	It's All a Struggle	KRS One	Kristyles
	Why	KRS One	The Sneak Attack
	The Nature	Talib Kweli ft. Justin Timberlake	Eardrum
	Where Is the Love	Black Eyed Peas	Elephunk
	Love Is	Common	Be
	U.N.I.T.Y	Queen Latifah	Black Reign
	Stopping All Stations	Hilltop Hoods	The Hard Road Restrung
	Brenda's Got a Baby	Tupac	2Pacalypse Now
	Love Is	Common	Be
	Get By	Talib Kweli	Quality
	I Tried So Hard	Bone Thugs n Harmony ft Akon	Strength & Loyalty
	5 Years From Now	Mike Jones	Who Is Mike Jones?
Economic Oppression	Black Cotton	2Pac	Loyal to the Game
	A Letter to the President	2Pac	Still I Rise
	The Message	Grand Master Flash	The Message
Racial Oppression	Letter to the King	The Game	Lax
	Cause I'm Black	Styles P	Super Gangster (Extraordinary Gentleman)
Personal Suffering	Day and Night	Kid Cudi	Man on the Moon: The End of Day
	Dance	Nas	God's Son
	Coldest Winter	Kanye West	808 and Heartbreak
	Fly Away	C-Mob	Hard Times and Hard Liquor

Table 6.1 (continued)   Songs and Therapeutic Themes

Subthemes	Song	Artist	Album
Theme 2: Social Empowerment			
Personal Empowerment	Off the Books	Beatnuts	Stone Crazy
	Changes	Common	Universal Mind Control
	The Food	Common	Be
	Gangsta	Dead Prez	Pulse of the People
	Last Line of Defense	Dialated Peoples	The Platform
	Pray for You	Husalah	
	Can't Stop Me Now	Jadakiss	The Last Kiss
	What If	Jadakiss	The Last Kiss
	Amazing	Kanye West	808s & Heartbreak
	See You in My Nightmares	Kanye West	808s & Heartbreak
	The Sky Might Fall	Kid Cudi	Man on the Moon
	Pray for Me	Mobb Deep	Infamy Album
	Analyze This	NAS	The Lost Tapes
	Hero	NAS	Untitled
	Surviving the Times	NAS	The Firm
	Never Dirty	Scarface	Balls and My World
	Ghetto Apostles	Shabazz	The Book of Shabazz
	Cause I'm Black	Styles P	Super Gangster (Extraordinary Gentleman)
	I Try	Talib Kweli	The Beautiful Struggle
	Listen	Talib Kweli	Eardrum
	More or Less	Talib Kweli	Eardrum
	Letter to the King	The Game	Super Gangster (Extraordinary Gentleman)
	My Life	TI	Urban Legend
	Successful	Young Chris	So Far Gone

Continued

Table 6.1 (continued) Songs and Therapeutic Themes

Subthemes	Song	Artist	Album
	My President Is Black	Young Jeezy	The Recession
	Keep Ya Head Up	Tupac	Still I Rise
	Dumb It Down	Lupe Fiasco	The Cool
	Krush Them	KRS One	The Sneak Attack
	Take a Minute	K'naan	Troubadour
	I Can	Nas	God's Son
	Get Your Self Up	KRS One	The Sneak Attack
	Hope	Twista & Faith Evans	The First Lady
	Wavin' Flag	K'naan	Troubadour
	Work It Out	Jurassic 5 ft. Dave Matthews	Feedback
	There Is a Way	Mos Def	True Magic
	Rocky Road	Chamillionaire	Ultimate Victory
	Heaven Only Knows	Eve	Ruff Ryder's First Lady
	The Fire	The Roots	How I Got Over
	Fly	Nicki Minaj	Pink Friday
	Slideshow	T.I. ft. John Legend	Paper Trail
	Kick Push	Lupe Fiasco	Food & Liquor
	Self Esteem	Nelly	Brass Knuckles
	I Am the Body Beautiful	Salt-n-Pepa	To Wong Foo, Thanks for Everything, Julie Newmar
	360 Degrees of Power	Sistah Souljah	360 Degrees of Power
	Independent	Salt-n-Pepa	Blacks' Magic
	I'm Not Afraid	Eminem	Recovery
	Rocky Road	Chamillionaire	Ultimate Victory
	Where Do We Go	Talib Kweli	Quality
	Umi Says	Mos Def	Black on Both Sides

Table 6.1 (continued)   Songs and Therapeutic Themes

Subthemes	Song	Artist	Album
Praise of Family Values	Letter to My Unborn	2Pac	Until the End of Time
	The Good Die Young	2Pac	I Still Rise
	I Miss You	DMX	The Great Depression
	Joy	Talib Kweli	Quality
	Dear Mama	Tupac	Me Against the World
	Grandma	Mike Jones	Who Is Mike Jones?
	She's Alive	Outkast	Speakerboxxx/ The Love Below
	Family Business	Kanye West	The College Dropout
	Just the Two of Us	Will Smith	Big Willie Style
	Umbilical Cord to the Future	Sistah Souljah	360 Degrees of Power
	He Say She Say	*Lupe Fiasco*	*Food & Liquor*
	Mothers Day	*Atmosphere*	*Leak at Will*
	Dance	*Nas*	*God's Son*
	Black Girl Pain	Talib Kweli	The Beautiful Struggle
Praise of Work and Achievement	Discipline	Dead Prez	Let's Get Free
	Game's Pain	The Game	Lax
	My President Is Black	Young Jeezy	The Recession
	Kick Push	*Lupe Fiasco*	*Food & Liquor*
Praise of Education	What If	Jadakiss	The Last Kiss
Praise of Women	*Dance*	*Nas*	*God's Son*
	Independent	*Salt-n-Pepa*	*Blacks' Magic*
	Black Girl Pain	Talib Kweli	The Beautiful Struggle

Continued

Table 6.1 (continued)   Songs and Therapeutic Themes

Subthemes	Song	Artist	Album
Theme 3: Humanistic Values			
Spirituality	Black Jesus	2Pac	I Still Rise
	I Wonder if Heaven Got a Ghetto	2Pac	R U Still Down
	Lord Take Me Away	DMX	...And Then There Was X
	Jesus Walks	Kanye West	The College Dropout
	Pray for Me	Mobb Deep	Infamy
	Holy Are You	Rakim	The Seventh Seal
	Heaven	Scarface	The Fix
	Someday	Scarface	The Fix
	What Can I Do?	Scarface	The Fix
	Hostile Gospel	Talib Kweli	Eardrum
Perseverance	Take a Minute	K'naan	Troubadour
	It Won't Be Long	Rakim	The Seventh Seal
Love	Coldest Winter	Kanye West	808 and Heartbreak
	Unconditional Love	Tupac	Greatest Hits
	Love Is	Common	Be
	The Light	Common	Like Water for Chocolate
	Nothing on You	B.o.B	The Adventures of Bobby Ray
Friendship	Decisions	Busta Rhymes	Back to My B.S.
Loyalty	Hustler Wifey	Jadakiss	Last Kiss
	Say Somethin	Drake	
Empathy	Walk With Me	Big Stan (feat. DMX)	
Theme 4: Negative Behavior Criticism			
Against Materialism	Pinoccio	Kanye West	808s & Heartbreak
	The Instrumental	Lupe Fiasco	Food & Liquor

Table 6.1 (continued)   Songs and Therapeutic Themes

Subthemes	Song	Artist	Album
	The Nature	Talib Kweli ft. Justin Timberlake	Eardrum
	Gone Going	Black Eyed Peas	Monkey Business
Social Complacency	The Instrumental	Lupe Fiasco	Food & Liquor
Against Parental Neglect	Cleaning Out My Closet	Eminem	The Eminem Show
	He Say She Say	Lupe Fiasco	Food & Liquor
Against "Thug" Lifestyle	Street Struck	Big L	Lifestylez ov da Poor and Dangerous
	December 4th	Jay Z	The Black Album
	Mothers Day	Atmosphere	Leak at Will
	Dead and Gone	T.I. feat. Justin Timberlake	Paper Trail
Against Substance Use	Day and Night	Kid Cudi	Man on the Moon: The End of Day
	I'm Not Afraid	Eminem	Recovery
Against Violence	Crossroads	Bone Thugs n Harmony	E 1999 Eternal
	Dead and Gone	T.I. feat. Justin Timberlake	Paper Trail

Specific Thematic Messages

Within these four broader themes there were several specific subthemes (i.e., 21 mini-thematic messages) that emerged from the lyrical analyses employed in this study. Concepts such as racial and economic oppression and praise of work, education, and women all emerged from these analyses. Additional concepts such as love, friendship, loyalty, empathy, and criticism of negative behavior like parental neglect, "thug" lifestyle, and substance abuse also were found to be part of the underlying messages of the songs analyzed here. These themes appear to be relevant themes that can be used for a number of prevention and intervention purposes. Further discussion of these results will be presented below.

Discussion

Limitations of This Study

There were several methodological shortcomings of this study. The use of two different sampling and coding procedures indicates that some of these results were obtained through nonrandom processes and may not generalize beyond the songs presented in this study. Moreover, the initial list of 325 songs that the random sample of 100 songs was selected from might not be representative of all the Hip-Hop music currently available. There are likely thousands, if not tens of thousands, of Hip-Hop songs currently available, and these results might not be representative of the entire population of songs. A third limitation of this study is that the coding procedures used in this study might be somewhat different from other approaches used to interpret the lyrical content of Hip-Hop songs. As a result, using a different protocol might reveal different results than those found in this study. Finally, although these researchers were able to identify thematic messages in the songs analyzed for this study, it is unclear the extent to which (i.e., number of words) each theme is represented in each song. It is possible that the ratio of words represented by each theme is minor and that there are other themes that are represented by a larger ratio of words in each song.

Implications of Major Findings

Despite the limitations of this study, this appears to be the first attempt to conduct a more comprehensive analysis of a fairly large sample of Hip-Hop music for the specific purpose of identifying potentially constructive and "positive" themes. These themes appear to have clinical and social significance and can be utilized in a number of treatment settings for a number of specific purposes. People are bombarded by a multitude of social problems that are addressed in these song lyrics. Past research has shown that for people who relate to Hip-Hop music, this medium can be used in therapy to engage clients in areas that they might not otherwise be inclined to address or discuss in therapy (Elligan, 2004; Kobin & Tyson, 2006). This study extends this previous research by including many more songs and using a more systematic and comprehensive analytic approach, which can be replicated and improved upon over time. Finally, therapists and other clinicians can now access suggested songs and themes for use in practice, without the need for personal knowledge of the song. In sum, this list represents a resource for clinicians that was not available prior to this study.

Conclusion and Future Research

Future studies should include a larger sample of songs. Additional analyses of additional songs might reveal different themes than those found in this study. Future research should also include an analysis of the ratio of words that each theme represents in each song. This approach would allow for an estimate of the relative weight given to each theme in each song and clinicians might use this information to guide their selection of a particular song for a specific purpose. This final gap is the impetus for the larger study currently in process (Tyson et al., *forthcoming*). Nonetheless, this study has important implications for clinicians and should be a valuable resource as we move forward past the infancy stage of this innovative practice of the therapeutic use of rap and Hip-Hop (Elligan, 2004; Tyson, 2002, 2003a).

References

Chang, J. (2005). *Can't stop, won't stop: A history of the Hip-Hop generation.* New York: St. Martin's.

Ciardiello, S. (2003). Meet them in the lab: Using Hip-Hop music therapy groups with adolescents in residential settings. In N. E. Sullivan, E. Mesbur, N. C. Lang, D. Goodman, & L. Mitchell (Eds.), *Social work with groups: Social justice through personal, community, & societal change* (pp. 103–117). New York: Haworth.

De Carlo, A. (2001). Rap therapy: An innovative approach to groupwork with urban adolescents. *Journal of Intergroup Relations, 27,* 40–48.

Elligan, D. (2004). *Rap therapy: A practical guide for communicating with youth and young adults through rap music.* Chicago: Dafina.

Jay-Z. (2010). Decoded. New York: Spiegel & Grau.

Kitwana, B. (2002). *The hip hop generation: Young Blacks and the crisis in African American culture.* New York: Basic Civitas.

Kobin, C., & Tyson, E. H. (2007). Hip Hop in therapy: Empathic connections and thematic goals for treatment with clients from urban settings. *Arts in Psychotherapy, 33,* 343–356.

KRS-One (2009). *The gospel of hip hop: First instrument.* Brooklyn, NY: Power House.

Lee, J. (2009). Battlin' on the corner: Techniques for sustaining play. *Social Problems, 56*(3), 578–598.

Lemieux, A. F., Fisher, J. D., & Pratto, F. (2008). A music-based HIV prevention intervention for urban adolescents. *Health Psychology, 27*(3), 349–357.

Liddle, H. A., Jackson-Gilfort, A., & Marvel, F. A. (2006). An empirically supported and culturally specific engagement and intervention strategy for African American adolescent males. *American Journal of Orthopsychiatry, 76*(2), 215–225.

Newman, M. (2007). "I don't want my ends to just meet; I want my ends overlappin": Personal aspiration and the rejection of progressive rap. *Journal of Language, Identity and Education, 6*(2), 131–145.

Pinn, A. B. (1999). "How ya livin'?": Notes on rap music and social transformation. *The Western Journal of Black Studies, 23*, 129–138.

Tyson E. H. (2002). Hip-Hop therapy: An exploratory study of a rap music intervention with at-risk and delinquent youth. *Journal of Poetry Therapy, 15*(3), 131–144.

Tyson, E. H. (2003a). Rap music in social work practice. *Journal of Human Behavior in the Social Environment, 8*(4), 1–21.

Tyson, E. H. (2003b, April). *Directions in rap music research: A content analysis of empirical studies published during a 15 year period.* Paper presented at the annual conference of the National Association of Black Social Workers, Jacksonville, FL.

Tyson, E. H. (2006). The Rap-Music Attitude and Perception Scale: A validation study. *Research on Social Work Practice, 16*, 211–223.

Tyson, E. H., Detchkov, K., & Eastwood, E. *(forthcoming)*. Constructive themes in Hip Hop music: A proportional analysis of a random sample of songs.

Tyson, E. H., Ryan, S., Gomory, T., & Teasley, M. (2008). Cultural issues: Diversity and child welfare. In R. Lee (Ed.), *Foster care therapist handbook: Relational approaches to the children and their families.* Washington, DC: Child Welfare League of America.

Weitzer, R., & Kubrin, C. E. (2009). Misogyny in rap music: A content analysis of prevalence and meanings. *Men and Masculinities, 12*, 3–29.

Williams, A. D. (2009). The critical cultural cypher: Remaking Paulo Freire's cultural circles using Hip Hop culture. *International Journal of Critical Pedagogy, 2*(1), 1–29.

Part 2

RAP AND HIP-HOP WITH AT-RISK YOUTH

Chapter 7

Beats, Rhymes, and Life

Rap Therapy in an Urban Setting

T. Tomás Alvarez III

Introduction

My work using rap music in a therapeutic setting first began in 2004. Since that time, I've focused my social work career on developing a community-driven model for treatment for urban youth of color resistant to traditional therapy by using Hip-Hop as a catalyst for change and development. This journey has been both enlightening and rewarding. Over the years, I have observed the efficacy of Rap Therapy among youth of color in need of therapeutic intervention. These youth come from communities where stigma to mental health services and negative experiences with therapy discourage many young people from pursuing services. Especially noteworthy has been the impact of Rap Therapy in a group work setting for African American young men, a population that exhibits some of the most unfortunate social, mental, and academic outcomes throughout the nation including in Oakland, California, where I live and work as a social worker.

My goal in writing this chapter is to document and share my work using Rap Therapy to provide strength-based, culturally responsive therapeutic services to at-risk youth of color in Oakland, California. My hope is that readers will develop a better understanding of the unique challenges that many young men of color face and how innovative models like Rap Therapy can be utilized as a tool for engagement and to help promote healthier mental health and social outcomes. In addition, I hope to offer a strength-based lens through which mental health providers can more fully comprehend youth behavior in the context in which it occurs, instead of subjecting youth to a system of pathology.

Mental Health and Social Outcomes for Young Men of Color

One is likely to encounter a large majority of youth of color when visiting any correctional youth facility, group home, teen runaway shelter, or continuation high school in an urban setting in California. Numerous studies focusing on outcomes for youth in California indicate poor results in multiple domains for youth of color, compared to their White counterparts. Most disturbing are the rates for African American and Latino male children and teens.

According to an executive summary combining research efforts by the RAND Corporation, PolicyLink, The Charles Hamilton Houston Institute for Race and Justice at Harvard Law School, and the Center for Nonviolence and Social Justice at Drexel University (Brooks et al., 2010), African American and Latino youth are more likely to experience the following:

- Grow up in poverty
- Not graduate from high school
- Experience a greater likelihood of going to prison
- Have a parent in prison
- Be born to teenage mothers
- Encounter higher mortality rates from homicide
- Be exposed to violence
- Suffer from post-traumatic stress disorder

The research mentioned above determined that these negative outcomes were the result of growing up in communities of concentrated disadvantage. In other words, there is a direct correlation between where a young person lives and the health and social outcomes they are likely to experience. Evidence of this has been observed in Oakland, where according to the Kids Count Data Center, in 2007 approximately one fourth of all children and adolescents under the age of 18 lived below the federal poverty line and 61% of children lived in low-income households (Tsoi-A-Fatt, 2009).

Oakland: A City Plagued by Violence

Rates for youth exposure to community violence are especially staggering in Oakland. In 2008, the city ranked fourth in the nation for its homicide rate. According to a report issued by Urban Strategies Council (Spiker et al., 2009), of the 125 people murdered in Oakland in 2008,

- 9 out of every 10 were male;
- 8 out of every 10 were African American;
- 2 out of every 3 were under the age of 30; and
- 9 out of 10 were shot by a firearm.

While homicide in Oakland impacts all ethnic communities, it has had an especially devastating effect on the African American community when considering the fact that African Americans account for only 37% of the city's population but account for 80% of all homicides. Another shocking fact is the rate of teen homicide.

Community Violence Impact on Teens

In 2009, eight of the homicides in Oakland were teenagers who attended Oakland public schools. At Oakland High, where I have been working for the last 3 years, between 2009 and 2010, two students died as a result of being shot. Several other students have survived shootings or lost close friends and family members to gun violence. The psychological and social ramifications resulting from community violence can be devastating. Children and adolescents who experience loss due to intracommunity violence demonstrate impairments in their emotional well-being and academic and social functioning. Community violence also impacts school staff and the school climate. Supporting youth affected by this type of violence can be extremely challenging and requires a collective effort and fundamental understanding of how trauma influences youth development and behavior. Unfortunately, many schools in Oakland are not always prepared to respond in a therapeutic manner that helps students cope and make sense of such tragedies. Instead, the common response from many adults has focused on the adverse behaviors exhibited by youth struggling with grief, loss, and trauma. In many cases, youth who withdraw or act out aggressively are dealt with punitively. Examples of this can be seen in rates for suspension in schools throughout Oakland among African American males.

In 2006, African American youth represented roughly 40% of Oakland Unified School District's K-12 population but accounted for 74% of all suspensions. The top three reasons that African American youth were suspended included injuring another person, classroom disruption/defiance of authority, and violence not in self-defense. These three incidents for suspension constitute over 75% of all suspensions for African American students. No data exists on how many of these youth suspended for the above behaviors have experienced some level of trauma in their life or have been exposed to violence.

The majority of the youth referred to me over the years for aggression or oppositional/defiant behaviors have been exposed to some level of violence and trauma. However, little discussion has taken place in the high schools in which I have worked about how exposure to violence impacts a student's behavior and emotional wellness. In recent years, mental health professionals have begun to look at the prevalence of post-traumatic stress disorder (PTSD) among urban youth with high exposure to violence. Research shows that PTSD among this population is often under-diagnosed and untreated (Schwartz et al., 2005). Some symptoms of PTSD include inability to concentrate, outbursts of anger, heightened anxiety, avoidance, and trouble sleeping. Youth suffering from these symptoms have a hard time dealing with the demands of school, including daily functioning.

Despite the prevalence of community violence in Oakland, there exists a lack of awareness of the impact of trauma on youth. The level of advocacy required to help parents, teachers, and school administrators understand the effects of trauma always surprises me. Sadly, I have encountered numerous skeptics that believe I am simply making excuses for a student's behavior. In their opinion, students who act out or become defiant are simply resistant to learning. Needless to say, these types of accusatory unsympathetic attitudes are not well received by youth who, in many ways, already feel misunderstood and marginalized.

These sorts of blaming practices have a multilayered effect. They confirm beliefs held by many youth of color that the people in charge who are supposed to help them cannot be trusted, which in turn has a profound impact on students' connectedness to school, the types of interactions they have with teachers and administrators, and ultimately how they perform academically. Blaming practices also perpetuate a system of institutional oppression that adds to the trauma experienced by these youth. For youth of color struggling with the issue of community violence, empathetic failures like these create additional hurdles to academic achievement and prevent youth from receiving the help they need to heal and develop healthy coping skills.

Barriers to Mental Health Treatment

For decades mental health professionals have searched for ways to engage diverse youth populations in therapeutically based services, which can be particularly challenging in urban settings. Over the last 10 years, I have noticed how certain barriers prevent youth of color from accessing services. These barriers include stigma toward mental illness, racial and cultural disparities among service providers and their youth consumers, and lack of strength-based and youth-friendly options for therapy.

Stigma toward Mental Illness

In many communities there exists a common notion that mental illness is shameful. This stigma is especially detrimental in African American and Latino communities where people are less likely to access mental health services due to cultural norms, gender expectations, and a general distrust of the mental health system. From a very young age African American and Latino boys are thought to be tough, conceal pain, hide emotion, and deal with problems on their own. These expectations discourage many young men from acknowledging when there is a problem and seeking help. Many youth in Oakland turn to marijuana and alcohol for relief, which contributes to additional health and social risks.

Racial and Cultural Disparities among Service Providers and Youth

A large percentage of the youth referred to me are opposed to traditional talk therapy. For many of these youth, the idea of talking to a stranger about their problems is a foreign and threatening concept, especially when the person on the other end does not look like them, share their values, or understand their cultural background. The mental health profession has its roots in the White middle class. There exist huge ethnic and cultural disparities among service providers and their consumers. In many clinical settings the racial composition of service providers does not match the populations being served. Agencies with staff shortages of people of color may experience a harder time engaging ethnically diverse youth. However, race alone is not the only barrier; a lack of culturally competent practices also makes it difficult for mental health agencies to engage diverse populations effectively. These racial and cultural barriers influence whether or not people of color utilize and continue services. As summarized by Gelso and Fretz (2001):

> Numerous researchers agree that the single most important reason both for the underutilization of mental health services by ethnic minority clients and for the high dropout rates is the inability of psychotherapists and counselors to provide culturally sensitive/responsive therapy for the ethnic minority client. (p. 153)

For service providers to be effective at engaging and treating diverse populations, they must be willing to explore their own biases, as well as be open to learning about the customs, culture, and worldview of those they serve. Furthermore, agencies that provide mental health services must learn how to adapt formal services to be culturally appropriate for diverse youth populations.

Lack of Strength-Based and Youth-Centered Options for Therapy

More often than not a young person of color's entry into the mental health system begins with pathology. For example, youth that present with certain acting-out behaviors are often labeled as oppositional defiant. Too frequently they are punished with suspension, mandated counseling, and, in some cases, expulsion. Unfortunately, this course of action makes it difficult to work from a strength-based perspective because it pathologizes youth from the outset, leaving many feeling guarded and turned off from therapy. Youth who do choose traditional forms of treatment are given few choices. In most cases, talk therapy and case management are offered. Both options present challenges to engaging the whole person. Once in treatment, emphasis is often placed on deficits and problem solving, which make it hard to embrace the interests and talents of youth.

To better serve youth, alternative models for treatment are needed. Treatment models that take into consideration the barriers mentioned above, appeal to diverse youth, and challenge notions about what therapy is and how it is offered can have a profound impact on youth engagement. One such model is Rap Therapy.

The Use of Rap Therapy with Youth of Color

Rap Therapy, also referred to as Hip-Hop Therapy, can be summarized as the purposeful integration of elements of Hip-Hop culture in a therapeutic setting to achieve catharsis and facilitate psychosocial development. Since the early 2000s, mental health practitioners have experimented with various applications of Rap Therapy and examined its efficacy in a variety of milieus and through different modalities. Numerous empirical studies have found Rap Therapy to be highly effective in improving therapeutic experience and mental health outcomes particularly among urban and minority youth (Allen, 2005; DeCarlo & Hockman, 2003; Tyson 2003).

The Origins of Rap Therapy

In 2000, Don Elligan, a clinical psychologist, coined the term *Rap Therapy* in a landmark article documenting his use of rap music in a clinical setting (Elligan, 2000). Although this may have been one of the first times Rap Therapy as a theoretical foundation for providing therapy was introduced to the mental health community, the notion of rap as a form of catharsis dates back to the early days of rap music and Hip-Hop culture. In the 1970s African American and Latino youth began using rap and other elements of Hip-Hop (i.e., break dancing, graffiti, and dj-ing) as cathartic and social outlets to deal with harsh conditions found in their neighborhoods. Through rap, disenfranchised youth were able to cope with stress, build support groups, speak out about the conditions in the neighborhood, and gain a sense of identity.

Rap Music through a Culturally Sensitive and Contextual Lens

Much has changed since the birth of Hip-Hop. Rap music is now a multibillion-dollar industry and critics of the genre argue that it reinforces misogyny, glorifies drug culture, and advocates violence. Some believe that it contributes to self-destructive behaviors for its youth consumers who try to mimic the attitudes and lifestyles of their favorite rap icons. However, for many youth of color, rap music is not seen as a destructive force; it's seen as an asset. It provides an outlet for expression and offers possibilities. Many of the youth I have encountered who rap have dreams of becoming the next rap star. However far-fetched or absurd these dreams may seem, they represent a hope for a better future. Hope is critical for a young person surrounded by despair and constant reminders of failure. Without hope, youth from communities of concentrated disadvantage are more likely to become discouraged and as a result more vulnerable to the risk factors that surround them.

Beats, Rhymes, and Life

For the last 7 years I have utilized Rap Therapy in my social work practice with youth in Oakland. In 2004, I pioneered a performance-based Rap Therapy program called Beats, Rhymes, and Life (BRL) to engage young men of color in therapy. This unique model for Rap Therapy utilizes the process of creating rap music to facilitate a therapeutic process and foster resiliency in a social work group setting. To date, I have operated over 10 Rap Therapy programs in schools throughout San Francisco, Berkeley, and Oakland. The model has been particularly popular and useful among African American young men, who make up the majority of the program's users. Through the BRL Rap Therapy program, participants learn to use rap as a springboard for discussion and as a conduit for positive peer interaction. Youth also learn to use the program to talk about their struggles, seek advice from peers, problem solve, and re-author their narratives from a strength-based perspective. For these youth, Rap Therapy makes mental health services more attractive and useful because it offers the possibility to receive psychosocial support and build life skills through a medium congruent with their worldview and culture. To date, two empirical studies have been conducted on the BRL Rap Therapy program (Alvarez, 2006; Gann, 2010). Both studies found the group to have utility in engaging youth in therapy and facilitating positive change and youth development.

Co-Creating Efficacy

Over the years the BRL program has attracted much interest and support from youth in the community, mental health practitioners, educators, policy makers, and community artists. Many have volunteered their time and donated resources to help develop the program. As a result, BRL has transitioned from a single therapeutic program into a budding community-based organization with programs in Oakland, San Francisco, and the South Bronx, New York. Although the basic principles behind every BRL program remain the same, individual programs are refined with feedback from youth participants. Undergirding this process is a belief that youth consumers deserve a seat at the table when it comes to deciding what mental health and youth development services should look like. Such a process empowers youth to advocate for their needs and co-construct the interventions necessary to bring about individual and community change through a community-driven approach that embraces youth culture and emphasizes strengths.

In Their Own Words

To illustrate the efficacy of such a culturally congruent strength-based method, I will allow the words and lyrics of youth in the BRL program to speak for themselves.

> Beats, Rhymes, & Life is a program for youth who are interested in music or rapping.

> We wrote a lot of lyrics on topics we all agree on, that we all feel about.

There's a lot of bad things in Oakland, but there's also a lot of good things in Oakland that people don't know about that the news probably don't talk about.

It's not as bad as people say it is. If you'd grown up in Oakland you'd probably say it too.

It's my hometown, I love Oakland. Oakland's where I'm from, born and raised.

When you hear about Oakland you just hear somebody got shot here or somebody got shot there.

Any one of those kids could be me right now. And as a young person, especially because there are more of us dying out here, it's always a worry, you just never know, like what's gonna happen to you.

Lyrics: Too many tears have been shedded from frustration,
            Discrimination, and segregation
            See brutality on the TV, I hurry up and change the station

I've seen a lot of things in here, but I still love it. Like seein' a lot of bad things makes me crumble down, but I still love it.

It just sucks that like people don't hear about the good things that happen in Oakland. You don't hear about how many honor roll students we had or how many people graduated or stuff like that. You don't hear that. You just hear somebody got shot.

Lyrics: I done seen a lot of things (I done seen a lot of things)
            I done heard a lot of things (I done heard a lot of things)
            I done felt a lot of things, I done been through a lot of things
            I still love a lot of things. . . .
            I done seen a lot of things out here in Oakland, California
            I done lost a lot of people that's why I bang this for my loved ones
            They done trapped us in this mess, got us afraid and all confused, bro
            I done seen a lot of things that's why my eyes is bleedin'
            And I been through hell and shit, that's why I always be leanin'
            Yeah I bet that's why it always be seemin'
            Like I got an attitude, no that's just me bein'
            That PG FTP RIP to all my peeps

Seeing things and just hearing a lot of things really affects you. And like it can just stay in your heart for a long time.

Being young and seeing people around me being killed, it traumatizes us, it makes us depressed and it makes our brains just really like distorted because you never know what's going to happen to you.

Sometimes if I be stressin', and just missin' my daddy . . . I just get a note-book and a pen and I just write. One day I was just goin' through it and I had wrote a whole song and we recorded it. It was called "Keep Your Head Up."

Lyrics: I've gotta keep my head up so I can stand on my feet,
Yeah, so I can stand on my feet
I've gotta keep my head up so I can stand on my feet,
Yeah, so I can stand on my feet
Never look down coz all that'll do'll just make me weak
Yeah, it just make me weak

Writing rap helps me a lot with stress. Whenever I get mad or anything like that I just write and then it really just helps me release everything ... like I can say anything I want on a piece of paper.

Lyrics: Each town has a definition of the word B I T C H
And then I pray til the day that that word will be erased
And replaced with beautiful queen
Ya'll know what I mean
I'm still a teen
And I've got plenty of dreams

Music is like my heart really. It's like the only thing that really keeps me moving. When I come here I just forget about everything that is happen-ing. It keeps me level. It keeps me wanting to come every day. I'm more than grateful for it. Coz it helps me communicate with other people. And it kind of showed me a different side I didn't know I had.

Lyrics: Nobody got shot, no cops
No sweat, not even no stress
Call today a god day
Because today was blessed
Fitted Mitchell & Ness
No bulletproof vest
Nobody trying to test
And I'm really lovin' the weather
Today's a good day
And it can only get better
I had great days
But never mind the rest
Because if days get better
Today will still be labeled my best

In a way, we all have something in common—a lot in common—and we need to put our voices together and help each other out.

Lyrics: And everybody's cheerful, nobody with a mug
         And there ain't no hate
         I only feel love,
         Oh. . . . (sings) What a day, what a lovely da--ay.

At some time in your life you will have to sit down, you will have to bring your abilities to the table to help other people get their abilities out and once you reach it, nothing that you do can stop it.

Conclusion

In 1999, the surgeon general issued a report on mental health that stated that in order for mental health services to be more useful and meaningful to diverse populations, formal services must be adapted to include the daily lives of the client. Yet, more than 10 years later, mental health agencies and systems of care continue to struggle with adapting services. In Oakland, the costs of failing to engage at-risk youth carries a high price tag, especially for young men of color. The negative effects on youth are clear. Youth that don't receive services are more likely to drop out of school, end up in the juvenile justice system, and experience poor mental health outcomes, all of which perpetuate a destructive system of inequality.

To bridge the opportunity gap and improve outcomes for young men of color, a shift must occur in how mental health services are packaged and offered. Innovative programs are needed that draw directly from the culture and lives of young people. In Oakland, and other urban settings, this means incorporating rap music and other aspects of Hip-Hop. Incorporating rap music into therapy, in the form of Rap Therapy or Hip-Hop Therapy, represents a community-driven approach to mental health and signifies a much-needed paradigm shift in the way services are offered to youth.

References

Allen, N. T. (2005). Exploring Hip Hop Therapy with high-risk youth. *Praxis: School of Social Work Journal, 5*, 30–36.

Alvarez III, T. T. (2006). *Beats, Rhymes and Life: Exploring the use of Rap Therapy with urban adolescents*. Unpublished master's thesis, Smith College School for Social Work, Northampton, MA.

Beats, Rhymes, Life. http://www.beatsrhymesandlife.org

Brooks, J., et al. (2010, June). *Executive summary. Healthy communities, healthy boys of color.* Retrieved from the California Endowment Foundation.

DeCarlo, A., & Hockman, E. (2003). Rap Therapy: A group work intervention method for urban adolescents. *Social Work with Groups, 26,* 45–59.

Elligan, D. (2000). Rap therapy: A culturally sensitive approach to psychotherapy with young African American men. *Journal of African American Studies, 5*(2), 327–336.

Elligan, D. (2004). *Rap Therapy: A practical guide for communicating with youth and young adults through rap music.* New York: Kensington.

Gann, E. (2010). *The effects of therapeutic Hip Hop activity groups on perception of self and social supports in at-risk urban adolescents.* Unpublished doctoral dissertation, The Wright Institute, Berkeley, CA.

Gelso, C. J., & Fretz, B. R. (2001). *Counseling psychology* (2nd ed.). Belmont, CA: Wadsworth/Thomson Learning.

Schwartz, A., et al. (2005, February). Posttraumatic stress disorder among African Americans in an inner city mental health clinic. *Psychiatric Services, 56*(2).

Spiker, S., et al. (2009, March). Homicides in Oakland. *2008 homicide report: An analysis of homicides in Oakland from January through December 2008.* Retrieved December 2, 2010, from http://www.cjgsu.net/initiatives/HomRates-2010A-01-21-City.pdf

Tsoi-A-Fatt, R. (2009, May). Focus on Oakland. In *Keeping youth connected.* Retrieved December 1, 2010, from http://www.clasp.org/admin/site/publications/files/Oakland-profile.pdf

Tyson, E. (2003). Rap music in social work practice with African American and Latino youth: A conceptual model with practical applications. *Journal of Human Behavior in the Social Environment, 8*(4), 9–21.

Chapter 8

Therapeutic Outreach through Bboying (Break Dancing) in Canada's Arctic and First Nations Communities

Social Work through Hip-Hop

Stephen Leafloor

Who Is Bboy Buddha? A Glimpse into the Work That I Do

First some background info as a starting point into my work as a Bboy/ social worker. My mother still calls me Steve, but to most other people I am known as "Buddha." This is my Bboy name that was bestowed upon me by my crew in the 1980s. I like to joke that it is because I'm the wise old man, but if the truth be known even when I was in my prime and very fit as a dancer, I always had a little belly. In fact, my crew used to rub my belly

for good luck moments prior to going on stage to perform. I have been dancing since about 1975 and have been Bboying (break dancing as it was known in the media) since 1983. I am the founder of the Canadian Floor Masters, one of Canada's oldest and most famous crews from back in the day, and our crew just recently celebrated our 27th anniversary in 2010. At the age of 51, I still perform but I'm not as quick or as agile as the young cats—but there is still the fire in my belly when the music drops and a cypher (Bboy dance circle) forms.*

It's important to me for you to understand the world that I come from so that you don't just think I'm just a social worker who loved dance as a hobby. I have a master's degree in social work and did my thesis on Hip-Hop back in 1985. I have worked many frontline jobs in the past 30 years, ranging from street outreach, child abuse investigations, and wilderness outreach programs to working in group homes and being a probation officer. However, I don't feel like this has ever defined me as a person. Don't get me wrong, I love helping people, especially angry young men. If you were to ask me who I am, I would shout to the world with pride that I'm a Bboy. It is strange to talk about Hip-Hop in words since those in the game all know that it's something you experience. And in my case it has been the lens through which I view and engage the world.

I didn't know all this in the early days; we were just doing our thing—channeling our anger and emotions into being the best dancers in our own world. Hell, no one really knew if Hip-Hop would evolve and still be around. We didn't think about that. We just felt blessed to be involved at a point in time where something seemed to make sense for us! There is a lot of talk about having stripes in Hip-Hop (earning one's reputation by commitment,

---

* I gotta make my Hip-Hop shout-outs here before I continue!!!

To my original crew: Flipski, Kid Quick, TrickyT, Lil Glen, Dexter, IceTeak, and Beat Street Kid, stay safe and happy fam—CFM foreva baby!!! Also to my BluePrintForLife team—"Each One Teach One"—you guys know what's up. And to the new generations of the Canadian Floor Masters! Knowing our past—to inspire the future! But also to my wife, Susan, for supporting my passions over the years and my children for mocking me about being one of the world's oldest Bboys.

getting down, shows, and battles). Well, my crew, CFM, had our stripes. We opened in the early years for James Brown, IceT, George Clinton, Public Enemy, Grandmaster Flash, LaLaLa Human Steps, Russia's Kirov ballet, and others. Sure these are things of great pride, but I'm not here to boast, but to try and get you to imagine the memories that I and my young crew had together as dancers and friends. We often joked that we were like a gang without all the negative shit. We were too busy beating up on the dance floor to get into fights and problems that were so close at hand. I'm not trying to over romanticize things, but when peeps talk about Hip-Hop saving their lives, it's often true. A number of our original crew members didn't have fathers and had mothers who drank way too much. Stories of abuse in people's lives were not uncommon, and there was this rage inside many of us that was always just beneath the surface. As for me, I was horribly bullied in high school because of my small size. I was even stuffed in garbage cans in front of 500 laughing students in the cafeteria. This was in 1975—years before Bboying would later become known to the world in 1983 outside of the South Bronx.

In retrospect, it seems clear to me that even in 1975 I was developing a Bboy mentality—learning how to channel one's anger and emotions through something positive. For many of us in southern Canada (growing up in the shadow of Detroit), it was getting down to funk music on roller skates. We called it "Rockin the Red Wheels." We would roller-skate 5 or 6 nights a week, mashing up the roller floor with dance moves and acrobatics on roller skates. I remember watching in amazement when entire skate crews from Detroit would come to our turf, wearing their colors, sporting tee shirts with "Rink Rockers" on it, and black panther picks shoved in their fro's. It was the epitome of cool, getting down to the Isley Brothers "Fight the Power" and strutting one's stuff. It was not for the faint of heart! The roller rink was aggressive and the place to meet the ladies. It was the perfect place for me to regain my sense of self and rebuild self-confidence. The bullies had tried to take this away from me, but I would reclaim who I was on the very same stage that they would venture onto. I channeled that rage to become the best and became that little White kid who could travel at full speed down the middle of the rink, spinning on one foot, diving into a roundoff back handspring, jumping into the splits, pressing up into a spin, and jumping back with a locker jump and an attitude and look that challenged all around me. It wasn't about size; it was about one's skills. It was about representing the music through our bodies and making a statement about who we were.

This is the canvas of my early years which eventually led me to the early 1980s when I first saw the movie *Flash Dance*. Like many old-school Bboys I had to see this movie many times, just to see that famous short clip when Jennifer Beals becomes inspired by the street dancers. I remember seeing the shot of a kid spinning on his back and I knew that I needed this.

I didn't really know why, but I knew I needed it. This was the magic of early Hip-Hop—to inspire and reach out to others. Hip-Hop was there for us to use, to express who we were and to use the dance cypher as a staging ground to explore our own identities.

Although 1983 seems like a long time ago, some of these core feelings and emotions have stayed with me. It was the internalizing of a sense of great pride and a vision of myself that allowed me to tackle the world and engage it on my terms. I traveled through Europe, North Africa, and Turkey where I used my gift of dance as a way to share with people from other cultures who I was as a person first! Not some kind of touristic bullshit or fluff about being a Canadian. I was Bboy Buddha and I presented myself to others with an honesty and urgency that most of society didn't understand. I celebrated being different with my Mohawk and punk rock fashion, and with my Bboy skills. My spirit was constantly nourished on the dance floor and I felt blessed to be alive. I perceived life as a challenge in all its shit and glory.

Being a Bboy is who I am. It is what defines me. It's hard to describe the feeling of battling some other cats in a cypher unless you've been there. All of this forms the backdrop out of which I developed our current outreach program, and it is some of these core experiences that have given rise to our current success.

Why the Arctic and Inuit and First Nations Communities?

About 5 years ago I helped write a proposal to engage youth in Canada's high Arctic with an intense 1-week program using Bboying as our connection point. I have a sister who lives in the Arctic and have three Inuit nieces. It was also out of concern for their future when they would become teenagers that I wanted to reach out and do something for the youth up North.

If you have never been to Canada's Arctic, it is very remote and very cold and can only be accessed by expensive flights. The communities there are small and are plagued by complex issues such as very high suicide rates, drug and alcohol abuse, sexual abuse, family violence, and a loss of culture and cultural pride. The Inuit have gone through so many changes adjusting to a modern world in the past 50 years, from many elders being born in igloos and living off the land, to present-day small communities with grocery stores, schools, housing, and so on. The Inuit people have had to adapt very quickly. But as in many indigenous cultures around the world, many Inuit parents and grandparents, when they were young, were removed from their families and sent to residential schools, which were run by the church. The effects of what happened as a result are still being felt, and it is often their grandchildren that our program currently focuses on.

There are many issues in Canada's North and in our First Nations communities that can be directly linked to the effects of colonization. I am, however, inspired by a strong sense of resiliency and a will to survive on the part of Inuit people. In fact, the Inuit survived for a few thousand years in one of the most hostile environments in the world.

Despite the underbelly of real pain and anger often experienced by the youth in Canada's North, there is still a strong passion to try new things, connect with the larger world, and scream out to everyone that they are here and that they count and that their voices are important. In many ways they feel like the rest of the world has forgotten about them and that they don't count. What is pertinent here is that this sounds like how the youth in the early days of Hip-Hop felt in the South Bronx (two different cultures, but similar contexts).

There are many strengths to build upon with the Inuit. Things like family and community are still important to them, and there is a great sense of storytelling, appreciation of oral traditions, and a love of humor that surfaces in profound and passionate ways.

I believe that it is not a coincidence that First Nations cultures around the world have embraced Hip-Hop and made it their own. They need it the most! Hip-Hop is adaptable and flexible in a way that speaks to creating a sense of self and culture in the modern world. They carve out a sense of themselves without feeling like they need to be Black or Spanish and from New York.

An example of this can be seen in the Maori of New Zealand, or in the slums of Nairobi, or in Cree youth in Canada who rap about growing up on the reservation and the issues they face. Rap is a vehicle to tell their story on their terms. I love this about rap/Hip-Hop, and this is why I believe it has so strongly rooted itself in Canada's Arctic.

There is also a sense of urgency and responsibility in Hip-Hop that is able to give guidance and discuss the positive gems and deep history that still thrive in this culture, but are not always front and center. Satellite TV is everywhere in the world, including Canada's high Arctic. When there is 24 hours of darkness and it is minus 50 outside, Inuit youth are inside watching MTV, BET, Much Music, and so on. So, the twisted versions of Hip-Hop that glorify violence, degrade women, celebrate bling bling, and so on, are ever present. To make things worse, these youth almost never see their own skin color or culture represented on TV and in music videos. This compounds already complex issues, making the youth up North feel like they could never be as cool in Hip-Hop as the images they see on TV. We fight to readjust how they perceive themselves against this backdrop of media exclusion.

What We Do/Intervention

Currently, we have completed intensive 1-week programs in 38 remote communities in Canada and have been described by government officials as the most important outreach that has ever happened in Canada's North.

We become the replacement school curriculum for 100 teenage youth in these communities. (Many of them don't attend school but regularly join in with us when we come to town.) From 9 to 5 each day for 5 days, it feels like Hip-Hop boot camp. The secret to our success, I believe, lies in the use of many different techniques of engagement and is based on the strength of the relationships that form between my team and the youth we work with. We bring with us some of Canada's top street dancers. Our team reflects a modern and complex vision of Hip-Hop: men and women, Black, White, Asian, First Nation, Inuit, Spanish. More importantly we are all true passionate Hip-Hop heads who bring our honesty about who we are to the youth as an open book. We often bring our own personal stories of abuse, depression, rape, anger, suicide, and so on, directly to the table. The youth are smart; they look directly into our eyes and size us up. There is no faking the funk. If you bring the realness about who you are as a person first and humble yourself before their culture, the door starts to open into their own lives. We see ourselves as passionate human beings that believe in bettering ourselves and our art day by day, and celebrating each other's presence along the way. We offer ourselves as possible new role models to consider for this complex world.

We teach the young people original street dance styles (Bboying, Boggaloo, and locking) and Hip-Hop history. After we exhaust their bodies from dance, we then engage their minds in discussions on all the issues going on in their lives.

Throughout the week we also partner with local cultural artists to explore how their culture can be brought into Hip-Hop. We also have a special afternoon on the fourth day where local elders get directly involved with the youth in our program as we make an effort to reconnect the generations that feel separated from each other.

All of this leads to a final showcase of Hip-Hop talent and a large dance battle that the youth perform in front of the entire community on the final night. It is a great sense of closure but also one of community hope. All of this always results in the youth wanting to continue with a regular Hip-Hop club that they run after we leave. It is like these microcosms of Hip-Hop have exploded in these isolated communities, empowering them as a result.

Guiding Theories

After I graduated from university with my master's degree in social work, I quickly went to work in frontline jobs working with families and teenagers. I remember clearly working with police and interviewing a 5-year-old girl who had been raped by her grandfather. Filled with various emotions and anger, I was also terrified that I would further traumatize the victim if I was not incredibly careful with the words I chose and how I presented them. I also remember investigating the family's history and thinking to myself that all that theory I learned in university did not seem to be helping me right now. As I rolled through a career of frontline work, it was the daily experiences of engaging with people that helped me connect with them and made my work more productive.

One day our child protection team had a guest speaker come and talk to us about an Adlerian approach to counseling. I was skeptical at first, then inspired as everything she discussed seemed to make sense in terms of my daily grind in the front lines.

What struck me about what the guest speaker shared was the emphasis placed on the strength of the personal relationships between people. It's the intensity of this that can help individuals create a moment and a movement for change in their personal lives. This made sense to me as I reflected back on years of frontline work.

This approach immediately reminded me of the story of the youth in Labrador Canada who were sniffing gas. The images of this went around the world on TV and it was a great embarrassment to the government of Canada. There was a person in Toronto who was so moved by this and wanted to help but didn't know what to do. He played harmonica. Using his own money, he bought 50 harmonicas and a flight to the community in Northern Canada. He gave these out to the youth and shared his time and passion with them. I don't know for sure, but I suspect he did more "social work" than all the academics and government strategists that spent millions considering relocating the entire community. Good work doesn't always require big bucks. Neither does Hip-Hop. It is the honesty and passion being shared between real people that gets the work done and creates an internal spark to change.

From that one lecture, I also recall emphasis placed on the guiding principle that healing takes place in the context of an entire community. I also believe this and it is firmly entrenched as a guiding principle in what we do even though it is a huge challenge.

Since we began our program, I have met some great people involved in working with Canada's Aboriginal cultures. Another concept that makes sense to me in the daily work we do is that "hope is a social determinant of health" (see "Feathers of Hope" by Steve Penderson and Dr. Len Syme). In the worlds we venture into, there are signs of post-traumatic stress disorder everywhere. We offer new visions of hope—not just in terms of the youth experiencing it in real ways themselves, but also in the parents and elders seeing it and feeling it, and the youth believing that the community has renewed hope in them as the new generation. I have come to believe that "hope is a key concept which could increase levels of control, social engagement, and social participation" (L. Syme, personal communication, 2009). I believe this and such concepts continue to shape our program's engagement techniques.

Another reason I think our program works so effectively is that we use a multitude of approaches. We often use one for a short time, then revert to a fun engaging activity, then return to an opportunity to connect the dots with the youth directly in their lives. When I lecture at universities, I point out examples of how we use the following techniques:

- Mentorship and role modeling
- Cognitive therapy
- Group therapy
- Resiliency training
- Humor and laughter therapy
- Anger management training
- Safety planning
- Sport, play, and art therapy—in a cultural context
- Disclosure and healing path stories
- Goal setting, daring to dream
- Self-regulating techniques and self-discipline
- Leadership training—cooperation skills
- Positive risk taking
- Meditation techniques

But I wouldn't talk like that with the youth we work with. They have already been counseled by professionals and are highly guarded and skeptical of counselors and social workers. Social workers are often seen as the ones who take children away from families—not as people who can help.

Our program works because it is fluid yet structured and highly intense, but also fun and engaging. But the net result at the end of the week is that some of the most shy and introverted youth on the planet come to hardly recognize themselves or each other. They experience real moments of change and confidence in their lives, and the parents and elders also see and feel this and a new sense of hope emerges.

To illustrate what we do, let me describe the dynamics of a cypher and the cognitive therapy that takes place. I believe we do real-world cognitive therapy, not armchair cognitive therapy. A cypher is a dance circle and an exchange of energy and passion. Let's say it's early in the week and I have just taught the youth a backspin. We now form a dance circle, and I suggest that we are all going to take turns getting down in the middle one by one and try out this new backspin technique. You can imagine the anxiety of the youth. Everyone is terrified and doesn't want to go into the circle. Well, in cognitive therapy terms the thought process is "Oh shit, Buddha's looking at me, oh shit, he's going to pick me!" The idea that they will be picked leads to real terror and anxiety that the youth all immediately feel. Some may even have a physical reaction as is often the case in anxiety—self-talk, sweating, trembling, and so on. I help ease the anxiety by stating a rule in Hip-Hop and a rule of the cypher. I explain to everyone that no matter what goes down we will all hoop and holla and clap in support of the efforts of each of us as we enter the circle. Well, the bullies are even thinking they better hoop and holla and cheer for everyone, even though they usually tease and bully, since they also want everyone to do the same for them. It's a great equalizer that everyone buys into. One by one, even the most shy youth enter the circle (sometimes with one of us if they are really terrified). Let's say that the backspin doesn't work out, that it turns into some sort of bum spin instead with a contorted body on the floor; it doesn't matter. Everyone would cheer and support them anyway. Their internal talk of fear and of being laughed at was belied by the group's response. It didn't roll out like that. In fact, the opposite happened and they felt supported and good inside. Many not only feel good inside, but ecstatic with the energy and support they just felt. We get them hooked on the therapy of the cypher, and every time they go in the dance circle it becomes easier to do and no longer a place of fear, but one of excitement. This is the same buzz that all us Hip-Hop heads experience sometime early in the game. Positive risk taking builds the confidence to try again, to engage life again, to take bigger risks next time.

At the end of all of this I might stop the music and talk to the youth about what just happened and how they felt while it is crisp and front and center in their minds. There's also strength that gets recognized as they realize they all share similar fears and anxiety, but are stronger when they support each other. We then immediately try and get the youth to visualize other bully-free zones. Imagine if this feeling of support and security happened outside of the cypher and in the classroom, or in the school, or in the community, or in the North, or in Hip-Hop around the world. The idea is to help them to connect the dots in small real-world ways and help create a broader vision of getting the youth to believe that they count and are connected to the bigger picture. They begin to connect the mind, body, and soul.

What Goes Down

In keeping with the importance of building honest personal relationships with youth, we progressively get into the more difficult topics as we progress through our 5-day program. It would not make sense to talk about sexual abuse and suicide on the first day, so instead we talk about it on day 5, as the relationships we now have with the young people are what I call "thick." There is more substance to our relationships and we are no longer being viewed as counselors or just dance instructors. As the week ebbs and flows we don't just stand at the front and teach dance, asking the youth to follow along. We are spread throughout them, in close contact, directly often working one on one. They may view us as Hip-Hop superstars when we first arrive, but we need this to quickly disappear. It's a great equalizer when they see this old man Buddha at age 51 trying all the stretches side by side with them, sweat pouring down my forehead. It sends a message that we are all in this journey and experience together. When we work with 100 youth with a team of 10 staff, we bring a wide range of different personality types to the table. This is important as the youth have a diverse range of options in terms of certain types of characters in my staff that they will start to connect with. Some youth might connect with me as I may represent the father (or grandfather) that they may be missing in their lives, whereas others may bond more with Frost as he's one of our Bboy philosopher kings and certain youth will dig this. Others may connect with Bgirl Lunacee as her life experience as a young Cree woman may echo much of their experiences. The point is that real human beings open up and connect with the youth, creating a different type of environment where the youth hopefully internalize much more from our difficult talks as it feels like honest and safe conversation among supported friends.

Early in the week we tackle issues like Hip-Hop history, bringing your own culture into it, media manipulation, and finding your own one mic in your life. Finding your "One Mic" is a metaphor we explore after watching Nas's video "One Mic." We challenge youth to talk about what "One Mic" they already use in their lives to combat all the anger and frustration they may feel. What do they do instead of breaking the windows in the school, or cutting their arms or burning them with cigarettes? Up north many youth will talk about things like sports and music, but often they will talk about a "One Mic" that involves hunting, fishing, or just going out for walks on the land. Being connected to traditional ways and the outdoors seems to be a great anger management technique they already understand.

We try to formalize these, exploring what they already know, and encourage them to explore many new "One Mic's" in their lives. We can promise that life will continue to throw a lot of shit at them, but it's how they will respond to this that really counts. Digging into a bag full of many options helps.

All of these are examples of the types of conversations we will have with the youth during the first few days of our program as the topics are not as difficult to talk about as those toward the week's end. All of this is placed within the context of intense physical activity through dance and celebrating culture.

As the week progresses, there will be lots of tears and lots of spontaneous gestures of healing and support for each other. It becomes really important for youth to realize that they are often not alone in their pain. We also make sure that we are partnered with local counselors so that they can be there for the needed follow-up support as some old wounds may be opened up. We also role-play and explore concrete ways they can be good listeners to a friend, or go with them to see a counselor if needed. In many of the communities we have visited, many of the issues we discuss have never been talked about openly. This in itself is a powerful first step in the healing of remote communities.

Breaking Down Bureaucratic and Academic Barriers

Something else magical happens on our projects. I try and insist that various adults come and participate in the program as equals side by side with the youth. Given that we become a replacement school curriculum, I strongly leverage the teachers and often the principal to participate. We don't allow adults to hang on the walls and just watch. We need to lead by example and show the youth that adults are willing to take new risks and learn things out of their comfort zone. (Otherwise how can we ask this of the youth?)

We strongly encourage local police, social workers, public health, and even the mayor and elders to participate. We often hear comments from this group like, "It's the most powerful professional dev they have ever experienced." But more importantly, it opens up the communication between adults and breaks down the perceived and often real barriers of power and control. It works both ways with adults and youth seeing each other from a different perspective. I had one teacher in an Arctic community tell me that she had been assigned as the primary person to keep watch on a teenage girl who had been on suicide watch for about 2 years. This teen refused to even say two words to her for 2 years. After a week of working together on dance routines, they seemed like best friends. We have heard similar stories with police who have done our program, stating they are now perceived by the youth in an entirely different way, one which now lends itself to the desired community policing model they were supposed to be operating under, but never really existed.

From my perspective, we forget quickly what it was like to be young. We forget about all the fears and anxiety, and all the excitement and spontaneity. We build a fence around our lives and become entrenched in our ideals, defending our positions and trying to make our children see things only our way. We become adult snobs, fearful of learning new things, reverting to using power and control as a way of managing younger generations. We even invest much of this way of thinking into all those bureaucratic systems that we have set up to "educate" and manage young people. Such systems tend to reflect our own insecurities and lack of faith in our own children. Yes, we become list and rule makers! We must learn to engage and reflect many of the positive values that the youth admire—spontaneity, side-by-side engagement, celebration, and so on. We are excited that our projects help break down some of the stereotypes in both worlds, offering new models of education and engagement that build communication.

Celebration of Culture

It's not only important to celebrate traditional culture as a way of youth creating their own cultural voice in Hip-Hop, but celebrating traditional culture is also important in building personal self-esteem. As mentioned, the youth we work with seldom see their faces represented on TV, in print media, and so on. This is why we are so proud of the fact that nine documentaries have been produced on our work and shown regularly on Canada's National Aboriginal Television Network (APTN).

It is important that our story gets told, but it is also very important that the youth get to see themselves reflected back to them on TV with all their passion and confidence. This is healing in a personal and a cultural sense. Every time *Readers Digest* or a newspaper does a story on our projects, I try to get them to interview the youth. Every bit of attention they get helps offset the fact that the media tends to cover largely the doom and gloom stories of our Inuit and First Nations people. We have produced a photo book of the youth of Canada's Arctic called "Arctic Hip Hop."* This was produced to help reverse the effects of a media that never shows the faces of these young people. Imagine the pride they feel seeing themselves in print.

Throughout our 5-day projects we collaborate with local cultural artists and athletes. We always explore traditional drumming, as every culture has a drum. And when I get down to "James Brown," my movements are hooking on the drumbeats. Whether it's a large handheld Inuit drum, smaller Dene drums, or a large Cree buffalo drum played by many at the

---

* You can preview 200 pages of it on our Web site at http://BluePrintForLife.ca.

same time, it is a drumbeat, it's a heartbeat, and it makes you want to move. We will often have a dance circle with just traditional drumbeats or perhaps explore adding a DJ scratch beat overtop the drum beats.

In Hip-Hop there is something called *beat box*, which is basically creating drumbeats with one's mouth. In Inuit culture they have something similar only it is not created in the chamber of the mouth, but much deeper in the throat. It is a very ancient tradition done by two women facing each other. It is called *throat singing*. We explore throat singing with all the youth, and we also explore freestyling it with beat boxing. The youth love it as it's something unique to Hip-Hop from their culture. We call it *throat boxing*.

There are also lots of traditional songs, traditional dances, and traditional athletic games in the Inuit culture. Such games require great skill, flexibility, concentration, and athleticism. They are similar to what Bboying requires. The games are connected historically to passing the time during long winters in a large communal igloo, as a way of staying in shape and having fun. We use these culturally specific games to "flip the script" as they are the experts. We have great fun as the Blueprint staff humble themselves before their culture and they get to teach us. We see ourselves as sharing human moments of laughter together as we fumble through something in terms of which we are inexperienced. Such experiences help to break down the barriers that can occur when we are seen as the "Hip-Hop superstars." We prefer to be just human beings, sharing with other human beings. We even take this a step further and explore this physical movement as we develop small battle routines for the final show. Often there will be movement in the dancers' toprock (what Bboys do before they hit the floor) or a small story that reflects traditional culture. I will never forget the eyes of the elders open wide, and the cheers from the parents, as the youth created a human dog sled in the cypher for the final battle.

When we have an elders afternoon on day 4, we always get elders up trying their hand at DJ scratching on the "Wheels of Steel." This is a powerful symbolic moment as it also shows that great-grandma is still willing to take a risk and share a human moment with others. There is always lots of shared laughter. This is in itself very healing. Because of the ongoing effects of residential schools, everyone always complains that nothing can be found in common between generations. We contend that creating these human moments is a great place to start. We will also get the youth to get their grandparents up dancing as they teach them a few gentle steps that they have learned so far. On our final night showcase before the entire community, we always get the elder DJs up scratching on the turntables as it is a moment of respect, pride, and joy for the whole community.

We also talk about Hip-Hop bling being carved out of gold and silver. Hip-Hop was always about adapting and using what was available in one's immediate space. The youth are encouraged to come up with their own arctic bling with things like a polar bear claw, or carving their name in graf letters out of caribou antler.

On every project we also create a large graffiti mural that is 5 ft × 9 ft on canvas. We cannot fly in spray paints as they explode in the small aircraft. So instead we bring lots of wide-tip markers. The youth work on a cultural graffiti piece with a powerful positive message that they want to communicate. We teach them basic technique, but the art is all theirs, often done in their traditional language and script (syllabics).

In one small community of about 1,000 people on Baffin Island, there had been six teenage suicides in the 2 months prior to our arrival. It is important to note that there are only about 250 teenagers in the whole town. This is a suicide rate among the highest in the world. The youth decided to create a graffiti mural stating "Never Give Up."

The art they create is unveiled at the final showcase and is always placed in a prominent location in the school or youth center, serving as a visual reminder to the messages and memories we all shared together.

Elders and parents may not understand Hip-Hop, but they do recognize the cultural significance of what is shown in the art, music, and dance produced during our stay. There is a great sense of pride in the community as the fear of losing one's culture and language is very real.

One might think that Hip-Hop is perceived as threatening to traditional culture. In our experience this is hardly ever the case. In contrast, many elders have thanked us for helping preserve their culture. One elder in Rankin Inlet had taught her granddaughter to throat sing, but she had given it up. After our program she was excited to learn from her grandmother again and her grandmother went out of her way to find a translator to help thank us.

Many elders tell us that various aspects of their traditional culture seem directly in sync with the battles and the challenge aspects that exist in all the elements of Hip-Hop culture. I have been told that drum dancing was used to settle disputes, as a challenge between two drummers, and that throat singing is a face-to-face challenge where one responds to the other person's rhythms and sounds and tries to trip up the other person or make them laugh.

The Final Event

The final event feels like closure to our intense week. Young people hardly recognize themselves in the new confidence they have discovered. We often joke that if you can outdo bingo on a Friday night in the North, then you are definitely doing something right. We hear over and over that the final show-case is often the largest gathering the community has ever experienced.

This is usually at least a 2-hour show where there are demonstrations of drum dancing, throat singing, throat singing with beat box, elder DJs, and the youth's dance battle, where often 50 youth battle 50 other youth.

This all ends in a performance by the BluePrintForLife team as a gift back to the community for trusting us with their kids. At the end of it all, there is so much excitement and positive energy in the community hall that it is at least 1 to 2 hours before we can pack up. At the end, it feels like we have signed every tee shirt and jacket in the community.

There are a lot of magical things that happen on this final evening, which has deep symbolic and cultural importance. There is also a great sense of hope and pride as the community witnesses the newfound spirit and confidence of the youth. More importantly, the youth directly feel the love and support of the community as they hoop and holla and cheer throughout the evening.

I have watched so many dance battles over the years that I tend to focus much of my attention on the audience, as I know the youth will be great. Many parents and elders are not just tearing up with pride, but many are openly weeping as they not only see the great potential in their youth but also see great moments of cultural pride where they realize that the youth have not forgotten where they have come from.

People are shocked to see some of the most quiet and shy youth in the community come out of their shell, or see the local bullies working side by side with those who are bullied in a dance routine.

We also unveil the large graffiti mural on this day and there is a great sense of pride in seeing a positive message created in their own language created by the youth. It is a great human moment where people start believing in themselves and each other. The smiles on the faces of the youth tell a story of healing, and parents are just happy to see the youth having fun and demonstrating a sense of community.

At this final event we also recognize, with awards, the extra efforts of a few youth who worked extra hard or went out of their way to help others. We also start off their newly formed Hip-Hop club by supplying them with lots of DVDs on the culture of Hip-Hop and music.

Sustaining a Program

Probably the biggest challenge is getting local adults and parents involved in their children's lives. Often there are a handful of people (many of them teachers) who are the ones to do everything supporting the local youth.

The trick seems to be in how to broaden this base of support. There is no question that the youth have the passion and desire to continue dancing and exploring the other positive elements of Hip-Hop in their lives. But many times this passion is sabotaged by adults. For example, the youth need a regular place to practice, a place that they can count on for a few nights a week. The venue needs to be supervised by adults and at a consistent time and place, not costing the youth to attend. Often it is hard to get a commitment from the local school or recreation center. Moreover, when there are adult gatherings, these almost always bump the youth's agenda. As parents and adults, we need to stop paying lip service that youth are our most precious resource and that they are the future when we don't mean it. We need to take responsibility and get involved in supporting the positive things our kids are interested in—in addition to Hip-Hop.

Many communities we have visited have very successful ongoing Hip-Hop clubs where they are actively supported by the community and elders. In Clyde River, Nunavut, the local Hip-Hop club shoveled snow for the elders in the winter and as a result the elders wanted to sew their traditional dance outfits for the Hip-Hop shows they performed in southern Canada. Many communities now have the older youth teaching the younger kids, and there are lots of Hip-Hop performances that are done at the local Christmas shows and festivals for the community.

To help sustain programs, we have also developed a "Leadership through Hip Hop" program where we bring potential young leaders together from many communities.

Indeed, we have often brought some of these youth to other communities as BluePrint staff in training. Having young Inuit youth in an elevated role as part of the BluePrint team is an important motivator.

But to me sustaining a program also means continuing the healing paths that many of the youth start to embark upon during our first week with them. As a follow-up support to this, we have also developed a program called "Healing through Hip Hop."

This program is also an intense week, but different in that we work more in smaller groups. We use 3 rotations of 10 youth per group (30 in total). The youth use spoken-word poetry, dance, and healing circles in the different rotations. Since we have already earned the trust of these youth and the communities from our initial program, we are able to get down to work in an honest and open way with the youth from the get-go. The entire process is like peeling back an onion a bit further to help keep them on a productive path of healing. For our healing circles we encourage the youth to talk about a whole range of emotional memories and encourage some of this to be used when they write their poetry. It is also very powerful when the youth do their poems or raps in front of the whole community again for a final showcase. This allows adults to hear directly from the youth about the joy, pain, and suffering in their lives. It takes a whole village to raise a child, but the village needs to know what's going on and feel connected in a deeply personal way.

Frost Graf—"Something Out of Nothing"

In Hip-Hop we use the term "Something outta nothing." It is a badge of honor to acknowledge the fact that Hip-Hop grew out of situations with very limited resources. Families couldn't afford to enroll their children in sports and dance classes, so we had to teach each other and invent stuff for ourselves. This process generated tremendous creativity. I believe it is one of the reasons that Hip-Hop still exists today and is still flowing and evolving. We inspired each other within contexts of often limited resources.

For example, if we didn't have a dance floor, we waited until garbage day at the furniture store to get a cardboard freezer box. If we didn't have a sound system, our homeboys laid down a beat with just their mouth in beat box form. If we didn't have an art studio or a canvas, we would put up graf on trains and old walls. We would scream out messages to the world that we were still here and couldn't be denied. Such graf expressions were ways of maintaining a sense of self and a sense of dignity. Hence, the essence of Hip-Hop is this creativity to let out art, music, dance, and fashion with whatever is available to you.

The following is a powerful story that illustrates this in terms of the youth we work with in the high Arctic. We had visited a community called Pond Inlet, which is a remote fly-in-only Inuit community at the top of Baffin Island. It is very remote with lots of the issues and challenges talked about earlier. After our project finished, the Hip-Hop club continued with about 50 youth showing up twice a week for practice. Many months later when I was back home in Ottawa I was on a conference call with the leaders from a number of Hip-Hop clubs when one of the teachers from Pond Inlet shared this story. It still makes me tear up with pride each time I talk about it because these kids not only get Hip-Hop, they are Hip-Hop.

A local teenage girl who attended the Hip-Hop club had passed away. That night at Hip-Hop practice all the youth were crying and hugging each other with support over missing their friend. According to this one teacher, this in itself was amazing because before this there was no formalized gathering for youth to grieve or support each other and this was often done in isolation. A discussion started among the youth that they should think of some way of honoring their friend. A creative idea was suggested that they should go out around the town (all 50 of them) and do "frost graffiti."

In Pond Inlet, under certain conditions, it is so cold that a thick frost forms on the outside of all the buildings. With the warmth of their fingers, having removed their sealskin mitts, they were able to trace and melt positive messages about missing their friend. It was like graffiti tagging without causing any vandalism or damage to anyone's property. These kids went out around the whole town all night, feeling like they were accomplishing something positive and powerful together. When the sun came out and the town woke up, everyone was talking about it and walking around town to read all the powerful messages celebrating life and saying things about missing their friend. The whole town was covered in art and messages!

If I was an adult or a parent in that community, I know what I would be saying to myself as I walked about town: "We have good kids!" Isn't this what is hoped for by every parent and community? Don't we want a sense of pride and hope generated from within the community itself, especially among the youth who are often underappreciated or simply written off?

I had never heard of frost graffiti, but now the story is out there. Wouldn't it be cool if Northern Russia, Finland, Norway, and Alaska all heard about this and a new form of graffiti caught on—tagging and art that lives for a brief moment, like sidewalk chalk drawings, but expresses great creativity as a voice from its creators and carries the importance of being read with great urgency?

Through frost graffiti, Inuit kids in the high Arctic in Canada are now adding their voice to the global Hip-Hop community. That's what I'm talking about: "Something outta nothing."

Final Thoughts

Next time you see a youth with baggy pants at the mall, don't turn your nose up with disdain and the arrogance that sometimes comes with age. Try to remember what it was like to be young yourself, and the need to put your own stamp on the world. Don't assume every youth involved in Hip-Hop wants to be a gangsta or mistreat women. Let's try and steer our children to the positive but always give them the flexibility to find their own voice. To me, Hip-Hop is a great gift, but as participants in this culture we also have a responsibility to try and take it back to some of its positive roots. Youth must be given the space to bring out who they are as people and what they want to say to the world, in a way that builds communities and celebrates the art forms and elements of Hip-Hop. If the world is dealing out bags of shit, then young people need to be able to talk about this. Hip-Hop to me is a great safety valve or survival mechanism that is needed in a world that sometimes feels like total chaos.

Therapists, social workers, police, and educators have a responsibility if they are working with youth to at least try and understand the current youth cultures that have been adopted as a youth voice. To not do this is disrespectful and it sends the all-too-common message that "adults know best" and will tell the youth of the world what to do. Clearly this has never worked. I contend that we need to understand the dynamics of what's going on in cultures like Hip-Hop, and then find creative ways to leverage all of this to help youth heal and find their own voice and identity.

Chapter 9

Hear Our Voices

A Music Therapy Songwriting Program and the Message of the Little Saints through the Medium of Rap

*Scott MacDonald and Michael Viega**

Introduction

This chapter details a unique music therapy songwriting program, Hear Our Voices, and the songwriting process of the Little Saints, a group of "at-risk" fourth-, fifth-, and sixth-grade children in Philadelphia, Pennsylvania. The authors, who were also the music therapists working with this group, discuss the relevance of Hip-Hop culture, and its musical framework, to the music therapy process, and to the success of the

* The authors would like to acknowledge Dr. Cheryl Dileo, director of the Arts and Quality of Life Research Center, and Dr. Joke Bradt, former assistant director, for giving us the opportunity to be a part of the Hear Our Voices program. We thank the Mid-Atlantic Region of the American Music Therapy Association for the generous grant that funded our work with the Little Saints. Thanks also to Exelon Generation for a generous grant that funds current Hear Our Voices programming. Of course, thank you to the staff and children at the afterschool program, as well as the neighborhood, who graciously welcomed us in and made us part of their community.

program. One particular song from that CD, "Superwoman/Superman," is examined for "the message" that emerged from the song's lyrical content. Lastly, interviews, conducted with group members after the songwriting program, are looked at to gain a better understanding of how the participants responded to being in the songwriting program, as well as evaluate aspects of the program they would keep and those they would change.

Hear Our Voices

The Hear Our Voices program is part of a larger initiative by the Arts and Quality of Life Research Center (Temple University, Philadelphia, PA) called *Arts at Your Side*. The Arts and Quality of Life Research Center works to create arts experiences that help to enhance the lives of the people in the communities of the Philadelphia region, especially those whose quality of life has been compromised by physical, mental, emotional, social, environmental, and/or economic problems. Initial funding for Hear Our Voices, which supported the work with the Little Saints, came from a generous grant from the Mid-Atlantic Region of the American Music Therapy Association.

Hear Our Voices is a music therapy songwriting program that serves at-risk school-aged children who attend Philadelphia-area afterschool programs. Participants of the songwriting program may be considered at-risk due to the fact that they are often surrounded by the pressures that come from growing up in low socioeconomic neighborhoods that struggle with such issues as gang violence and drugs. The songwriting program, run by board-certified music therapists, uses a "theme-centered approach aimed at providing the children with a creative outlet for exploration and expression of issues relevant to their lives (violence, gangsterism, family situation, drug use, anger management, school, and peer pressure) and an opportunity to collaboratively create strategies for personal safety and success" (Arts and Quality of Life Research Center, 2003). Each 14-week cycle culminates in a CD release party to celebrate the songs created by the youth.

Hear Our Voices began in 2007 at an after-school program run through a Christian ministry in the Kensington section of Philadelphia.* The program provides a meal, study time, and recreation activities for school-aged children, serving a neighborhood with a diverse ethnic and religious makeup (African American, Caucasian, Latino, Muslim, Christian). The center has a close-knit, community feel, and is situated on a residential block on which some of the children who attend the program live. The parents who bring their children to this center for after-school programming

---

* Thanks to the initial success of the songwriting group presented in this chapter, the Hear Our Voices program continues to thrive at this site.

represent working families that make an effort to give their children structured time in a safe environment to work on homework, play, and experience opportunities beyond what school alone is able to offer.

Research shows that children exposed to factors such as violence, drug use, school truancy/drop out, family problems, and poverty are at risk for developing unhealthy behaviors, and when exposed to more than one of these behaviors, the risk increases (YouthARTS, 1998). Hear Our Voices is an attempt to address the needs of a community where these factors are prevalent and threaten to further cycles of poverty, criminal behavior, and violence. Philadelphia's Kensington section was chosen as a site for this program in an effort to offer an arts-based program to a neighborhood that was struggling with such problems. In 2007, 46.2% of the population in the zip code in which the center is located was below the poverty level (City-data.com, 2009). According to the most recent census data for the area, the percentage of individuals over the age of 25 who had received high school diplomas is only 29.16% (U.S. Census Bureau, 2000). As of the 2000 U.S. Census data, over 20% of households in this neighborhood have a single parent with children less than 18 years of age, almost half the total number of households with children (Philadelphia NIS neighborhood-Base, 2009). Additionally, at the time that the Hear Our Voices program began, Philadelphia as a whole was in the midst of a wave of violence that became the focus of national attention. The murder rate for the year 2007, when the program began, reached its highest level in 9 years, with the highest per-capita incidence of juvenile victims within that same span of time (Philadelphia Police Department—Research and Planning Unit, 2009). In the district that encompasses Kensington, the rates were similarly on the rise (Philadelphia Police Department, 2006). While the factors that classify the Kensington neighborhood as at-risk are irrefutable, there are nonetheless problems with this term. However true its socioeconomic realities may be, the people who live in this community may nonetheless refuse to see themselves in this light. While their children live in a community with many risk factors, parents, particularly those of the children at the afterschool program where Hear Our Voices takes place, work hard to ensure that the at-risk cycle does not come full circle.

The Little Saints

Thirteen children, ages 9–12, took part in the first Hear Our Voices program. The group was made up of seven girls and six boys, including two sets of siblings. The racial makeup was predominantly African American and Latino. The kids attended several different nearby schools, both public and parochial. A handful of the group members had previous musical experience, both formal and informal, including singing, rapping, and study on instruments such as trumpet, drums, and piano.

An important factor in determining the direction to take in song-writing with this group was to find out what they listened to. The music they preferred ranged from rap, including artists such as Lil' Wayne and Playaz Circle, reggaeton artists like Daddy Yankee, to American R&B and pop singers, such as Ciara and Miley Cyrus. In a way, the musical tastes of the children seemed to teeter between childhood and adolescence, bridging artists popular with children such as Miley Cyrus with the more adult and controversial themes contained within the music of Playaz Circle and Daddy Yankee.

As they worked on their music over the first half of the program, with expectations of recording a CD of their own songs, it became apparent that the group would need a name. After discussing it, they decided to call themselves "The Little Saints," a name that reflects the core, though not fully defined, spiritual compass point of the group. Although as children they continued to exhibit such behaviors as teasing, competitiveness, occasional disputes, and mischief, what comes through in their words and music are beliefs concerning humanity, social consciousness, and spirituality, even though the surrounding milieu included the specter of drugs and violence.

The Songwriting Process

As a new program in a new setting, the songwriting approach with the Little Saints was an evolving one. Given the age of the group members, we knew that the approach we took would have to account for the energy level of the children, as well as their unique developmental learning needs. It seemed prudent to take a multimodal approach to songwriting where we could derive ideas from the musical improvisations, discussions, and focused art tasks. The goal was to create situations where creativity could flourish and provide a direct link to issues and ideas that were relevant for the children, with regard to their view of the world around them, and specifically, the community that they lived in.

In working toward this goal, we found the need to be flexible, to allow the music to occur spontaneously, and to work from the interests and strengths contained within each child. We learned to tolerate a process that at times seemed unruly, but recognized that the real creative energy lay within this chaos. Several factors emerged from this approach that made it a meaningful one for the children. These factors included using a free-style rapping style, focusing on the unique strengths and style of each individual's contribution to the group, allowing the songs to contain and reflect these various contributions, and lastly, a tendency toward socially conscious themes in the songs. In hindsight, it became apparent that these very factors connect the music of the Little Saints to the larger context of Hip-Hop music and culture, a connection that strengthened their investment in the collective goal of creating their songs.

The musical ideas that seemed significant for the Little Saints often emerged in unexpected moments, sometimes before and after the group, with one or two kids, who, seeing the handheld recorder, wanted their chance to show what they could do. These ideas came in the form of spontaneous melodies and raps about themes that came up in the group, but also about what was going on in the immediate vicinity. After an initial frustrating session where the group seemed unable to coalesce in writing songs together, we packed up for the day and made our way out of the center. One participant, "American Diva,"* followed us out, telling us about her interest in music and eager to demonstrate her skills. With the aid of a handheld recorder, we were able to capture her melody, riffing on the theme from the group, that "life is crazy."† After a similarly challenging second session, "Roc Boy" and "IG" traded verses in the pastor's office, first riffing on their faith in God and then transitioning into a commentary about the pastor, who entered the room as they rapped into the microphone.

For the Little Saints, planning the songs in a formal way was often met with distraction and feelings of boredom. The ideas that came in the moment, when the inspiration hit, seemed to motivate the group and made their connection to the music stronger. With the challenges facing us in helping this group write songs, we brought what we had from these voice recordings to serve as a foundation around which the group was able to construct their first song. As a result, the formation of the Little Saints music links directly to Hip-Hop culture and rap music, in that it utilizes such approaches as sampling and freestyling. With a digital recorder, we would record moments of each session, sample significant moments of music or vocal interplay, splice and layer them together using laptop-based recording equipment, and then bring it back to the group for them to expand upon, usually through improvising lyrical ideas.

Naturally, the sound of the music that would support the lyrical ideas was important to the Little Saints. Although we came prepared with percussion instruments to engage the musical process, we encountered a challenge in bringing the group together in a productive way using these instruments. Though they were able to expend a great deal of energy, the acoustic drums had the effect of driving the group apart, creating disruptions and disputes, not to mention a wall of sound that overpowered the

---

* To protect confidentiality of the group members, nicknames were chosen by each child and became his or her "stage name" for the remainder of the group.
† This recording became the primary sample for the first song on their CD.

voices. In an effort to approach sounds that more closely matched their pre-ferred music, we began using a trio of interactive electronic instruments that allowed the Little Saints to manipulate the sounds and grooves for their music in a way with which they immediately resonated. The sounds of the drum machine, sampler, and synthesizer may be preprogrammed, yet with the push of buttons, a turn of the dials, and the use of a touch pad that could be controlled by "scratching" it as a DJ might manipulate a record on a turntable, the sounds could be embellished in an infinite number of ways. A few members of the group gravitated toward these instruments and found sounds that seemed familiar and satisfying. The rest of the group members responded immediately with a noticeable shift in energy and identified this new sound as their own.

The sound palette of Hip-Hop music, and the role of technology in creating it, played a significant role in what made these instruments attrac-tive to the Little Saints, motivating them further toward the creation of their songs. Hip-Hop has relied on technology from its inception, manipulation of turntables and mixer sliders, the twiddling of knobs, and the use nowadays of computer-based software that makes the creation of music an almost exclusively studio-centered production. Through the mastering of the tech-nology used to create it, those who produce it have been able to gain artistic control and power through it, and thus have a greater chance to be heard (Dyson, 2007). This electronically facilitated sound palette was immediately attractive to the Little Saints, and the ease of use of such electronic instru-ments gave those who played them a level of control that they could not access as a group with drums and other acoustic instruments, which often resulted in an unwieldy sound that any one person was unable to control for very long and negatively impacted the effort needed to develop the lyrical content of the songs. In a way, the technology was a shortcut, but one that nonetheless added a significant element of authenticity for the children.

Another avenue in which technology impacts the sound of Hip-Hop music is in the way that it has allowed artists to create music that can draw on many sources and styles at once, recycling and reinventing the music which becomes more than the sum of its sources. Dyson (2007) describes this as a *bricolage* effect, represented by the disparate samples, break-beats, and cut-and-paste construction that has been a cornerstone of so much of Hip-Hop since its inception. As it has evolved, it has been able to absorb a wide variety of influences, branching into styles that at times seem far removed from rap (as with Run DMC's collaboration with rock artist Aerosmith, Jay-Z's sampling of the song "Hard Knock Life" from the musical "Annie," or Nas's interpolation of Beethoven's "Für Elise" in the song "I Can"). Another aspect of this bricolage effect can be seen in the development of distinct styles within Hip-Hop, from more popular rap music that frequently mixes rapping with sung soulful choruses (such as in the emergence of West

Coast rap in the 1990s) to less commercially driven music that eschews mainstream acceptance and at times addresses more controversial themes and decisive stances (such as hard-core or "gangsta" rap).

As mentioned above, the Little Saints as a group contained a mix of musical interests that went beyond Hip-Hop alone. While some of the boys clearly gravitated toward Hip-Hop, taking roles in rapping the lyrics and mixing the beats, many of the girls aspired to sing their contributions. Hip-Hop again provides a useful model, acting as a stylistic container that contains multiple styles at once in music that makes sense as a whole. The second song by the Little Saints, "Homeless," exemplifies just such a crossover style, with elements of Hip-Hop, R&B, and pop, echoing countless collaborations between these stylistic worlds.

Developing a theme that emerged in their first song, "Everyday Life Is Crazy," "Homeless" constructed a hypothetical situation involving a person struggling with homelessness. As the story took shape, drawing was used to flesh out the ideas, creating an image of a woman failing in school, turning to drugs, and sleeping outside in a cardboard box. The group brainstormed about this, but as their tolerance for focused discussion began to reach its limit, smaller cliques broke off and freestyle lines emerged, coming to the rescue of the song's progress: "She wanted to go to college to get more knowledge, then she went to Jupiter to get more stupider." One group member, "Juju," added a fitting melodic chorus, "and now she's homeless, homeless, homeless." Causes, effects, and solutions were considered, such as the reasons for and effects of dropping out of school and drug use, as well as the value of prayer, family support, and rehabilitation programs.

In their first two songs, the Little Saints began to emerge as a cohesive group when the children gravitated toward specific roles that reflected their individual strengths and interests. Some were clearly motivated to sing and develop lyrical ideas, while others showed interest in the instruments and devices. Considered another way, some of the kids wanted to be up front with their voice being heard and their musical ideas realized, while others gravitated toward a behind-the-scenes role, writing lyrics but reluctant to sing or perform them. Other roles included making artwork for the anticipated CD, dance choreography, and filming footage for a video. Some kids fell into a role quickly and assertively, while others struggled to find a place that felt comfortable. In many ways, these roles are analogous to the various roles and personalities that are part of the social and financial reality in Hip-Hop (at one point early in the program, "Roc Boy," when asked if he would sing or rap something, stated, "I want to be the producer!"). In today's world of popular music, and particularly in Hip-Hop, the making of the music is only part of the experience. The clothing, product affiliations, onstage choreography, and perhaps to a decreasing extent, the music video, all play a role in defining the wholeness of the musical experience. It is not simply an artist making his or her music, but a product of larger "extended families" of production teams, fashion designers, and entourages, where the lines between the artist, the business, and the merchandise/style are blurred (sometimes these lines are blurred within one person, as with Jay-Z, as artist, CEO of Roc-A-Fella Records, and creator of Rocawear clothing). Within the Little Saints, there was an inherent awareness that making music must include more than just the songs themselves. The various roles that each child chose were crucial in the process of bringing the whole group together to make a CD and communicate their message to the community.

Through their various roles and a broader conception of what the music should be, the Little Saints, in a way, represent something akin to the kind of larger group formations that have existed since the beginning of Hip-Hop, from the early collective of Afrika Bambaataa's Universal Zulu Nation (Chang, 2005), to groups like Wu Tang Clan and G-Unit, who spawn a cadre of different artists, each with unique styles, while maintaining a unified "brand" identity. This coming together of different styles and perspectives under one banner allowed the Little Saints to become unified in the common focus of their musical message and the shared experiences of living in Kensington. This allowed them to organize some of the chaos that exists to an elevated degree in their community at that time, most notably the heightened crime rate, and communicate it through their songs.

When we look at the content of the music emerging in the Little Saint's first two songs, a clear social consciousness emerges. While Dyson (2007) identifies Hip-Hop as an art form that attempts to act as a catalyst for social change, more than anything, he argues, it is a reflection or product of those struggles. And whether or not the stories told by rappers bear some resemblance to their own lived experiences, what is most significant is that the stories that are told have truthfulness and reality to them. When we began to write songs with the Little Saints, our initial prompt was to get them to talk about life as they see it. What came from this was an honest and at times bewildered reflection of life as they saw it. As the title of the first song came to be known, an initial response to this question was that "everyday life is crazy!" This phrase seemed to resonate with the kids, and what followed was a litany of examples of how life is crazy, from violence in the streets to the catastrophe of Hurricane Katrina. As this discussion moved forward, feeling words emerged: "It makes me feel sick, it makes me feel upset, it makes me feel bad." When we asked them what could be done about these things, the responses were sometimes clear and forceful: "It makes me want to make some noise!" Other responses included prayer: "Oh Lord, help me pray for them"; ambivalence: "but sometimes it makes me happy because I get bored with things"; and insight resulting from reflection: "When I'm mad, it makes me wanna smack someone. But I know I'll get in trouble, so I throw my anger back in the trash, 'cause it's garbage." The song "Homeless" carried on this socially conscious message as well. However, much in the way Hip-Hop has been accused of ambiguity toward social ills, particularly when focused on the world of the ghetto, drug dealing, and gang violence (Dyson, 2007), "Homeless" began amid laughter, poking fun at the predicament of the homeless woman, described in the song as "walkin' around actin' all stank." Nonetheless, the group supports the central character of the song, identifying a means by which she gets needed help (spirituality, family support, and treatment).

"The message," a term often used in Hip-Hop to denote authenticity within the artistic and cultural expression contained in rap music (Sylvan, 2001), plays a critical role in the interpretation of the songs of the Little Saints. This interpretation provides insight into the music therapy process and the impact of the songs on the community as a whole. This message crystallized in the third and final song that the group members wrote, "Superwoman/Superman." The following section will describe how this song materialized, and will be considered from the framework of Kobin and Tyson's (2006) analysis of therapeutic themes in Hip-Hop.

Developing the Message

On October 31, 2007, a Philadelphia police officer walked into a Dunkin Donuts where a robbery was in progress. The burglar shot and killed the officer and escaped. For the next several days the shooting and the search for his killer dominated the headline news in Philadelphia. This police shooting appeared to heighten the unfortunate fact that the murder rate in the city had been escalating for several years.

The Little Saints met at their regular time, which was 6 days after the shooting, but was also the same day the police officer's murderer was apprehended. The song "Superwoman/Superman" began to take shape that day. "DJ JJ," "M&M," and "Joey" played with the drum machines and synthesizers, while "American Diva" and "Lil' Spicy" improvised a vocal melody repeating the refrain "superwoman, superman." With the beat and the melody forming, each group member began participating in the development of the song. "Roc Boy," "The I.G.," and "Lil' Spicy" began MC'ing on the microphone and freestyling lyrics, blending with the drumbeat and the improvised melody of the refrain.

The vocal improvisations appeared to become more focused, evolving from a fantasy version of superheroes toward recognition that firefighters and police officers were real-life superheroes, and then finally touching upon the events of the past week concerning the slain officer and the search and capture of his killer (Excerpt 9.1). Other group members began to dance, some joined in on electronic or acoustic percussion instruments, while others sang along with the refrain "superwoman, superman."

EXCERPT 9.1

A TRANSCRIPTION OF THE FREESTYLE LYRICS FOR "SUPERWOMAN/ SUPERMAN"

Roc Boy:

John Lewis killed that cop
There's an example that violence need to stop
he robbed Dunkin Donuts just for some money
he didn't get none and that was funny
He got caught in Miami
The shelter turned him in for some money
He was on his knees, clutching a Bible and cryin'
When he should be in the cells lyin' and cryin'

Lil' Spicy:

(Paying for that guy's life)

Roc Boy:

He took a cop's life for no reason…
Everybody don't like him and they have a right
just because he took that man's life
He should have never killed that cop
Again, violence needs to stop
He shot Officer Cassidy through the eye, and the bullet went
    through the head
Then he went and robbed Dunkin Donuts just for some bread
That's a shame that he did that thing
Now people don't call him a person, he's a thing

Lil' Spicy:

He has to pay for that life cuz there gonna lock him up or kill
    him
They say that it's better that they locked him up
It's good that they caught him before his funeral
because if they didn't, he'd have to pay with his life

Once all the Little Saints songs took form, the pastor's office was transformed into the group's recording studio. The children came in one or two at a time and recorded their vocals and instrumental parts. Their first two songs, "Everyday Life Is Crazy" and "Homeless," followed a traditional verse-chorus structure and were mostly completed and recorded as they were written in the group. The song "Superwoman/Superman," however, remained a work in progress. The recording studio became a secondary place for the group members to continue to explore the themes of the song and its musical and lyrical possibilities.

The music track was created using three separate beats co-created by "DJ JJ," "M&M," and "Joey" on the drum machine and synthesizer. The music therapists recorded these parts into GarageBand, the recording software that comes standard with Macintosh computers. Each drum section was given enough time for the students to improvise freely over the track when they recorded their individual vocal parts. Working either in pairs or individually, each group member recorded his or her own vocal parts to the song, sometimes freestyling lyrics in the moment. Group members chose where their vocal parts would fit into the song and how their voice would sound. These cut-and-paste and editing choices allowed for each group member to have creative input into the all aspects of the song's development, from writing and arranging to the recording and final production of the song.

By the end of the recording process every voice combined to make one clear message they wanted to share with others: "Stop the violence!" Excerpt 9.2 shows the final version of the lyrics as recorded by the Little Saints. Note that the final version discusses complicated issues of forgiveness and redemption for the murderer, as well as finding possible solutions to violence through shared communication, themes that did not emerge during the group portion of the songwriting process but came out during the recording process.

EXCERPT 9.2

"SUPERWOMAN/SUPERMAN" BY THE LITTLE SAINTS

American Diva and Lil' Spicy:

Superwoman, superman x4

The I.G.:

There's crime goin' on in the street.
People talkin' bout they gonna get the heat.
The Lord is watching over us,
Being baptized is a prize to us,
We should climb on the heaven bus.

Joey:

Elderly people getting shot for no reason,
That is why that cop got shot too.
There's no reason why these people get shot,
They didn't do anything to you.

DJ JJ:

He shot Officer Cassidy through the eye,
And the bullet went through the head.
Then he went and robbed Dunkin Donuts,
Just to get a little bread (Now everybody raise your hands up!)

American Diva and Lil' Spicy:

Superwoman, superman x4

M&M:

He did something bad, but he also repented.
God's a wonderful man, so he'll forgive him.

Pooky:

He has to pay for that life that he took away,
They say that it's better that they locked him up anyway.
It's good that they caught him before the funeral
So he can pay his honors and be respectful.

American Diva and Lil' Spicy:

It's emotional, very emotional
It's sad, very sad

Roc Boy:

Officer Cassidy, he had a nice family
But instead he died over something silly
Man that's crazy how he died
Because the bull wanted some pie
Man you got pie, what you gonna do with that?
What you killed a cop and so now you want to clap?
Check-it, I feel sorry for his family
Yo, that's crazy
No more violence

American Diva and Lil' Spicy:

Superwoman, superman x4

American Diva and Lil' Spicy:

It's emotional, very emotional,
It feels like you're gonna lose your own family member. X3
It's sad, very sad,
Innocent people get shot every day (Innocent, very innocent)
The people who did, it will have to pay.
They're Innocent, very innocent.

Ramsey:

Crime is going on in the street, it's a problem I recognize.
Everybody should just look in each other's eyes and apologize.
It's scary but sometimes you have to make a sacrifice.

American Diva and Lil' Spicy:

It's emotional, very emotional
It's sad, very sad

Baby Girl:

It's crazy, it's hard to believe, but people have to compromise.

Baby Girl and Destiny:

It's crazy (it's scary) but people have to sacrifice

The I.G.:

Jesus Christ has to cry because a guy came to him and said
  goodbye.

"The Message" of Superwoman/Superman

The emphasis on the potency and power of the spoken word in rap music is steeped in oral traditions that anthropologist Robin Sylvan (2001) traces back to West Africa. Poets and musicians within the tribes of West Africa, also known as *jalis* or *griots*, had to possess a high level of oral skill to deliver the potency of words in a way that would evoke supernatural and sacred messages for the members of a tribe (Sylvan, 2001). These powerful spiritual messages were known in Africa as *nommo* (Berry, 1994). Today, rap music has often been seen as a way for modern poets and rappers to express culturally germane problems and issues facing our world today and speak for and to all those whose voices have been suppressed by society (Sylvan, 2001; Chang, 2005; Kobin & Tyson, 2006).

Kobin and Tyson (2006), in an analysis of therapeutic themes in Hip-Hop when working with clients in urban settings, recognize that rap music can be "a catalyst for culturally relevant self-expression" (p. 346). One of the themes that emerged was that certain Hip-Hop artists voice an empowerment perspective, which the authors found useful for therapists to draw from when working with clients in low-income neighborhoods and minority backgrounds. In the article, Kobin and Tyson identify four ways in which rap lyrics can empower ethnic and cultural minority populations: "increasing self-efficacy, developing group consciousness, reducing self-blame, and assuming personal responsibility" (p. 347). The Little Saint's song "Superwoman/Superman" focuses primarily on two of the steps to empowering an audience through lyrics: (1) developing group consciousness, and (2) assuming personal responsibility.

Using Kanye West's 2004 song "Jesus Walks" as an example of development of group consciousness, Kobin and Tyson (2006) note that the song empowers its listeners by "bestowing unconditional, spiritual acceptance on hopeless members of society" (p. 347). This theme permeates the first half of "Superwoman/Superman." While wrestling with why people commit such violent acts ("There is no reason why these people get shot, they didn't do anything to you"), throughout the song the group members also offer their community unconditional spiritual acceptance, reassurance, and offerings ("The lord is watching over us. Being baptized is a prize to us. We should climb on the heaven bus"). The Little Saints show empathy for all the families and victims of violence. In a complex stanza by Roc Boy, which was improvised at the moment of recording, he shows concern for the family of the fallen officer while also struggling to understand why someone would kill another human being for some money ("Officer Cassidy, he had a nice family, but instead he died over something silly. Man that's crazy how he died, because the bull wanted some pie"). One of the most surprising and powerful messages in the song was finding empathy and forgiveness for the murderer in such lines as "He did something bad, but he also repented. God's a wonderful man, so he'll forgive him."

Lastly, the group members did not shy away from the violent images of murder, reminding the listener that just because they are young they are not immune from the images displayed on the nightly news. At the end of the following stanza, the singer asks everybody to raise their hands up, as if asking the community to recognize the pointlessness of such senseless acts of violent murder and also offering empowerment by coming together as a community and not shying away from difficult realties. "He shot Officer Cassidy through the eye and the bullet went through the head. Then he went and robbed Dunkin Donuts just to get a little bread (Now everybody raise your hands up!)"

In the second half of the song, the theme of assuming personal responsibility occurs at both an individual level and a collective level. Group members voice the emotional qualities that come when dealing with the shock of violent acts occurring within a community. This deepening of feelings toward violence is expressed within the song as a collective trauma: "It's emotional, very emotional. It feels like your losing your own family member." The Little Saints ask the community as a whole to take responsibility in helping stop the violence. This request comes in the stanza, "Crime is going on in the street; it's a problem I recognize. Everybody should just look in each other's eyes and apologize. It's scary but sometimes you have to make a sacrifice." Though at first glance this appeal may appear to be the naïve pleas of a young child, upon further reflection one sees that it is a complex message for people not to be afraid to sacrifice their own pride and take ownership for their mistakes. The Little Saints ask the community to take on the responsibility of talking through their problems and find compromise among one another.

Celebrating the Message

The community block party plays an important role in ritual expression of Hip-Hop culture (Sylvan, 2001). Block parties provide a space where neighbors can eat and socialize. The DJ, the sound system, and the music become the focal point for such socialization. The location of the block party is typically in a location that serves as a common meeting place for community members. Sylvan recognizes that these events become a spiritual space where family and neighbors can connect and interact in music and dance. It is an event where community members receive the message contained in the MC's raps. The musicians and the MC take on the role of a priest or priestess, and the message can often sound like a sermon, empowering friends, family, and neighbors to unite and rise above their current circumstances (Sylvan, 2001).

The Little Saints CD release party occurred in the church where the CD was made. This is a place where community members meet to pray together and discuss topics that affect their lives, a place that they trust to watch and teach their children after school. It was a fitting place for the message of the Little Saints to be heard and for their CD to be celebrated.

That evening, community members brought food, socialized, and gathered for the presentation that introduced the Little Saints and the work they accomplished. A music video was viewed as the children sat in front of the audience and received accolades for their achievements. Each group member was presented with several CDs to keep for him- or herself and give out to friends and family. After the presentations, community members listened to the Little Saint's CD on a sound system, ate, and socialized. The group members autographed CDs, danced, and glowed in the attention they deserved.

Especially exciting for the group members were the local news cameras that were there to cover the CD release. The Little Saints' message was being broadcast across the city, and with cameras rolling, group members and parents were interviewed, their voices being heard citywide. In the liner notes of the CD, the Little Saints expressed how their message is not only local but global as well. "The Little Saints would like to dedicate this album to: Officer Cassidy and his family, all the victims of violence in Philadelphia, all the victims of violence in Iraq and around the world."

Response to the Message

The members of the Little Saints were interviewed at the end of the 14-week songwriting program. The purpose of these interviews was to gain a better understanding of how the participants responded to being in the songwriting program and to allow them to evaluate aspects of the program they would keep and those they would change. To provide a space where the children could be open and honest without feeling pressure to give positive feedback only, a music therapist, trained in open-ended interview techniques and who was not part of the Hear Our Voices project, conducted the interviews. The interviews were taped and transcribed. Quotes that summarized the group members' answers to the questions were extracted.

The following questions were asked:

1. How did you feel about the program/what did you like?
2. Has the program helped you in any way?
3. What would you change?
4. What else would you like to sing about?

The majority of the Little Saints reported how important the music-making experiences and recording sessions were for them on an individual level and how these experiences allowed them to feel a part of the group. "[My favorite part] was being with all my friends; being able to control the tape recording, music and record, writing songs, making certain sounds, and videotaping." Another group member mentioned, "I got to open my heart and sing for people . . . I get to finally show them what I'm singing and how

I sing, and just show them what I believe in." This ability to open up to other group members appeared to improve confidence and self-esteem for some individuals, with one participant stating, "Now I know that I have a lot more abilities to do things if I put my mind to it, because before I used to just give up." Others commented on the group process of finding their own unique roles in the group and how it allowed them to get to know others in a different way, with one group member commenting, "[I liked] how all the kids could pick their parts and put them together and just practice, record, and put [the CD] together." Another added, "Well I already knew these kids, but it showed me a little bit more about them."

Group members also remarked about the importance of the therapeutic relationship with the music therapists, with most focusing on the playful environment that the therapists allowed in the group setting. One participant observed that "[the music therapists are] willing to let us prepare and tape, and joke around." Another added, "They came and pushed me in a good way, so I could be more intelligent." It appears by these comments that a musical environment (one shaped primarily through the medium of rap music) that is fun and allows for individual autonomy helped the Little Saints feel connected to other group members and to the process of creating their own CD. In guiding the group to find their individual voices through the possible roles needed in creating a CD, participants reported that there was authenticity contained within the group's collective message. One group member observed, "The [songs] were true. What they were saying about crime is true."

Group members, reflecting back on the songs' content, felt that they would like to expand the topics they would like to write about in the songwriting group. Songwriting topics that some participants suggested included "love," "family," "friends," "school," and "songs that teach lessons by focusing on fun." Interestingly, some group members commented that the songs "were kind of sad" and "emotional." Another added that he/she would have liked to have written a "different song, like about happy stuff, not the crazy stuff." The music therapists considered this important feedback; however, they also felt that adults who had voiced similar concerns might have influenced these reactions, causing a bias in the participants' responses. This left the therapists wondering whether the group members' comments toward their chosen subject matter—the songs—might not have reflected their true feelings. It could be that even though the children were observing the violence around them, the adults in the community still wanted to protect them from these aspects of their community. However, it was the children who primarily suggested many of the themes that were important to them in the spontaneous, creative moments of each session. The music therapists decided that for future Hear Our Voices projects at this site they would remain culturally sensitive to the community's need to spotlight the positive aspects of their environment, while also allowing the children to create spontaneously in a group setting that focuses on how each individual makes a contribution to the larger group collective.

Conclusion

Hip-Hop culture provides a unique perspective in music therapy by focusing on empowerment and community. It is both the group members and the music therapists who must go on a journey together to discover what these words mean to each of them in the music therapy setting. Hip-Hop music provides a head-bopping groove in which these issues can be explored through rap and vocal freestyle, allowing each individual to have their voice heard, making an impact on the health of the community as a whole. For children and adolescents in neighborhoods that face daily struggles such as violence, drugs, and poverty, Hip-Hop culture and its music provides an outlet for group members to express their concerns and fears, while also looking for and discovering solutions in a way that impacts both the group members and the communities in which they live.

References

Arts and Quality of Life Research Center. (2003). *Hear Our Voices: Songwriting with at-risk youth*. Retrieved January 26, 2009, from Temple University, Boyer College of Music and Dance, http://www.temple.edu/boyer/ResearchCenter/MARgrant.htm

Chang, J. (2005). *Can't stop won't stop: A history of the Hip-Hop generation*. New York: Picador, St. Martin's Press.

City-data.com. (2009). *19122 zip code detailed profile*. Retrieved December 15, 2009, from http://www.city-data.com/zips/19122.html

Dyson, M. E. (2007). *Know what I mean? Reflections on Hip Hop*. New York: Basic Civitas.

Farnum, M., & Schaffer, R. (1998). *YouthARTS handbook: Arts programs for youth at risk*. Washington, DC: Americans for the Arts.

Kobin, C., & Tyson, E. (2006). Thematic analysis of Hip-Hop music: Can Hip-Hop in therapy facilitate empathic connections when working with clients in urban settings? *The Arts in Psychotherapy, 33,* 343–356.

Philadelphia NIS neighborhoodBase. (2001–2009). *Neighborhood reports—Zipcodes: 19122—U.S. Census Data*. Retrieved December 15, 2009, from http://cml.upenn.edu/nbase/

Philadelphia Police Department—Research and Planning Unit. (2009, November 12). *Murder analysis 2006–2008.* Retrieved December 15, 2009, from http://www.ppdonline.org/pdf/det/MurderAnalysis.pdf

Philadelphia Police Department. (2006). *Philadelphia Police Department: Patrol district crime statistics—2006.* Retrieved December 13, 2009, from http://www.ppdonline.org/hq_statdist_06.php

Sylvan, R. (2002). *Traces of the spirit: The religious dimensions of popular music.* New York: New York University Press.

Tyson, E. H. (2002). Hip Hop therapy: An exploratory study of rap music interventions with at-risk and delinquent youth. *Journal of Poetry Therapy, 15*(3), 131–144.

U.S. Census Bureau. (2000). *DP-1. Profile of general demographic characteristics: 2000 data set: Census 2000 summary file 1 (SF 1) 100-percent data geographic area: 19122 5-digit ZCTA.* Retrieved December 15, 2009, from http://factfinder.census.gov/servlet/QTTable?_bm=y&-geo_id=86000US19122&-qr_name=DEC_2000_SF1_U_DP1&-ds_name=D&-_lang=enz

Chapter 10

"Just So You Know, I Miss You So Bad"

The Expression of Life and Loss in the Raps of Two Adolescents in Music Therapy

Katrina McFerran

The relationship between adolescents and songs is profound, yet the nature of this relationship is hotly contested. Teenagers perceive a powerful positive role of music in their lives, describing the ways they use music to regulate their emotions (Saarikallio & Erkkila, 2007) and describing how music therapy can make them "feel better" (McFerran, 2010b). Contemporary music can be a forum for presenting the voice of young people, or at least their consumer instincts since it is they who purchase the music and make it popular (Mark, 1988). Some adult activists worry about the nature of this voice, with the Parent-Teacher Association of America arguing that the aggressive, pejorative, and sexist lyrics commonly found in some genres of music have a negative influence on the development of their children (Scheel & Westefeld, 1999). Researchers have sometimes adopted this perspective, claiming that music can have a causative influence, determining the thinking of young people and priming them for aggressive or suicidal thoughts and behaviors (Anderson, Carnagey, & Eubanks, 2003; Rustad, Small, Jobes, Safer, & Peterson, 2003). Hip-Hop music, along with metal, has been a major focus of such criticism. Evidence from correlational studies frequently identifies a relationship between "psychological vulnerability" and a preference for rap or metal music (Lacourse, Claes, & Villeneuve, 2001; North & Hargreaves, 2005; Stack, Gundlach, & Reeves, 1994; Tarrant, North, & Hargreaves, 2001), but the limitations of survey research mean that the direction of the influence within the teenager-music relationship cannot be determined. The idea that music leads to negative behavior is not well supported, and therefore the suggestion that Hip-Hop music may be contraindicated for vulnerable teens is a simplistic reading of a complex topic.

Many commentators on adolescence view the role of music, and the different perspectives about its influence, as reflecting the inherent process of differentiation during adolescence. Becker describes the ways that teenagers "create walls of sounds that repel adults" in order for them to make a space in which they can reflect on the past and dream of the future (1992, p. 78). The movement away from time spent in shared family spaces into the solace of the bedroom (with music blaring) marks a natural transition for teenagers as they focus on their peers in preference to their parents (Poole, 1994). Music not only blocks parents because of its unfamiliar sounds but also connects young people to a peer group, with music preferences providing a "badge of identity" (Frith, 1981). Ruud (1997) has described the function of musical affiliation as allowing for the "performance of identity," a concept that neatly captures both the public and private aspects of music's use for identity formation.

A more active performance of identity is fostered by music therapists when they use songwriting to work with adolescents. The everyday music-listening habits of young clients often serve as the first point of verbal encounter in the therapeutic relationship, with the simple but potent probe of "So, what kind of music do you like?" being used to great effect (McFerran, 2010a, p. 87). Drawing on this affiliation and using it as the motivation for creating original songs takes the therapeutic encounter beyond the directly familiar world of music listening and into new domains. The affiliations that teenagers have to different genres of music continue to be an important part of the songwriting process and usually inform decisions that are made between the music therapist and teenager. Whether working individually or with groups, this influence can be seen in many of the steps of songwriting previously outlined by McFerran (2004) and adapted in Table 10.1.

Once adolescents choose to focus on working within the genre of Hip-Hop for songwriting, a number of musical decisions are implied. The prominence of beats as a major musical influence will be assumed, and rapping will be the dominant strategy for conveying lyrics. As illustrated in Table 10.1, a number of musical details still need to be negotiated and this

Table 10.1   Songwriting Process with Groups of Adolescents

Step		
1	Introduction to idea of songwriting	What do you think makes a good song?
2	Selecting song style	What type (genre) of song will we write? Hip-Hop, rock, pop, grunge, folk, country, opera, other?
3	Identifying musical roles	Who will play, who will sing, what other roles in a band can people take on? Who's going to be the producer, for example?
4	Brainstorming song concept	What do we all have in common that we could write a song about? What issues can we communicate with this song?
5	Brainstorming lyrics	What ideas do you have about the song concept? Individual words; sentences; stories; anything?
6	Selecting ideas for inclusion	Which of these (pages of) ideas shall we use? What is going to be in and what will we put aside?
7	Determining song structure	Do we need a chorus to repeat the most important idea? Is there a short but powerful sentence that would serve as a bridge? Is this a story that should be through-composed?
8	To rhyme or not to rhyme	If a song doesn't rhyme, is that OK? Does it have to rhyme all the time?
9	Creating lyrics	How can we turn these ideas into lyrics? Will we have a consistent length of phrase? What meter suits this style of song?
10	Creating melody and harmony	Can you sing or rap the words as you hear them in your head? Do you like the way that any of the alternatives I have offered sound?
11	Finalizing musical features	Is this the right speed (tempo)? What is the best accompaniment style? Is it too loud or too soft (dynamics)? Does anything need to be changed to make this better?
12	Rehearsing	How many times, and over what time period, are we going to practice this?
13	Final performance	Are we going to record this, perform it to a known or even unknown audience, or keep it private and play through it when we're together?

process will be described in detail in the following case studies. However, what Table 10.1 does not address is the lyrical content of the songwriting process, and it is usually assumed that this will be related to the context for therapeutic intervention. Yet research shows that the content of songs written by teenagers are more likely to be focused on developmental issues than the specific need that has led the young person to therapy (McFerran, Baker, Patton, & Sawyer, 2006). In a retrospective lyrical analysis of songs written by adolescent girls with disordered eating, the dominant themes that emerged from the lyrics were relationship dynamics, identity formation, and aspirations for the future. Reference to the disorder and its impact ranked fourth, after these other issues, followed by references to emotional issues.

The main themes identified in the lyrics of songs written in music therapy by the 15 teenage girls match neatly with the focus found in the literature describing music therapy with teenagers. A systematic review of descriptive literature revealed identity formation and social goals as the main focus of interventions (Gold, Saarikallio, & McFerran, 2011). The emphasis on these two types of clinical goals was not related to the challenges being faced by the teenagers (behavioral, emotional, physical, or cognitive) or even the approach adopted by the therapist. Fifty-seven percent of music therapists of all orientations and working with a range of adolescent clients across various services focused on either identity formation or social goals, and 46% addressed both. "Taken together, this shows that many music therapists of all orientations were focusing on their clients achieving goals that improved their understanding of themselves and/or their relationships with others" (McFerran, 2010a, p. 41). The literature suggests that in music therapy there is a focus on adolescent growth and development that is positive and health oriented (salutogenic), rather than symptom focused (pathogenic). This reflects broader trends in adolescent health that see this as a time of great potential with both the adolescent brain and body peaking in capacity (Epstein, 2007). Adolescence is a complicated time for these reasons, but rather than adopting a conservative approach based on managing the Sturm und Drang of adolescence, a focus on resources and healthy development is more appropriate (Rolvsjord, 2010). Hip-Hop may be seen as such a resource.

In the remainder of this chapter, I will examine the lyrics of two very different young men whose affinity with the genre of Hip-Hop was used as a resource. Each young man will be described and located in his unique personal, cultural, and systemic context before a search for parallels with the literature is undertaken for each. Following this important assertion of their individual identities, the lyrics composed for their rap songs will be considered in relation to the themes of relationship dynamics, identity formation, and aspirations. Differences and similarities based on gender, needs, and cultural background will be discussed.

Working with Joel

I met and worked with Joel in a 10-week music therapy group at a school that had been devastated by bush fires 6 months earlier. Joel was part of a group of six Caucasian students who were 15–16 years old, and one of the three young men who attended the group diligently. Joel was the loudest in the group and was challenging initially—cracking jokes and teasing other group members, and frequently jumping on the kit and smashing the drums very loudly when the rest of the group was in discussion. Our attitude* toward Joel in the early sessions was led by the reaction of the other students, who seemed to accept his need for attention and to find him amusing rather than being frustrated by his behavior. Joel expressed an interest in Hip-Hop music on a number of occasions and I encouraged this, noting that he was the only one of all the young people we worked with in this school who was interested in this genre. In Week 2, I played him a *Hill-Top Hoods* track on my iPod and he listened to it, but didn't engage with me in a focused discussion afterward. In Week 3, we were doing group songwriting with the other members and Joel was hanging around the outside of the group, distracting us occasionally with a story. Suddenly, he pulled me aside and asked if I had a piece of paper and a pen. I obliged and he went to sit at a table at the back of the room. He sat there for the next 30 minutes before returning to the group and pulling me aside again. "Look at this," he whispered. "What do you think?"

The rap song that Joel began writing that day continued to emerge over the next few weeks and was created solely within the confines of the group meeting times, although Joel would sometimes arrive with lyrics memorized that he simply wanted to write down. The lyrics of his song were as follows:

We Were BB

Verse 1:

Man I miss those Friday nights
when we used to get drunk and get into those fights
Despite the fact
that we made a pact
never to think about death

---

* This work was co-facilitated with a colleague, Kate Teggelove RMT.

till we took our last breath
Man it's crazy, why do I miss you so much
now your grave is growing daisies
I remember the last punch when we used to muck around
and we went to the "lost and found"
coz we thought we lost our mate
but really it was only fate
You left us with a wound
now you're locked inside a tomb

We were BB it was fucken sweet,
you guys were my brothers now I have to live for two others

I remember the last time
when we listened to those rhymes
We missed him so much
but when it came to the crunch
we just missed the three of us
And when we used to kick up a fuss,
coz we wanted a toke
but we only had a couple of smokes
And now there's two
can it be true
Now I'm stuck with these mates
and I'm scared of their fates
Now you've passed
you're locked inside a caste
never being able to take your last breath
and only hope you didn't think of death
So Rest in Peace
you won't need to see the police
ever again

We were BB it was fucken sweet,
you guys were my brothers now I need to live for two others

So there's only one
and it aint gonna be fun,
I'm dealing with all these feelings and I'm trying to express
but also trying to impress
all my mates
but I'm full of hate
Still feel crappy
and I can't be happy
knowing that my best mates are gone

hope they've got reborn
I'm living in a desperate life
hoping that I'll settle down and find a wife
I'll always remember that crown that we had
Just so you know, I miss you so bad

We were BB it was fucken sweet,
you guys were my brothers now I need to live for two others

Similarly to many of the young people we worked with during those weeks, the traumatic impact of the bush fires were not the only challenges being faced. For most of the group members, the fires had added to a situation that was already complicated. By the end of the group process we were able to understand that Joel was describing his "Best Buddies"—BB. One of the trio had died in a reckless accident some months prior to the fires and Joel attempts to separate out the stages of loss in the rap, as first the BB are "only two" and then, tragically, he is left alone when the second young man is killed in the fires.

It is worth emphasizing that Joel did not articulate this story at any point in the group, but each time he created a new verse he would bring it to me and sit beside me as I read through it. I would then compliment him on the rhythmic qualities of the lyrics and comment on the intensity of the situation being described. The verses did not appear in order, and the lyric lines were not always clear before being edited and placed in the context of the whole song. I did not know who or what BB was for most of the time we worked together, and it was only by the conclusion of this process that I had a sense of Joel's whole journey. Direct probes usually resulted in nonverbal responses. For example, one time I asked, "Are you talking about someone who died here?" and Joel responded with a very serious nod. He obviously felt that he was communicating to me through the lyrics and was both satisfied and comfortable with that. I did offer to rap the lyrics to the group on a number of occasions, and Joel agreed, but was not willing to do it himself. The group would compliment him for the lyrics on these occasions and he appeared proud of his achievements.

Once the song seemed to be complete, I brought my PC laptop to the sixth session and introduced Joel to Sony ACID Music Studio 6.0. ACID software is user-friendly and contains a good number of prerecorded beats that can be looped and used as the background for Hip-Hop tracks. I spent around 10 minutes explaining the mechanisms of the program to Joel and another young man in the group and then left them to play with it while I worked with other group members who were also composing their own songs. This stage in the group process was marked by individual projects, perhaps influenced by Joel's initial decision to "go it alone." I noticed the young men leave the room about 5 minutes later, and when I followed them to make sure they were not breaking any school rules, I found them huddled over the computer at an outside table. "It was too loud in there," they insisted, so I left them to it. By the end of the following session, Joel had recorded his track onto my computer. I had spent another 10 minutes with them that day, helping to attach a Sony mini condenser microphone to the computer and showing them how to record into another line of the track. Joel played the song for the group, and the group also played their songs for him. We decided to make a CD.

Working toward the recording of a CD can be a complicated process, and in this project we decided to focus on achieving a quality recording. A community musician became involved in the project and took responsibility for the production of the CD while we continued to work with the emerging content of songs and the personal issues that surfaced in terms of group dynamics and individual needs. After some discussion, Joel agreed to remove the swearing from his song in order for it to be included on the compilation CD of songs written by all the young people in the program. We also recorded a single version for him that included the swearing. In the final week of sessions we were discussing a way of launching the CD and Joel offered to host the launch at his father's pub.* From his initial presentation as someone unable to engage in the group process, he had slowly matured to take on a significant leadership role and was willing to take responsibility for the group and its achievements.

Relationship Dynamics

The rap song describes a tight-knit friendship between three teenage boys. It is the tale of love and loss, in typically male adolescent terms. There are references to intimacy, or play-fighting, as seen in the lyric "I remember the last punch." When probed, Joel explained that they used to "muck around" a lot, a response that was later included in the lyrics. In response to further queries, he reassured me that usually this was not violent, but rather physical expression—they were having fun. These descriptors of their friendship as it existed before the sequence of losses contrasts sharply with the emotional commentary offered by Joel when reflecting on his continuing connection with his deceased friends. He speaks clearly to the young men, directing the story to them, as if to let them know what has been going on. The last line is poignant: "Just so you know, I miss you so bad."

---

* Which the school agreed to do after establishing some limitations in regard to having an alcohol free room for the event.

Identity Formation

There are a plethora of references to typical adolescent rebellion within the lyrics of this rap song. At a cognitive level, adolescence is known as a time of risk-taking, with many young people having a poor sense of the potential ramifications of dangerous behavior. Psychosocially, identity formation occurs through a process of differentiation from parents, and this often involves young people attempting "adult" behaviors themselves. The descriptions of substance use in the form of smoking ("wanted a toke, but just had a smoke") and alcohol ("used to get drunk") are proudly touted, and the explicit language in the original version also serves a similar process. "Friday nights" are recalled as an important opportunity for fun-filled and somewhat dangerous social encounters, with the usual adolescent experimentations. This young man is asserting his identity as daring, energetic, and defiant. Reference to these kinds of behaviors fits well within the Hip-Hop genre, with its emphasis on rebellious attitudes and illustrating the strength of the individual rap-artist. Joel shows an awareness of this function, clearly stating that he is trying to "impress his mates." This kind of transparency is also popular in Hip-Hop, particularly in the work of White artist Eminem.

Aspirations

This rap song focuses most powerfully on the past rather than anticipating the future. Rap provides a forum for storytelling that lends itself to these kinds of action-based reflections. Nonetheless, some aspirations are described in the more hopeful moments of the lyrics. Most conspicuous is the expression of a desire to "settle down and find a wife," and during the project Joel did become involved with one of the young women in the group, proudly flaunting their relationship by holding hands and cuddling. The reference to new mates confirms the continuing focus on relationship building and emphasizes the importance of connectedness to the future of this young man.

Working with Raheem

Raheem was a 17-year-old Sudanese refugee who joined the media-arts program halfway through the year. The program was designed to support youth who had lost their connection with the traditional education system, providing innovative and supportive programming to reengage young people with learning and career opportunities. When Raheem learned that I was a musician and that I was there to help people record tracks, he approached me immediately. "I want to be a famous rap artist. I have some songs. Will you help me?" I was hesitant to collude in developing a fantasy about achieving fame with this young man and I qualified my acceptance of his request by emphasizing the difficulties of making a living from being a rap star. Raheem's English language comprehension and expression were both quite poor, and as I tried to explain myself in simpler language I realized that it was more important to reach out to this young man than to defend against impossible goals. I asked Raheem to show me the lyrics he had written and he reached into his bag and pulled out a piece of paper. The words to his first song are presented below, although at the time I found it difficult to understand his writing. After spending some time examining the paper, I asked him to rap the lyrics to me and he launched immediately into the song. It was well rehearsed and precise according to an internal sense of timing, and yet the tempo changed considerably and frequently, making it impossible to beat-box with or tap along to. I praised Raheem for his confident performance and his use of language and we agreed to work in the studio the next week to begin recording his work.

Bitter Sweet Life

Bitter sweet life, believe me, life is bitter sweet

You beware, I'm gonna tell about my shadow
When God lived on earth, people broke his windows
His peasants lied down in his house
You got to respect, fine,
Looking at me, my way, down town,
Summer town
Shadow looming, the thing, you don't like is me

You accept this thing in life
When it hurts, it cuts you like a knife
We spend hours of life just around the corner
Fingers in a glove, comes with warning

Don't shit on me
Never bullshit me
You've got to respect my right to be free
Some things are evil of mankind
When I lean my head I can feel it in my heart
Life no promise, it's shame someone gotta die
Live your life like you gonna win

You told me son, this is my time
I don't feel ashamed
I see life from different angles
I don't know from God it's sent
Or if it's all sin

Bitter sweet life, believe me, life is bitter sweet

When the next week arrived, the studio was booked out and Raheem and I chatted for a while before I suggested that we could prepare for our turn by using hand drums to practice rhythms. I passed a standing Klong Yaw to Raheem and began to play a simple, traditional African rhythm on a doumbek. He echoed my rhythm immediately and we began to take turns playing short simple patterns back and forth. The tempo was still fluctuating, and if I offered more complex rhythmic patterns, Raheem would simply ignore them and repeat the previous pattern. We played together for nearly 90 minutes on this day, passing rhythms backward and forward. I stopped on three occasions to provide positive feedback and asked open questions about being willing to keep playing. On each occasion, he responded briefly and began playing again immediately after I offered another pattern.

The following week we were more successful in pushing our way into the studio, and we took the drums in with us. I played a repeating beat and encouraged Raheem to clap along with me initially, and then to try to tap while he read his rap in time with the beat. This strategy was somewhat successful and Raheem began to develop a greater connection with an external rhythm than previously. Over the next few weeks, we experimented with different preprogrammed beats on the user-friendly Mac software "Garage Band" and practiced recording with, and without, the drums playing. Raheem's attention span was short and he was not interested in taking control of the computer keyboard or in spending too much time refining details. It was clear that he wanted to record his lyrics over a beat and to take the burned CDs with him. He had written a number of raps, and we focused on three over a 15-week period. The other two were love songs ("Don't Die on Me" and "Low Mamma") and described his feelings for a woman he was courting. Although the words were distinct, the creative process was similar for each of the tracks. We worked hard to establish a sense of rhythm and listening to improve the sound of the raps, an important consideration for a young man who was planning to share his material with others.

As the rhythm of Raheem's rapping improved, he was more able to participate in the studio at an equal level with his peers. Although his grasp of English as a second language meant that spontaneous rap battles were too difficult to attempt, he was able to play his own recordings to the other young men and garner some respect from them. The lyrics were hard to understand for the others, and for myself, but it was clear that there was intensity and religion in his material and both of these elements meant that he was addressing new topics for the group. I was focused on assisting him to integrate with his peers and used the live music element to capture their attention. One of the other young men could play piano, and I invited him to record a version of Pachelbel's Canon along with a backing beat that Raheem then rapped over the top of. This meant that the shared studio time was focused on Raheem's material and that he played a central role in some of the encounters with his peers. By the end of the year, Raheem was happy with the three tracks and used one as the basis of his video-media project.

Relationship Dynamics

The lyrics for "Bitter Sweet Life" reflect on a number of important relationships in Raheem's life. The role of God is central in his considerations, and this appears to be a traditional relationship grounded in understandings from the Bible and of following in the steps of God ("When God lived on earth, people broke his windows"). This sense of worship is sharply juxtaposed against his assertive nature with "the other/s" being referred to in the lyrics ("You've got to respect my right to be free"), and his contemplation of violence within that ("Fingers in a glove, comes with a warning"). The two other love songs that Raheem worked on were almost exclusively focused on relationship dynamics, primarily describing the beautiful qualities of the woman protagonist and how this made him feel, both physically and emotionally.

Identity Formation

The group of young men who attended the program was culturally diverse, but mostly of European or Asian descent, whereas Raheem was the only African man in the group. Hip-Hop was a shared interest of all the group members, and therefore having dark skin was an advantage for Raheem within the group of young men who admired and identified with African American artists such as 2-Pac and Kanye West. However, his challenges with language were significant and it was often difficult to feel clear about the content of conversations. The lyric material above was spoken with a strong accent and therefore the potent life circumstances and existential reflections that Raheem seems to be offering were not always understood. Nonetheless, the intensity with which he spoke and his determination to rehearse and record his songs conveyed a similar attitude to those portrayed in the lyrics. Raheem asserted his personality into a complex group dynamic of these dissociated young men, many of whom struggled with attention and behavioral problems and were not simple to engage. Hip-Hop provided a different kind of cultural bridge for him to connect with the group, and this affiliation meant that his participation was not questioned by the others.

Aspirations

The lyrics of "Bitter Sweet Life" are more retrospective than prospective, but they do speak to Raheem's aspirations. The words attempt to make meaning out of a complex situation, which seems to be based on encounters with violence ("Life no promise, it's shame someone gotta die") and exclusion ("You got to respect, fine, Looking at me, my way"). Yet Raheem is focused on moving forward, gathering strength from his reflections that even God was treated badly during his time on earth, and focusing on a positive future ("Live your life like you gonna win"). He uses all of his songs to outline the life he wants, not the life he is actually living.

Discussion

There is some overlap with the main themes identified in the (mostly R&B) songs of young women with disordered eating and the raps written by these two young men struggling with the expectations of the school system. The clearest overlap is the prominent focus on *relationship dynamics*. Although the young women were mostly discussing parental relationships (McFerran, Baker, Kildea, Patton, & Sawyer, 2008), these young men are discussing other forms of significant relationships—best friends and God. There is some intersection between references to relationship dynamics and identity formation, since peer relationships in particular are an important part of establishing an independent sense of self.

This striving for independence as a strategy of *identity formation* is not just apparent in the lyrics; it was also a prominent aspect of the songwriting process selected by the young men. In both cases, I was presented with completed sets of lyrics that had already been rehearsed privately and were rhythmically predetermined. This independence may be related to the choice of genre. Many authors argue that choosing, for example, "isolating" music reflects a sense of feeling isolated, rather than results in feeling isolated (Roe, 1987). This contrasts with the causative influence sometimes proposed by commentators. What is clear from these two individual examples is that writing rap songs feels *accessible* and inspires these young men with *confidence* to tell their story. Rap artists are renowned for "keepin' it real," and these young men had real stories to tell and utilized the depth of their losses to enhance the credibility of their material. The possibility of expressing their personal and existential grief in words is further underpinned by their personal belief that they could rap. Paul Edwards (2009) suggests that the three defining features of rap are content, flow, and delivery. In both cases, the content and delivery were strong, despite their challenges to stay on a consistent beat. Neither had an overt connection with external rhythms, yet their internal rhythm was so strong that they were sure they had flow, and in the context of music therapy this perception is valued as the basis for growth.

In addition to an inclination to write and perform rap songs, these two young men share some other features. Gender is one important influence; socioeconomic status is another. Although Raheem was a recent refugee, he was living with family members in a house in the outer suburbs of the city. Joel's family lived in a small country town and owned the local pub, making a living, but possibly not a large profit. These young men were isolated from their peers—both due to the loss of their previous social network, although the specific nature of their situations is distinct. Both young men seemed to be focused on meaning-making, trying to process their experiences, and to move toward a better life. The relative lack of reference to *aspirations* provides the greatest contrast with the songs written by the young women with disordered eating. Instead of the sometimes fantastical aspirations outlined in the previous study, these young men combined aggression, emotion, and existential contemplation in their lyrics. They moved smoothly between descriptions of violence and descriptions of love—for a wife, friends, or God. This may be fueled by testosterone, or it may be that the intensity of their life experiences is a part of what draws them to the rap genre. Although there has been some investigation of links between rap and aggression, more exploratory investigations that incorporate the perspectives of the young people would be valuable. In neither case did their involvement in writing rap songs lead to an increase in their levels of aggression; instead it led to greater connectedness with peers and more prominent and positive roles within their networks.

A lack of verbal processing was another shared characteristic of the music therapy work with these two young men. The intensity with which both of them handed me their lyrics suggested a strong desire to communicate, and the material they alluded to was personal and challenging. However, neither of the young men responded with much detail to probes or attempts to extend conversations around the content of their songs or their current lives. The level of rapport between us felt strong and both expressed a desire for further music therapy when our interactions came to a natural close due to school holidays or the end of the project. The contrast between their ability to express themselves in rap and in conversation is striking.

Conclusion

The major themes identified in a prior analysis of lyrics written by adolescent music therapy clients have been considered in relation to two rap songs. Although the context for the young women with disordered eating and the two young men struggling with the school system are very different, their focus is reasonably similar. A review of the music therapy literature predicts such a conclusion, with music therapists regularly addressing goals related to identity formation (where aspirations could also be categorized) and social connectedness (including relationship dynamics) rather than symptom specific objectives.

Some striking differences have emerged, however. The choice of musical genre is the most obvious, with the young women predominantly choosing to write R&B songs, while the young men described here have elected to use a Hip-Hop framework and have focused on writing rap lyrics. Both styles rely heavily on looping (repeating) backing beats, although melody often plays a more dominant role in R&B than rapping. The image of Hip-Hop is more streetwise and reflects the real-life contexts of the young men compared to the more protected lives of the young women with disordered eating who were institutionalized at the time of the songwriting. A musical reflection of these different contexts is also apparent in their sense of rhythm. Both these young men struggled with achieving a regularity in tempo and their connection to an external beat was initially tenuous. The young women, in contrast, were more likely to be rigidly in time, lacking any flexibility in their use of rhythmic shape and style. Music therapists expect to see reflections of pathology in the music making of clients, and Rickson (2006) used improvements in the steadiness of rhythm as an indicator of outcome in her study of young men with ADHD. However, it is rare to reflect on the function of internal and external rhythm in the context of songwriting and further exploration is recommended, particularly in relation to genres such as Hip-Hop in which rhythmic flexibility and stability are both central.

References

Anderson, C., Carnagey, N., & Eubanks, J. (2003). Exposure to violent media: The effects of songs with violent lyrics on aggressive thoughts and feelings. *Journal of Personality and Social Psychology, 84*(5), 960–971.

Becker, C. S. (1992). *Living and relating: An introduction to phenomenology.* Thousand Oaks, CA: Sage.

Edwards, P. (2009). *How to rap: The art and science of the Hip-Hop MC.* Chicago: Chicago Review Press.

Epstein, R. (2007). *The case against adolescence: Rediscovering the adult in every teen.* Sanger, CA: Quill Driver.

Frith, S. (1981). *Sound effects: Youth, leisure and the politics of rock 'n roll.* New York: Pantheon.

Gold, C., Saarikallio, S., & McFerran, K. (2011). Music therapy. In R. J. R. Levesque (Ed.), *Encyclopedia of adolescence.* New York: Springer.

Lacourse, E., Claes, M., & Villeneuve, M. (2001). Heavy metal music and adolescent suicide risk. *Journal of Youth and Adolescence, 30*(3), 321–332.

Mark, A. (1988). Metaphoric lyrics as a bridge to the adolescent's world. *Adolescence, 23*(90), 313–323.

McFerran, K. (2004). Using songs with groups of teenagers: How does it work? *Social Work with Groups, 27*(2/3), 143–157.

McFerran, K. (2010a). *Adolescents, music and music therapy: Methods and techniques for clinicians, educators and students.* London: Jessica Kingsley.

McFerran, K. (2010b). Tipping the scales: A substantive theory on the value of group music therapy for supporting grieving teenagers. *Qualitative Inquiries in Music Therapy (A Monograph Series), 5,* 2–49.

McFerran, K., Baker, F., Kildea, C., Patton, G., & Sawyer, S. M. (2008). Avoiding conflict: What do adolescents with disordered eating say about their mothers in music therapy? *British Journal of Music Therapy, 22*(1), 16–23.

McFerran, K., Baker, F., Patton, G., & Sawyer, S. M. (2006). A retrospective lyrical analysis of songs written by adolescents with anorexia nervosa. *European Eating Disorder Review, 14,* 397–403.

North, A. C., & Hargreaves, D. J. (2005). Brief report: Labelling effects on the perceived deleterious consequences of pop music listening. *Journal of Adolescence, 28,* 433–440.

Poole, M. (1994). Australia. In K. Hurrelman (Ed.), *International handbook of adolescence* (pp. 31–50). London: Greenwood Press.

Rickson, D. J. (2006). Instructional and improvisational models of music therapy with adolescents who have attention deficit hyperactivity disorder (ADHD): A comparison of the effects on motor impulsivity. *Journal of Music Therapy, 43*(1), 39–62.

Roe, K. (1987). The school and music in adolescent socialisation. In J. Lull (Ed.), *Pop music and communication* (pp. 212–230). Thousand Oaks, CA: Sage.

Rolvsjord, R. (2010). *Resource oriented music therapy in mental health care.* Gilsum, NH: Barcelona.

Rustad, R. A., Small, J. E., Jobes, D. A., Safer, M. A., & Peterson, R. J. (2003). The impact of rock videos and music with suicidal content on thoughts and attitudes about suicide. *Suicide & Life-Threatening Behaviour, 33*(2), 120–131.

Ruud, E. (1997). Music and identity. *Nordic Journal of Music Therapy, 6*(1), 3–13.

Saarikallio, S., & Erkkila, J. (2007). The role of music in adolescents' mood regulation. *Psychology of Music, 35*(1), 88–109.

Scheel, K. R., & Westefeld, J. S. (1999). Heavy metal music and adolescent suicidality: An empirical investigation. *Adolescence, 34*(134), 253–273.

Stack, S., Gundlach, J., & Reeves, J. L. (1994). The heavy metal subculture and suicide. *Suicide and Life-Threatening Behavior, 24*, 15–23.

Tarrant, M., North, A. C., & Hargreaves, D. J. (2001). Social categorization, self-esteem and the estimated musical preferences of male adolescents. *The Journal of Social Psychology, 141*(5), 565–581.

Chapter 11

Naming My Story and Claiming My Self

Mandana Ahmadi and Helen Oosthuizen

Introduction

One of the things that struck me when I* first started working as a music therapist at a school in Heideveld was the seemingly never ceasing sound. Children call out to one another, voicing their opinions freely and strongly; there are sounds of laughter, teachers shouting (rather loudly), balls bouncing along the corridors. Community members residing in small tenement buildings or houses neighboring the school add to the sounds as they greet one another (loudly), or perhaps engage in a heated argument outside a local shebeen.† Cars and donkey carts pass by on the roads surrounding the school. The sounds of domestic life, of a vibrant, energetic community, are amplified by the close proximity of living quarters and the large number of unemployed people spending their days on the streets that wind through the community. The community sounds are continually permeated with music. Children seem to come out of the womb already drumming or "kap-ping the drums" as they call it. Music abounds in school corridors, on desks in the classroom, with boys, for the most part, using pencils, sticks, or just

---

* This chapter refers to clinical work conducted by Mandana Ahmadi.
† A liquor store in a township.

their hands to beat out Kaapse Klopse* rhythms with which everybody is familiar. Adding to this spontaneous music-making, the latest 50 Cent or Black Eyed Peas tracks can often be heard blasting out from cars and taxis. As they pass the school, groups of children eagerly join in with the music, reciting all the words and sometimes adding their own break dances as well.

As an introvert and someone who has grown up in a culture that places much value on personal space and privacy, at times I feel bombarded by sound, and crave some silent time to reflect and process my thoughts. People within this community embody a culture that is celebratory, expressive, and outgoing, which has been quite something for me to get used to. In Heideveld, sound is perhaps a creative coping mechanism for the reality of living in a disenfranchised and politically voiceless community. Perhaps music drowns out the despair felt by the community and transforms it into a thing of beauty, into something that animates and energizes people. The sounds shout out, "This is who we are. This is the story that we want to tell. This is Heideveld."

Context: Heideveld

One of the lingering side effects of the Group Areas Act of the apartheid regime is the segregated housing in the form of townships assigned to different racial groups in the city of Cape Town, South Africa. The city was planned in such a way that the most scenic and therefore valued areas were allocated to the White population, which was politically dominant during apartheid. Less attractive and barren areas, most of which are some distance away from the city center, were earmarked for the marginalized Xhosa and "Colored†" population groups. Heideveld, one such "Colored" township, forms the backdrop for the work described in this chapter.

Although the violent and oppressive apartheid regime was abolished over 15 years ago, the oppression was replaced by violence that occurs on

---

* Kaapse Klopse are minstrel bands associated with so-called Colored cultural groups and comprise a cross section of community members from young boys to men. The origins of the Kaapse Klopse date back to the Civil War in America, when many White performers blackened their faces and wore bright costumes to impersonate African American slave minstrels (Hutchinson, 2006). When introduced in Cape Town, this idea became very popular. Performers dress in colorful carnival costumes and perform annually at parades, competing against other bands. Some troupes still blacken or paint their faces. While some initially felt this made a mockery of Black people, it has become a symbol of pride for "Colored" people in Cape Town.

† South Africans use the non-derogatory term Colored to refer to "people of color"—a group of the population that includes Cape Malay and Khoisan people, and those with mixed racial lineage—thus all those who, according to the system of apartheid, were not classified as either Black or White, Asian or Indian.

two levels, the first of which is continuous and nonspecific. This form of violence manifests in Heideveld through poverty and unemployment, inadequate access to medical facilities, under-resourced educational services, and neglect of children (Pavlicevic in Sutton, 2002) by adults who may themselves be grappling with personal issues. As a result of these stressors, a second form of violence emerges. There is a strong presence of gang activity, high levels of violence and criminal activity, sexual and physical abuse, drug and alcohol abuse, disintegration of families, large numbers of school dropouts, and high teenage pregnancy rates. Sociopolitical imbalances contributing to the above-mentioned stressors feed into a vicious cycle that results from and also leads to a community defined by a sense of apathy and disempowerment, which negatively affects children and youth by eroding their sense of self-worth, diminishing their sense of agency, and tarnishing their hopes and dreams for the future. When already vulnerable children and youth fall prey to a specific traumatic or violent event such as abuse or death of a close family member, this experience further contributes to a "sense of loss of security" as well as to "an intense feeling of powerlessness" (Sutton, 2002, p. 31). Psychosocial support in the area is limited, meaning that children and youth rarely have the opportunity to process trauma. Unfortunately, evidence suggests that unless victims of violence receive some sort of therapeutic intervention, they themselves are at risk of becoming perpetrators of violence (Camilleri, 2007).

In the midst of the sounds of Heideveld, there are sounds of celebration and joy, but also of despair, pain, and hopelessness. It is important that these other voices are also given space to be heard and acknowledged.

The Music Therapy Community Clinic in Heideveld

It was in Heideveld, in 2004, that the Music Therapy Community Clinic, a nonprofit organization (NPO) offering music therapy services to under-resourced communities who cannot otherwise afford these services, began its first project: the Heideveld Music Therapy Project. Music-making in Heideveld offers the community a valuable resource for drawing together and celebrating the community's identity and vibrancy. Thus it seemed a natural progression for the Music Therapy Community Clinic (MTCC) to establish a music therapy program to cater to the needs of the multitude of young people referred by teachers from a number of schools in the community for reasons including exposure to violence, abuse, death in the family, parent(s) in jail, aggression, or withdrawal. Although these children are mostly "Colored," this group includes Xhosa children who travel from the nearby Xhosa townships to attend school in Heideveld. Thus, a mixed group of children from different gang territories and schools, and from different race groups, joined together in our music therapy room with two things in common—their stories of trauma and for the most part their love for music.

What follows is a case study of one of the groups I recently worked with, where each boy ended up composing his own rap as a major part of the therapy process. This case study powerfully indicates how by writing their own raps, the boys were able to tell their stories; how refining raps helped the boys to process events in their lives and explore a new, positive identity; and how performing raps enabled the boys to voice their stories to others and to be heard.

The Group

Most of the music therapy work we do in Heideveld is group work, as members of a group with similar referrals offer some support to one another, thus helping individuals to feel safer about bringing their stories and lives into the therapy room. Groups usually attend an average of 14 sessions of music therapy. Music therapists run groups either as a team serving as therapist and co-therapist, or together with "music therapy assistants." The latter are members from similar communities to Heideveld who have some musical background, and whom the MTCC has trained to assist with managing sometimes challenging group dynamics or providing translation if required (children in Heideveld schools may speak English, Afrikaans, or Xhosa as a first language).

Nokuzola,* my Xhosa music therapy assistant, helped me to run this group consisting of four 12- to 14-year-old boys from different schools, who were all referred for the loss of a loved one. I had very little information about the ways in which the loss of a loved one had affected these boys as a result of referral forms that had a paucity of background information. All I gathered was that Adrian had a parent in jail and was playing truant; Nathan had spent much of his life in children's homes and held a lot of anger inside him, sometimes disregarding authority; and Mark was described as demonstrating violent behavior. The only information I had for Sandile was that his mother had recently passed away.

Sandile was a Xhosa boy, Adrian and Mark were "Colored," and Nathan was White. I am highlighting the racial and cultural diversity of the group because of the complicated dynamics that this would normally generate, particularly in a community like Heideveld. Although Xhosa children attend school in Heideveld, it is quite unusual for the different cultural groups to mix because of racial tensions stemming from apartheid.

---

* All names of clients and coworkers have been changed to protect their privacy and safeguard confidentiality.

Nathan was attending a school for young people who have had interrupted schooling because of unstable home situations and was not a resident of Heideveld. Politically, White people have typically been born into privilege. This unearned privilege tends to bring with it a sense of superiority and thus some White people may alienate themselves from other cultural groups and simultaneously may be despised by these other less privileged cultural groups. However, Nathan's life experiences, his socioeconomic status, as well as his accent and mannerisms were culturally very similar to those of his "Colored" counterparts, enabling group members to relate to him and to establish a form of trust. Nathan's participation in our group did stand out as it very quickly became apparent that he had powerful leadership skills. However, the leadership roles he took on within the group seemed less a result of his White identity, but more due to his confidence and his willingness to invest in the music therapy process and to share important details of his life that others could relate to. Examples of how Nathan galvanized the participation of other group members will become clear shortly.

Telling My Story

Session 1: Drumming

Three boys enter the music therapy space. The session begins with a greeting ritual in the form of a drumming activity, with each boy introducing himself by offering the group a different short, rhythmic sequence while I play the piano in accompaniment. The energy of the group is low. The boys appear awkward, looking at one another, playing softly, tentatively. I wonder whether these boys think that music therapy is a very serious activity so they had better behave, or perhaps they feel they are being punished by being sent here. Maybe they are apprehensive of me. Will I despise them as some others in positions of authority have done in the past? Will I understand them, their actions, their stories, their pain? Why are they here?

I join the circle to do some more drumming after the greeting ritual. I demonstrate a beat and get the boys to mirror it back. Each boy in turn gets a chance to lead a beat that the others reflect back. We are laying the groundwork for each person to voice himself in his own unique way, to be heard, and to have his ideas reflected back by others. This will also feature later in the process of writing and performing raps. During the activity, Nathan enters the room, late, and instantly tries to draw attention to himself by joking around. I suspect it is to cover up his initial discomfort of joining the group, which already appears to be cohesive. He needs to find a way to feel included. I offer a brief opportunity for group members to introduce themselves to one another and then quickly carry on with the activity, feeling that I would rather help Nathan experience a sense of belonging through participating in the music than by letting him dominate the session. After the activity Nathan pulls up his shirt to show the group the scars from his stab wounds and uses this to begin to tell his story. Not a nice, pretty story, but a story he wants others to hear, a story he needs to tell.

Nathan offered me a clear idea of the direction this group needed to take. Each boy in this group, it seemed, needed a space to verbalize his story of loss, to allow others in the group to know and to share his burden of pain. Due to the ongoing trauma in Heideveld experienced by practically all community members, children learn to "suck it up," not feeling entitled to experience the luxury of sharing their pain with others who might themselves be going through their own challenges. In such a close-knit community where people live in such close proximity and know their neighbor's business, it might also be difficult to know who you can trust with stories that might make you feel vulnerable. For these boys, this music therapy group may be the only space where they would be able to feel safe enough to share and reflect on their stories.

As not all group members were completely comfortable with sharing with the group immediately, I decided to begin with a free word association activity to initiate this "storytelling" process. I have often found it useful to hear a group's spontaneously offered words, as a complementary method of mapping a more complete picture of my clients in addition to them sounding themselves through music. Some of the young people I have worked with possess greater confidence expressing themselves verbally. In such instances, using music in isolation limits expression. Hearing a person's music and words helps me to direct my clinical compass.

Session 1: Word Association

I begin by introducing a short, repeated rhythmic motive on my drum, with a rest between each repetition. I play the sequence until the whole group is playing together, beating, then resting as one unit. Then I add a word in the first rest: "music." I indicate that Adrian, who is sitting next to me, should similarly offer a word of his own during the next rest. He hesitates, then offers: "Happy." Slowly, between drumbeats, words begin to flow from the group, all held within the phrasing of the music. As Nathan takes his second turn, he changes the tone of the activity. "Gangs," he says. Mark, sitting next to him, continues: "Fighting." And Sandile: "Drugs." The group becomes more animated; it is clear they are connecting with the activity. They are talking about life in Heideveld ... their lives.

The activity comes to an end. I fetch a large sheet of newsprint paper, and ask the boys to call out words they heard during the activity. I write them down randomly on the page and guide the boys to group the words into the categories of "emotions," "family," and "what they know about where they live." I sense immediately that these are important ideas being offered and that group members are keen to share more. I want to encourage this and so suggest that we write a rap together as a group. The response is immediate and shared by all group members—yes, they would love to write a rap.

The offer to write a rap changed the energy of all in the group almost instantly. From a tentative group of boys indicating apprehension or even negativity toward the music therapy process, the boys were ready and eager to become a part of this process.

Music is exceptionally important to young people and forms a large part of their lives (North & Hargreaves, 2000). Although active music-making in the Heideveld community predominantly revolves around the Kaapse Klopse bands, which arrange popular tunes, many young people also enjoy listening to rap music. Rap music appeals particularly to the older boys we see, from age 10 upward. It may be the strong beat or the way that rap music often incorporates loud city sounds—something very familiar in Heideveld—that draws these boys to the music. It is also the ability of the rappers to account stories artfully of violence and gang fights, drugs, and sex in a powerfully poetic, musical form that gives the music its appeal. These boys can relate; they understand. There are rap artists who have experienced life as they have, who depict "ghettoes" not unlike Heideveld, and who can offer them a sense of remaining strong, rising above their circumstances, and looking to the future with hope (Kubrin, 2005).

The use of rap in therapy sessions has been meaningful and profound for many of these young people. While we may occasionally play a well-known rap song in a session to encourage some discussion or practice our own rendition of a song, many of the children have their own stories to tell and are eager to create their own raps. I felt that the form of a rap may help the boys in this group to share what they needed to without feeling too vulnerable, and may also help them to order and thus reflect on their thoughts more deeply. Using rap artists as examples for these boys is helpful because they are able to detail stories of pain, confusion, and loss, but still hold images of being strong male figures, suggesting that sharing your pain with others is not a weakness. If the rap artists so highly regarded by this group are able to share such personal stories through their work, these boys could now do the same. The rhythmic, musical flow of raps could also offer the group a way of telling their stories that would enable these stories to embody all the emotional quality that telling them would require (Laiho, 2004). Anger could be expressed through the hardness of a beat or the sharpness of lines rapped out. Sadness might be expressed through a short pause within a flowing rap, or a slowing down of a beat-box. Further, by writing their own raps, these boys could work as artists; their stories would become valuable, aesthetic, musical products, which is a stark contrast to the many disappointments some of these boys have faced in their lives.

I am not much of a "rapper"; my inability to relate to the often hard-edged lyrics inhibits my ability to rap with "attitude" and I sound more like a schoolchild reciting a nursery rhyme. And yet, the opportunity to write a rap has grabbed the attention and interest of these boys in a way that our drumming, and perhaps many other activities I may prefer in terms of my own aesthetic tastes, has not. Placing the need of young people to use rap to express themselves at the forefront supersedes any insecurities I might have about my limitations to use this art form. My less than convincing rapping compels me to support the process in other ways—namely facilitating the emergence of stories or structuring raps where needed, among other things. I have often found that the process of enabling boys to write raps encourages them to support one another with some beat-boxing, rhythms, additional lines, or even a break-dance. Thus the boys in the group are encouraged to support and accompany one another as they tell their stories.

Although the initial ideas generated through the word association activity were not directly related to their reason for referral, namely the loss of a loved one, I decided to see where the writing of a rap based on spontaneous contributions might lead the group process.

Session 2

Only Adrian and Sandile are present. After our greeting, I start to write down the boys' observations of what they witness and experience in their communities as raw material for the group rap. Ideas that keep resurfacing include drug abuse and violence. This opens a space for Adrian and Sandile to begin to talk, sharing openly about loved ones they have lost through violence and illness. Adrian explains how his father shot his mother. Sandile, who also lost his mother, demonstrates great inner strength, drawing on his belief in the afterlife and his continued relationship with his mother's spirit as he talks about her death. As I listen to these painful stories, I am aware that the specific traumatic event for which the boys were referred to music therapy is intricately linked with the continuous and nonspecific violence that they experience on a daily basis.

The boys, perhaps longing that each one have his own stories documented and expressed through music, then ask whether it will be possible for them to work on their own verses for the rap rather than creating a group product. As we think about how to go about this, Sandile asks if he can write his rap in Xhosa—but shows some ambivalence about this request. He explains that he wants to express himself in his home language, but at the same time he wants very much to be heard and understood when he performs his rap for me and the other group members, who do not speak Xhosa. I feel that it is important for Sandile to be able to express himself in his own language. We decide that he can work with Nokuzola in Xhosa, and later he can translate his rap for us, with Nokuzola's help, so that we can all be a part of hearing his story. Nokuzola sits with Sandile, and they begin. I turn to Adrian, and as his thoughts begin to flow, I write down a rough draft describing some of the social issues he identifies in Heideveld as a backdrop for his story.

Although many young people in Heideveld favor American rap and Hip-Hop artists, Kwaito (an eclectic musical style with echoes of traditional African music and Hip-Hop) is also popular. The lyrics of most Kwaito music are in African languages such as Zulu or Xhosa, which sends a message to young people that their own culture and language is important. By writing his rap in Xhosa, Sandile was not only telling his own story but also expressing an important part of his identity as a Xhosa boy.

Session 3

All the boys except for Nathan arrive, excited to work on their raps. In this session, Nokuzola and I have decided that it will be helpful for the boys to each have a chance to brainstorm their ideas for their individual raps together as a group. This may offer group members the opportunity to be a witness to each other's stories and to support each other. This support is demonstrated by Mark, who listens intently as Sandile, who is very forthcoming, expresses his thoughts during the brainstorm session. When he struggles with his English, Mark carefully reflects back his contributions to ensure that I understand what he is saying.

This is one of the most integrated groups I have worked with, particularly given that the different represented cultural groups valued and encouraged each other's contributions, showing respect for one another. My sense is that it was their common interest in this medium of rap and the overlaps in their individual stories that enabled these boys to draw together, working against racial and other prejudices in their community. This spirit of respect created a safe space in which these young people could share painful aspects of their lives with each other, recognizing that they were not alone in their suffering.

After Session 3...

Although Nathan missed this session, I see him later in the day at his school when I go to sort out some administration issues with the principal. He comes up to me and (rather proudly) hands me a notebook asking me to read the rap he has written. Once back at the music room I begin to read:

> 'Since age 3 I was sent away
> Because my mommy never had a place to stay...
> 'And at the time I never said much
> Cause I was just a young boy growing up'...
> 'I never had a chance to pick up the phone and say
> Mommy can I come home for the holiday?'

> I am stunned by how musically and linguistically coherent this rap is, not to mention honest.

Nathan's rap showed echoes of well-known rap artists, indicating his keen interest in and knowledge of rap music as seen for example from the lines he borrowed from T.I.'s song "Live Your Life" featuring Rihanna:

> Never mind what haters say
> Ignore them 'til they fade away

His rap told his own story, but he was helped to tell this story using phrases and words borrowed from rap artists he enjoyed. As Nathan developed his rapping skills by listening to and imitating other rap artists, he developed the vocabulary to be able to say what he was unable to verbalize as a child. The many similarities between life stories told by rap artists and those of the boys in Heideveld offer resources and artistic ideas that can guide boys toward reflecting on their stories, even if they may struggle initially to express these.

To inspire his peers, I asked Nathan if he was happy to share with the group the rap that he had invited me to read in his notebook. I thought it would be important for him to share because he was often very dominating and quite attention-seeking in sessions, suggesting that he urgently needed to voice his story. Writing a rap in his own time further confirmed this need—a need to express stories that, as the first lines of his rap suggest, had remained unfulfilled since childhood.

Session 4

Although it takes some coaxing, Nathan decides he will share his rap in the group, under the condition that we will not just watch him but will also participate in some way. He may feel anxious about sharing his vulnerable self with the others for fear of being judged. The rest of the group members quickly decide how they want to contribute to the rap. Mark provides a beat on a djembe drum while Sandile adds his own beat box. I join in, taking a drum to add to the rhythm that is forming. Nathan listens to the forming rhythm. He looks at me and tells me to stop my playing, assertively—demonstrating self-assurance and trusting that I will not reprimand him. Then, with growing confidence, he recites his rap.

As our group began to work together, to support one another, the boys began to tell their stories. Besides Nathan's rap, the other three boys' raps were for the most part prosaic, although they did contain inklings of rhyme. Their thoughts, observations, and experiences were captured as raw material on paper, ready to be shaped and refined.

From this point, while the boys worked on their raps individually, it was important that each boy's story was actually heard and voiced to others. So, there were a number of opportunities for the boys to read their raps to one another.

Refining Raps to Make Sense of Our Inner Lives

Session 5

Most of the boys have completed the process of writing their raps in their "raw" form and it is time to refine these. I decide that this should be done together as a group, so that group members can help one another to process and elaborate on the thoughts and feelings expressed in the individual raps.

We decide to begin by helping Mark refine his rap. He starts to read "My father died on my birthday. I was 7. I can't remember the time or the place." "Hmmm, how could we reword these so that it's easier to rap the words?" I ask. My limitations as a rapper mean that rather than relying on me predominantly for input, the group is obliged to tap into its own internal resources. Nathan suggests getting a better flow in the rap, maybe by starting with "When I was 7, my father died on my birthday." The group looks to me for my opinion for something to rhyme with "birthday." I offer "That's what I want to say." Nathan looks at me jokingly and threatens to fire me for this suggestion, which he does not feel will work at all. Nathan goes on with "I was not OK, No way." "Ah," I say—"and then we could add something like 'I didn't know what to say.'" "Maybe," says Nathan, "or, 'I couldn't find the words to say.'" "Yeah, I like that," says Mark.

While I was occasionally asked for my opinion about a rap, the boys took charge of this process. For teenage boys who had struggled or may well still have been struggling with authority figures, this might have been a powerful experience of engaging with an adult in a position of authority—namely me, who is not only White and the therapist, but at the same time I try to work in a collaborative, empowering, and nonauthoritarian way. Further, this "role reversal" was important in our group. These boys— who to teachers or many authority figures would be seen as difficult, in need of help or therapy, perhaps with little to offer—became the experts, the professionals, the ones who were needed *to* help or even "manage" the therapist. This offered them feelings not only of power but also of having something valuable to offer society, of having skills and worth.

Thus the process of refining the raps led to a process within the group where members explored new roles and had to learn to work together, particularly when dealing with material that was very personal to each group member. In an environment filled with conflict and violence, to be able to sit together and work creatively to form a product encourages the development of valuable skills of negotiation, listening, and teamwork.

As well as this, the process of refining raps offered each group member a sounding board, and, sometimes without any intervention from myself as the therapist, led group members to discuss and explore important issues within their lives.

Session 6

Adrian has chosen to work on his rap with the group. He begins to read: "I come from Heideveld. People is drinking on the street. One fire one hit."

I stop him. I have misheard his pronunciation of "hit" and ask what he means by this. He explains: "It's about people using TIK*—they light a flame under the bulb with TIK in it—that's the fire. And this makes fumes which they sniff—so taking a 'hit.'"

The rest of the group members are listening carefully and soon volunteer more information about the drug. This leads to a general

---

* TIK is the common "street" name given for a methamphetamine drug, commonly used in Heideveld. This drug is highly addictive and destructive, and also easily and cheaply obtainable.

conversation about drugs. I am shocked by how much these boys know about drugs, given my lack of exposure to it in the circles I move in. It is something that is all around them in Heideveld. The discussion soon turns to the boys' personal stories. Group members seem to feel safe enough to share their stories with each other and encourage one another as they pick up similarities in their stories. Nathan, Mark, and Adrian admit to having tried marijuana, known in South Africa as "dagga," and some of the group members also admit to having tried TIK. Mark starts to discuss corrupt police who confiscate drugs and use the drugs themselves. Adrian highlights the dangers for community members of reporting drug activity to the police as there is a possibility that they could get killed for doing so. As tempted as I am to point out the dangers of drug use, it seems like the boys are able to identify these by themselves, unprompted by me. As the discussion moves to a close, the boys agree that drug use leads to crime, causes hallucinations, and keeps you from achieving your dreams. Mark explains that his friends use TIK, but that he will not do so.

This group conversation was instigated by the process of refining raps and was valuable to our group in many ways. It deepened the trust between group members and offered space for group members to share and discuss many issues affecting them on a daily basis.

Finally, the process of refining raps helped to build group relationships, to the point where group members supported one another, enabling individuals to express themselves in ways they felt unable to do on their own.

Session 7

The group has decided to listen to Mark's rap. The group energy is low, and Mark seems to really be struggling to express what he wants. Eventually I suggest arranging the rap in such a way that other group members occasionally rap a few words in unison with Mark, for greater impact. We try it out:

When I was 7 my father died on my birthday

I wasn't OK, *No way,* I couldn't find the words to say

Adrian becomes more engaged in this process than usual and even adds a bit of freestyling to Mark's rap. This seems to encourage Mark, and he starts to become more animated and confident as we run through his rap again.

As with Nathan, Mark needed to feel accompanied by the others as opposed to performing for the group, which may have been much more daunting. The group served to affirm Mark's expressions that at first were tentative. Thus, the group helped Mark to begin to own his life experiences, and express who he was with confidence.

Forging Positive Identities

One of the major tasks for adolescents to achieve is identity development—the process of deciding who I am and who I will become one day (Laiho, 2004; Campbell, Connell, & Beegle, 2007). During adolescence, young people begin to move beyond their family circles to experience a range of different worldviews, ideas, and concepts, and need to decide for themselves in which ways they want to become different from their families or peers, and in which ways they want to follow examples set through these relations. In Heideveld, this decision is often particularly difficult. Young people need to decide whether they will join gangs and engage in acts of violence, or find alternative ways of seeking status and power. They need to decide whether they want to be part of building up their community or breaking it down.

In this rather challenging phase of development, music often serves as a beacon for young people, enabling them to "construct, negotiate and modify aspects of their personal and group identities, thus offering strategies for knowing themselves and connecting with others" (Campbell et al., 2007, p. 220). Through the choices adolescents make about the music they listen to, or the way in which they participate in musical activities, they offer others a message about who they are and to which groups they belong.

This places the music artist in an important position as song lyrics communicate important attitudes and ideas concerning issues to which teenagers can relate. Some rap music, especially rap containing controversial lyrics, is often seen as sexist and violent, glorifying images of criminals, gangsters, or pimps, and could be argued to impact adolescents in a negative way, enticing them toward this kind of life. Rappers sometimes express themselves as violent people and justify violent acts and violence in itself as a means to acquiring power (Kubrin, 2005). Given this, it may be argued that the elevated status of rap artists among boys such as this group could negatively affect decisions these boys make in their lives.

Rap music, however, also offers a depiction of life in the inner-city "ghettoes" of America, a depiction that is, for these boys, very close to their own reality. They do not need rap music to teach them that the most notorious and violent gangsters earn the greatest respect in their communities, and that it is important, in their community, to be seen as tough—and thus violent—in order to gain status. While some may argue that rap music itself may draw young people toward violence, for the boys in Heideveld, this music offers the boys an opportunity to explore the realities in their community. Rap music helps them to express what happens in their lives, and perhaps helps them to understand some of the violence they see all around them, and also often, within themselves. Rap artists let these boys know that it is OK to be angry and OK to talk about what is going on around them—even if these subjects are usually not socially acceptable to discuss. Indeed, the use of rap music with previous groups of children has at times enabled them to share shameful stories openly, such as the experience of being victims of abuse.

Further, "many of the violent (and patriarchical, materialistic, sexist, etc.) ways of acting that are glorified in gangsta rap are a reflection of the prevailing values created, sustained, and rendered accountable in the larger society" (Kubrin, 2005, p. 376). In many ways, the community of Heideveld remains a victim of apartheid, and it could be argued that some of the violence within this community is a response to the greater violence of this system. Encouraging boys to express their own violent feelings eloquently through a rhythmic, rhyming rap rather than through acts of physical violence offers boys more beneficial ways of coping with these feelings.

However, in my own past experience, even with boys from similar communities to Heideveld, rap music can potentially have a negative effect on the therapeutic process. The language used in raps has caused tension in groups where some feel that the genre of rap gives them the freedom to use the language they need to express their feelings and others feel this language is unnecessary and offensive. Some group members have also used particular phrases or language choices in an attempt to shock the therapists rather than simply express their own experiences. There are also times where group members have written their own raps or commented on their favorite raps in such a way that gives the impression that they feel it is OK or excusable to engage in the violent or sexual activities depicted by some of their favorite artists.

Thus, it remains important that rap lyrics are discussed and explored within the therapy process and that the boys are encouraged to seriously consider what they are expressing (and why) through their choice of words. In Nathan's rap, he tended to embody the persona of a gangster, including lines such as "What you waiting for? Pop dat bitch." Nathan had in the past been involved in a gang, and yet the rough and violent persona shared through his rap was often very different from his behavior in our group. Although he often took on leadership roles in the group, he also demonstrated a lot of insecurity. He was nervous about sharing his rap with others for the first time, and his music-making was often unsteady and uncertain—which isolated him from others who could not make music together with him as a result. The therapy space appeared to offer Nathan an opportunity to let down his defenses and enable the group to see glimpses of another side of his character. While the final version of his rap remained unchanged, through group discussions about some of the lines I gained a sense of what Nathan was expressing through his choice of words. The gangster he describes in his rap could be thought of as a protective persona he adopted as a means of survival when he most needed protection. Also, he possibly needed some way to protect himself while becoming vulnerable in the group by sharing his story.

In their raps, each of these boys expressed their own life stories, but also expressed hope for something more, for change, for a new, positive identity. When talking about his rap at a later stage with me, Nathan said writing the rap helped him to get rid of some of the "rage" he felt inside of him. It seems like the process of writing a rap was cathartic for him. He described his past in the following way:

> I couldn't go back again
> No one can imagine the pain
> That I've been through
> All my friends telling me "what you're gonna do"
> I told them "can't you see?"
> I put it behind me now that's history

Although he did "go back again" by retelling his story to the group, it was in light of his knowing that he would not remain there and that he would be able to move forward with his life.

Mark narrated the painful reality that his father was a drug dealer when he died, with the words:

> I remember only one thing about him, being a drug dealer
> He wasn't a killer or a stealer
> It was heartbreaking for me to lose a father

He attributed the demise of his father to the ills in his community and had a very clear idea of the changes that his community needed as described in one of the earlier versions of his rap:

> Every neighborhood needs to look after themselves
> People must stop doing drugs, stop walking with guns
> The drugs can kill you if you don't stop; guns will hurt you if you pop
> To look for a better life
> The struggles are hard on the streets

When an external evaluator visited the group a couple of weeks later, she gleaned, during an informal interview with Mark, that voicing this information helped him decide that he did not want that life for himself. Perhaps there was something about concretizing an idea in black and white that enabled Mark to see the reality of his situation. In a community like Heideveld where young people have very few positive role models, they are greatly at risk of perpetrating the crimes of those they look up to. Here was a young man making a profound decision not to follow in the footsteps of his father.

In an early version of his rap, he also describes a dream that he would like to protect:

> I just want to look out for other people's children on the streets
> I love to play with babies to see how they grow up
> I don't want children to grow up without a future
> My dream is to be a rapper one day

Mark is one of the few young men in Heideveld I have come across who wants to do something proactive to ensure that other young people do not have go through the difficulties he did. His own story of pain has led him to dream of helping other children, so that they do not have to grow up with the struggles that he faced. He is also voicing his own hope of having a future, one which includes being a rapper. Rappers can be seen as socio-political commentators, and being a rapper might afford Mark the opportunity to act as an ambassador for himself and other "voiceless" young people in his community.

Adrian's relationship with his father seemed somewhat more ambivalent as seen from the words in his rap:

> My father let me play with guns. He's now sad for what he's done
> But he's still my father after what he's done but still one fire one hit

One can only imagine how confusing and painful it must be for a young person to have to come to terms with having a parent whom he loves but who also hurts him. And yet, through the process of writing and refining his rap, Adrian, too, was reflecting on his own life and making decisions about the future he wanted to have for himself.

Performance and Closure

The group was meant to continue with another three sessions, but the ninth session ended up being our last as a group, as three of the four boys became busy with examinations that were being held the following week. At the time we did not know that it would be the final session, which meant that there was no closure for the majority of group members or for myself.

Session 9

The group energy is low. Nathan describes how he was attacked by gangsters yesterday because they thought he was still part of a gang. Mark is not feeling well and sits slumped over his djembe drum, saying that he does not feel like talking. Adrian chooses to work by himself to finish his rap.

Toward the end of the session, as we begin to share our raps together, for the last time, the medium of rap music enables these boys to end the group with a celebration, a celebration of one another, of their stories. Nathan and Mark start experimenting with free-styled sections in Nathan's rap. Suddenly Mark becomes energized. It seems like the formal writing down of a rap restricted his creativity. What I had originally intended as an aid to help the young people feel a sense of safety to express themselves seems to have worked against him.

Now, he spontaneously offers lyrics to Nathan's rap and high fives abound between the two. As the two take a hold of the process, the energy of the whole group increases, making for a vibrant last session. As we're about to end, Sandile even demonstrates his break-dance moves as he recites his rap.

Even though we were unaware that this group would not share another session together, the performances of each boy's rap in this session were important. Performance enables us to be heard and thus validated and affirmed by others. Here was a group of boys—yes, with painful stories, but now also a group of rappers … and good rappers at that. While I am not suggesting that the process of writing and performing raps miraculously transformed the young men, as I am only too aware of the societal pressures and forces that act on them, this process helped them to question and reflect on their lives and to begin to make sense of the "ugly" and "hopeful" parts of their lives as coexisting narratives. The incentive of a great-sounding rap of their very own as an end product kept some group members motivated when they struggled to describe and explore difficult ideas through their raps, and when challenged by others musically and personally. Following the example of their favorite rap artists who depict their lives in explicit details, the boys were enabled to confront issues in their lives, including the hurt and pain caused by family members they looked up to through the music. The opportunity for each boy to write and reflect on his own rap offered space for the boys to freely construct and create their stories, as they were in reality, but also as they wanted them to be in the future. Thus, the group members were able to engage in a process of individuation. They recognized that while up until now they had been a product of their past relationships, they could now claim their lives as their own and could take responsibility for their own choices. As each performed for the others, they performed identities of musicians and rappers; they performed identities of hopeful, energetic young people, not gangsters, not taking drugs together, but moving forward, dreaming, hoping, looking up.

References

Camilleri, V. A. (Ed.). (2007). Outcomes for at-risk children in the inner city. *Healing the inner city child* (p. 42). London: Jessica Kingsley.

Campbell, P., Connell, C., & Beegle, A. (2007). Adolescents expressed meanings of music in and out of school. *Journal of Research in Music Education, 55*(3), 220–236.

Hutchinson, M. (2006). *Bo-Kaap: Colourful heart of Cape Town*. Claremont, South Africa: David Philip.

Kubrin, C. E. (2005). Gangstas, thugs and hustlas: Identity and the code of the street in rap music. *Social Problems, 52*(3), 360–378.

Laiho, S. (2004). The psychological functions of music in adolescence. *Nordic Journal of Music Therapy, 13*(1), 47–53.

North, A. C., & Hargreaves, D. (2000). The importance of music to adolescents. *British Journal of Educational Psychology, 70*(2), 255–272.

Pavlicevic, M. (2002). Fragile rhythms and uncertain listenings: Perspectives from music therapy with South African children. In J. P. Sutton (Ed.), *Music, music therapy, and trauma* (p. 100). London: Jessica Kingsley.

Sutton, J. P. (Ed.). (2002). Trauma: Trauma in context. In J. P. Sutton (Ed.), *Music, music therapy and trauma: International perspectives* (p. 31). London: Jessica Kingsley.

Chapter 12

Yo, Can Ya Flow! Research Findings on Hip-Hop Aesthetics and Rap Therapy in an Urban Youth Shelter

Aaron J. Lightstone

Background Information

In 2003–2004 while I was enrolled in the Master's of Music Therapy program at Wilfrid Laurier University, I conducted research on the use of Hip-Hop with youth in an urban shelter. I was very interested in Hip-Hop as it seemed to be the most direct way in which I, as a music therapist, could meet the aesthetic needs and interests of the music therapy participants. With limited Hip-Hop specific experience, skills, and equipment, I developed makeshift methods of *approximating* the Hip-Hop musical aesthetic* in the music therapy sessions and engaging the youth in music making. This study was done before my own personal journey into the world of software-based recording and music making. If I were working with youth and Hip-Hop today, I would use a laptop computer with MIDI controllers as my primary instrument with the much more flexible and powerful tools available in modern DAW (digital audio workstation) software. The fact that the data was so rich in content, despite my relative inexperience with the equipment and the genre, is a testament to the power and potential of this unique musical form that has so captivated and become so firmly embedded in youth culture around the world.

Rap Music as a Therapeutic Intervention

When I began in the youth shelter, I had some interest in, but relatively little experience with, Hip-Hop. As a relatively inexperienced music therapist working with what was at the time an undocumented medium in music therapy, I found it difficult to reconcile what I understood about therapeutic practice, cultural sensitivity, media stereotypes about Hip-Hop, and the sometimes violent, misogynistic, and generally antisocial content of the participants' rap lyrics and the lyrics of some commercially successful artists.

One purpose of my research study was to determine whether the participants' rap lyrics carried meaning for the creators, and if the expression of this meaning was of potential therapeutic value. I was also interested in some of the ethical and clinical questions that this new medium seemed to raise. As a clinical practice, music therapy endeavors to make music making accessible to all, yet rapping requires quite a bit of skill and practice, and the musical accompaniments are technologically mediated. So, although one can get started making beats† with limited musical skill and knowledge, technical skills are still required. Some aspects of Hip-Hop seem to encourage verbal threats, aggression, and misogyny. As a cultural outsider and a less experienced therapist, it was difficult to determine where the boundaries should be. The nature of working in a situation that used unconventional music therapy techniques, a relatively unfamiliar musical paradigm, and a musical form that has generated significant controversy in the

---

* According to Rose (1994), Keyes (1996), and Salaam (1995), Hip-Hop is an art form that emphasizes key aesthetic features such as lyrics, flow, layering, rupture, sampling, emphasis of rhythm, and de-emphasis on melody and harmony as understood by Western musical theorists. For a more complete discussion of the Hip-Hop aesthetic please refer to Lightstone (2004).

† In Hip-hop culture, making beats refers to the creative act and skill of creating the musical accompaniments for rappers. Beats refers to the entire accompaniment sequence, not just the drum parts.

popular media created many challenges. It became apparent that some of these challenges could become the core of a research project.

The purpose of the study was as follows:

1. To discover and share findings on how the use of Hip-Hop aesthetics can impact the music therapy process with youth
2. To come to a greater understanding of the meaning of the lyrical expression of youth participating in Hip-Hop music therapy
3. To develop further Aigen's (2002) notion of groove-based music therapy[*]

The research questions for this study were as follows:

1. What is the therapeutic potential of producing and recording rap music as a clinical technique in music-centered therapy?
2. What meaning is contained in the improvised and precomposed rap songs of youth, as recorded during music therapy sessions?
3. When residents of a youth shelter are given the opportunity to create spontaneous rap songs, what is the content and nature of this form of self-expression? Is the content expressed in those songs potentially therapeutic, harmful, or neutral?

Once I started the data analysis, I quickly discovered that the lyrics created by the therapy participants were rich in content and often related to multiple categories or themes. This suggested that the participants embedded many layers of meaning into their lyrical expression. The process of creating rap music lyrics allowed the participants to express a range of emotions and aspects of their spirituality. Further, it allowed them to experience a sense of empowerment through the critique of oppressive social structures, experience a sense of mastery in the context of familiar musical vernaculars, and possibly strengthen their ego through adoption or expression of African American oral traditions such as *signifyin'*[†] and *boasting*. Rap

---

[*] Aigen (2002) investigates the role of "groove" as a defining characteristic of popular music styles. He expands on the ideas of ethnomusicologists Keil and Feld (1994) and applies their ideas to understanding the role of groove-based music in the music therapy process. Groove-based musics tend to be hybrids of Afro-diasporic styles and genres and thus contain many elements of the above-mentioned Afro-centric musical aesthetics. The power of groove rests largely in its power to invite participation.

[†] Campbell (1995) defines signifyin' as a practice in African American oral culture that is a "way of rendering powerless through language an uncompromising oppressor ... I see signifying ultimately as the use of language or discourse to affirm cultural identity and community in the face of the imposition of cultural dominance and oppression" (Campbell, 1995, p. 1).

music gives voice to those who are, or feel, marginalized through realistic expressions of despair, hopelessness, and existential angst (Rose, 1994). In addition to expressing their ideas, emotions, and traumas, the participants were able to engage in a creative group process and work together to create musical experiences in the context of their musical vernacular.

One of the main objectives of many music therapists is making the experience of *musicing** accessible to a wide range of people who might not otherwise have access to such experiences. Rap music and Hip-Hop aesthetics can be used in music therapy to facilitate culturally appropriate and meaningful music interactions and experiences. This was demonstrated in this study with the often marginalized and inaccessible street youth population.

The popularity of rap music, in youth culture, requires that music therapists working with youth familiarize themselves with rap music and its specific techniques of music production. The transformative power of rap and other African American musical forms is well documented (Pinn, 1999) and is potentially an effective and overlooked tool for music therapists.

About the Research Study

Over the course of a year and a half I conducted weekly, 2-hour, drop-in, group music therapy sessions in an urban youth shelter. Sessions were largely based around improvised music experiences in the framework (Wigram, 2004) of a variety of popular music styles. The improvisations were all recorded and those that fit into a Hip-Hop musical aesthetic were selected for transcription, detailed analysis, and coding following a modified approach to grounded theory (Strauss & Corbin, 1998). The drop-in nature of the group meant that there was no predicting how many sessions an individual might attend.

The data was rigorously coded following the principles of grounded theory adapted to suit the demands of the particular data set (Strauss & Corbin, 1998; Kenny, 1996). The data was reanalyzed a number of times until the final nine categories and subcategories emerged from the data. The final categories were:

1. Authenticity & emotional expression (9 subcategories)
2. Rapper as critical theorist (5 subcategories)
3. Boasting (6 subcategories)

---

* Elliot (1995) proposes the term musicing to reflect the basic reality that music should be treated as an action rather than an object. According to Stige (2002) this term is gaining increasing popularity with music therapists as it is seen to reflect the "*process aspects*" (p. 101) of what music therapists do.

4. Rap battles/insults (3 subcategories)
5. Drugs (5 subcategories)
6. Evidence of group process (4 subcategories)
7. Spirituality (6 subcategories)
8. Violence (4 subcategories)
9. Musical wordplay (3 subcategories)

During the first stages of data analysis, I had formed two preliminary expectations:

1. The self-expression articulated in most raps was rich in meaning and was of potential therapeutic value. However, there was content in a number of songs that was of questionable therapeutic value, or seemed to raise a number of questions regarding its therapeutic value, or even its potential to be harmful.
2. Creating Hip-Hop music requires an attention to technological devices that is not typically found in other types of music therapy work. I worried that the attention the technology required, and the drop-in nature of the group, was interfering with group process to the extent that there may not be enough group process occurring to call the process "group therapy."

The data supported the first expectation and challenged the second. The codes that emerged strongly paralleled the issues, topics, or categories that one would expect to hear people expressing in various forms of verbal therapy.

Authenticity & Emotional Expression—Keepin' It Real

Not trying to put ya off
And make ya feel bad
'Cause inside you know I be the man
Who feels sad

—Sam*

...Nevah fuckin' spit fake rhymes we always stay true
Me and my crew we got to do what we got to do
To survive, just to get by everyday nevah lie
We walk the streets with a mean ass look
'Cause I aint no half way crook...

—SN

---

* Names of the participants have been changed.

As illustrated in the second example there were a number of references in the songs and the literature on Hip-Hop (Keyes, 2002) related to the importance of authenticity or *keepin' it real* as a cultural value in Hip-Hop culture. It is of great importance for expression in rap songs to be *real* and to reflect the lived experiences or direct observations and thoughts of the rappers. For members of youth culture who are involved in Hip-Hop, this makes rap music a compelling therapeutic tool. Music therapists generally hope to engage participants in authentic, self-reflective self-expression. It is usually assumed that when people express and connect with their emotional states and triggers, they will develop greater insight into their own human condition, and become better able to develop creative ways of improving their circumstances (Yalom, 1980). For rap music fans and members of Hip-Hop culture this is a natural step when using rap music in music therapy. The expectation to be authentic and self-expressive is built into rap music.

The participants in this research study expressed sadness, frustration with life on the streets, hope for the future, hopelessness, loneliness, abandonment, hatred, and other emotions. Table 12.1 illustrates the subcategories that emerged during the process of axial coding of this category, with one example from each category.

The category of expression of emotions had important overlaps with all the other categories. This suggested that emotional expression is at the root of, or motivating, most of the expressions in the other categories. It is clear from the data that rap music is a useful tool to share and vent both positive and negative emotions. This is important in group psychotherapy for cathartic reasons and for group process, thus allowing the group to capitalize on the therapeutic factors of *universality* and *instillation of hope* (Yalom, 1995).

An important subcategory was *Frustration With Shelter Life*. The stresses of poverty, unemployment, and disconnection from family and the stress of over 60 youth living under one roof were expressed in this category. In the following example, Calvin uses the spoken word subgenre of rap to express his frustration with the daily routines in the shelter.

> You know what happen today
> I was upstairs
> And I had a chore
> And the lady who works in the building
> Told me to go wash some dishes
> But I refused
> And then she said
> The key words

Table 12.1 Expression of Emotions

Subcategory	Example
Hope/Hopelessness 7 examples 5 participants	But here we are as young people we are We have to think positive toward the future And learn from the mistakes we make Tami
Sadness 8 examples 5 participants	God send me an angel from the heavens above God send me an angel to wipe the tears from my eyes... "Send me an angel to heal my broken heart from being in love Cause all I do is cryin' God send me an angel to wipe the tears from my eyes." Angel
Anger 3 examples 3 participant	Yo cops ya'll deserve to die Yo bitch niggaz ya'll deserve to die Yo rats ya'll deserve to die Yo FBI ya'll deserve to die Yo government ya'll deserve to die F & D
Loneliness 3 examples 3 participants	My life is endless no limit to it[a] My destiny is vague, I look up I see nothing but rain Many say life is all struggle, yes indeed it is Come Jah oh please Oh Jah don't leave me Jah please My life is the dark moon I don't know who to follow James

Continued

Table 12.1 (continued) Expression of Emotions

Subcategory	Example
Frustration with hardships	*Our visions getting faded*
	So tired of livin' this livin' we are livin'
6 examples	*Make you weak minds feel*
	they gotta give in
5 participants	*Now's the time to live prosperity...*
	Sue
Hatred	*Yo my brain's sharper than thistles*
2 examples	*I hate you blow you up into evaporated sweat crystals*
2 participants	*Bill*

^a This example was categorized in the subcategories *loneliness* and *hopelessness*.

If you refuse
You shall be abused by gettin' discharged
And I said that's not fair
Because I don't want to stick hands in no water
But no
This lady was disrespectful
and immune to a man's feelings
But
in the end
I did for mine
My heart and soul
Because I need a place to sleep for the night
Ya know
As I look at it
It is not too much to ask
For one lonely guy
to do some dishes
But the fucked up thing is
I was already assigned to a chore
But instead the lady crossed my name off a that one
and put my name and put it on another one
So what am I supposed to do?

—Calvin

It is also important to investigate negative cases, or examples in the data that contradict the main findings (Strauss & Corbin, 1998). Chris was a participant who came to many sessions. He had a very good voice and could *flow;* that is, he could ably rhyme within the rhythmic parameters of rap music. Music from Chris reveals lots of wordplay and verbal/musical impro-visations by an individual with strong musicality and musical sensibilities. However, he expresses and says very little. He rarely engaged in (verbal) self-expression. Because he came to so many sessions as an active partici-pant, I do not think that the sessions were any less valuable to him than to the other participants. Although he did not express much in the way of deep thoughts, emotions, or reprocessing previous experiences, he was deeply involved in a satisfying music-making experience. The implication of this finding is further discussed in the analysis of the category *Musical Wordplay*.

Rapper as a Critical Theorist (RACT)—Signifyin'

And so the need for greed causes that one to lead
Can't no one believe
How much one can deceive
So while they're dreamin' and sceamin' and claimin' truth and their lies
Somebody really needs to tell 'em they need a better disguise
Cause real eyes, realize
Real lies...

—Karen

This category was formed in response to the observation that rap-pers (both commercial rappers and my participants) often performed lyrics that critique social institutions and structures. Commercial rappers tend to represent young, urban, Black America. The creative use of language to attack oppressive social structures is an African American oral tradition that goes back to the times of American slavery (Jackson, 2004; Levine, 1977; Campbell, 1995). In African American oral culture this practice is referred to as *signifying:*

> "signifying"—meaning, in this case a way of rendering powerless through language an uncompromising oppressor ... I see signifying ultimately as the use of language or discourse to affirm cultural identity and commu-nity in the face of the imposition of cultural dominance and oppression. (Campbell, 1995, p. 1)

The participants in these groups represented a wide variety of cul-tural backgrounds. However, as street youth, my participants represented a distinct marginalized group irrespective of their individual ethnic back-grounds. Many come from traditionally marginalized ethnic groups such as First Nations Canadians, West Indian immigrants of African and Indian descent, African immigrants, and other immigrant communities. Their personal identities are a complex matrix of life history, ethnic group, religion, age, race, class, and education level.

> Now, see my name is me
> I'm young and Cree
> I'm almost legendary
> I grew up with no family
> This makes me crazy in my mind
> Makes me rewind
> Makes me go crazy
> Makes me almost go blind

—Mel

Mel was a young Cree man from Saskatchewan. He participated in a number of music therapy sessions using a number of popular music styles. He was comfortable improvising songs in the classic rock genre and in a number of rap music subgenres. The above example illustrates the richness of the data. The power of poetry or song lyrics rests in how much meaning can be conveyed with so few words. In this example, Mel is expressing awareness about how his difficult past and early traumas had led him to his difficult, current life situation as a drifter.

A significant amount of the therapeutic work occurred before and after the sessions as participants helped to set up and tear down the equipment. I learned from Mel that he had a difficult background. He was born on a Cree reserve to alcoholic parents and was adopted out to a White missionary family who raised him as a Christian. He explained that he had little connection to his adopted family and their religion. In the brief passage transcribed above of only 38 words, Mel critiques, or *signifies on*, the social structures that are causing him mental anguish. The metaphor that he uses in the last line could be read in a number of ways, including an example of *signification*. Being a young Cree and raised away from his family are all factors that point to Mel's sense of disenfranchisement. The mentally ill and the disabled represent other groups that are marginalized by society, and Mel suggests that he might join their ranks as well. Embedded in the subtext of this passage is the suggestion that the traumas of life place sufficient mental stress and anguish upon Mel that he might go "crazy" and "almost go blind." This could also be read from a psychodynamic perspective. Mel's life circumstances are difficult to cope with and he knows and feels the risk this poses to his mental health. The line "makes me almost go blind" suggests that there is something in his past that he does not want to see. Many of the Aboriginal youth who I worked with who were receiving treatment for addictions spoke about how their substance abuse began in attempts to obliterate traumatic memories of abuse.

Commercial rappers offering critical theory or *signifyin'* about the structures and institutions they live under have been identified in the academic literature (Stephens & Wright, 2000; Lunine, 1995; Perkins, 1996; Rose, 1994). I was surprised by the depth and clarity with which some of my participants were able to *signify* in the context of improvised rap songs as can be seen in Table 12.2.*

Construction of an earlier version of this table revealed that one individual participant (Faisal) was represented in every subcategory. During each stage of analysis there were a number of subcategories with only one example. These single examples were all the creations of Faisal. It is clear from this analysis that this is an important theme to Faisal. Despite the possible lack of saturation, the quantity of examples in the data point to the importance of this category.

The arts therapies operate under the assumption that creative self-expression is therapeutic. In work with marginalized and/oppressed groups an individual's empowerment is frequently seen as an important factor in personal growth and development (Bishop, 2002). When rappers identify, name, and critique the instruments of their oppression and marginalization, they are engaging in an empowering experience.

The fact that this category and its subcategories (critique of the media, the war in Iraq, hypocrisies of governments, residential schools, the aftereffects of slavery and indentured servitude, commodification of music, etc.) represented a significant amount of the data suggests that these rap therapy experiences offer an uplifting, creative, and empowering experience. As individuals who identify with Hip-Hop culture, the participants know that *signifyin'* is a frequent theme in commercially produced and available rap music. I suggest that they often come ready to engage in this type of critical dialogue because it is a cultural norm. It follows that the creation/production of rap music as therapy with this population may have great therapeutic potential, not just because it is the music of their culture, but because of the themes and issues that one is expected to convey when engaged in this type of musical expression.

Faisal was able to *signify* and offer critical theory related not only to his immediate socioeconomic conditions but also to the historical circumstances of his ethnic group. Faisal was an immigrant with Indo-Guyanese cultural background. His Guyanese heritage was a point of connection in our therapeutic relationship, because during the year that I worked with him I had led three humanitarian trips to Guyana. We were involved in a group improvisation where each group member had a turn to shout out

---

* Professor Joel Amernic, a social scientist at the Rotman School of Business (University of Toronto), provided invaluable advice and acted as a sounding board and outside observer at critical phases of the research.

Table 12.2 Rapper as Critical Theorist (RACT)

Subcategory of RACT	Sub-Subcategory	Example
We are fed propaganda	By the government 3 examples 1 participant	*but people criticize* *don't want to sympathize* *cause it ain't they lives that die* *or deny* *by government illusion* *pump our minds with pollution* *Faisal*
	By the media 7 examples 3 participants	*Media feedin' us all this* *propaganda* *Conceptions manipulated* *Our visions getting faded* *Sue*
	By schools 1 example	*Then sometimes we don't even* *hear it on the news* *How victims get abused and put* *in these schools* *But bettah yet man we all gettin'* *treated like fools* *The way they put us in institutions* *and make us go to school* *Faisal*
Society is abusive/ apathetic to the oppressed	Mainstream society 3 examples	*And nobody else gets to choose* *to be violated and abused* *While the public does nothing* *and is always amused* *Faisal*
The War (in Iraq) is not justified	3 examples 2 participants	*I shake I quiver* *for the breaking news* *has just been delivered* *Bombs over Baghdad* *Shock and awdamn I think* *We got that damn Saddam* *But as we often are*

Table 12.2 (continued) Rapper as Critical Theorist (RACT)

Subcategory of RACT	Sub-Subcategory	Example
		Could be wrong so
		Bear with us as we continue to bomb
		Karen
Stop racism	6 examples	Black on Black crime has to stop
	4 participants	White on White crime has to stop
		Black on White crime has to stop
		Everything needs to stop
		Cause really and truly
		We are all one inside
		Yo
		'Cept for you're White
		and I'm Black
		He's blacker than me
		That don't matter
		We still come from the same country
		Or continent
		I wasn't born there that has nothing to do with it
		My ancestry comes from der
		Yeah we don't come from fuckin' Mars...
		Calvin
Critique of capitalist/ consumer culture	Capitalist society has commodified our cultural expression	Our principals of true Hip Hop have been forsaken
	2 examples	It's all contractual an' about money makin
	2 participants	Kyle
	Youth culture is caught in this too	Yo livin' in this world of sin
		I'm just a brown kid I'm outside lookin in

Continued

223

Table 12.2 (continued)   Rapper as Critical Theorist (RACT)

Subcategory of RACT	Sub-Subcategory	Example
	1 example	*At the white man he's starin straight down at me*
		Saying I shouldn't be here this ain't my country
		If I don't know where I been
		Then where will I go
		Yo all I see is all these hos
		Yo, they sellin they souls
		Cockin out their legs for
		The chu chump change
		Hence ya best remember what I say
		The White man run this land
		And You ain't gonna get a han'
		Unless you shed the blood of another man...
		Faisal

a word to him. He would improvise a rap until he ran out of ideas and then the next person in the circle would shout out a word. When it was my turn, I shouted the word "Guyana." In response, he improvised the following:

> Guyana used to be a beautiful country
> Got everything stole
> Yeah that was the stories that was tol'
> Because a president was elected
> Rhymes that came up
> In a section
> He wanted to take everything
> Was too greedy
> Conceited
> And that's the way we always gotta found treaties
> Meanin' that people was signing contracts
> So we could come from India and work like that
> And they brought the Africans over too
> So that we could all be abused
> And be treated like fools
> Like the tools implemented in this world this society

That's the way I be watchin' things from my forefathers
Because they here and they never wanna botha
With that lifestyle
And they used to have to go wild
And provide for the kids
And the kids getting raped
And then now a days ya hear on tape
And that's why I speak
So that I can reach through your speakers
With my hands
But bettah yet with my voice
Right to your brain and attached to your ears
Pull you in yeah and you gonna feel the tears
That they used to shed in those fields pickin' cotton

—Faisal

It is clear that Faisal was more able and/or interested in this form of expression than the other participants. A final search through the transcripts for more information on this category revealed that he explicitly stated his interest in *signifyin'* in improvised raps.

Spittin' like the spiritual
And I'm comin' like its literal
Bettah know I be critical

—Faisal

But bettah yet I'm turning from concepts to understand
Processin' in my mind and that's why I freestyle*

—Faisal

Faisal was clearly an exceptionally creative and able rapper, in both improvised and precomposed raps. It seems that creating raps with these themes is difficult, especially producing coherent critical thought under the pressure and structures of improvised rapping. The difficulty in creating raps with these themes does not diminish their importance or therapeutic potential.

Signifyin' or critical theory was an extremely rich and interesting category of data but appears to be difficult to execute and thus was the expression of a very small number of participants. Further investigation in this area is recommended.

---

* Freestyling is the act of creating an improvised rap.

Battles

> Yo nevah wanna take the life of another man
> But if he's comin' for me I'll leave that in God's han'
> Try to avoid confrontations, physically
> But if he wanna go, I'll kill him verbally

—Faisal

Battles emerged as a category early on in the research process. The rap battle is a well-known phenomenon in Hip-Hop culture. In a battle, two or more participants engage in a ritualized form of verbal sparring. It was a relatively common occurrence in the sessions that one or more participants would pose challenges to other participants to perform battles. Not all challenges to battle were accepted, and not all battles were recorded (due to occasional technical challenges with the equipment). In the data, two types of battles emerged: direct battles and rhetorical battles. *Direct battles* are defined here as the traditional verbal sparring that two or more participants engaged in, trying to outdo each other in facility, ritualized insults, or rhymed threats. The following examples contain violent imagery in verbal threats or attacks on various aspects of the opponent's character, musical ability, or lyrical expression:

> Mel: Now you may think that you're high class
> You may think that you can whup my ass
> But when you see me in the dark
> I be killin' you and leavin' you down the road in the park

> Eddie: Bang, the mothafucker's down on the groun'
> You hear the sound of the gun shots hittin' his frown
> I said the guy thought the mothafucker was checked
> Thinks he can Leave' me in the park
> His rhymes are wrecked

—Mel & Eddie

This subcategory of battles represents a small amount of the recorded data. Often battles happened at the end of the sessions. Perhaps this was because participants tended to enact them after they had achieved a certain amount of comfort in the group. Many challenges to battles were not accepted by potential opponents. When the challenge to battle was not accepted, those challenged usually offered one of two reasons:

1. They did not feel confident in their rap abilities and felt unable to meet the musical challenge of a battle.

2. They simply did not *want* to battle, feeling that it was counterproductive. Some participants critiqued this aspect of Hip-Hop culture, suggesting that it ran contrary to positive messages of community building and empowerment that Hip-Hop is *really* about. One participant who did not want to accept the battle challenge made a joke out of the entire ritual.

> ...I'm standin' right here with nobody to battle
> 'Cause you know I put on the session
> Let go like a green light
> Yo my guns smoke when I squeeze this clip tonight...

Then, off microphone Sam can be faintly heard trying to cajole the other participants into a battle. To which Calvin responds:

> You suck!
> That's my battle nigger
> That's my battle
> I just killed you
> Yo, You suck
> (laughter)

The subcategory *Rhetorical Battles* emerged more frequently from the data than *Direct Battles*. I use the term *Rhetorical Battles* to describe the subcategory of raps that had the flavor of a battle because the rapper was communicating insults or threats, but they did so in the context of a solo performance or group performance with no clear target of who was receiving the verbal attacks.

> Holy shit
> Whose style you fuckin' with
> It better not be mine or I'm gonna start to hit
> Don't even try to bump my crew
> Special delivery but not to you
> You a bitch, a coward
> Homey you're so fake
> I put your motherfuckin' life at stake
> You phony homey
> You don't even know me
> You don't own me homey

Though this piece has the flavor of a battle, it is rhetorical because it is not clear toward whom the sparring is directed. This was a precomposed song that Carl read from his journal as he performed the recording.

Battles were difficult to come to terms with as a therapist. I wanted to be sensitive to the musico-cultural norms and practices of my participants' cultural group. Yet I initially felt that as a therapist there could be clinical and ethical issues around encouraging expression that is potentially hurtful. Even when the battles were consensual and clearly in jest, they were often quite vicious and I had many concerns about the clinical appropriateness of this mode of expression. Yet various forms of ritualized verbal sparring are a pervasive feature of African American oral culture (Jackson, 2004; Hanson, 2002; Levine, 1977) and have served a cultural purpose. Groups or individuals living in socially difficult and oppressive conditions have many real and symbolic battles to fight on a daily basis. Surviving these battles requires a certain degree of psychological armor.* Though it may seem controversial and counter-therapeutic to expose participants to ritualized insults, this may in fact be quite therapeutic as it allows participants to sublimate aggression into a creative ritual and build their emotional and psychological armor. Faisal demonstrated explicit awareness of this point as evidenced by the following quotation that occurred toward the end of a 15-minute improvised rap duet. The two participants rapped about a variety of topics and toward the end of the rap, Dollah started getting very verbally aggressive with disturbing and violent imagery:

> I'm gonna crush your knees step on your face until you pee
> I'm gonna kick you in your belly till you get HIV
> From rats eatin' it out after I step on your stomach till it gets grout
> And more I'm kick your head down the floor
> …
> You want some positive
> I still curse nothing
> And made it still derogative
> To ya
>
> —Dollah

Following these disturbing and violent images, there was some laughter and the other participant proceeded to rap:

> Yo, yo we was just playin'
> And the words that we was just sayin'
> Didn't mean nothing

---

* The editors want to note that while as therapists it is important to consider the psychological processes necessary to survive some forms of battling, sometimes these battles are simply humorous and fun. Playing the dozens/Yo Mama jokes, while a category of battling, is an example of a humorous and enjoyable form of battling.

Except that we was just jokin'
Almost like we was just laughin', smoking
And that's the way we do it when we all fuckin' locin' (ha ha ha
simultaneous)
But that's just fun
Instead of goin' and pickin' up a gun
And sayin' fuck that niggah
What the hell he just said?
But man yeah right
I be not thinking about that stuff in my head
I got more stuff to think about
And that's the way I be finding myself on another route
And no doubt we gots to keep it positive

—Faisal

This example reveals a potentially important difference between the data and ritualized insults that are described and depicted in the literature on African American oral culture (Levine, 1977; Jackson, 2004; Hanson, 2002). At the roots of battles are toasts and ritualized insults. They have their origins in the West African folk tales about the *Signifyin' Monkey*. The monkey was a character in folklore who could get out of difficult situations by outsmarting his opponents. This tradition continued during the times of slavery with clever stories of those enslaved outwitting their enslavers/"masters." I suggest that this illustrates the close connection between ritualized insults, boasts, and *signifyin'*, and the psychologically protective and empowering way in which these modes of expression operated for African Americans during centuries of slavery, poverty, and oppression. It follows logically that these traditions would be picked up by other groups that are in need of similar psychological coping strategies.

Most battles in African American oral culture involve double meanings and sophisticated, clever insults (Jackson, 2004; Hanson, 2002). This underscores an important difference between that tradition and the data. There are examples in the data of ritualized insults, but they are not particularly sophisticated. Most of the battles found in the data are verbal sparring in the form of threats. It might be argued that this is a healthy sublimation of aggression that could prevent actual physical violence. The data demonstrate that Faisal believes this argument. Bishop (2002) cautions helpers to be aware of when the liberation of one group or individual inadvertently increases the oppression of another. The release of aggression that takes place in a battle may be helpful to the participant who "wins" the battle, but I wonder if the exposure to threats and insults can be oppressive or psychologically wounding to the other participants. In related fields such as art therapy, therapists use materials to help participants sublimate and engage in creative expression, and boundaries are placed on actions and activities that are harmful or hurtful to others (Fisher, 2002). Music therapists should follow similar guidelines, but in music therapy this becomes more complicated as the battles are consensual and some participants perceive battles as an important and legitimate component of their culture. Further, battles might assist consenting participants to build the psychological armor needed for the tough realities of their world. The phenomenon of rap battles raises important questions about the meaning of aggression and cultural sensitivity in therapy.

As outsiders to Hip-Hop culture (the majority of music therapists), it may be problematic to suggest which aspects of the music culture are appropriate and which are not. After taking all of these thoughts into consideration, I would argue that the clinical appropriateness of rap battles is still under question and requires further study. Clinicians working in similar situations should be very aware of the potential conflict this could create.

Boasting

> Her name is Alice
> She came to my palace...
> ...She knew that she loved it
> Then I had to rubbah glove it
> Twice just to feel nice
> It was all day and all night freakin'
> I'm the man that's super for the weeken'

—Dollah

Boasts appeared frequently in the data. This category is closely related to battles as they often merged in and out of each other.

I found many examples of the participants boasting in the data with subcategories that included boasts about their musical/rapping ability; sexual exploits (real or imagined); drug use and drug dealing; athletic ability; and being a *badman*.* (See Table 12.3.)

---

* The badman is a character that appears frequently in African American folk tales. He is a hero/trickster/ruthless figure who "directly confronted the power structures through the exhibition of 'badness' ... these badmen struck out at any time and at anyone. Although they defied social norms and the power structures created by White Americans, they also wreaked havoc within the Black community" (Pinn, 1999, p. 12). Readers interested in a comprehensive account of the badman phenomenon are referred to Pinn's engaging analysis.

Table 12.3 Boasting

Subcategory of Boasting	Example
Musical/rap abilities	I don't care who I rap with my style stay drastic I make a rapper look slow They head like molasses Sun
Sexual	Any day of the week I'm the super freak I got it wrapped up In ten thousand Sheik Condoms Yo I ain't got no mothahfreakin problems Dollah
Drug use and dealing	We never run on empty always on high (singing) You wanna step into our world well we be getting spliffed everyday and even all night Karen
Being a *badman*	Yo I be like Andre The Giant One thing I'm not as quiet Ya check me out I'm not quite a delight To be around I'm serious, the type of shit that makes a brother delirious Ya hearin this I don't think ya are So what ya doin kid Whatcha wanna do When I come around with a 22 Bustin people straight up leavin em fat bruised Yo with the bottom of my shoe My feat make the beat for me to speak Wisdom with em Sam

Giving participants the opportunity to boast in the context of a musical/social experience where such expression is socially acceptable may be therapeutic. For those who have something to be proud of, the boast allows them to express and affirm confidence in themselves. Youth who live in a shelter have suffered many ego wounds. They may have experienced rejection at work, at school, in the family, and by society. Boasting provides an immediate method to begin to rebuild ego strength. Arguably, it may not be the most effective or psychologically mature strategy for building ego strength, but in the brief contact of a drop-in group, the participants need to be heard, acknowledged, and validated.

Drugs—Bluntin' Kronic

What you talk about pain?
Yo certain people use mary jane to maintain
Certain people use cocaine
Certain people use heroins
Injected in they mothafuckin' vein
Yo Your brain is full of fog...

—Sun

Twenty-eight musical excerpts in the transcripts make references to drugs—17 references were to cannabis, five to crack cocaine, two to alcohol, while mushrooms, crystal methamphetamine, and heroin each receive one reference. There is one nonspecific reference to drugs. (See Table 12.4.)

The fact that there are so many references to drugs in the data is reflective of the role that drug use (especially marijuana) plays in the lives of many of these participants.

Evidence of Group Process—Preachin' Positive

Right now a young lady is walking into the room
...
And she did a brave thing yesterday
Accepting somebody else's energy and holding it for her own

—Calvin

Group process occurred in rap music therapy and was coded in three distinct subcategories: (1) verbal encouragement (off microphone); (2) lyrical interplay; and (3) lyrical encouragement. The first subcategory

Table 12.4 Drugs

Subcategory	Example	Specific Drug Mentioned
Boasting—drug use	You don't understan' I'm the man	Cannabis
7 examples	With the power spliff	Alcohol
2 participants	and I came with the gif'	
	I am on this rhyme	
	and I'm a half bent over	
	I'm not drunk I'm a little sobah	
	Dollah	
Boasting—drug dealing	Make your fuckin head drop Like the last refuser	Crack cocaine
2 examples	He can refuse my weed but I got him back	
2 participants	Took a big shank sprinkled with Crack	
	Now you talk shit	
	Homey you dead	
	All that crack numbed your brain and your head	
	Carl	
Drug use as a coping strategy	In this life we all gain to loose Either you deal with it	Cannabis
5 examples	with weed or booze	
	Or let reality eat at you	Alcohol
4 participants	until you're consumed	
	I did not mean to be rude	
	Faisal	
Drugs will harm you	Crack cocaine makes me insane	Crack cocaine
4 examples	cause I know the dope'll	
4 participants	fuck with my brain	
	Garry	

Continued

Table 12.4 (continued)   Drugs

Subcategory	Example	Specific Drug Mentioned
Expression of drug use	And I don't give a fuck cause I be smoking that spliffah	Cannabis
4 examples	That's the way I get much rippah or tipsy or tipper	
6 participants	Faisal	
Glorification of cannabis use	And I want to reach out to everyone in this room	Cannabis
4 examples	who does drugs	
	Or not	
4 participants	Weed is okay but not drugs	
	Smoke all the kronic	
	you want to smoke cause	
	I smoke kronic too	
	No, kronic came from the earth when God created it	
	Calvin	
Glorification of drug dealing	Now Tic Toc I hear my clock	Crack cocaine
	I still got the pocket full a rock	
2 examples	I'm a sellin 'em to your little kids on your block	
	What are you gonna say	
2 participants	What are you gonna do Today	
	Nothing, nothing at all	
	'Cause I got myself an eight ball	
	I'm ready to rock…	
	Mel	

includes examples where the music is under way and participants encourage one another to participate. The second subcategory was characterized by musical moments when a section of a group or duo improvisation would end and the following rapper would make reference to or repeat phrases from the previous rapper's rap, demonstrating that they were listening to each other. One example of this took place during a group improvisation. The first rapper in the excerpt makes a comment about the frequency of marijuana use in the shelter; the second rapper is clearly referencing her phrase when he joins in:

well we be getting spliffed everyday and even all night
4 beats
(1:35 re-enter F)
And all night in sight and
That's the way we be keeping it
From broad night to the broad day light

—Karen

An even more striking example of this phenomenon occurred during a later session.

T: That means ya need to quit the smoking
The hydro the sex whatever
Okay?

S: even in the bad weather
It sounds like you got a cold
your lyrics are old
You need something new huh huh hu

T: It's okay it's okay your hurting
But like I'm saying all of us
We're hurting inside ooh
Hurting deep inside oh oh oh
We have to think positive
For another day

C: Oh /yeah

T: Another day oh oh oh oh oh

—Sam and Tami

Two participants, Sam and Tami, did most of the rapping in that session. Sam was a young man who identified strongly with Hip-Hop culture. Tami was a strong-willed young woman who was constantly encouraging the other group members to be positive, set personal goals, and take individual responsibility for improving their situations. Sam kept trying to engage Tami in a rap battle and launched musical/verbal attacks on her abilities as a rapper throughout the session. The entire communication took place within the musical interaction, yet it had strong parallels with the processes of group psychotherapy that Yalom (1995) describes. Tami responded to Sam's verbal attacks in a way that may be therapeutic for both of them. Throughout their interactions, Sam kept trying to bait her into a rap battle but she would not bite. She kept reminding him that he must be in deep emotional pain if he felt the need to attack, and that she understood this and would accept him anyway. Furthermore, when she sang about her own pain, she sang in the first person plural. Her statements that "We're all hurting deep inside" were made a number of times during the session in response to Sam's verbal attacks. She had the insight to understand that, at least in this case, his machismo was rooted in a sense of vulnerability.

> I woke up this morning with tears in my eyes
> I wonder I wonder I wonder
> Why?
> These tears are pourin' down
> I look out my window I see blood shed
> On my door step
> I wonder
> Why?
> I try and I try and I try
> To understand this world that I live in
> This world that gives you so much opportunity
> but then can step on you in an instant
> we've been through so much
> Pain and suffering
> and we wonder why
> I don't know but I speak for myself
> And I wonder why
> Where's my parents when I need them
> When I need the spiritual one above to look upon me and guide me
> But here we are as young people we are
> We have to think positive toward the future
> And learn
> from the mistakes we make
> I wonder why
> I wonder why
> We're all hurting
> Hurting deep inside*
> Deep inside
> And they tell us to make a couple of goals
> And try to do those and accomplish them
> Accomplish them, can we?
> When we have no support

—Tami

---

* This is evidence that group process was occurring. Here Tami was referring to a previous song in the same session. Sam was on a verbal negative attack, trying to engage her in a battle. She would not have any of it and called him on it. She told him that he must be hurting inside if he felt the need to verbally attack her.

This example illustrates a number of therapeutic factors (Yalom, 1995) occurring within the rap musicing.

1. By singing about her own pain in the first person plural, Tami was emphasizing the factor *universality,* letting Sam know that everyone carries emotional wounds and the repercussions of early traumas.
2. By constantly singing to the other group members that keeping a positive attitude was the key to moving on to a better place in life, and by performing spoken word about her plans to go back to school and become a nurse (example not shown), Tami was emphasizing the therapeutic factor of *instillation of hope.*
3. Tami's explicit acceptance and understanding of Sam despite his verbal aggression toward her conveyed *altruism.*
4. Tami's interactions became a trigger for Sam's anger and discomfort and he almost left the room. Tami convinced him to stay in the session, and staying allowed him to learn more about how his interactions could be hurtful to others. This emphasized the therapeutic factor of *development of socializing techniques.*
5. Not only did Sam stay, but by his fourth improvisation in that session, he began to shed some of his verbal machismo armor and to sing explicitly about his own emotional pain, thus potentially achieving greater levels of authenticity and *catharsis.*

Not trying to put ya off
And make ya feel bad
'Cause inside you know I be the man
Who feels sad

—Sam

In these examples, the rappers used their lyrics to encourage a positive and optimistic attitude and outlook in themselves and fellow participants. A number of different ideas were found in this category, including encouraging others to stay in school, the need to stop youth crime, the need for self-respect, and the need for maintaining optimism.

Spirituality—Leavin' It in the Hands of Jah

Open up your mind and let your
Light shine far
Nobody can judge me
But the splendid one of creation
We are all made in this nation
To be our own revelation

—Sue

Spirituality emerged from the data as an important and frequent theme. Arguably, people need religion or spiritual experiences even more when their lives seem meaningless or when they are in difficult life situations. Detachment from family, education, and work can create a sense of meaninglessness in life. According to Yalom (1980), patients are seeking therapy with accelerating frequency because of complaints associated with a sense of meaninglessness in life. Yalom (1980) argues that the problem of meaninglessness can be a matter of life and death as it is frequently mentioned or implied as a rationale in suicide notes. Conditions that are typically described as giving meaning to life tend to be absent or diminished in the lives of individuals living in a shelter. Sylvan (2002) argues that involvement in popular music subcultures fulfills social and spiritual functions that have replaced the traditional role of religion in the task of meaning-building in people's lives. This is especially true for youth whose struggle for meaning is complicated by the developmental tasks of adolescence (Sylvan, 2002).

> Many young people, caught in the difficult transitional time between adolescence and adulthood, seem to crave the intense initiatic experience, the sense of solidarity, and community, the expression of oppositional values which these sub-cultures provide. Some feel intuitively drawn to the underground stream of West African spiritual power implicit in the music, as well as the ritual forms of the live concert which still contain elements of traditional possession practices. While the mainstream religious institutions become more and more irrelevant to the lives of many young people, they find some fundamental need for spiritual expression fulfilled by these musical sub-cultures. So, even though the West African religious complex has gone through a myriad of major transformations on its journey into American culture and is now tied into a white youth audience and a corporate economic structure, its transformed expressions still thrive and have the capacity to profoundly affect people's lives in powerful ways. (Sylvan, 2002, p. 75)

The data in this study strongly supports Yalom and Sylvan's findings. (See Table 12.5.)

I was struck by how poignantly the following piece expressed prayer, faith, meaninglessness, loneliness, encouragement, witnessing violence, and instillation of hope. In addition to serving as a striking example of spiritual themes in the data, this piece also is a further example of how a single unit of datum can convey a range of meaning and can fit into multiple categories.

James was performing improvised spoken word, while Kenny listens and provides occasional encouragement. It was a very moving piece

Table 12.5 Spiritual Themes

Subcategory	Sub-Subcategory	Example
Prayer 5 examples 5 participants	Thanks	Thank you moma for de nine months ya carried me through All de pain and sufferin' Ya never heard that? It sounds tough eh! Calvin
	Request	Well My mind is filled with sickness Sexual disease Come Jah, fill me Jah Oh Jah oh you have forsaken me Jah Please do not leave me Jah Fill me Jah I am the only one left And I'll still be the only one left James
	Praise	yeah comin' through praise the life that I be livin' Tryin' to survive And the way I be livin' Everyday survival of the fittest
Spiritual/mythical/ supernatural beings 7 examples 4 participants		...But the truth shall remain The devil'l bring the pain Open your third eye and fuck them devil lies To all my warriors and my Souljahs Rise like Jehovah Sue
Spiritual concepts 5 examples 2 participants	References to specific scriptures	I seen the truth through his eyes a black man in disguise he showed me the seven seals he made my mind appeal (Book of Revelation) Sue

Continued

Table 12.5 (continued) Spiritual Themes

Subcategory	Sub-Subcategory	Example
	General concepts	born into sin
		but societies perception is demonic
		Faisal
Rastafarian influenced spiritual expression 4 examples 3 participants		Spoken Word Nov 7th line 10 Praise thee Jah Emperor Sal ah ah ah sie[a]
Death/mortality/ afterlife 9 examples 5 participants		Battle like snake Came back tryin' to open up the heaven's gate. I never knew how a situation turns so Cause I came back and I am trying to let my life flow I never knew How a situation turns so J.J.
Spiritual practices 1 example		Red from the things I said Cause ya smoking it up From the knowledge Meditation when ya thinking Faisal
Search for meaning/ release from meaninglessness 3 examples 3 participants		Livin for the dollah But what is our life really worth Just to struggle and survive the hurt And not get filthy from all this dirt Spending our last piece of change and expensive shirts Faisal

[a] A reference to Emperor Haile Salassie, the former emperor of Ethiopia who is revered by Rastafarians as a messiah.

that was rich in content so I transcribed it and included it in this and other sections of analysis as appropriate.

> J: Well My mind is filled with sickness
> Sexual disease
> Come Jah, fill me Jah
> Oh Jah oh you have forsaken me Jah
> Please do not leave me Jah
>
> K: Feel it
>
> J: Fill me Jah I am the only one left
>
> K: Got nothin'
>
> J: And I'll still be the only one left
> Jah all my life can no longer be in repentable minds
> But the strugglin'
> Strugglin' and fane*
> I see no point to this
> My life is almost like a
> Magnificent fable it's endless
> No limit to it
> My destiny is vague
> Or I look up and I see nothing but rain
> Many say that life
> It's all struggle
> Yes it is
> Yes indeed it is
> Come Jah Please
> Oh Jah don't leave me Jah
>
> K: Feel it
>
> J: Please
> All my life is so in the dark moon
> I don't know which way to go
> Which way to follow
> Who do I see
> Who do I follow
> There ain't nobody
> I look around I see nothing but guns and knives
> So the story of Lucifer
>
> K: You said it red man

---

* Profane?

J: Oh come Jah
Do you understand me Jah

K: I understand

J: Do you actually understand me
Do you understand Jah
Understand me Jah follow me Jah
Oh come Jah
Please Jah don't leave me

The themes of death, mortality, and the afterlife appeared in the data nine times with a direct connection to spiritual themes.

The *Spirituality* theme emerged in Bill's improvisation, illustrating the diverse ways in which spiritual ideas and themes were expressed in the data.

...Yo, yeah it's not getting that brighter
We need some sunlight in here
Yo, or maybe a couple a beers
Or maybe some tunes and fuckin' tears
People getting around campfires yo I'm a vampire
Suck all the blood outa you
Yo, I got the powers ah Goku
On the fuckin' cartoon
Yo, I need a car soon
Or maybe a house (laughter)...

—Bill

His train of thought moves quickly from a desire for hope (expressed metaphorically by "Yo it's not getting that brighter. We need some sunlight in here") to what may be interpreted as the use of alcohol to manage difficult emotions ("Yo or maybe a couple a beers. Or maybe some tunes and fuckin' tears"). He then raps about two beings with supernatural powers. His allusion to being a vampire and Goku* alludes to the afterlife and the desire to possess supernatural powers. A psychodynamic reading of this statement might be that this was an expression of a wish for supernatural powers that in turn was a statement of the powerlessness that Bill felt in his life. It is interesting that after stating his desire for supernatural power, he alludes to the practical frustrations of poverty ("Yo, I need a car soon, or maybe a house").

---

* Goku is a popular character in Japanese animation, which is an art form that is gaining increasing popularity in youth culture. Goku is a young, handsome Saiyan. Saiyans are humanoid creatures, with supernatural powers (Anime central, 2004, p. 1).

A wide variety of themes emerged during the analysis of the *Spirituality* category, which suggested that the involvement in Hip-Hop culture and the enactment of its artistic expression may provide important opportunities for shelter residents to experience and express their spirituality.

Spirituality emerged as a theme that not only was rich in data but also revealed complex and interesting connections to other theme areas such as drugs, violence, boasting, and expression of emotions.[*]

Violence

With all the media controversy surrounding the violent content of rap lyrics (Binder, 1993) it is not surprising that various depictions of violence occurred in the lyric analysis. Like the other categories, violence involved overlap with the *Death, mortality, and the afterlife* subcategory of *Spirituality,* with the *Badman* subcategory of *Boasting,* and with *Battles.* As a relatively new immigrant from Somalia, I wondered if J.J.'s violent expressions were depictions of events he witnessed during his childhood in Somalia, or whether they were simply imitations of some violent aspects of the Hip-Hop he listened to. (See Table 12.6.)

According to some theorists (Rose, 1994; Perkins, 1998; Stephen & Wright, 2000), the violence in rap music is not always gratuitous. It is reflective of the harsh realities that many rappers have experienced during their upbringing in the urban ghettos of America. In some cases raps by artists such as 2Pac Shakur (1991) contain lyrics with violence aimed at upsetting the status quo. Tired of oppression, he wants to trigger a revolution. It is not clear if the revolution is literal or metaphorical. The subtext of these artists clearly is one of social transformation (Stephens & Wright, 2000). In analyzing a small number of songs by 2Pac and listening to songs by Public Enemy, Wu-Tang Clan, and Eminem, it became clear that there was a very different quality and subtext to the violent content of lyrics in the small sample of commercial rap music that I looked at and the violent content in the raps of my music therapy participants. For the most part, the violence in the commercially produced music had a strong subtext of the rapper acting as a critical theorist.

During my clinical work I was troubled by the violent content of the lyrics that often came out in my sessions. I was uncertain of what the violent content meant, and, more importantly, whether I should challenge it, subvert it, unconditionally accept it, or accept it with some limitations. Doing this research has provided me with the opportunity to look into this issue in some depth. The data suggest that much of the violent content from raps

---

[*] For a full description of these connections please refer to Lightstone (2004).

Table 12.6 Violence

Subcategory	Example
Threats 11 examples 7 participants	Yo the state of mind I'm in They call me Black Terminator Snap your neck Snap your neck Like it was a gator Infiltrator, rebel hit to rebel wars Reclip retie reach for more amo Feelin' my type shoot back never retire shoot back shoot back, I aint never gonna retire Your fuckin fire hits to the fear..., J.J.
Depictions of violence experienced, witnessed, or imagined 10 examples 4 participants	But we all drenched in blood We got so much of it we might cause a flood And now look at what we doin' to each other Bustin' caps we might just take a babies motha What happened to that kid Go live in an orphanage not even knowin' who his moma is Faisal
Call to avoid or stop violence 2 examples 2 participants	Never wanna Never wanna Yo nevah wanna take the life of another man But if he's comin' for me I'll leave that in God's han' Try to avoid confrontations physically But if he wanna go I'll kill him verbally Faisal

in my sessions is of a different content from critical artists such as 2Pac. The data contain little in the way of a detectable subtext that is advocating for societal transformation. It appears that the violent content is both imitative of the successful rappers that my participants listen to and a form of posturing. The violent images and threats that are frequently depicted in the music therapy raps seem to have a therapeutic/psychological purpose. Participants who are creating these raps seem to be posturing as the badman, or putting up a tough facade in an effort to conceal their vulner-ability. This was connected to the theme of being a survivor that was also found in the data. To survive in street/shelter life there are many obstacles and one has to be strong and tough or at least appear that way. Rapping about experience with weapons, fights, or sending threats (direct or rhe-torical) is one way of posturing and posing as a badman. This is one way of armoring oneself for the realities of the street.

Themes of violence seem to be connected to feelings of vulnerabil-ity; the witnessing, imagining, or experience of trauma; the expression of anger; expression of existential angst and feelings related to guilt, remorse, and meaninglessness; and some aspects of African American oral culture such as boasts, the badman, and verbal sparring. There were a small num-ber of examples in the data of violence that seemed to be connected with the expression of critical theory, but not to the same extent, depth, or sophistication as is found in the music of commercial rappers such as Paris, Public Enemy, 2Pac, KRS-One, and many others. This still leads to some important clinical questions for music therapy clinicians.

Musical Wordplay—Just Rhymin', Ya'll

This was initially a very large category defined by rhymes with no inter-pretable meaning. Three subcategories emerged: musical wordplay, shout-outs, and play-by-plays.

Musical Wordplay

Musical wordplay is a category of phrases and sections of songs where I could not detect any specific referential meaning. From my experience in the shelter and various work experiences around the Caribbean, I have a fairly high level of comprehension of both urban North American and West Indian street slang. So this category contains song sections that, even after attempt-ing to translate from street slang, appear to contain no discernible meaning.

> And the Nelly* in his tutu the fuckin' belly
> Or bettah yet I could call him up on his celly
> And he could come meet me at a disclosed location
> And I be holding this shit down because I got much patience
>
> —Faisal

---

* Nelly is a popular rapper.

Shout-outs

Shout-outs was a category that was reminiscent of lyrical practices in Hip-Hop and West-Indian genres such as Soca and Calypso. The performance of a shout-out is not meaningless rhyming but a way of affirming one's identity and giving respect to one's geographical context. Rappers typically include shout-outs to their crew, or respect to their neighborhood, by naming it or shouting out its zip code or area code (Forman, 2000). In West Indian forms the shout-outs often display the cultural unity among Caribbean nations by naming many Caribbean locations. Calvin, a participant from Antigua, perfectly illustrated this tradition in one of his spoken words that began to take a distinctly West Indian flavor when he rapped:

> You know what?
> I want to go home
> I want to go back to Antigua
> Antigua, Barbuda
> St. Lucia, Dominica
> Guadeloupe, Trinidad, Tobago
> St. Kitts, St. Nevis
> But you know, there is one place that is not an island
> But is still part of the Caribbean
> Somebody else wanna say?
> Guyana
> Bajans
> ...

The shout-out seems to proceed along a stream of consciousness as Calvin tried to remember all of the islands he can recall. Later in this rap the British Virgin Islands came to mind, he (mistakenly) identified them as U.S. territory and he begins to *signify* on the relationship to the United States and its colonies.

Play-by-Plays

This category was used to describe the lyrics when rappers simply described the action in the room going on around them in very concrete terms.

> And know I'm in the basement by the big screen TV
> Four people just licking up some beats
> Me Jesse a Black guy and a White guy
> I don't know his name
> I just know he is playing the guitar
> And me he is sitting in front of the drum

This is a great African instrument you know that
I feel so happy
This connects you with home a little more

—Calvin

In this example, the wordplay seems to function as a filler to keep the musicing going while the participants either wait for a new idea to rap about or are
in between expressing different ideas.

Play-by-plays occurred frequently near the beginning of improvisations. They seemed to function as a warm-up. As rappers got comfortable in the space and the group, it often seemed that play-by-plays were
being used to gain comfort and test the group atmosphere before launching into more serious issues and expression. Other rappers seemed to
use the play-by-plays and musical wordplay as a lighter way to engage in
the experience.

Yo check it
I'm yo and I'm on the mic
My name is Chris
Half-Black, Half-White
I'm runnin' it
(32 beats instrumental)
Bidy be bit bit
I don't know what to sing
I don't know what to do
I never sang this song
I never sang for you
My name is Chris
I said Chris
Bitty yop
Yeah yeah yeah
Ugh Ugh Ugh Ugh
Ticky ticky tickyticky ticky

—Chris

There is no way to know if this type of self-expression reflects an
awareness of the value in musicing regardless of meaning, or if it is some
kind of therapeutic resistance, or if some of Chris's needs are met by being
the center of attention for a moment, or if there is some other reason why
this seems to be Chris's preferred mode of expression. It may not always
be possible or important for a therapist to make such a conclusion. It is,
however, important to consider what the possible meanings of any given
expression might be for music therapy participants.

Conclusions

It cleanse our state of mind when the music sounds sublime

—Sue

Rap music is a relatively new resource that has yet to be fully explored and utilized by music therapists working in a music-centered, improvisational approach. Rap music is rooted in Hip-Hop culture and expresses the values of that culture. Some of those values reflect a musical worldview that sees rap music as a vital, alive, life-affirming sound that is capable of pushing forward personal development and social transformation. Though Hip-Hop is becoming an increasingly popular, mainstream, and commercialized subculture, its roots and many of its messages are countercultural. This makes it a potentially useful tool in therapy, because it is easily used to give a strong, creative voice to the voiceless. The adoption of rap music and aspects of Hip-Hop culture may also be problematic for the therapist as it may contain and communicate cultural values that may contradict traditional thinking in therapy. Commercial rap music frequently contains violent and/or misogynistic lyrics. This may create an expectation for some participants that when using rap in sessions this type of expression is condoned. This can place the therapist in a double bind. Telling an individual that his or her music culture is unacceptable is not something the therapist wants to do. Without careful handling of such expression, the emotional safety of other group members may be compromised. Therapists using rap music should think very carefully beforehand about how they plan to handle such challenging clinical situations. Thought needs to be given to the balance between cultural sensitivity and therapeutic boundaries. This is a potentially complex issue for cultural outsiders (most music therapists) to negotiate as there is no consensus within Hip-Hop culture as to what the boundaries of appropriate creative expression are. Some founders of the movement maintain that rap battles and antisocial expression run against the spirit and message of Hip-Hop. Feminist rappers criticize the misogynist rap groups but simultaneously defend their right to freedom of expression (Keyes, 2002). "Gangsta" rappers claim that the violence and depictions of criminal activity in their lyrics are simply depictions of their lived realities.

Many music therapy studies of improvisational processes in music therapy attempt to understand the meaning of the participant's experience (Amir, 1996; Lee, 1997; Lee, 2000; Arnason, 2002). This study adds potential richness to these discussions because the creativity of the participants was articulated through their musical and verbal expression. The raps seem to be laden with multiple layers of meaning, allowing the therapist to come to an understanding of possible representational/referential meaning of the improvisations in music therapy. In a similar sense, this study can be seen as a point of dialogue between two approaches to music therapy that often seem divergent. The study of clinical improvisations that occur within the framework of rap provides a point of contact and discussion between music-centered approaches to music therapy (Lee, 2003; Ansdell, 1995), and the music psychotherapy approaches that rely on the verbal ability and musical creativity of participants (Ahonen-Eerikainen, 2003).

This study gives support for the assertions of Lee (2003) that music therapists "should be knowledgeable about multicultural styles, and recognize the organization of modes/scales and general theoretical makeup of different music from around the world" (Lee, 2003, p. 33). This study demonstrates the complexity of carrying out Lee's suggestion. Rap is a musical system that is considered by many in academia and the popular press to be a very simplistic musical system. Immersion into the field of rap reveals that this is not the case. The amount of time, thought, and energy that went into following Lee's statement was considerable and ongoing, and that was just for one of the world's thousands of unique musical systems.

The deep bass, street sounds, record noise, layers of samples, groove, and aggressive beats that are all part of the Hip-Hop aesthetic reflect the world in which the participants in this study live. This allows those sounds to penetrate and affect them in ways that other sounds and musical aesthetics may not. I believe that this, in and of itself, is a strong justification for the use of rap music as a clinical resource with youth shelter residents and similar populations, despite the complex problems that come with it. I look forward to dialogue with other music therapists working with youth and rap music. The benefits of working with this medium outweigh the difficulties. I hope further research can be directed toward finding and sharing creative solutions to some of the inherent challenges that come with working in this medium.

References

Ahonen-Eerikainen, H. (2002). Group-analytic music therapy. *Nordic Journal of Music Therapy, 11*(1), 48–54.

Aigen, K. (2002). *Playing in the band: A qualitative study of popular music styles as clinical improvisation.* New York: Nordoff-Robbins Center for Music Therapy, Steinhardt School of Education, New York University.

Amir, D. (1996). Experiencing music therapy: Meaningful moments in the music therapy process. In M. Langenberg, A. Aigen, & J. Frommer (Eds.), *Qualitative music therapy research: Beginning dialogues* (pp. 109–130), Gilsum, NH: Barcelona.

Anime Central. (2004). *The legend of Son-Goku.* Retrieved June 9, 2004, from http://www.animecentral.net/goku/info/gokulegend/gokulegendintro. html

Ansdell, G. (1995). *Music for life: Aspects of creative music therapy with adult clients.* London: Jessica Kingsley.

Arnason, C. (2002). An eclectic approach to the analysis of improvisations in music therapy sessions. *Music Therapy Perspectives, 20*(1), 4–12.

Binder, A. (1993). Constructing racial rhetoric: Media depictions of harm in heavy metal and rap music. *American Sociological Review, 58*(6), 753–767.

Bishop, A. (2002). *Becoming an ally: Breaking the cycle of oppression in people* (2nd ed.). Halifax: Fernwood.

Bushman, B. (2002). Does venting anger feed or extinguish the flame? Catharsis, rumination, distraction, anger, and aggressive responding. *Journal of Personality and Social Psychology, 28*(6), 724–731.

Campbell, K. E. (1994). The signifying monkey revisited: Vernacular discourse and African American personal narratives. *JAC 14*(2). Retrieved June 5, 2004, from http://jac.gsu.edu/jac/14.2/articles/8.htm

Eliot, D. (1995). *Music matters.* New York: Oxford University Press.

Fisher, K. (2002). The role of art in child and adolescent group therapy. *The Group Circle.* Retrieved June 6, 2004, from http://www.groupsinc.org/pubs/GC_0802_art.html

Forman, M. (2000). Represent: Race, space and place in rap music. *Popular Music, 19*(1), 65–90.

Hanson, C. (Director), & Mathers, M. (Lead actor). (2002). *8-Mile* [DVD]. Hollywood, CA: Universal Studios & Dreamworks LLC.

Jackson, B. (2004). *Get your ass in the water and swim like me: African American narrative poetry from oral tradition.* New York: Routledge.

Keil, C., & Feld, S. (1994). *Music grooves.* Chicago: University of Chicago Press.

Kenny, C. (1996). The story of the field of play. In M. Langenberg, A. Aigen, & J. Frommer (Eds.), *Qualitative music therapy research: Beginning dialogues* (pp. 55–80). Gilsum, NH: Barcelona.

Keyes, C. (1996). At the crossroads: Rap music and its African nexus. *Ethnomusicology, 40*(2), 110–125.

Lee, C. A. (1997). *Music at the edge: The music therapy experiences of a musician with AIDS.* New York: Routledge.

Lee, C. A. (2000). A method of analyzing improvisations in music therapy. *Journal of Music Therapy, 37*(2), 147–156.

Lee, C. A. (2003). *The architecture of aesthetic music therapy.* Gilsum, NH: Barcelona.

Levine, L. W. (1977). *Black culture and Black consciousness: Afro-American thought from slavery to freedom.* New York: Oxford University Press.

Lightstone, A. J. (2004). Yo! Can ya flow?: A qualitative study of Hip Hop aesthetics and original rap lyrics created in group music therapy in an urban youth shelter. Retrieved September 1, 2010, from http://www.wlu.ca/soundeffects/researchlibrary/

Lunine, B. J. (2000). Genocide and juice: Reading the postcolonial discourses in Hip-Hop culture. In C. R. King (Ed.), *Postcolonial America*. Urbana: University of Illinois Press.

Perkins, W. P. (1996). *Droppin' science: Critical essays on rap music and Hip Hop culture*. Philadelphia: Temple University Press.

Pinn, A. B. (1999). "How ya livin'?" Notes on rap music and social transformation. *Western Journal of Black Studies, 23*(1), 10–21.

Rose, T. (1994). *Black noise: Rap music and Black culture in contemporary America*. Hanover: Wesleyan University Press.

Salaam, M. (1995). The aesthetics of rap. *African American Review, 29*(2), 89–97.

Shakur, T. (1991). *2-Pac: 2pacalypse now* [CD]. Santa Monica, CA: Interscope Records.

Stephens, R. J., & Wright, E. (2000). Beyond bitches, niggers, and ho's: Some suggestions for including rap music as a qualitative data source. *Race and Society, 3*, 23–40.

Stige, B. (2002). *Culture-centered music therapy*. Gilsum, NH: Barcelona.

Strauss, A., & Corbin, J. (1998). *Basics of qualitative research* (2nd ed.). Thousand Oaks, CA: Sage.

Sylvan, R. (2002). *Traces of the spirit: The religious dimensions of popular music*. New York: New York University Press.

Wigram, T. (2004). *Improvisation: Methods and techniques for music therapy clinicians, educators, and students*. London: Jessica Kingsley.

Yalom, I. (1980). *Existential psychotherapy*. New York: Basic.

Yalom, I. (1995). *The theory and practice of group psychotherapy* (4th ed.). New York: Basic.

Chapter 13

Rap Composition and Improvisation in a Short-Term Juvenile Detention Facility

Florence Ierardi and Nicole Jenkins

Introduction

This chapter explores the use of rap music in the context of music therapy in a short-term juvenile detention center. Music therapy was administered within the educational program at the transitional facility, where youth await decisions on their placement. The vast majority of the center's population is African American; thus the music therapy supervisor (Flossie) and intern (Nicole) maintained a cultural emphasis on African-influenced drumming, blues improvisation, and rap music improvisation and composition. A background of mental health needs and services in juvenile justice will be presented, followed by brief placement of rap as a medium of expression within the trajectory of African and African American oral traditions. Rhythmic applications for groups will be recommended, based on the authors' experiences at the center. Description of group and individual cases, including the use of drumming and music technology to support expression of rap lyrics, will be presented with reference to theoretical orientations of client-centered humanistic and supportive psychotherapy models.

Background

The county detention center, located in a suburb of a large urban area, is a short-term facility where youth await further placement or possible return home. The average length of stay is 18 days. Many of the youth, ages 10–21, live in low-socioeconomic areas of this county in which drugs, crime, and underfunded schools parallel those of the inner city. The vast majority of youth at this detention center is African American. There are four male units and one female unit. Behavioral health services are state and county funded and include case managers as well as a psychiatrist and psychologist, primarily for evaluative functions due to the short-term nature of the setting. Educational services are provided by the county intermediate unit, which is responsible for the educational needs of all students residing at the center. The intermediate unit faculty at the detention center includes a lead teacher, a teaching assistant, and several state-certified classroom teachers including a part-time art teacher who is trained as an art therapist. All students receive academic grades that are sent to their home school upon their release. The center is a 66-bed facility where the educational staff work with approximately 1,200 students per year. The facility saw a 77% increase in admissions between 1997 and 2007.

Early in 2008, Flossie Ierardi began weekly music therapy sessions at the request of the education program's lead teacher, simultaneously supporting a practicum experience for two pre-internship students. Flossie and her students provided three music therapy group sessions and two individual sessions each week. Groups were divided by residential units at the facility and were facilitated by Flossie, and each student had the opportunity to work with one individual under Flossie's supervision. Therapeutic goals included decreasing anxiety and depression resulting from the incarceration and its transitional nature, increasing self-esteem related to personal strengths and cultural background, and providing opportunities for healthy interactions. Due to the short-term placement, the approach was strength-based and positioned within supportive psychotherapy and client-centered models. After a 10-week pilot program was deemed successful for the youth and for the academic program, an internship experience was planned for the following academic year. Sharing of client information occurred on an informal basis; generally, we did not have access to files and were not aware of reasons for incarceration or mental health history.

Mental Health and Juvenile Justice

Despite high rates of mental disorders among juvenile offenders, estimated at over 66%, many youths in the juvenile justice system do not receive treatment for their disorders (Cauffman, 2004). Abram, Paskar, Washburn, and Teplin (2008) further clarify the above estimate, reporting that 70% female and 60% male juvenile detainees meet the criteria for a psychiatric disorder other than conduct disorder and approximately half have two or more disorders. Some incarcerated youth who do not meet criteria for formal diagnoses nonetheless exhibit depressive and trauma-related symptoms (Cauffman, 2004; Pajer, Kelleher, Gupta, Rolls, & Gardner, 2007). In addition to accurate diagnosis and access to mental health services, Cauffman states that developmental and ethnic factors should be considered when providing services for detained youth. In a study examining identification of mental illness among juvenile detainees, Rogers, Pumariega, Atkins, and Cuffe (2006) evaluated 120 detained youth, half of whom had been referred for treatment. Among both groups (referred and non-referred), they found disruptive behavior disorders and anxiety disorders were the most common diagnostic categories, with more of the referred youth presenting with affective disorders. Also present in both groups, but higher among referred youth, were symptoms of psychosis, although not necessarily thought disorder.

Cultural Contextualization

The most commonly used music therapy experiences in our group sessions at the detention center were improvised drumming, spontaneous vocalizing, most often rap, and blues instrumental and vocal improvisation. Rap, described by Keyes (1996) as "talking in rhythm over music or to an internally realized beat" (p. 225), is believed to have its origins in West Africa (Keyes, 2002). The griot, a storyteller and cultural historian, represents West African bardic traditions that have influenced the evolution of orality in the African diaspora. The trajectory can be traced to the southern United States through blues music and other oral traditions, and eventually to the Bronx in the 1970s (Keyes, 1996). Smitherman (1997) has identified the rapper as a "postmodern African griot" (p. 4). The rhythmic speech of the bard and the repetitive accompaniment of a kora (stringed instrument) and/or drum are thought by Keyes (2002) to prefigure rap. Vocal communication with drumming is also common in Ugandan society in East Africa, where specific messages can be transmitted through the use of these "indigenous media" (Mushengyezi, 2003, p. 108). Specific drumbeats, for example, may be used to call people to work or for rituals such as the crowning of a king.

Drumming and vocalizing, usually rapping and/or call and response forms, occurred regularly in group music therapy sessions at the center. As described in the group examples below, spontaneous rapping, consisting of improvised, preexisting, or client-composed lyrics, often occurred in groups in response to a familiar rhythm played on the drums. In a paper presented in South Africa in 2002, Maiello drew a parallel between the drumming/dancing ritual and the mother-infant relationship, both of which contain a regular and reliable beat, crucial for the establishment of trust (as cited in Berg, 2003). Rhythmic improvisation and acknowledgment of drumming traditions in West Africa, through presentation of video material by master drummer Babatunde Olatunji (1993), seemed to create an initial level of trust and credibility when the music therapy supervisor began implementing groups at the detention center. Also helpful were informational materials, that is, books and pictures of blues musicians prior to active engagement in instrumental blues improvisation. With the added opportunity for melodic improvisation offered by the blues progressions, the music therapist and/or intern pointed out that the xylophone, which was available to the group members, also has roots in West Africa.

While the music therapy sessions offered an environment of trust and safety, as noted above, some issues that emerged reflected the development of Hip-Hop culture and rap as a resistance against Eurocentric dominance and the survival of African Americans despite abandonment by the dominant culture, that is, racism (Smitherman, 1997). Resistance to active participation was a therapeutic issue in earlier music therapy groups; however, as the concept of music therapy became more familiar to the facility, trust began to develop and fewer group members refused to participate. This improvement could also be attributed to the professional growth of Nicole, who became more of a nurturing presence as the internship progressed. The issue of abandonment also emerged during group rap improvisations, but was most obvious in the individual rap compositions that will be described. While the use of rap, often containing images of crime and misogyny, may seem contraindicated in a detention center, early Hip-Hop culture/rap music seemed to be a response intended to address the increasing violence in the Bronx (Keyes, 1996). Furthermore, the lyrical content in existing rap music is often clearly reflective of the life experiences of this population. Since the education program and the detention staff discouraged the use of language that could be considered racially and/or sexually offensive, Flossie and Nicole encouraged group members to self-monitor when improvising and composing rap lyrics.

Theoretical Orientation

Several factors have influenced the underlying theoretical or clinical orientation of music therapy at the detention center. The short-term nature of the setting contraindicates the use of uncovering and/or confrontational techniques that would be more appropriate in long-term treatment settings or where co-occurring diagnoses, such as substance abuse, might be addressed. It was determined by the music therapy team and educational staff that the detainees, heretofore referred to as clients due to their relationship in the therapy process, would possibly present with one or more of the following symptoms or features: low self-esteem, shame resulting from the incarceration, lack of trust and/or feelings of safety in the forensic environment, loss of control over everyday experiences, anxiety about their future placement, and temporary or long-term challenges involving affect regulation. It is also likely that some or most of the clients have experienced complex trauma, or "multiple, chronic and prolonged, developmentally adverse traumatic events" (van der Kolk, 2005, p. 401), as revealed in self-disclosure during groups or informal conversations. In a study to determine prevalence of post-traumatic stress disorder and trauma in detained youth, Abram et al. (2004) found that most (92.5%) of the 898 randomly selected participants had experienced one or more traumatic events. A trauma-based approach, informed by brief therapeutic models and influenced by a person-centered orientation, became the focus for music therapy groups and individual sessions.

Supportive psychotherapy has been defined as the amelioration of symptoms or restoration to healthy levels of functioning in the areas of self-esteem, ego functions, and adaptive skills (Winston, Rosenthal, & Pinsker, 2004). Ego functions are described as those abilities that help us assess the environment to determine our responses. Ego functions relevant to this population include relation to reality, such as true consequences of behaviors, and regulation of affect. In addition, Perry (2006) describes brainstem dysregulation, with resulting impulsivity and increase in anxiety, as a consequence of complex trauma. He then states that the patterned and repetitive stimulation of rhythmic experiences are successful in helping to modulate the dysregulation. Adaptive skills, as addressed in supportive psychotherapy, include those behaviors in which individuals engage as a response to their assessment of events (Winston et al., 2004). Many youth in detention have not mastered adaptive skills, as demonstrated by impulsivity, misjudgment of the consequences of their anticipated behavior, and perhaps long-standing perception of needed survival skills. The three target areas of self-esteem, ego functions, and adaptive skills made a supportive approach the most applicable in our clinical perspectives. Techniques of supportive psychotherapy include advice giving, praise, and cognitive restructuring (Winston & Winston, 2002). The last technique can be considered within the context of trauma thinking—that is, that early and repeated trauma contributes to one's view of oneself and may result in cognitive distortions.

Music therapy in the clinical environment described here included a humanistic approach, due to the client's relationship to music, the therapist, and the group, when applicable. In describing the inherently humanist qualities of music therapy, Nolan (2008) states that it attracts that which is well in the person (growth-motivation and self-actualization), provides for peak experiences, stimulates inner resources of creativity, accesses personal history of music as well as the ancestral culture of one's music, engages the client with beauty as a link to one's own spirituality, and emphasizes a here-and-now experience.

Another theory that is relevant to the use of rap in music therapy, according to Weinstein (2005), is Winnicott's theory of play. She compares the process of freestyle rapping, which requires associative thinking and wit, to Winnicott's theory of play, or free association that relies upon trust among those involved. The concept of trust is again influenced by trauma-based care, which requires trust, connectedness, and expression of emotions (Bath, 2008). Weinstein later states that when trust exists to the extent that play is possible, it allows for experimentation with roles and behaviors that are not generally available to the participants.

Music Therapy in Juvenile Detention

Flower (1993) described a non-directive approach in music therapy work with adolescents in secure care, making efforts to provide opportunities for choices. Through the use of improvisation, Flower encouraged in the teens the ability to play, an experience which may have been missing from their childhood due to trauma. Wyatt (2002) includes percussion improvisation as a clinical resource in work with juvenile offenders, especially for those who prefer the strong rhythms of rap music. Rio and Tenney (2002) described work with a 16-year-old male placed in a residence for sex offenders. Music therapy goals included increased self-control, learning ways to relax (to assist in anger management), and appropriate self-expression, addressed through songwriting in his preferred style of rap. Through the individual music therapy process, he was able to modify his use of language so that his second song, performed for peers upon request, reflected positive thinking and contained lyrics that did not include expletives. He also demonstrated the ability to follow a productive task through to completion. This kind of ability was seen in a case reported by Ierardi, Bottos, and O'Brien (2007), when two boys in an after-school prevention program performed a rap song consisting of a poem one of them had created for a large audience of peers. In this example, the music therapist used a very basic rap rhythm played on two differently pitched drums to accompany the precomposed poem. Two boys who had had difficulty working together and completing tasks successfully were able to perform the song for the appreciative audience. In the two previous examples, the primary goal areas of supportive psychotherapy—self-esteem, ego functions, and adaptive skills—were addressed via song composition and performance using the rap genre. Rickson and Watkins (2003) describe a client-centered humanistic approach in a pilot study where music therapy was implemented to promote prosocial behaviors in adolescent boys who displayed aggressive behaviors. Among the musical experiences were rhythm-based ensembles, call and response, and improvisation, where the group members were encouraged to support each other as well as be supported in the music. Their study suggested that music therapy may help adolescents become aware of their own and others' feelings, as well as assist in internal organization and impulse control in those who are able to attend to the stimuli.

Therapists in other disciplines have reported the use of rap music with adolescents in detention. Ciardiello (2003), while describing a rap music program consisting primarily of lyric analysis and opportunities for composition in a residential setting, stated that youth who have experienced loss, rejection, and abandonment identify with the rappers' life struggles. Baker and Homan (2007) report an increased understanding of the role of rap and other popular music in the lives of teens, especially those with criminal histories. They described a project during which detained youth planned and produced a CD of their work as a group. They described the project as music lessons in this facility and stated that little is known about arts programs in juvenile detention facilities. All of the aforementioned treatment and programming occurred in longer-term facilities or residential treatment for juvenile offenders.

Music Therapy in the Short-Term Detention Center

Throughout the pilot program and the internship, drumming and rhythmic improvisation remained an anchor in the music therapy experience in typical group sessions. Male detainees were first placed on an admission unit and moved through the units depending on behavioral improvements; thus the group membership changed frequently because of new admissions and residents moving through the privilege system. There was one female unit, allowing for more consistency in the female detainees' groups; however, there were changes due to new admissions and short stays. Students occasionally missed music therapy because of appearances in video court.

During the 10-week pilot program, Flossie felt that it was helpful with this population to first present an African drumming video recording. This not only was an educational and perhaps validating experience for the clients but also was intended to communicate that this middle-aged Caucasian female music therapist respected the genre and the well-known African drummer Babatunde Olatunji (1993). It was also hoped that this could provide a safe environment in which we could address cognitive processes via attention to musical techniques, instruments, and rhythmic invariants. If the group appeared interested in the instruments and eager to participate upon arrival, the therapist instead gave a brief introduction to the instruments and basic techniques, followed by a warm-up improvisation or imitative call-and-response, depending on the therapist's determination of the need for structure. Many clients tended to be guarded at first, especially if they were new to the facility and dealing with issues such as anxiety about further disposition, anger and/or shame due to the incarceration, concern about their own safety, and fear of appearing vulnerable. It was not unusual for several group members to refuse to participate and sit passively in the circle. Disruptive behavior was not typical, since detention staff was always present and the clients were aware that their behavior was observed. In this environment, refusal to participate in therapy was perhaps one of their only options for control. With patience and occasional interaction, and the avoidance of direct confrontation, most group members gradually became less guarded. Several approaches were used when a majority of group members refused to participate:

- Music listening, as chosen by one or more group members, was encouraged if the group tended to be passive. Musical choices, made from a collection provided by Nicole based on the preferences of the clients, were generally current rap music and occasional rhythm and blues recordings. This experience would generally lead to (1) lyric analysis, (2) lowering of defenses and thus willingness to participate in instrumental improvisation, or (3) increased interaction among group members as discussion of various artists and songs ensued.
- Flossie has experience in rudimental drumming, seen in *Drumline*, a popular movie among teens. Performance of rudimental compositions often led to reactions of surprise and laughter or verbal comments among the students, due to Flossie's age and gender. This experience, as in the African drumming video, could reinforce a sense of safety through reliance on cognitive processes.

Discussion of the movie's favorite scenes and the overall message was therapeutic in this context.

Group Case Description

The following examples are based on recordings and group notes for two sessions that occurred 10 days apart, with group 2B (unit name changed). During each of the two sessions, there were two recorded examples that will be described here. Due to the short-term nature of the facility, some of the group attendance was consistent from the first to the second session and some were new to the group. Ages ranged from 13 to 17 years old. Most members were active participants, although at least one preferred to contribute verbally but not musically. The groups were facilitated by Nicole. Audio recordings were analyzed by Flossie and Nicole.

Musical Example 1, Session 1

One of the group members began the improvisation with a shaker and made a vocal sound that seemed to be imitative, perhaps humorously, of African music. This vocal call occurred intermittently throughout the improvisation. Dwayne, who had been quite enthusiastic about the music, initiated a rhythm at approximately 96 bpm on a djembe, an African drum with a range of high and low resonance. He began with a commonly used rhythm, one which the boys had attributed to rap artist Meek Millz:

The group members chose to play various sized drums, xylophone, shaker, and later claves and tambourine. The xylophone was arranged in an e minor pentatonic scale (EGABDE) for all examples. The patterns during example 1 were repetitive and in close range, similar to high-pitched keyboard figures heard in some existing rap songs, for example:

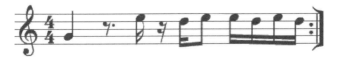

After about 1 minute, Nicole introduced a pattern of a one-measure rest on the fourth measure of each phrase. This intervention seemed to raise the energy level further, as the participants' musical responses became freer during those breaks, although the group as a whole was able to return to the "groove" or structure after each break. At 2:00 in the recording, there was talking during the drumming, one boy mentioning a solo. Several seconds later, the drums stopped playing and the tambourine and shakers were featured with a tremolo. There was some laughter from the group and one group member enthusiastically cued the others to begin the groove again. At 2:50, there was again talking/planning and at 2:58, Dwayne said, "When I say 2 you say B," initiating a call-and-response section. This was repeated several times; however, the only person to respond verbally was Nicole while the others continued playing. Dwayne initiated a countdown, similar to the cues given by Nicole, to signal the end of the music. He then ended with a last stroke on the drum and said, "Yeah, you know we're champions." There was agreement and laughter from other group members as the tambourine continued to roll.

Remarks: Dwayne had emerged as the leader, although it is unclear whether that was his role on their unit, that is, prior to the group session. This was supported by Nicole, as Dwayne was modeling healthy behavior without monopolizing the group. Although the improvisation did not result in a rap per se, the rhythmic foundation throughout was based on a popular rap artist's style. The call and response can certainly be considered reminiscent of the African call and response idiom, part of the tradition of orality that weaves through the group improvisations and a common practice in rap. This example contains an interesting mix of African traditions (drumming, vocal calls, and chants) with current musical styles via the rap rhythm. The three supportive psychotherapy goal areas were evident: (1) self-esteem was demonstrated by the group members' musical intention and interdependence, as well as the obvious "champions" statement at the end; (2) ego functions of reality-based thinking and regulation of affect as demonstrated by (3) the adaptive skills of impulse control and appropriate group interactions of leadership and support.

Musical Example 2, Session 1

Dwayne continued in a leadership role; however, there was more vocal/verbal expression from other group members. He began vocalizing an existing rap with a few drums accompanying. While Nicole offered a strong and stable repetition of a groove similar to that of the first example, the group's rhythmic responses were somewhat less organized at first. At 0:17, Dwayne cued the group to stop and "start over," resulting in increased synchrony, although it was still necessary for Nicole to maintain a very strong rhythmic ground. This example seemed more challenging as it was based on a current existing rap song by the same artist, Meek Millz. The style resembles what Krims (2001) describes as percussion-effusive flow, that is, the rhythmic placement of the lyrics may emphasize offbeats and in this case, many of the vocal phrases begin on the upbeat, or just prior to the strong beat of the rhythmic pattern, thus making it more difficult to accompany with an ongoing repeated pattern. Nicole's role here was more supportive and stabilizing due to the challenging musical nature of the piece. At 1:35, another group member, Michael, began to chant syllables in support and when Dwayne, the original soloist, could not remember all of the words, Jamal, a younger group member, took over the rapping. Eventually, other group members were rapping in unison, as this song was familiar to them. The music continued with improvised vocal contributions, such as repetition of the soloist's words and other brief verbal encouragements (e.g., "oh yeah").

Remarks: While this example sounded less organized, the recording contains a higher level of vocal participation and group interaction than the first improvisation. Similar to African styles, the group members received vocal support from each other while rapping, a practice that Keyes (2002) states "synchronizes speakers and listeners" (p. 26). The preexisting song that was initiated by the group in this example contained some expletives. In favor of the increased group participation and supportive verbal and nonverbal interactions, Nicole decided to support the musical process instead of setting limits and/or focusing on the content of the lyrics. The participants were able to demonstrate impulse control and regulation of affect, despite their exuberance within the creative process. Adaptive social skills were apparent within the music as they encouraged each other vocally and instrumentally. They worked cooperatively by assisting each other with words (with a healthy dose of braggadocio—a component of Hip-Hop culture and rap music) to preserve the integrity of the musical process, demonstrating a commitment to the music itself and to the group.

Musical Example 3, Session 2

This session occurred 10 days later with a smaller group, six members, from the same unit as the previous recordings. Dwayne assumed a leadership role again, this time using another existing song by the same artist. This time the rhythmic pattern began with a skeletal rhythm and was gradually filled in until it became the following rhythm with slight variations:

The last two notes of the rhythm became an important predictable point that was sometimes duplicated by several instruments. The vocals began almost immediately, with some slurring of lyrics that were explicit, as he was encouraged by Nicole to self-monitor. The xylophone played throughout this 2:27 example, but more randomly than in the previous examples. After 1 minute, Dionte began to use the keyboard, playing a repeated note in the bass on each downbeat; however, this stopped after about 30 seconds. At 1:19, the tambourine entered with a well-placed note, but this was not repeated. As the song ended, the therapist continued the above rhythm on the djembe and the xylophone continued as the lyrics came to an end.

Remarks: This example contained less interaction, cohesion, and creativity than those of the previous session. Several of the group members dropped out and just listened, and the keyboard and tambourine had very brief gestures. For this group, some of whom were new to making music with each other, there seemed to be a lack of interest in having one person simply reiterate previously created lyrics. In an effort to increase participation for those who may have been reluctant to self-disclose, Nicole used the experience as a segue or transition to a more creative, interactive process by asking the group, via chant within the rhythmic improvisation, to rap about "plans for the future." As some of the young men in this setting had little motivation to aspire about life goals, Nicole chose to use an intervention of positive thinking to suggest a shift from negativity and aggression to a reality of adaptive possibilities.

The following example lasted more than 16 minutes with occasional pauses, but the group members' expressions included true responses to the directive, plays on words, reflections on the past, and a return to the previous week's chanting of their unit name.

Musical Example 4, Session 2

Dwayne chanted "plans for the future" and Nicole matched his tempo with the following rhythm:

This slightly slower tempo, about 88 bpm, and the space in the measure seemed to create a feeling of openness that invited thoughtful vocal responses from two of the young men in the form of freestyling, described by Weinstein as improvisational composition relying on verbal dexterity and often competitive (2005). As the instruments entered, the rhythm eventually returned to that of the previous example, but continued in this slower tempo, possibly in an attempt to make it more conducive for freestyling. Dionte, still playing keyboard, experimented with two pitches, a minor third apart, until he developed a pattern with that interval using the rhythm heard earlier in the session:

Vocals returned with the chant "plans for the future." Dwayne again began by listing things that he wants: *nice house, nice wife, nice car.* He then vocalized about things he is "tired of": *being on the block, selling drugs, running from the cops.* An older group member, James, took a turn with similar content and when Dwayne reentered for his turn, he began to play with words and syllables, as though encouraged by the competition. Nicole musically reminded him of "plans for the future" and there was a brief call and response between them using those words. As the rhythm continued, there was verbal interaction among group members and Nicole. He soon returned to what he was tired of (e.g., *hearing about Black people getting shot*).

There was a pause in the rhythm as there was group discussion and working out of lyrics. When the lead teacher suggested from the periphery that they might want to use a poem from the center's book of original poetry, Dwayne seemed to be encouraged competitively again and initiated a new round of spontaneous improvisation, again using wordplays such as "pop to the top" and "top to the pop." James began rapping at 7:00, with similar words that reflected life on the streets and the inability to move forward. Dwayne reentered around 9:20, with lines such as the following:

> I'm livin at the speed of light; My mom always told me you have a life; My dad told me sell drugs and get with it; That's all I know; But now I'm tryin to change my life.

James also began to disclose more personal information, his lines including the following:

I was 13 when I had my son; Now I'm tryin to be a father to my son; He said hey Dad when you comin home, I say I don't know; I'm a strong man.

After continuing in this way, with intermittent entrances on instruments, Robert, who took over the keyboard, played a preprogrammed beat that was approximately 126 bpm, which the group called a "party beat." For the next couple of minutes the group played along, with the clave taking a strong role:

The group allowed themselves to be reined in by this rhythm, joining in with instruments as James chanted syllables intermittently. The keyboard player again changed to a slightly faster beat, about 132 bpm, and Nicole played the following rhythm on the djembe to maintain consistency:

Dwayne began chanting the name of the unit on the first two beats of the measure, creating a variation on the original theme of the first musical example of the prior week. He would intermittently chant, "This is what we do." When the group stopped playing, he said it again to end the piece.

Remarks: Example #4 was a long experience with occasional pauses in attention to the music and group focus. It seemed that throughout the 16:17, there was participation and interaction from some or all members of the group. This example differed in that Nicole took a more active role at times, engaging in the rap and sometimes verbally encouraging more positive thinking, observing that the group members always returned to lyrics about life on the streets. She also periodically allowed for the rappers to return to the more familiar material that they needed to express, and to take breaks from the intensity of the material, as seen in the few periods where the group focus was rather diffuse and lacked direction. For the last few minutes, when the keyboard player introduced "party beats," the group seemed to be attracted by the faster tempo and basic beat that were more conducive to dancing than rapping. Perhaps this was a relief from the reflective lyrics of this example, and provided for reduction of anxiety and the sealing over that was needed to end the experience.

Possible Contraindications: Since the group approach described in the examples above was improvisational, Flossie and Nicole generally supported stylistic preferences that emerged during the group process. Rap vocal improvisations often developed naturally from rhythms used in drumming initiated or supported by the facilitator, so the genre itself would not have been contraindicated at those times. In some instances, the use of highly stimulating rhythmic music was not supported if one or more members of the group appeared to be easily overstimulated. Flossie and Nicole relied upon observations of the need for structure when making clinical decisions regarding stylistic elements of music to initiate and/or support.

For groups that needed increased structure due to impulsivity and agitation, they would incorporate harmonic support, such as familiar progressions on keyboard or guitar, in lieu of purely rhythmic improvisation. Another option for increased structure was the use of basic rhythmic imitation or call and response to assess whether the group could tolerate the unpredictable nature of improvisation. Within the music therapy approached described by Flossie and Nicole, clinical judgments were made based on assessments of group tolerance for certain musical elements rather than the musical genre.

Individual Case Descriptions

The following descriptions are based on music therapy sessions with two individuals. They each worked on an original rap composition that they recorded during their sessions with Nicole.

Individual: Kevin

Kevin was 17 years old when he was seen for music therapy. He reported that his father was in jail and his mother was a drug addict. He was awaiting placement at another facility. He had expressed a desire to live with his uncle, but this was not approved by the authorities. He had a 2-year-old son whose birthday is the day after his, and around the time of his incarceration.

In group music therapy sessions, Kevin's participation varied according to his mood. After one session during which he seemed particularly sullen and angry, Nicole and the lead teacher discussed individual sessions. He readily agreed and shared with Nicole during the first session that he was upset at not being able to see his son for their birthdays. Music therapy goals included elevating mood, increasing frustration tolerance, and awareness of coping strategies. During the first of 6 sessions, which occurred during 3 weeks, Nicole gave Kevin an overview of the keyboard and the recording technology. He had apparently had exposure to recording studio equipment, so he was eager to begin immediately. Nicole suggested that he begin with the drum track, as this would be the foundation for the other tracks. He used the following rhythm:

He worked methodically on the five available tracks from one session to the next, with assistance from Nicole. The three middle tracks were sustained synchronized pitches, each lasting 2 to 4 beats. The highest-sounding track was a rhythmic pattern using the sound that emulates scratching of vinyl records, often heard from rap DJs. Kevin was then encouraged to create lyrics and a title for his recording. The title he chose for the 2:14 recording was "Harsh Life." He expressed a sense of hopelessness early on, stating *I don't even want to feel no more.* Other lyrics reflected the title including lines such as *I don't want these cuffs and I don't want this life.* He also wrote about intermittent homelessness, mentioning *Nothin to eat* and *Nowhere to sleep.* He ended the song by expressing frustration at himself and others *"out here."* Kevin's vocal style had a monotone quality. He recited the lyrics in a rhythmic fashion; however, after the first few lines, the rhythmic flow of his speech was not in synchrony with that of the underlying music, as though anxious about the lyrics or pressured and eager to finish. He was speaking softly into the microphone apparently because he was somewhat intimidated by the presence of the detention staff person. It is interesting to note that he finished recording the lyrics at about 1:06 and the recording continues, with the same repeated loops, for another 1:08 before the piece ends. He chose to stop the mid-range tracks first, then the beat, and finally the scratch.

Remarks: Despite the lyrics being about difficulties in his life, Kevin was very pleased with his achievement. He was able to complete all steps of the project, including choosing sounds and recording each track, picking a topic and writing lyrics, and finally recording the vocal part, in time for Nicole to make a copy on CD for him prior to her academic break. He demonstrated excellent planning and problem-solving skills with gentle encouragement from Nicole. During verbal discussions with Nicole, he was able to express frustration at his current situation and a desire to have his "own place." While this may be unrealistic at this time, it appeared that his sense of hopelessness may have mitigated somewhat. He also stated that he wanted to get out of "the game," as that could lead to lengthy incarceration or worse. The static nature of the accompaniment, especially after the vocals ended, seemed to demonstrate a need for predictability and consistency. Based on Kevin's background, it is possible that he experienced complex trauma and is currently struggling with identifying options that will allow him a better future than that which he may be facing now. The individual music therapy sessions incorporated trauma-based care by providing safety, connectedness, and a vehicle for expressing emotions.

Individual: Tanisha

Tanisha was 17 years old at the time of this incarceration for violation of probation. She apparently had an explosive temper and had several experiences of "failure to adjust" at residential settings. Her mother had died of a drug overdose before Tanisha was 10 years old and currently her father was her primary caregiver. She had disagreements with her father, who wanted her to follow all Islamic traditions; however, she preferred to choose certain customs. Tanisha had played drums in a community drill team and proved to be quite a talented and enthusiastic group member and leader during music therapy sessions. During one session, however, she presented with a flat affect and was somewhat withdrawn; Nicole asked her if she would like some individual time. Nicole hoped to give Tanisha an opportunity to express her immediate concerns without becoming impulsive.

Tanisha chose for the first few measures to use percussive sounds of snare drum and a whistle effect, perhaps based on her drill team experience, at a tempo of approximately 100 bpm. At the same time, she used a very high sustained pitch, along with a mid-high-range melodic motif in quarter and eighth note motion. On the fourth measure, she began the lyrics over a drum pattern that became variable but was based on the following rhythm:

After she had recorded the instrumental tracks, she began working on the words during the session and then continued independently as their next session would be Nicole's last day. When they returned, Nicole had imported the tracks into her computer and Tanisha recorded the words. Her speech velocity was rather quick as though she had practiced the song. The words as they appear here are taken exactly from Tanisha's writing; however, her recitation was metrically synchronized with the accompaniment pattern, that is, the following structure does not indicate beginnings and endings of lines as vocalized.

> Home is were its at thats were we need to
> be, waking up in da morning without of familys.
> We can make it all we got to do is believe, Being locked
> up aint a place for you or me? Think about we can do any
> thing we want to, the world is an opportunity for
> me and you, I never would of thought I would
> be in this position, Dad telling me to be good
> I should of listen, Now look Im locked up in
> a cage day and night, when trouble come my way
> I should of took flight, Err-nite I think about
> my life, praying to god that I can get it right
> Im almost 18 my adult life, So this is a
> message from me to you do the best that
> you can do, cuz'n be in trouble is for fools.
> Stay in school, get a good job, and I promise
> in the end you'll make yourself proud.
> Think about it is ya life
> So live it up and all that
> Street life man just give it
> up its to much out here
> for us to see so love yaself
> BE FREE

Clearly, some of Tanisha's words are misspelled and others are deliberately spelled in language consistent with rap. Her words indicate a sense of abandonment as she continues to deal with the loss of her mother, regret for the behavior that led to her incarceration, and yet a sense of hope on her fifth line and again at the end of the song. The underlying rap rhythm ended at 1:00 and for the last 10 seconds, the music returned to snare drum, whistle effect, and the melodic tracks. The last tracks heard were the very high sustained pitch and the mid-range track, a g which had the sense of the tonal center, plus a higher track with a toggling b^1 and c^1. As the instrumentation thinned, the last sounds were the b^1 and c^1, and then finally ending on the latter, leaving the listener with a sense of incompletion given the musical tendency for the fourth degree of the scale to want to resolve rather than be an ending point.

Remarks: Tanisha took full advantage of the two individual music therapy sessions through this songwriting experience. Her verbal material is an eloquent expression of numerous feelings related to her life and her choices. As with Kevin, she has a desire to change her life, yet Tanisha demonstrates awareness of adaptive skills as she makes appropriate suggestions even though she seems to be telling someone else. Perhaps she feels it is too late for her, or she is playing a nurturing and encouraging role for herself in the absence of her mother. At the end of her recording, the remaining instrumentation seemed rather telling of the various aspects of herself that she may have been experiencing: a centering/grounding g, along with a very high almost birdlike sound. The toggling b^1–c^1, finally ending on c^1, may have indicated an ungrounded vulnerable feeling or a sense of more to come (i.e., future). As with many clinical musical examples, we are led to more questions that could be explored with further treatment, where goal areas of self-esteem and strengthening of ego functions may be addressed to curb impulsivity. At the time of this recording, Tanisha was able to channel multiple feelings and issues into one composition through her preferred genre of rap music.

Conclusion

In recent years, the use of culturally informed music therapy methods has become an ethical responsibility. Ginwright and Cammarota (2002) state that rap music, as part of Hip-Hop culture, is used by young people to express pain, anger, and the frustration of oppression. Rap music can also express joy, appreciation, and hope for the future. This phenomenon can certainly be seen in the above clinical examples, where incarcerated youth have used rap lyrics to express loss, regret, abandonment, and eventually the hope of change. As the current iteration of orality in the African and African American traditions, rap music has carved a place in music history by bringing to consciousness the issues of racism, poverty, and oppression. While this is significant for all Americans, it appears to be especially true for young African Americans who have been exposed to violence, crime, and poverty as the result of racism in our society. As these young people begin to interface with the justice system, where they may experience blame rather than an opportunity to heal, issues of identity and self-esteem emerge. Through the use of music that speaks to young people's identities and life stories, the music therapist can begin to facilitate a process in which youth may experience validation, learn new ways to view the world and themselves, and discover the capacity for change. Through the introduction of African drumming and blues music, the youth were exposed to a rich cultural past and were also supported in their need for expression of present life experiences through rap composition. Successful musical/instrumental risk taking and expression of "plans for the future" via rap improvisation were part of a therapeutic approach in this short-term environment to encourage the envisioning of their full potential and a more positive future.

References

Abram, K. M., Paskar, L. D., Washburn, J. J., & Teplin, L. A. (2008). Perceived barriers to mental health services among youths in detention. *Journal of the American Academy of Child and Adolescent Psychiatry, 47*(3), 301–308.

Abram, K. M., Teplin, L. A., Charles, D. R., Longworth, S. L., McClelland, G. M., & Dulcan, M. K. (2004). Posttraumatic stress disorder and trauma in youth in juvenile detention. *Archives of General Psychiatry, 61*(4), 403–410.

Baker, S., & Homan, S. (2007). Rap, recidivism and the creative self: A popular music programme for young offenders in detention. *Journal of Youth Studies, 10*(4), 459–476.

Bath, H. (2008). The three pillars of trauma-informed care. *Reclaiming Children and Youth, 17*(2), 17–21.

Berg, A. (2003). Ancestor reverence and mental health in South Africa. *Transcultural Psychiatry, 40*(2), 194–207.

Cauffman, E. (2004). A statewide screening of mental health symptoms among juvenile offenders in detention. *Journal of the American Academy of Child and Adolescent Psychiatry, 43*(4), 430–439.

Ciardiello, S. (2003). Meet them in the lab: Using Hip-Hop music therapy groups with adolescents in residential settings. In N. E. Sullivan, S. E. Mesbur, N. C. Lang, D. Goodman, & L. Mitchell (Eds.), *Social work with groups: Social justice through personal, community and societal change* (pp. 103–117). New York: Haworth.

Flower, C. (1993). Control and creativity: Music therapy with adolescents in secure care. In M. Heal and T. Wigram (Eds.), *Music therapy in health and education* (pp. 41–45). London, England: Jessica Kingsley.

Ginwright, S., & Cammarota, J. (2002). New terrain in youth development: The promise of a social justice approach. *Social Justice, 29*(4), 82–95.

Ierardi, F., Bottos, M., & O'Brien, M. K. (2007). Safe expressions: A community-based creative arts therapy program for at-risk youth. In V. Camilleri (Ed.), *Healing the inner-city child: Creative arts therapies with at-risk youth* (pp. 254–267). London: Jessica Kingsley.

Keyes, C. L. (1996). At the crossroads: Rap music and its African nexus. *Ethnomusicology, 40*(2), 223–248.

Keyes, C. L. (2002). *Rap music and street consciousness.* Urbana, IL: University of Illinois Press.

Krims, A. (2000). *Rap music and the poetics of identity.* Cambridge, UK: Cambridge University Press.

Mushengyezi, A. (2003). Rethinking indigenous media: rituals, "talking" drums and orality as forms of public communication in Uganda. *Journal of African Cultural Studies, 16*(1), 107–117.

Nolan, P. (2008). Existential/humanistic music therapy: Theory and practice. Paper presented at XII World Congress of Music Therapy, Buenos Aires, Argentina.

Olatunji, B. (1993). *African drumming.* [VHS]. Brattleboro, VT: Interworld Music Associates.

Pajer, K. A., Kelleher, K., Gupta, R. A., Rolls, J., & Gardner, W. (2007). Psychiatric and medical health care policies in juvenile detention facilities. *Journal of the American Academy of Child and Adolescent Psychiatry, 46*(12), 1660–1667.

Perry, B. (2006). Applying principles of neurodevelopment to clinical work with maltreated and traumatized children: The neurosequential model of therapeutics. In N. B. Webb (Ed.), *Working with traumatized youth in child welfare* (pp. 27–52). New York: Guilford.

Rickson, D. J., & Watkins, W. G. (2003). Music therapy to promote prosocial behaviors in aggressive adolescent boys: A pilot study. *Journal of Music Therapy, 40*(4), 283–301.

Rio, R. E., & Tenney, K. S. (2002). Music therapy for juvenile offenders in residential treatment. *Music Therapy Perspectives, 20*(2), 89–107.

Rogers, K. M., Pumariega, A. J., Atkins, D. L., & Cuffe, S. P. (2006). Conditions associated with identification of mentally ill youths in juvenile detention. *Community Mental Health Journal, 42*(1), 25–40.

Smitherman, G. (1997). "The chain remains the same": Communicative practices in the Hip-Hop nation. *Journal of Black Studies, 28*(1), 3–25.

van der Kolk, B. A. ((2005). Developmental trauma disorder. *Psychiatric Annals, 35*(5), 401–408.

Weinstein, S. (2005). Free style: The role of play in rap composition. In D. Shepherd (Ed.), *Creative engagements: Thinking with children* (pp. 103–106). Oxford, UK: Inter-Disciplinary Press. Retrieved from http://www.inter-disciplinary.net/publishing-files/idp/eBooks/CE%20 v1.9.pdf#page=110

Winston, A., Rosenthal, R. N., & Pinsker, H. (2004). *Introduction to supportive psychotherapy.* Washington, DC: American Psychiatric Press.

Winston, A., & Winston, B. (2002) *Handbook of integrated short-term psychotherapy.* Washington, DC: American Psychiatric Press.

Wyatt, J. G. (2002). From the field: Clinical resources for music therapy with juvenile offenders. *Music Therapy Perspectives, 20*(2), 80–88.

Chapter 14

Song Communication Using Rap Music in a Group Setting with At-Risk Youth

Amy M. Donnenwerth

Some have called it a fad that would eventually go away. Others have said that it isn't actually music and have insistently labeled it noise. However, as George (1998) asserts, "Hip Hop has outlived all its detractors and even surprised most ardent early supporters by always changing, and with each change, expanding its audience" (pp. x–xi). Rap music didn't go away, but the judgments continue.

For almost 10 years I have used rap music in song communication sessions with teenagers at a residential treatment center for youth offenders. As a classically trained musician, I knew very little about rap when I started the program. What I ascertained almost instantly was that Bach, Beethoven, and Mozart were not going to be the best "musical tools" for reaching these adolescents. I quickly surmised that I must meet them where they were musically, in the world of rap music. Thus began a journey into the therapeutic use of rap music.

Validation Theory

Time after time I have witnessed young people put their guard down when they have been validated through their musical preferences. Stone, Patton, and Heen (1999) state, "Telling people to change makes it less rather than more likely that they will. This is because people almost never change without first feeling understood" (p. 29). What better way to have teenagers feel understood than through the portal of their musical preferences? If you tell them that their music is "bad" or "sends a negative message," you run the risk of losing them from the start.

Just because we have validated our clients by allowing them to pick their own songs does not mean that we have agreed or promoted the message in the songs they have picked. Feil (1993) states, "Painful feelings that are expressed and validated by a trusted listener will diminish. Painful feelings that are ignored or suppressed will gain strength. Validation is based on the notion that there is a reason behind all behaviors" (pp. 29–30). With this in mind I have validated clients who have chosen rap music. This has allowed unproductive behaviors that are presented in some rap lyrics to be acknowledged and then discussed in a clinical setting.

Program Inception

Before I began the song communication program with rap music, I carefully assessed the population and spent a great deal of time researching rap music and its origins. To best understand Hip-Hop culture, I have read many things about it, including information about graffiti art, break dancing, MC-ing, and mixing. With the goal of reaching clients by understanding their musical lives, I have read biographies, newspaper articles, magazine articles, historical perspectives, cultural commentaries, and even the Sunday newspaper comics, which have often presented satire about this cultural force. I have searched the Web for Hip-Hop sites and learned about various artists, including news about their careers and personal lives. Through all of this, I have been careful not to pass personal judgment and have done my best to be open and receptive to a world that was quite different from my own. I have been excited about learning new things and intrigued by the many facets of rap music. As I began this process, I almost immediately learned that coworkers and peers were not always supportive of Hip-Hop culture and specifically rap music. I remember one coworker with a sneer tossing a rap CD at me saying sarcastically, "Here is your 'therapeutic' CD!" Other coworkers commented, "What does a little white girl like you care about rap music?" Once I developed some credibility with both clients and coworkers, we began to learn from each other. Through open and sometimes intense but productive discussions, we made bridges across cultural, ethnic, socioeconomic, and gender barriers. This process has been invigorating and inspiring, but certainly not without challenges.

Purpose Statements

Just when I have started feeling a measure of confidence about knowing something about Hip-Hop and rap music, a client would bring in an underground (not commercially popular) rap selection and my knowledge would go to a new level. The payback has been immense and I have discovered that the more I have been equipped with Hip-Hop and rap music knowledge, the more I have been able to relate to and work with clients. Out of these discoveries, I have developed purpose statements that have been helpful when explaining the song communication with rap music program to peers and coworkers. The statements have helped clarify the logic for using rap in a therapeutic manner.

Purpose statements:

1. After a music therapist assesses that rap music is the preference of the clients, rap music can be used to acknowledge and recognize the clients' choices.
2. This acknowledgment promotes a positive, trusting relationship between the clients and the music therapist and thus creates an environment where the clients feel at ease and in their own element.
3. A safe environment enables clients to share during clinical discussions and helps them with the development of their personal and interpersonal skills.

I view the purpose statements as an overall mission statement for the therapeutic use of rap music. The purpose statements are followed by a protocol. This protocol has been critical to the success I have had in helping clients with their transformation process.

Protocol

Lyric Discussion and Song Communication Definitions

The protocol starts by examining the differences between song lyric discussion and song communication. Bruscia (1998) describes song lyric discussion as follows: "The therapist brings in a song that serves as a springboard for discussion of issues that are therapeutically relevant to the client. After listening to the song, the client is asked to analyze the meaning of the lyrics and to examine (in dialogue) with the therapist (or other clients) the relevance of the lyrics to the client or the client's life" (p. 124). In contrast, Bruscia describes song communication: "The therapist asks the client to select or bring in a recorded song which expresses or discloses something about the client that is of relevance to the client or the therapist selects a recording that communicates something of relevance to the client. Both parties listen to the recording and explore what the music communicates about the client, the client's life or therapeutic issues" (p. 124). The protocol I created specifically employs the song communication technique. I use this method because it empowers the clients to make a choice when they often feel that so many choices have been made for them. It is also a form of validation for the clients. If the clients feel validated from the beginning, they are often more likely to open up and share during discussions. Regarding terminology, though, I have discovered that clients are more agreeable to the term *lyric discussion*, and thus this is the term I often use with them.

Assessment

The next step in the protocol is assessing how well the clients can introspect and reflect, including the consideration of their resilience and ego strength. If the assessment reveals that clients have poor introspection and reflection skills, song communication will not likely be the technique that will prove to be most effective for the clients.

Self-assessment is also important. Wheeler (1983) maintains that music listening activities may be used in a psychodynamic framework to elicit emotional or cognitive reactions needed for insight into feelings and behaviors. She states that music therapists who utilize these music listening techniques "must have advanced clinical training and be thoroughly aware of individual psychopathology" (p. 11). Therefore, it is critical that music therapists not only thoroughly assess their clients but also carefully and objectively assess their own abilities and skills.

Activity-Based and Insight-Based Music Therapy

Once these assessments have been made and there is a strong indication for moving forward, the next step in the protocol involves discerning whether to conduct an activity-based session or an insight-oriented session using song communication. Wheeler (1983) describes activity-based sessions as focusing on the music and what the clients might like about the song. She explains insight-oriented sessions as focusing on what the clients might think the lyrics mean and how they might feel about the song. I have found the insight-oriented structure has worked best for the song communication sessions with rap music. I have also found that when working with a group, insight-oriented song communication works best in a closed group setting. In other words, this technique works best if group members do not change so trust can build over a period of time.

When individual group members have been asked to select a song for a group, some clients have initially said to me, "I just like it." I then reply, "It is important that you are able to talk about how and what connects you to this song." Sometimes they have needed a little more time to think about their song choice, but usually the time they have been allowed has helped them carefully consider their choice. When the clients are trying to avoid talking about various therapeutic issues, having the clients articulate a specific reason for their song selection has often helped them hone in on a particular clinical concern.

Researching Songs and Rappers

Once the clients have selected a rap song and related their connection to the song lyrics, the next step in the protocol involves me listening to and researching the many aspects of the song. This involves thoroughly researching the song's artist(s), including the biography of the artist(s) and, if possible, the reasoning and story behind the song's lyrics. While many popular artists sing songs written by other lyricists, rappers are often the ones penning their own song lyrics. The stories about the writing of various rap songs have often been significant to why the clients selected the song and why they have related to that particular song. The more information the therapist has about the rap song, its background, and the artist, the more prepared the therapist is to guide, reflect, and facilitate clinical discussions.

Reviewing Clients' Histories

The next step in the protocol is to comprehensively review the clients' histories. This step is vital to the success of using rap music in song communication. The links between clients' histories and the songs they have selected can be basic or complex. Some clients I have worked with come from a single-parent home and many times that parent is their mother. An example of a basic link would be the song "Dear Mama" by Tupac Shakur. The basic link with the clients' histories and the song lyrics is that both the lyricist and the clients are sorry for the pain and suffering they have caused their mama and they want her to know how much they love her. A more complex link would be the many rap songs that describe witnessing the killing of a "homie," a discourse reference to a person/friend from the same neighborhood and/or gang. Many of the clients that I have worked with have seen or been a part of violent acts. A considerable number of them have reported that they have not willingly or easily discussed this topic during daily group time with their social worker and/or primary therapist. Time and again clients have reported that it wasn't until they experienced a song communication group with rap music that they opened up and shared stories about their grief, guilt, trauma, and more associated with the violence in their lives. All this considered, knowing as much as possible about the clients' histories cannot be overemphasized.

Preparation for Client-Centered Discussions

When preparing for client-centered discussions, I have found it most helpful to explore the rap song and the clients' history from as many angles as possible. After doing so, I have felt fully prepared for what might transpire during the song communication sessions. Some group members don't understand aspects of the rap, and because I have done my homework, I feel more prepared to guide them through discussions. If the group discussion has veered off to what seems to be a gratuitous topic, I have been prepared to refocus the group onto a clinical issue. The vigilance and attentiveness to preparatory steps has paid off repeatedly, considerably improving client-therapist rapport. The clients have sensed that I have done my homework and seem to appreciate that. Many of the positive evaluation reports from clients have attested to the transformative powers of song communication with rap music.

It is noteworthy that I have had the luxury of doing a once-a-week session with a closed group that meets for approximately 12 weeks. Group trust has been built over time and by the end of the 12 weeks most clients have reported significant bonds with other group members.

Other Considerations

Song Types and Purposes

Another angle to consider when preparing for song communication groups with rap music is assessing the song type or the song purpose. Some songs fall into more than one category. I have created the following list of song types and have found it helpful in the preparation process. Sometimes if the group has seemed cohesive enough, I have integrated the teaching of song types and song purposes into the session. While this is not the main thrust of the group, some clients have often reported feeling positive about learning something new. Additionally, some clients have reported feeling affirmed about what they already know.

The following are song types and rap song examples:

1. Story—"Real Gangsta" by SPM
2. Descriptive—"The Streetz of Compton" by The Game
3. Inspirational—"Save the Music" by NAS
4. List*—"21 Questions" by 50 Cent
5. Holiday—"Santa Goes Straight to the Ghetto" by Snoop Dogg
6. Situation—"Ms. Jackson" by Outkast
7. Love—"Dear Mama" by Tupac Shakur
8. Social message—"Why We Thugs" by Ice Cube
9. Religious—"Order My Steps" by Bone Thugs-N-Harmony

Group Process

I have started each song communication session using rap music with a mood check-in. All clients have been asked to give a brief description of their current mood state and if they feel so inclined, they have also shared something about the events in their day. After listening to the rap, I have started the group discussion by saying to the clients, "How do you physically and emotionally feel after hearing this rap?" Clients are encouraged to give their initial physical and emotional reactions to the music and the lyrics and we talk about the physical aspects of active music listening. Since the group members have taken turns selecting the songs, we have also talked about the importance of giving an opinion without being judgmental. This is a life skill that many of the clients I have worked with have not been taught. Gang allegiance, neighborhood loyalty, and other street living factors have played into the clients not liking or supporting specific rappers and their songs. Therefore, giving an opinion in a respectful manner has been a huge and sometimes difficult lesson for the group members to learn. A typical client

---

* Citron (1983) reports that list songs are as old as Gilbert and Sullivan and he cites their song "A Modern Major-General" as an example of such. He asserts that writers of list songs should combine the list with an interesting concept. He further advises writers to not combine several different lists within a song. He gives "50 Ways to Leave Your Lover" as another example of a list song.

evaluation report has been, "I have learned something new by expressing myself without judging other people or their music."

Another important factor during the listening portion of the session has been to carefully monitor the body language of all the clients. While some clients have smiled and bobbed their head to the beat, other clients have begun to clench their fists and their jaws. Rap lyrics are sometimes filled with intense words and can also conjure up intense images. After listening to a fast-tempo rap song with angry, violent lyrics, some clients have said, "I feel really good. I feel relaxed and calm," while other clients have reported, "I want to go hurt someone." With careful acknowledgment, guidance, and facilitation, productive conversations have ensued.

In-Depth Discussions

After the initial check-in questions, the real depth of the therapeutic process using rap music begins. The person who chose the song for that session has been asked to talk to the group about his/her reason for choosing the rap and how he/she specifically relates to the lyrics. While most of the clients have been able to articulate to me as the music therapist how they connect to the song lyrics, it has been another step and milestone for them to relate their song relevance to their peers in a group setting. Some of them initially put up a front or lie about their reasons for selecting the song. If this has occurred, I redirect them to share sincerely. Others put their heads down, mumble, and struggle to talk and have needed encouragement from me and their peers. This has often been a real bonding moment for the group members since many of them are going through similar issues and don't even know it until they become connected through the rap they have just experienced together. Time and again during this sharing step I have watched amazing connections occur between clients who in the past would hardly look at or speak to each other. In this regard, a goal has been achieved and a life lesson has been learned through the therapeutic use of rap music.

Once the song selector has spoken about how they relate to the song, I then facilitate a deepening of the discussion with the entire group. If the group was struggling to bond and communicate from the beginning, then a simple, less clinical question typically has helped the group transition to find common ground and then move on to a more clinically based discussion. If the group has been cohesive from the beginning, then in-depth clinical discussions have been likely to occur more quickly. Sometimes the group discussions have been more focused on the person who selected the song because this person feels so attached to the lyrics. This has often motivated that particular client to speak more freely. Once again, validation has played a huge role in the sharing of clients. Parents, teachers, social workers, therapists, counselors, and other adults have sometimes shunned their rap music. The fact that they have been able to make their own song selection, regardless of its Parental Advisory label, has been a supportive validation for them.

Many therapists I have worked with in a team setting have reported that the clients rarely open up and share during their daily talk therapy groups. They are surprised and excited when I tell them that these same clients speak openly and in-depth during song communication groups with rap music. Additionally, the clients' willingness to share in song communication with rap music has often inspired them to increase their participation in other areas of their program.

Client Goals Achieved in Sessions

Many goals have been worked on in our song communication groups with rap music. While the following list is not exhaustive, it has been encouraging to reflect on the many issues that can be addressed during these sessions.

Expressing Emotions

One of the goals achieved during the sessions has been to help the clients express a variety of emotions. Like most musical genres, rap music runs the gamut by presenting a multiplicity of emotions through both the lyrics and the music. Discussions about various emotions and how to express them productively have been a regular occurrence in the song communication groups that I have led.

Problem Solving

Improving problem-solving skills has been another goal that has been addressed. This has often been done by discussing the dysfunctional problem-solving skills that rap lyrics sometimes present. Through clients identifying with the dysfunction, an opportunity has been afforded to discuss more productive ways of dealing with upsetting situations. Specific examples have included rap songs that include lyrics about using violence as a form of coping with frustrations. Fruitful discussions that have offered alternative methods of dealing with various situations have helped clients learn new, productive coping skills.

Communication Skills

Communication skills have been improved in a variety of ways. Many rap songs include profanities, derogatory terms, and racist and sexist words. Rewarding discussions have occurred about learning to communicate without using offensive language. If the rap lyrics promote productive communication skills, I have reinforced and commended these skills. On the other hand, if the rap lyrics endorse unproductive communication skills, I have offered and encouraged more constructive ways of communicating with others.

Impulse Control and Attention Span

Improving impulse control and increasing attention span has been discussed and achieved. If rap lyrics present the idea of being destructively reactive, discussions about thinking things through and acting rationally rather than irrationally in a variety of situations have transpired. Many clients have reported, "I learned to deal with problems physically instead of talking them through. Until now, no one ever told me that there are other options for dealing with my problems." Additionally, if the clients themselves have chosen the music selections, they have been more apt to pay attention and focus during group discussions, which has then been praised and reinforced by me.

Social Interactions

Since many rap songs detail a variety of social issues and situations, improving social skills has been another goal that has been encouraged during song communication groups. Many clients have shared that they have never learned how to interact well with others. Joining and participating in negative peer groups have often been glorified for them in their neighborhoods. I have facilitated discussions about using socially productive behaviors and how using these behaviors can open new doors and lead to better, exciting opportunities.

Discrimination has been a topic that presents itself in rap lyrics and has opened up discussions about acceptance and tolerance. Many of the clients I have worked with were told from a very young age to hate and discriminate against people who were different from them. Playing raps that have included these issues has been a good venue for opening up the minds of clients who have been repeatedly taught to discriminate and not associate with those outside their culture and race. Many clients have admitted, "I thought you would not care or know anything about me because you are white. Now I have learned that I shouldn't just assume these things." This has supported many clients to explore and form new relationships in their lives with therapists, teachers, social workers, and many others.

Another potentially challenging topic in the lyrics of some rap songs is that of discrimination against homosexuals. Just like cultural and racial discrimination, many clients have reported that they were taught to "hate gays." By talking about these issues in a safe, contained setting, clients have learned to open their minds to identity issues, especially important at the sensitive time of adolescent development. I have witnessed clients who initially refused to acknowledge gay peers then build bridges with them and even stand up for them.

Self-Esteem

Many clients present and struggle with low self-esteem and a poor self-image. Finding their voice by participating in song communication groups with rap music has helped them increase and improve their self-image. Sometimes clients have picked rap songs that contain lyrics about rappers bragging or boasting about who they are and what they have done. This has been a springboard for discussions about self-worth. While many of the clients I have worked with portray themselves as confident and full of bravado, this has often been a cover for their self-hatred. When individual clients have been unable to come up with positive self-statements, group peers have spoken up and named several positive qualities they have seen in these individual clients. This has been powerful since peer acceptance is so important at this age.

Rap lyrics often espouse gaining empowerment by acquiring large sums of money. Discussions related to this topic have aided with conversations about how clients can gain empowerment by other means, instead of focusing on just money. Clients have been offered alternative empowerment strategies including but not limited to getting a good education, focusing on having a healthy body and mind, and discovering productive things that draw upon their strengths and gifts. These discussions have also led to productive conversations about goal-setting and how to work realistically on reaching objectives and aspirations.

Academic Skills

Rap songs and rap lyrics have been used to help improve academic skills in clients that lag far behind in their educational level. Many rap lyrics contain historical snippets and present important information about individuals both famous and infamous. I have watched clients get very excited about being given an assignment to research a particular historical figure mentioned in rap lyrics. Additionally, many rappers are prolific writers and use words that many clients do not know. This has been an amazing way for clients to increase their vocabulary. I will never forget the time a client learned the word *exquisite* and how he spent the next week using the word in a sentence wherever he went.

Addictions

There are many rap songs that deal with addiction issues, including the use of drugs and alcohol. Instead of shying away from these songs I have strongly encouraged clients to pick them since addiction has been one of their main issues. Clients have recounted stories about when their drug use began, who they used with, where they used, how often they used, and how they obtained drugs and alcohol. While substance abuse treatment with a substance abuse counselor has been mandatory for many of the clients, addiction and addictive behaviors have also been important issues to address during music therapy sessions. Many clients have shared that they have gained strength and insight by discussing their addiction issues in-depth during song communication groups. They further report that this has inspired them to share more in their substance abuse groups.

Family Issues

By far the number one song chosen by clients in the past 10 years of my work has been "Dear Mama" by Tupac Shakur. The lyrics in this song have addressed many family issues that the clients feel relate to their own lives. There are many other rap songs that are full of family and relationship issues. Time and again I have heard clients relate to rap lyrics that speak of family abuse, family violence, family heartache, family neglect and abandonment, family loss, appreciation for particular family members, and so much more. These songs have allowed clients to go beyond their shame and to speak up about family and relationship issues.

Trauma Issues

Carefully bearing in mind the ego strength of the clients, I have facilitated discussions about trauma issues that are played out in the lyrics of various raps. A significant number of the clients I have worked with have witnessed someone being hurt or killed. These have been very sensitive conversations and great care has been taken to keep all group members feeling safe and connected. Time after time during sessions clients have reported that they have revealed a traumatic event in their life for the very first time. It has been on these occasions that I have called upon the support of the entire treatment team, including the main therapist or social worker and the psychiatrist if needed. In many cases, these revelations have been the beginning of a significant clinical breakthrough for the client.

Anger Management

One complaint often heard from adversaries of rap music is that it sounds angry and the lyrics contain angry messages. Anger management has been a core issue for the majority of the clients at the agency where I have worked. With careful monitoring and well-prepared facilitation, discussing rap lyrics that are full of anger has proven to be very successful. Many clients have reported feeling tired of being labeled as angry and have opened up about what fuels their anger and why they hold on to it. This has presented a great chance to discuss productive anger management skills and tools that are practical and achievable for the clients' developmental stage.

Gang Issues

Another frequent complaint heard about rap music is that it promotes a gang lifestyle. Gangs have been an issue for centuries and continue to be present throughout our country. For the clients I have worked with, gangs have been a reality in their lives, some of them since birth. Talking about gang issues has certainly been a challenge given that members within the groups can be from rival gangs. It has taken diligent work to know as much as possible about the clients' gang backgrounds and their gang rivals. This has proven to be quite difficult since the gang world is an ever-shifting phenomenon. In a positive regard, after having discussions about gang rap lyrics and the possible negative outcomes of this lifestyle, I have witnessed some clients express a willingness to explore the idea of living without their gang or gang lifestyle. While numerous clients have reported that they have been in for too long and they are now in "too deep to get out," I have still heard some of them convey their desire to live life in a different, better way.

Testimonials

Whatever the rap lyrics have been in the songs selected, they have been viewed and used in such a way that they have been beneficial and transformative for the clients. Ten years of conducting these groups has shown that song communication sessions using rap music have helped clients work through a variety of clinical issues.

Here are some client testimonials: "These groups helped me think about why I'm so upset at my father and to stop stealing. I figured things out." "These groups helped me get in touch with my feelings." "These groups helped me learn how to talk to my mom and now I know what I need to do to be successful." "I learned how to share my feelings with others and to be more open with others." "I learned ways to control my anger better." "I learned to not hold things in because that is why I explode." "I learned to open up to new things and to participate more." "After these groups I have started to think about what I want to do and be when I leave treatment." "I learned that I am a part of my problems."

Reports and feedback from clients indicate that using rap music in song communication sessions with at-risk youth can be therapeutic. Week after week I have witnessed life-transforming conversations that have been clinically significant in the lives of youth in a residential treatment facility.

Contraindications

While the majority of at-risk youth in this particular program have reported many benefits from using rap in clinical song communication groups, there have been occasions when using this specific technique proved to be counterproductive. Vigilant assessments, consultations, and evaluations have been valuable tools for deciding if this avenue of treatment has been helping clients toward transformation or contributing toward a cycle of dysfunction.

This specific program has worked well for almost a decade in a long-term residential setting. In this setting, I have been able to attend individualized treatment team meetings for most of the clients. During these meetings I have interfaced with numerous staff who have worked with the clients in various facets of their program. The specific departments have included an on-site school program, an accredited substance abuse program, a recreation program, a daily clinical group program, and, if called for, the client's psychiatric program. During the treatment team meetings at this facility the clients have been allowed to pick which music therapy group they would like to participate in, thus affording them the opportunity to "buy into" the treatment. The music therapy group choices have included song communication, rhythm and drumming, songwriting, and a show choir performance group. All of the groups have used some component of rap music.

Over time, specific indicators have arisen as to when song communication with rap music has not been useful for at-risk youth. One such indicator has been when a client is experiencing active hallucinations and paranoid thinking as a result of substance abuse detoxification. It has been observed that many clients who are experiencing strong withdrawal symptoms or serious side effects from heavy drug abuse over a long period of time struggle to take part in a clinical talk therapy group. These clients have had difficulties staying focused even for short periods of time and they have often alienated themselves from other group members by making bizarre and completely off-topic statements. Therefore, clients exhibiting these behaviors have been dissuaded from taking part in the song communication groups using any genre of music, including rap, until these drug-induced symptoms have sufficiently decreased.

Another indicator is resistance toward treatment. Since most of the clients at this particular facility have been court-ordered to participate in the rehabilitation program, many of them have reported feeling resentment about being "forced" into therapy. The majority of clients have been able to work through their initial resistance and have gone on to become active group members. However, some clients have maintained a strong resistance and a strong commitment to their delinquency. These clients tend to choose songs that are aggressive and they seem to want to hinder the therapeutic process. Grocke and Wigram (2007) state, "Sometimes the therapist has to make a choice between allowing a client free expression of an aggressive song, versus the good of the group" (p. 171).

Of course, as with any genre of music, when the majority of the clients in the group do not relate to rap music or when the majority do not choose rap as a musical preference, there would be a strong indication for not using this genre in a song communication group. At the facility where I have worked for nearly 10 years, rap music has consistently been the musical preference for the majority of the clients. However, there have been occasions when a client selected a song from a different genre. When this has happened, I have let the group know that a different type of music will be discussed during the upcoming session. This type of situation has afforded the opportunity for group discussions about biases, judgments, closed-mindedness, discrimination, and other interpersonal learning issues. In turn, group and individual growth has followed.

References

Bruscia, K. (1998). *Defining music therapy* (2nd ed.). Gilsum, NH: Barcelona.

Citron, S. (1983). *Song writing: A complete guide to the craft.* New York: Proscenium.

Feil, N. (1993). *The validation breakthrough.* Baltimore: Health Professions Press.

George, N. (1998). *Hip Hop America.* New York: Penguin.

Grocke, D., & Wigram, T. (2007). *Receptive methods in music therapy.* Philadelphia: Jessica Kingsley.

Stone, D., Patton, B., & Heen, S. (1999). *Difficult conversations.* New York: Penguin.

Wheeler, B. (1983). A psychotherapeutic classification of music therapy practices: A continuum of procedures. *Music Therapy Perspectives, 1*(2), 8–12.

Part 3

RAP WITH CLIENTS IN SPECIFIC CLINICAL SETTINGS

Chapter 15

Hip-Hop Healing

Rap Music in Grief Therapy with an African American Adolescent Male

Edgar H. Tyson

Introduction

Popular discourse and scientific research on rap music and Hip-Hop culture has become increasingly important given the prevailing presence of Hip-Hop culture in the lives of contemporary youth (Chang, 2005), particularly many youth from urban and economically disadvantaged communities. During the past decade, Hip-Hop-based interventions have become more prevalent as well, given the relevance and meaning that some of the messages found in rap lyrics have in the lives of many youth and young adults (see Kobin & Tyson, 2006, for review). This chapter features a case example and application of principles and techniques associated with a specific Hip-Hop intervention. First, a brief overview of Hip-Hop culture and a review of Hip-Hop-based interventions are presented. After this broad review, a detailed description of a specific intervention called Hip-Hop Therapy (H²T; Tyson, 2002, 2003; Tyson, Ryan, Gomory, & Teasley, 2008) is provided, along with the theoretical foundation and preliminary research evidence for this intervention. Next, the case example is presented, including background information, a synopsis of the treatment process, and follow-up assessment of the outcomes associated with the goals established during treatment. Finally, this chapter ends with a discussion of future research directions that might further demonstrate the efficacy and promise of Hip-Hop-based interventions with youth.

Hip-Hop Culture: It Is More Than Rap

There are volumes of academic textbooks (e.g., Chang, 2005; Dyson, 1996; Kitwanna, 2002; Ogbar, 2007; Rose, 1994) on the definition of Hip-Hop culture. Most of these authors at some point address central questions such as what it is and what it is not, when it began, and who began it. Hip-Hop scholars and historians appear to agree that Hip-Hop culture grew out of a set of political, economic, social, and cultural conditions that existed in the Bronx, New York, in the early to mid-1970s. If this was the case, then a similar set of conditions must have existed in many other urban communities as well, due to the rapid growth of Hip-Hop culture throughout the United States and the world that began during the early 1980s and has not yet waned. Another well-documented fact about Hip-Hop is that it began with four key elements: music/deejaying, graffiti art, dancing, and rap/poetry (Kitwanna, 2002; Ogbar, 2007; Rose, 1994). Ironically, it appears that industry forces (i.e., economic conditions), gender inequality (i.e., social conditions), free speech (i.e., political/legal conditions), and the ever-present force of contemporary youth culture (i.e., cultural conditions) also are responsible for rap being the most popular, salient, and controversial element of Hip-Hop in contemporary discourse and academic research. However, neglecting to integrate all of the founding elements in an attempt to define Hip-Hop results in an incomplete and misguided understanding of its potential significance and relevance as a tool in practice (De Jesus, 2003) and youth intervention research (Tyson, 2003).

Practitioners utilizing Hip-Hop-based technologies with youth should be well trained and educated on how each element of Hip-Hop can be incorporated into treatment depending on the goals, skills, talents, and desires of the young person in need of service (De Jesus, 2003; Tyson, 2003; Williams, 2009). The principles and meaning behind each of the four elements can be conceptualized and co-constructed with youth in such a manner that has clinical utility. For example, as one historian demonstrates in a personal reflection on his experience with graffiti, "Tagging was a youth rebellion. It was also fun. It was artistic, creative, destructive, and cool. It was hip-hop" (Ogbar, 2007, p. 2). These qualities attributed to graffiti indicate that it can be as constructive and effective as other forms of visual arts currently being used in a therapeutic manner (Hogan, 2001; Riley, 2001). Indeed, some youth intervention researchers have found the application of graffiti-based interventions to be useful in helping youth cope with collective trauma (Klingman, Shalev, & Pearlman, 2000).

Because rap music has been conceptualized as a form of poetry (e.g., Tyson, 2002) and its application as a therapeutic tool has been shown to be similar in scope, approach, and technique to poetry therapy (Mazza, 1999), helping professionals appear to have little difficulty understanding how it might be incorporated into their work with youth. Nonetheless, a brief history of how so-called rap has evolved as a concept might reveal a more complete understanding of how it can sometimes differ from traditional views of Hip-Hop and might best be reconceptualized as being multidimensional. One of the most complete analyses of rap in the social scientific literature was conducted by Smitherman (1997), who wrote that in the African American community, rap originally referred to romantic sexualized speech used by men for the purpose of winning affection and favors from women. Smitherman suggests that, over time, rap began to represent any kind of strong, aggressive, highly fluent, and powerful speech. Both aspects continue to define rap in contemporary Hip-Hop. However, rap has additional qualities as well. Rap is a form of poetry and has been defined as poetry by several rappers in their music (e.g., Ice Cube, 1991; KRS-One, 2003; West, 2005). It has also been defined by rappers as a form of therapy, an outlet and a platform for ventilating views and feelings and exercising strengths and talents that would have otherwise been used for negativity and self-destructive outcomes. It is these latter dimensions of rap that makes Hip-Hop-based technologies a unique fit for therapeutic engagement (Kobin & Tyson, 2006; Elligan, 2004; Tyson, 2002), treatment (De Carlo, 2002; Elligan, 2004; Tyson, 2003), and outcome assessment (Tyson, 2006) in youth work. Below is an overview of a growing body of research on the use of Hip-Hop-based technologies in youth intervention work.

Synopsis of Research on Hip-Hop-Based Interventions

A significant advancement made in youth intervention research is the increased use of culturally specific interventions that are, for example, race, class, gender, and age appropriate. An emerging trend in this area is the use of Hip-Hop culture, and rap music in particular, as a culturally specific approach to intervention research, and this approach has been found to enhance the effectiveness of youth interventions (Liddle, Jackson-Gilbert, & Marvel, 2006). The infusion of Hip-Hop-based technologies has influenced positive changes in youth behavior (Lemieux, Fisher, & Pratto, 2008; Tyson, 2002; Tyson et al., 2008; Williams, 2009) and critical thinking skills (Newman, 2007, 2009; Tyson, 2003). These models have also been used to better understand the complex nature of Hip-Hop culture (Lee,

2009; Newman, 2007; Williams, 2009), improve the quality of relationships between youth (Tyson, 2002), and enhance the therapeutic relationship (Kobin & Tyson, 2007; Tyson et al., 2008). Hip-Hop-based models range from utilizing Hip-Hop as the central focus of the intervention (e.g., Tyson, 2003; Williams, 2009) to applying a Hip-Hop-based technology as a supplement to a traditional or existing intervention (Liddle et al., 2006). A more complete review of the research in this area is absent from the literature and would fill a significant gap in this area. Nonetheless, it is clear that practitioners and intervention researchers have begun to give greater attention to Hip-Hop-based interventions as an important contemporary development.

Hip-Hop Therapy: Research and Practice Outcomes

Almost 10 years ago now, I conducted an early study of my Hip-Hop Therapy (H²T) Model with a small group ($n = 11$) of delinquent youth in state custody (Tyson, 2002). H²T is a culturally specific, prosocial, and critical thinking youth development model based on well-established principles of social cognitive theory (Bandura, 1991) and social information processing (see Landsford et al., 2006). As a therapeutic model, its process and application also is compatible with that of music therapy, bibliotherapy, and poetry therapy (see Tyson, 2002, for complete review). In this preliminary study, I found that although youth in H²T condition ($n = 5$) had higher peer relationship scores, an analysis of covariance revealed that pretest scores may have influenced posttest results. However, it is possible that the null hypothesis was falsely accepted because of low power associated with this sample.

Moreover, I found that qualitative interviews revealed that youth in the H²T group expressed wide support for the model (Tyson, 2002). Specifically, four youth stated that they appreciated the "respect" for "their" music that was demonstrated by using this approach, their friends in the shelter had "beef" (i.e., resentment) with them for being in the H²T groups, and they created their own rap songs and shared these songs during succeeding groups. In a subsequent paper, I presented the steps of the model and a sample of qualitative, process recordings collected during the study, further demonstrating the ability of the model to facilitate youth critical thinking skills (Tyson, 2003). Process recordings showed that youth were able to deconstruct the lyrics in rap songs and apply them to their individual struggles and reality. The actual steps and processes of the original H²T are not presented here because, following the approach used by some colleagues and me (Tyson et al., 2008), the steps for H²T were adapted and tailored to meet the specific needs and circumstances surrounding the case study used for this chapter. My colleagues and I (Tyson et al., 2008) presented an individual case example that prescribed how H²T, which was originally conceptualized and tested as a group intervention, can also be used in individual therapy. Other practitioners have demonstrated the use of Hip-Hop-based technologies in individual therapy as well (e.g., Elligan, 2004).

Essentially, the H²T model requires that the practitioner discusses the history and significance of Hip-Hop and how the music is much more complex than what might be gleaned from listening to the type of rap music consistently aired through mainstream media outlets. Some youth may come to the therapeutic process with this understanding and this step can be very brief, depending on the level of understanding of these complex issues that the youth has developed prior to entering treatment. The next step is to explore whether the youth prefers to utilize established rap songs to listen to and discuss or whether the youth wants to create a rap song that addresses or explores an issue(s) relevant to the reason for treatment. In the case used for this chapter, this latter approach was taken because it was discovered in the initial session that the client had written a rap song as a means of expressing his thoughts and feelings surrounding the death of his estranged biological father. Below is a synopsis of the treatment process and outcomes associated with this case, along with part of the rap song. This material is reproduced here with permission from the young client, his guardian, and the university-partnership.

Malik: A Case Example Utilizing H²T in Grief Work

Background Information

During the fall of 2007, while an assistant professor for a state university located in the southeastern United States, I worked part-time as a volunteer in a mental health clinic at a high school that was a university-partnership with the local school district. The case presented here involves Malik (a fictitious name), a 16-year-old African American male who presented with school problems that were exacerbated by the death of his father, whom he referred to as Jackson throughout the therapeutic relationship. We initially met in a group setting. After our first talk, we mutually decided that he and I would also meet one-on-one because of some unique issues that he did not feel comfortable sharing in group. It was explained to Malik that speaking with me was very similar to working on his "jump shot, dribbling, or defense" in practice, as he was a second-string forward on the high school basketball team. I told him that we would need to meet regularly, in a similar manner that he practices basketball along a schedule to be ready for game time. We would need to meet regularly in order for him to better deal with a recent family tragedy that he wanted to process outside of the group. We agreed to not set an end date for our meetings and that we could possibly meet for the remainder of the fall or the entire school year, if needed. Malik was assured that the length of our involvement would be entirely up to him.

Malik lived with his mother and younger sister, who was 14 years old. According to Malik, he did not know his father very well before the months leading up to his death. After his father and mother separated when he was roughly 3 or 4 years old, Malik reported that they only had sporadic encounters when Jackson would take him to get something for his birthday or Christmas, which, he made a point to report, did not happen every year. Roughly 3 months prior to meeting Malik, he found out through his mother that Jackson was hospitalized due to complications associated with cancer. Malik's mother informed him that his father wanted Malik to come to the hospital to spend time with him because the early prognosis was very bad. Malik's father was diagnosed late and his condition had progressed to the debilitative stages and doctors gave his father less than a month before his body would shut down completely. Malik reported that he went to see his father and the two of them met and talked extensively about many things, including family, girls, school, and Malik's future. The young client also stated that he learned a great deal about his father and the two of them became very close during his final month of life and this was very important to him. The mutually agreed upon initial goals of treatment were to (1) help the young client begin to resolve his feelings toward his father's death and (2) improve his school outcomes.

Beginning Phase of Treatment

During the first session, we discussed rap music. In keeping with the H²T model, I first assessed the level of Malik's understanding and appreciation for the history and complexity of Hip-Hop. He had a fairly extensive understanding of these issues, and we were able to establish a good therapeutic bond through our mutual interests in several contemporary and "old school" (i.e., rappers with recordings prior to 1990) artists. More importantly, in this initial session, I discovered that Malik wrote and produced a rap song to express his thoughts and feelings regarding his father's death. We immediately agreed that discussing and processing the song in our meetings would be a valuable use of our time.

In the second session, Malik brought his rap song to the meeting. The title of Malik's song was "Lord Change My Life," and it is presented in full here and then it is demonstrated how the song was deconstructed and processed in treatment and used as the primary mechanism through which we were to achieve the goals for this young client.

> (Chorus)
> Lord Change My Life, Lord Change My Life,
> I know U Love me even though I cheat, steal & lie
> Lord Change My Life, Lord Change My Life
> I know U Love me even though I cheat, steal & lie
> (Verse 1)
> Lord, he instilled me this 1, I'm down on me knees just praying 4 forgiveness.
> They telling me that my life going 2 end, Can U have mercy on me and forgive me 4 my sin
> My head hurts & I don't fill the same, My stomach hurts lord can U get rid of the pain
> I'm getting shorter of air & it's hard 2 breath, My muscles getting tight can U tell it 2 leave
> (Chorus) (Then Verse 2)
> My eye's closing slowly & I filling so soe, I'm getting scare now Lord is it time 4 me 2 go
> Tell my family I love them even though I act this way, when time get ruff Lord help them 2 pray
> Now I'm getting in bed & I'm closing my eyes, All I hear in my ears is my family cries
> I hope I go 2 heaven not 2 hell 2 stay, & if I make it in heaven I see U soon someday.
> (Chorus)

In the second and third session, we processed the title and chorus because it had such a powerful and significant meaning to Malik. Consequently, we discussed the implications of his decision to use the specific words in the title and chorus to the song. Malik stated that one of the things his father initially said to him when he first visited was that Malik should "change his life" and not end up like his father with very few accomplishments to show for 40 years of living on this earth. Malik had been in minor trouble with the police, including truancy, a shoplifting incident, and possession of cigarettes. His school problems were another issue that his father discussed with him and was something that Malik wanted to improve upon. According to Malik, the chorus was created out of something his father told him and something about himself that he knew. Malik says that his father would tell him that he hoped God would forgive him for all the bad things he did in life, such as cheating on women, stealing things, and the lies that he told. Malik says the unique aspect of his song's chorus was that it simultaneously represented his father's plea to God and Malik's plea to God regarding his own shortcomings and weaknesses. Malik stated that every time he sung the chorus he would feel the connection to his father in ways he never felt before. In these first few sessions, Malik was asked to and did sing the song several times. By the fourth session, Malik became somewhat emotional as he again recounted why he chose the words to the chorus. We processed how the creation of the song was paying off for him because he was able to use the song to capture a special moment with his father that would last in his heart and mind forever. Malik agreed and appeared further convinced that writing the song was a good idea.

Middle Phase of Treatment

Roughly during the next few sessions we began decoding and processing verse 1. According to the young client, the first line (i.e., "Lord, he instilled me this one") refers to how both God and his father inspired this rap song and that he was always taught to get "down on his knees" (line 2) when he prayed as a sign of respect for God. Malik's spirituality became a theme we discussed in great detail throughout the time we shared, as it was a "self-identified strength and coping strategy" (Tyson & Baffour, 2006; Tyson, Baffour, & DoungTran, 2010) that we utilized. During subsequent discussions, Malik stated that the second line referred to how his father knew he only had a short time to live and his father wanted, more than anything, to be forgiven for the wrong he did in life. Again, this allowed us to reflect and process the meaning and significance of spirituality in his life and his family's lives. The fourth line included some of the complaints his father would make while he visited him. Specifically, his father was in a great deal of pain during most of his time in the hospital and this bothered Malik. We mutually reinterpreted this experience as helping his father bear the pain a little better because Malik was there with him. Malik then recalled that this is something his father actually stated to him once.

Consistent with the H²T model, throughout our work together, we listened to, read the lyrics of, and discussed several contemporary rap songs that addressed similar issues of grief and loss. For example, a few of the songs we processed were "I Miss You" (DMX, 2001), "Heaven" and "Someday" (Scarface, 2002), and "Teardrops & Closed Caskets" (2Pac & Outlaws, 1999). Throughout the middle phase of treatment we compared and contrasted some of the themes in Malik's rap and the songs listed above (as well as several others). It was Malik who suggested we listen to "I Miss You" (DMX, 2001) because he accurately interpreted that the song essentially was about the rapper's grandmother who had passed. Malik insightfully stated that this song most closely mirrored the thoughts and feelings that were expressed in his rap song. This therapeutic approach appeared to give Malik a great deal of relief and solace, as he stated several times that he was not aware of how prevalent these types of songs were and that he now "related to" many of the rap songs and artists more than he did prior to our sessions.

Termination and Follow-Up Phases of Treatment

The final few weeks of our work together consisted of a series of conversations about bringing some of these ideas back to the group that had continued to meet. The song and our individual meetings had been mentioned by Malik in a subsequent group session and the positive response he got from group members appeared to give him the courage and comfort level needed for him to decide he would bring the song to the group. It was a major step toward healing for Malik because he initially did not want to discuss his song and his father's death with the group. The group liked his song a great deal and we played it dozens of times in the group. Malik went online and added a very creative and quality beat to the lyrics and recorded the song on a CD. In fact, at the end of the fall, the high school had a talent show and Malik was encouraged to enter the talent show and perform his rap. However, he refused, stating that he was not comfortable performing in the show. Nonetheless, in our final individual session, Malik acknowledged that the fact that his peers in the group thought so highly of his song that they believed he could have won the talent show gave him a profound sense of belonging and competence. Also, Malik indicated that the respect and support from his peers made him feel that his father's death was not in vain and that something really good resulted from the two of them being able to spend that final month of his father's life together.

At termination, which was roughly 11 weeks after meeting him, Malik had (1) better teacher reports (i.e., had not been sent to the office for his behavior in eight successive weeks), (2) better school grades (i.e., completed all homework assignments and had not received a grade lower than a C), and (3) decided he did not need to come to the mental health clinic any longer due to experiencing more manageable emotional states whenever he thought of his father.

For follow-up assessment, I met with Malik and his mother 6 months and again 1 year after terminating our involvement. Six months later, Malik was doing very well and had begun to consider college as an option after high school. This was significant because college was something that he initially stated he was not interested in. The 1-year follow-up report showed that Malik was able to resolve some of his issues with his father and his father's death. Malik and his mother's relationship improved as a result because Malik had resented his father for not being in his life and now had forgiven his father for this shortcoming. Malik also continued to do well in school and had not been sent to the office for his behavior for an entire year and a half. Malik also continued to write rap songs that expressed his thoughts and feelings about different issues in his life and in his community. During each follow-up assessment he shared several of his new songs with me. Malik indicated that he now feels that he can express anything through a rap song and enjoys doing so, not because he hopes to be a rapper, but because it allows him to ventilate some of his frustrations in a way he is most comfortable with.

Limitations of H²T

As with most interventions, H²T has several limitations that must be considered before drawing any firm conclusions from the information presented in this chapter. First, I have previously reported that this model might not be useful with all young clients from urban communities (Tyson, 2002, 2003). Equally important to note is that the model might be useful with young clients from suburban and rural communities. The salient issue is that the young client must have an affinity for Hip-Hop and rap music. The assumption that all youth in urban communities have similarly high levels of interest in rap music is misguided and perpetuates an insensitivity to individual differences that is too often observed in underserved communities. A second limitation of H²T is that many rap songs have what some perceive as an excessive level of obscene and offensive language that many parents and others might object to or be troubled by. For example, the songs we listened to and processed during our work together include much of this type of so-called offensive language. However, the contexts within which much of the obscenities are embedded produce a more clear and different interpretation of the meaning and intent of the artist. Usually, the obscenity is not intended to be negative and from the rappers' perspective it might be intended to express and emphasize a point that is best understood by contemporary youth when couched in the form of an obscenity. Moreover, there are edited versions of nearly all mainstream rap songs, and practitioners working with youth who have parents that might object to certain rap lyrics can access and utilize these "clean" versions in their work with youth.

A final limitation that must be noted here is that H²T is a fairly new model and remains in its developmental stage. There is more research needed to support the notion that H²T is an effective youth intervention. The anecdotal evidence presented in this chapter is not sufficient for claiming that H²T is effective and more research, including more stringent experimental designs, is needed to support the efficaciousness and effectiveness of this emerging model. However, taken together, the information from this case and previous youth work using H²T (Kobin & Tyson, 2006; Tillie-Allen, 2004; Tyson, 2002, 2003; Tyson et al., 2008) suggests that this model has significant promise in practice with youth and in youth intervention research.

Conclusion

This chapter highlights a significant advancement made in youth intervention research over the past 15 years. Specifically, it appears that the use of Hip-Hop culture, and rap music in particular, as a culturally specific approach to intervention with youth is a growing and increasingly important development in youth intervention research (Lemieux, Fisher, & Pratto, 2008; Liddle, Jackson-Gilbert, & Marvel, 2006; Tyson, 2002; Tyson et al., 2008; Williams, 2009). While there are a number of different models that exist (e.g., Watts, Abdul-Adil, & Pratt, 2002), the model discussed in this chapter has been cited in several previous studies and continues to show promise as a potentially effective approach to youth intervention work (Kobin & Tyson, 2006; Tillie-Allen, 2004; Tyson, 2002, 2003; Tyson et al., 2008).

More research is needed on H²T, including controlled trials, either randomized or nonrandomized, with larger and more diverse samples, reliable and valid measures, and practical outcomes that are targeted to meet specific goals developed collaboratively by researchers, practitioners, and youth. As evidence for this and other Hip-Hop-based models continues to be generated and made more widely available, practitioners working with youth should consider the H²T model as an alternative to traditional and conventional intervention techniques. These models would be particularly salient when working with youth who demonstrate an appreciation for and interest in rap music and Hip-Hop culture. Failure to explore the utility of Hip-Hop-based models in youth practice might represent a missed opportunity to validate an underutilized talent that many youth have. In addition, neglecting to utilize and examine these Hip-Hop-based technologies in youth work also might represent a missed opportunity to successfully intervene in the lives of one of society's most vulnerable populations.

References

Bandura, A. (1991). Social cognitive theory of self-regulation. *Organizational behavior and human decision processes, 50*, 248–287.

Dyson, M. E. (1996). *Between God and gangsta rap: Bearing witness to Black culture.* New York: Oxford University Press.

Elligan, D. (2004). *Rap therapy: A practical guide for communicating with youth and young adults through rap music.* New York: Kensington.

Kitwana, B. (2002). *The hip hop generation: Young Blacks and the crisis in African-American culture.* New York: Basics/Civitas.

Klingman, A, Shalev, R., & Pearlman, A. (2000). Graffiti: A creative means of youth coping with collective trauma. *The Arts in Psychotherapy, 27*(5), 299–307.

Kobin, C., & Tyson, E. H. (2007). Hip Hop in therapy: Empathic connections and thematic goals for treatment with clients from urban settings. *Arts in Psychotherapy, 33,* 343–356.

Landsford, J.E., Malone, P. S., Dodge, K .A., Crozier, J. C., Pettit, G. S., & Bates, J. E. (2006). A 12-year prospective study of social information processing patterns and externalizing behavior. *Journal of Abnormal Child Psychology, 34*(5), 709–718.

Lee, J. (2009). Battlin' on the corner: Techniques for sustaining play. *Social Problems, 56*(3), 578–598.

Lemieux, A. F., Fisher J. D., & Pratto, F. (2008). A music-based HIV prevention intervention for urban adolescents. *Health Psychology, 27,* 349–357.

Liddle, H. A., Jackson-Gilfort, A., & Marvel, F. A. (2006). An empirically supported and culturally specific engagement and intervention strategy for African American adolescent males. *American Journal of Orthopsychiatry, 76*(2), 215–225.

Mazza, N. (1999). *Poetry therapy: Interface of the arts and psychology. Innovations in psychology.* Boca Raton, FL: CRC Press.

Newman, M. (2009). "It's all concept: It's not real" Reality and lyrical meaning in rap. In H. S. Alim, A. Ibrahim, & A. Peenycook, (Eds.). *Global linguistic flows: Hip hop cultures, youth identities, and the politics of language,* (pp. 195–213). New York: Taylor & Francis.

Ogbar, J. (2007) *Hip hop revolution: The culture and politics of rap.* Lawrence: University Press of Kansas.

Rose, T. (1994). *Black noise: Rap music and Black culture in contemporary America.* Hanover: Wesleyan University Press.

Smitherman, G. (1997). The chain remain the same: Communicative practices in the Hip-Hop nation. *Journal of Black Studies, 28*(1), 3–25.

Tyson, E. H. (2002). Hip-Hop therapy: An exploratory study of a rap music intervention with at-risk and delinquent youth. *Journal of Poetry Therapy, 15*(4), 131–144.

Tyson, E. H. (2003). Rap music in social work practice with African-American and Latino youth: A conceptual model with practical applications. *Journal of Human Behavior in the Social Environment, 8*(4), 1–21.

Tyson, E. H. (2005). The Rap-music Attitudes and Perception (RAP) scale: Preliminary analyses of psychometric properties. *Journal of Human Behavior in the Social Environment, 11*(3/4), 59–82.

Tyson, E. H. (2006). The Rap-music Attitude and Perception Scale: A validation study. *Research on Social Work Practice, 16*, 211–223.

Tyson, E. H., Baffour, T. S., & DuongTran, P. (2010). Gender comparisons of self-identified strengths and coping strategies: A study of adolescents in an acute care psychiatric facility. *Child and Adolescent Social Work Journal, 27*(3), 161–175.

Tyson, E. H., Ryan, S., Gomory, T., & Teasley, M. (2008). Cultural issues: Diversity and child welfare. In R. Lee (Ed.), *Foster Care Therapist Handbook: Relational Approaches to the Children and Their Families.* Washington, DC: Child Welfare League of America.

Watts, R., Abdul-Adil, J., & Pratt, T. (2002). Enhancing critical consciousness in young African American men: A psycho-educational approach. *Psychology of Men and Masculinity, 3*, 41–50.

Williams, A. D. (2009). The critical cultural cypher: Remaking Paulo Freire's cultural circles using hip hop culture. *International Journal of Critical Pedagogy, 2*(1), 1–29.

Chapter 16

Beat It

The Effects of Rap Music on Adolescents in the Pediatric Medical Setting

Nicole Steele

Music Therapy with Adolescents in a Pediatric Medical Setting

Working at a children's hospital, I have often heard teens referred to as the "lost population" in pediatric medical care. They struggle with the standard insecurities of adolescence, compounded by the confusing unfairness of medical complications. It's hard enough to be a teenager. It's even harder to be a sick teenager.

Add to that the fact that they are being treated in a place that is designed for children, a bright and cheery wonderland, festooned with cartoons and barnyard animals—a virtual Kiddie Land. The children's hospital I work in houses a wonderful teen lounge, with pool tables and video games and an only-12-year-olds-and-older rule, but the environment was still designed overall for a younger demographic. Teens are not just asking, "How do I fit into the world?" They're asking, "How do I fit into this hospital?"

My role as a music therapist grows when I work with teens. It is more than about breaking down barriers of age. Sometimes, it's also about breaking down barriers of race, socioeconomic status, gender, and sexuality. I can do this by accepting their musical preferences and meeting them where they are. In this chapter, I will provide case vignettes of the varying ways I use Hip-Hop in music therapy. In these short vignettes Hip-Hop is used as an icebreaker and in songwriting, song discussion, playing instruments, improvising, recording, musical instruction, and movement.

In a hospital setting, there is a kind of transient nature about the work we do. Sometimes, the people we work with have short hospital stays. Sometimes people are discharged earlier than we expect. On the other hand, sometimes we have patients who stay for extended periods of time and we have patients who are repeatedly hospitalized due to their ongoing medical condition. The brief vignettes in this chapter help to illustrate the multifaceted nature of the work done in hospital settings.

Vignette 1: Gaining Trust

"I don't wanna sing no 'Old MacDonald,'" Layla huffs as I stand in the doorway to her hospital room, guitar in tow. Before I take another step, the 17-year-old patient mumbles, "And I don't do no 'Kumbaya' either."

"Well, good," I sigh and smile, "because if I have to sing my ABC's one more time today, my head might explode."

This earns enough of a smile out of her for me to slip through the door.

"Do you mind if I sit here?" I ask, pointing to the chair stacked with the latest issue of *XXL* magazine, a half-smiling Jay-Z on the cover with his trademarked New York Yankees hat, crisp and cocked to the side, and an old *Rolling Stone* with Hip-Hop goddesses Missy Elliot, Alicia Keys, and Eve on the cover.

She shrugs, seemingly uninterested, and I sit. "I'm Nicole. You're Layla, right?"

"Yeah," she groans. Just before I break into my spiel about who I am and what I do at the hospital, she scowls, "I know. I know you are the music lady; I always see you carrying that guitar around." She pauses. "And is that all you do all day long? Just roam around the hospital and play 'Old MacDonald'?"

"No, not exactly," I chuckle, "but I do have an impressive repertoire of animal noises that I could break out for you if you want."

She gives me a half smile and says, "Then why you here?"

Layla has sickle-cell anemia, a genetic blood disorder in which the body produces sickle-shaped (or C-shaped) red cells that are ridged, restricting blood flow to areas of the body, and resulting in a pain crisis and often organ damage. She has been in and out of the hospital her whole life, but this admission was much longer than others. By the time I was consulted, she had been an inpatient for about 2 weeks.

"I'm just here to hang out," I say. "Tell me what music you like to listen to."

She shrugs.

"Do you like Jay-Z?" I offer, using her magazine as my hint.

"Yeah ..."

"Yeah? So, do you know 'Song Cry'? That track is one of my favorites."

She smiles.

"I've listened to Jay-Z for a long time," I say, "even before he started dating Beyonce."

She raises her eyebrows.

"You like Beyonce?"

"Yeah ..."

"I'm guessing by the *Rolling Stone* cover that you also like Missy and Eve."

Her smile widens. "And Alicia and Mary J."

"Yeah, girl! I love Alicia Keys!" I light up. "Her piano skills are amazing! Did you see her perform 'No One' on MTV when she played that gorgeous white grand piano? Why don't you scroll through your iPod with me. Show me what you have, and tell me some things that I should be listening to."

She obliges.

When we get to Missy Elliot, I say, "Ooo, do you know the track 'Friendly Skies,' featuring Ginuwine? She sampled part of that track from Earth, Wind, and Fire ... . You know, Earth, Wind, and Fire is the group who sang, 'New World Symphony'—"

"—I know who they are." She seems pleased to get me back.

She scrolls to "Ladies Night," the new one by Missy Elliot, Lil' Kim, and Angie Stone. "You know they bit this one off of Kool and the Gang's 'Ladies Night,' then."

I am impressed.

We don't play instruments in that first session. I think of it more as a trust-building session. I am giving her a reason to let me come back tomorrow. I try one more thing before I leave:

"You know I just don't play guitar," I say. "My major in school was percussion."

"Oh, you know drums?" she looks interested. "I can play drums."

She could. I later learn that drums were something that she played in school and with friends. And she is good.

I start to bring drums to our sessions, and sometimes we turn on the radio. Or I ask her about a song that is on her mind, and we drum out the beat. The emotive Hip-Hop grooves are always very solid and reminiscent of something you would hear on the radio, things we could bob our heads to.

One day, in the teen lounge, En Vogue's "Free Your Mind" is playing softly over the radio. I bust out with the chorus. I know her tastes well enough to know that she'll like the song—and will laugh at me.

That afternoon, Layla opens up about how people don't believe in her pain, about how sometimes it's so intense that she cannot move. She is attached to intravenous opioids, which come with side effects, like itching and skin irritation, and more seriously, the debate over opioid tolerance and addiction. She talks about nurses and doctors who ask her questions about how much pain she is "really" in and comment about her heavy sleep habits. Her medication often makes her tired. "But they all look at me like a lazy teenager," she says. "They don't know what it's like to have pain like this."

Sometimes we drum through her pain, breathing with the groove—in through our noses for four beats and then out through our mouths for four beats, almost trancelike, rhythmically. This is subscribing to the theories of Frank Bosco:

> As the mind orients itself to the physical mechanism of the breathing process, it literally invests in this function as a singular focus. The breath becomes a conduit for the mind to stay in touch with the body's relaxation process. (Bosco, 1997, p. 15)

There are times that, more than playing, Layla needs someone to listen to her talk about her pain, about the hospital, about music, about what it is like to be absent from school for large periods of the school year, and to feel like an outcast at school when she is there. Sometimes, we just bob our heads to the songs playing in our minds.

I know that respecting her musical choices proves to be pivotal in building trust. She is a patient with sickle cell, a teen, and an African American, and we use her love of Hip-Hop to validate both her emotions and her physical pain.

Vignette 2: Song and Rap Writing

Most teenagers who have a love for Hip-Hop culture think they can write a rap song. There is usually a mix of feeling invincible and overwhelmed by amazing insecurity and angst. Many times, the themes in rap songs deal with alienation or a sense of being wronged. It's no coincidence that I've met a lot of patients, teens with various medical conditions, who can relate.

Kara is one of them. She has Gardner's syndrome, a disorder characterized by polyps and tumors in and on the colon. She was physically abused as a child, expediting the progress of her disease to the point where she had to undergo a complete enterectomy—her intestines had to be removed. Her father died of the same disease, her mother is often absent, and her sister is also hospitalized.

"Let's pretend I'm Mary J. [Blige] for a minute," I say, standing up and puffing out my hair. "Now, pretend my skin is much darker, that I'm taller, that I'm prettier, and that I have really expensive glasses and shoes on." I make her laugh.

We have spent the morning listening to "Just Fine," one of the most positive songs by the artist, with a chorus that reinforces that her life's just fine.

It's very upbeat. But the song also provides the opportunity to talk. Mary J. Blige sings about liking what she sees when she walks past the mirror. I ask Kara how she feels about what she sees when she walks past the mirror. I keep things light and silly, warping back to "Mary mode" with my invisible shades on. Sometimes, it's just about improving our outlook.

The song continues with Mary J. stating that she wouldn't change her life, because her life is just fine. We start our songwriting experience as I ask Kara if there are things she would like to change about her life. She talks about being "normal" and a "regular kid." She speaks about missing being able to eat and drink (as her disease process has prevented her from eating by mouth for years at a time and she is currently fed via feeding tubes). She is provided with a safe space to talk about things in her life that she would like to change. I listen and jot down ideas that she says and we begin to brainstorm on how to incorporate these thoughts into lyrics. "You see I would change my life …" This is how we start talking about ideas of things that she would like to change. "I wanna eat real food with the rest of my friends, and I wanna have candy too." "I wanna go home and chill in my own house, don't wanna be told what to do." "I don't wanna be on these meds no more, wanna walk without this pole [she points to the IV pole where she runs at least 10 different medication and nutrition infusions] … See these are the things I'd change but I am still fine, fine, fine, fine, fine, fine … [she repeats the original chorus right after]." We discuss knowing that some of these things she cannot change right now but also try to keep the focus on some things that we can work on improving. Kara is happy to "freestyle" her new lyrics as I slow down the groove and tap out the beat on the back of my guitar. Her favorite line in the song talks about keeping your head up high and believing in yourself.

I am counting on Kara's inspiration to write her own lyrics—or to substitute her own words into songs that she loves. We found themes similar to "Just Fine" in India Arie's "Video." India Arie sings about not being the average girl from a video, not being built like a supermodel, but having unconditional love for herself. We also used Janet Jackson's song "Control," which talks about being in control of what she says and what she does. She goes on to state that this time she is going to do it her way because she does have control over what she does. We discussed what control means to Kara and how we could come up with plans and effective ways to assert control over her medical condition, hospitalization, and life. This is a song that Kara often played on days that she was feeling frustrated or upset. Sometimes she was upset about her condition, about pain, or about her family, and at times it was more about being upset over the "normal" teenage things such as a lights-out time or restrictions on computers and video games. She substituted her own thoughts of control or restriction and belted it out to the groove we drummed out on hand drums.

Kara loves Michael Jackson, too. She refers to him as "The King," and his calendar hangs in her room. She often talks about how he is misunderstood. It is a pivotal day when we rewrite "Beat It." We talk about everything that makes her feel "defeated" and more importantly all the things that she does to turn it around. She often uses outlets such as journal writing, music, and arts and crafts. Music has always been a powerful release for Kara and at times she has requested jazz and classical music. When I ask her to talk about what she likes about these genres, she states that sometimes she does not want to listen to any words; she "just wants to close her eyes and let the music just play."

Mary Priestley states, "Music is always an expression of some kind, but sometimes it is the expression of acceptable feelings and at other times it is the expression of a defense against an unacceptable feeling or impulse" (Priestley, 1994, p. 136). I never push positive Hip-Hop or rap songs. Kara has often wanted something fun—"Single Ladies," by Beyonce, or "Scream," by Michael and Janet Jackson—and we play them. Once I gain her trust, I can introduce songs with themes I think she can relate to, songs that might be therapeutic for her to hear, play, sing, or rewrite.

I know that some therapists have a hard time with the subject matter in rap songs. And there are times when I, too, struggle with some of the language and subject matter. At these times, I rely on the insights of Caroline Kobin and Edgar H. Tyson, who write about Hip-Hop in therapy and its ability to strengthen the bond between the therapist and the client by breaking down implied cultural barriers and relatedness. "In practice, it is not the subjective perception of the lyrics that is important, but the client's personal response to these lyrics" (Kobin & Tyson, 2006, p. 343).

It might be difficult to write or rewrite a rap song with a teen who's taking notes from Eminem's more violent and "vulgar" tracks, or who is especially inspired by Ludacris's "Move Bitch." I try to focus on the patient's interpretation, his or her personal connection. I try to take my bias or judgment out of each session, meeting a patient where they are before attempting to move them, to move *with* them.

I've learned that an unconditional positive regard goes much further to break down barriers and to build trust. This has allowed me the opportunity to reframe rap lyrics that I may have found offensive or challenging.

Edgar H. Tyson, credited for doing some of the first studies on Hip-Hop therapy, called it "an innovative synergy of hip-hop, bibliotherapy [poetry therapy], and music therapy" (Tyson, 2002, p. 132). He uses rap music as an intervention. I find the intervention is most successful when it is an invention, too.

Vignette 3: Lyric Discussion

Juan is a 19-year-old patient, awaiting his third multi-organ transplant. He has spent years in and out of pediatric hospitals due to rejection of his previous transplants and infection.

Juan's face is familiar in the transplant unit, and admission after admission, he routinely but politely turns down music therapy services. Instead, he spends most days in his room with the lights off and the shades drawn, an oversized hooded sweatshirt pulled over his head and zipped to cover his extremely frail body.

I stroll past late in the afternoon and poke my head in just to say hello and to ask if he needs anything. Without lifting his head, and in the softest tone, he mumbles, "No, thank you."

His illness progresses at a faster pace, and there is talk of him becoming too sick to survive another transplant. He denies all support services, and the staff begins to notice more withdrawal. Juan knows and understands his condition very well and openly speaks with his mother, who spends most of her time at his bedside.

One afternoon, I notice that the lights are on, and he is sitting up in a chair. His arms are uncovered, revealing a beautifully colorful tattoo of the Virgin Mary. Underneath are the words *Mi Madre es Mi Hero*.

"Wow, that is a beautiful piece," I say. "Does it say, 'My mother is my hero'?"

He looks up and squints through his eyebrow rings. "No one's ever asked me that. And, yeah, you're right."

He has other large colorful tattoos, filled with words, pictures, and lyrics, covering both arms and parts of his neck and chest.

On the far wall of his room, there is a poster: "Hip-Hop's 100 Most Influential Faces." He notices me staring at it. "You know who those people are?"

"Well, I probably couldn't name them all, but ...."

"I bet you couldn't name ten," he chuckles.

I bounce over to the poster. "Easy," I smile back and point to faces I know, like Notorious B.I.G., Snoop Dogg, Lil' Kim, Eminem, Queen Latifah, and was sure to include the groundbreakers like The Sugar Hill Gang, A Tribe Called Quest, The Roots, and Run-D.M.C. I peer over my shoulder to see Juan crack a slightly smug smile.

"Okay, so I guess you can," he says. "I have always been into rap. It's what gets me through a lot. I know all kind of people just think it's crap, and it's got no meaning, but it does. You just gotta listen."

He goes on to tell me more about his favorite artists and songs and how he believes that rap is more like storytelling and poetry. The next day, and for many sessions after that, we share music and printed-out lyrics to Hip-Hop songs with themes of struggle, triumph, defeat, death, life, and power.

One day, we use Kanye West's "Jesus Walks" to talk about judgment passed on Juan in his life. The young Latino man looks tough; his tattoos give him edge, and his attitude and language are not always positive. He loves the shout-out in the song, "to the hustlers, killers, murderers, drug dealers, even us cripples." He is religious and uses this song to explain his faith to me, as well as his hardships.

I attempt to share with him some songs of hope and inspiration as well as struggle and pain. "Hope" by Twista, featuring Faith Evans, is one such song. In this song, it talks about being hopeful, about using music to help get you out of your current state, and about finding solace in religion. The song also provides empathy to the listeners by acknowledging that even though it isn't easy to go through the things they are going through, it is okay if you have hope.

One afternoon, he shares the lyrics from "Dear Mama," a song by Tupac Shakur, while his mom is in the room. I can see Juan making a connection with some of the lyrics as he is reciting them with his mom sitting close beside him. We let it play sort of softly in the background as he points out some of his favorite lines on the lyric sheet. These are the lyrics that talk about being able to depend on his mother and that even when he was sick as a child there were no limits to what his mother did for him. He wants his mother to know how much he appreciates her.

This was an emotional session that provides the space for them to communicate more about their relationship and how grateful he is for the care that she has shown him, as they both know he is near the end of his life. Shortly thereafter, Juan was moved to the palliative care service.

Vignette 4: Drumming

Sean, another patient with sickle-cell anemia, and I would play off of each other's rhythms: He would beat box, and I would repeat it back to him on a djembe drum. Sometimes, I would start, and he would answer back. We would groove together, taking turns to solo in between. Using the technique of call and response in drumming and other music I have often found has led to opening the lines of communication both verbally and nonverbally. Today call and response has found its way into rap, R&B, rock, country, jazz, blues, and most other forms of music, but its roots are in the African culture of sacred music and communication. Call and response has been used by the Baptist and Methodist churches as a way to get the congregation more involved in the service. This same technique was used by some of the first DJs and rap artists in New York City to get the crowds more involved at their shows. It has always been utilized as a means of communication and a way to unite people.

It was a great communication exercise—to listen to each other, to not use our words. He would call it "battling" or "freestyling," terms he borrowed from rap. Sean was often known on the unit as being shy, but when he was drumming and beat boxing it was a different story. He would often invite his nurses and doctors into his room to watch a session and sometimes even to participate. For Sean this was an important exercise in building his self-esteem and self-confidence as well as normalizing his hospitalization.

Often with this age group making friends and building relationships is hard enough when they are healthy and becomes more complicated when they are hospitalized (especially for an extended stay). Group drumming has been an effective way to bring some of these patients together and enhance communication inside and outside of the drumming experience. In using call-and-response experiences each member of the group is provided with an opportunity to lead the group in a short rhythmic phrase and to have that phrase answered back to them. We go over the importance of listening to what is being played to be able to play it back to them. Once we have established cohesiveness between the group we often go into creating a group song or beat. We discuss the importance of listening to everything that is being played by the group members so they know to make their rhythm fit the "song/beat" it must also fit with the others. In this setting I give the group members an opportunity to lead by taking turns on creating the call rhythm for the group to respond to.

Vignette 5: Recording and Improvisation

Veronica is a 13-year-old patient with Gardner's syndrome, who is frequently hospitalized for the surgical removal of desmoid tumors and cysts caused by her disease. She is used to the hustle and bustle of the hospital, but her tumors and cysts often cause her a lot of pain and gastrointestinal irritability.

She is easy to work with: She loves music. She loves old-school pop, some of the influences in Hip-Hop music today. I learn quickly that I can share with her my passion for Prince, funk, and rhythm and blues. Together, we can talk about pioneers in the industry and their relationships to contemporary artists.

I gained some of her respect (and some credibility) when I talk about and play songs by James Brown. I gained even more when I tell her that "Keep Ya Head Up" by Tupac Shakur has a chorus that came from "Ooh Child, Things Are Gonna Get Easier" by The Five Stairsteps. Then, we play The Fugee's "Killing Me Softly," followed by the original by Roberta Flack.

One day, I arrive in her room to find three harmonicas that she had purchased in the gift shop. I pluck a 12-bar blues out on my guitar and let her play what she feels on the harmonica. She plays and plays and plays. She sounds great.

The next day I come back with my computer to record her (a practice I sometimes use for patients in palliative care, providing the family with another way to remember their loved one). I play guitar while she plays the harmonica. When we roll the playback, she beat-boxes over it, bringing in more of a Hip-Hop feel. So we record that, too.

She learns she can do no wrong. It is expressive and passionate and multilayered. After we burned her "album," we have a CD release party for all of her friends, doctors, and nurses. When we play her tracks, Veronica takes out her instruments and plays over the recordings. Her expression has found release, and it won't stop.

Vignette 6: Musical Instruction

My job is never easier than when a patient tells me what he wants. Such is the case with Chris, who has epilepsy, but who desperately wants to learn how to drum and, then, how to record.

"I want to be a producer," he tells me.

I quickly gather resources, as Chris's hospitalization requires testing that confines him to his room and his bed. I bring him a MacBook with Garage Band on it, a user-friendly program for beginning producers. Then, I begin simple drum instruction. He loves the rap artist Flo Rida, so we began with the beat in "Get Low." Sometimes we clap along or tap along to it. And then we record it. I show Chris how to make drum loops and how to sample other instruments on the program.

Oftentimes, he calls our sessions "music class." It helps to normalize the situation for Chris—it was his favorite class in school.

Vignette 7: Movement

Melissa is a 17-year-old patient with epidermolysis bullosa, a disorder that causes her skin to break down constantly. She is depressed and demonstrates a low self-esteem that is due in large part to her illness, but also as a result of being adopted, having little family support, and compounded by gender identity issues.

She begins to refuse physical therapy and occupational therapy. She stops getting out of her bed.

"I used to play guitar," she says when she sees my instrument. Immediately, I try to devise a way for how her fingers, now webbed together, could strum. She isn't into it.

She confesses to also playing drums in her high school band. I arrive the next day with three full-sized congas. We are both delighted that the "mittening" of her hands makes a really good tone on a drum. We play beats from some of her favorite songs. Each has whole, heavy sounds that she can beautifully duplicate.

Soon, the physical therapists approach me about her treatment. Melissa hasn't gotten out of bed in weeks. I make a plan for our next visit, incorporating her favorite Hip-Hop songs.

"We should totally have a dance party," I say.

She laughs and gives me a hard time. "You know how to dance?"

"Well, I bet you could teach me something," I offer. "Do you know the Cupid Shuffle?" It is one that fits safely inside of the genre of mainstream Hip-Hop that she has been requesting for our drumming sessions. She knows it, of course.

"If you teach me the Cupid Shuffle, I'll teach you the Cleveland Shuffle," I say, choosing a Hip-Hop song and dance that was not as mainstream, one I know would challenge her.

At first, she laughs this off. She is reluctant.

"I'm not kidding," I say. "I want to learn."

I bring the tracks to our next session, along with other dance tracks like the Macarena and the Cha-Cha Slide.

"So are you going to teach me or not?" I ask.

And then a girl who wouldn't get out of her bed is kicking and sliding and shuffling around her hospital room.

When I teach her the Cleveland Shuffle, she can't wait to show off her new moves.

We gather a couple of nurses and support staff to join us for our Cupid/ Cleveland Shuffle out in the hallway of the adolescent unit, where everyone could see. It was a party that drew doctors and more nurses from the entire floor. Other patients peeked out of their rooms.

Conclusion

It is a privilege in my profession when I can call on the powers of movement, instruction, improvisation, drumming, song discussion, and songwriting as they apply to the world of Hip-Hop and rap music when I work with adolescents. These are genres born out of struggle, and it is because these patients struggle that they can so thoroughly relate. They are pioneers in pediatrics: Their pain is compounded by their age, their status, and their race.

Literally tapping into a teen's musical preference—and respecting that preference—is the most effective way to create trust. It gives me an in, and it gives them a safe space.

The "lost population" doesn't have to stay lost. The music finds them. And then, I can find them, too.

References

Bosco, F. (1997). Sensing and resonating with pain: A process-oriented approach to focusing the body/mind using music therapy. In J. V. Loewy (Ed.), *Music therapy and pediatric pain* (pp. 7–15). Cherry Hill, NJ: Jeffrey.

Kobin, C., & Tyson, E. H. (2006). Thematic analysis of Hip-Hop music: Can Hip-Hop in therapy facilitate empathic connections when working with clients in urban settings? *The Arts in Psychotherapy, 33*, 343–356.

Priestley, M. (1994). *Essays on analytical music therapy.* Phoenixville, PA: Barcelona.

Tyson, E. H. (2002). Hip-Hop therapy: An exploratory study of a rap music intervention with at-risk delinquent youth. *Journal of Poetry Therapy*, 15(2), 131–142.

Song List

Arie, I. (2001). Video. On *Acoustic soul* [CD]. Motown.

Big Mucci and the 71 North Boyz. (2007). Cleveland Shuffle. On *Cleveland Shuffle* [CD]. School House Records.

Blige, M. J. (2007). Just fine. On *Growing pains* [CD]. Geffen.

Cupid. (2007). Cupid Shuffle. On *Time for a Change* [CD]. Atlantic.

DJ Casper. (1996). Cha-Cha Slide. On *The original slide album* [CD]. Universal.

Earth, Wind, & Fire. (1975). New world symphony. On *Gratitude* [CD]. Columbia/Legacy.

Elliot, Missy (featuring Ginuwine). (1997). Friendly skies. On *Supa Dupa Fly* [CD]. The Goldmind, Elektra.

En Vogue. (1992). Free your mind. On *Funky divas* [CD]. Eastwest Records.

Evans, F., & Twista. (2005). Hope. On *Kamikaze* [CD]. Capital.

Flo Rida. (2008). Get low. On *Mail on Sunday* [CD]. Atlantic, Poe Boy.

Jackson, M. (1982). Beat it. On *Thriller* [CD]. Epic.

Jackson, M. (featuring Janet Jackson). (1995). Scream. On *HIStory: Past, Present, and Future, Book I* [CD]. Epic.

Jay-Z. (2001). Song cry. On *The Blueprint* [CD]. Roc-A-Fella/Island Def Jam.

Keys, A. (2007). No one. On *As I am* [CD]. J.

Kool and the Gang. (1979). Ladies night. On *Ladies night* [CD]. DeLite Records/Polygram.

Los Del Rio. (1995). Macarena. On *Fiesta Macarena* [CD]. RCA.

Ludacris. (2001). Move bitch. On *Word of mouf* [CD]. Def Jam South.

Shakur, T. (1995). Dear mama. On *Me against the world* [CD]. Interscope/Atlantic Records.

Shakur, T. (1993). Keep ya head up. On *Strictly 4 my N.I.G.G.A.Z.* [CD]. Interscope/Atlantic Records.

The Five Stairsteps. (1970). O-o-h child. On *The stairsteps* [CD]. Buddha Records.

West, K. (2004). Jesus walks. On *The college dropout* [CD]. Roc-A-Fella/Island Def Jam.

Chapter 17

"Must Be the Ganja"*

Using Rap Music in Music Therapy for Substance Use Disorders

Felicity A. Baker, Genevieve A. Dingle, and Libby M. Gleadhill

Introduction

Over the last decade, music and music therapy approaches have been increasingly reported in the literature as playing a valuable role in the rehabilitation of people with substance use disorder (SUD). Music therapy is especially suitable to substance abuse treatment because of its ability to motivate and engage clients with SUD (Cevasco, Kennedy, & Generally, 2005; De l'Etoile, 2002; Dingle, Gleadhill, & Baker, 2008; Gallagher & Steele, 2002; Ghetti, 2004; Silverman, 2009), counteract isolation (Soshensky, 2001), elicit surfacing of emotions and positive mood changes (Baker, Gleadhill & Dingle, 2007; De l'Etoile, 2002; Ghetti, 2004; Jones, 2005; Soshensky, 2001), decrease stress and anxiety (Cevasco et al., 2005; Hammer, 1996; Silverman, 2003), and decrease impulsivity (Silverman, 2003). The types of music activities that have been used in treatment for substance abuse include guided relaxation, lyric analysis, songwriting,

---

* Eminem, 2009.

singing, instrument playing such as drumming, and improvisation on a particular theme (Silverman, 2003).

Treder-Wolff (1990) suggests that music therapy provides opportunities for clients to access feelings that are both integral to the addiction and pose obstacles to recovery. Doughtery (1984) stated that one of the primary goals of the music therapy program, which possibly lies intrinsic within the act of music making/listening, is to teach the client how to cope with emotions without resorting to substance use. Recent studies that we conducted (Baker et al., 2007; Dingle et al., 2008) found that music combined with cognitive behavioral therapy was effective in exploring clients' emotions and feelings around their SUD, and in facilitating the discussion of topics addressed in their programs. The clients tended to learn to tolerate their uncomfortable feelings without the need to use substances.

Substance Use Disorders and Treatment

The 2007 (Australian) National Drug Strategy Household Survey reported that 83% of Australians aged over 14 years had consumed alcohol recently, and that 10% had consumed alcohol at levels considered to be harmful in the longer term. The proportion of Australians over 14 years who had used an illicit drug in the previous 12 months was 13%, most commonly marijuana, ecstasy, and amphetamines. Despite this widespread use of alcohol and illicit drugs, only a small percentage of these substance users go on to develop addiction problems. For these individuals, the substance abuse causes significant problems with their health, social relationships, occupational functioning, and financial status. Some also have legal problems relating to possession and/or dealing in illicit substances or stemming from illegal activities associated with obtaining the substances. For many addicted individuals, there is a strong sense of guilt and shame associated with their ongoing substance use in the face of the obvious problems that it causes. Depression and anxiety disorders are much more common among people with an addiction than in the general population. According to the National Survey of Mental Health and Wellbeing, Australians with an alcohol use disorder were 10 times more likely to have a drug use disorder, four times more likely to have a mood disorder, and three times more likely to have an anxiety disorder than a member of the general population (Burns & Teesson, 2002). The link between substance abuse and negative emotions is one that we explore in further detail below.

There are many types of treatment available for individuals with an SUD, including community support groups such as Alcoholics Anonymous; hospital detoxification and treatment in public and private hospitals, often with longer term treatment and relapse prevention provided at a community clinic; shared care between a medical practitioner, a private psychologist, and a registered pharmacist in the case of opiate replacement therapy; and therapeutic communities. Individuals with an addiction experience significant barriers to treatment, including practical difficulties (such as substantial treatment or health insurance costs, having to travel to a major metropolitan area to access treatment, and having to take several weeks off work or away from the family to enter a rehabilitation service) and psychological difficulties (such as having to accept that the substance use that is a predominant way of coping with life stress is going to stop). These internal barriers are further compounded by the negative reactions and stigma that such individuals face from members of the community and also from health professionals—many of whom view addiction as a moral issue rather than a health problem. These factors may explain why addicted individuals have difficulty in engaging in therapy.

Engaging and Keeping Clients in Substance Abuse Treatment

Based on prior statistics, it is estimated that only 28% of those with an alcohol use disorder and 36% of those with a drug use disorder sought help in the past year (Teesson, Hall, Lynskey, & Degenhardt, 2000). An even smaller number continue with treatment. For example, the Australian Treatment Outcome Study (ATOS) investigated the treatment course for 745 people entering heroin treatment services across three states and reported that more than 40% had discontinued treatment 1 year later (Teesson et al., 2006). One review reported that between 52% and 75% of patients in alcohol treatment drop out by the fourth session (Baekeland & Lundwall, 1975). These findings are not unique to Australia. Similar findings were reported in a study of 419 consecutive clients undergoing assessment at a specialist alcohol clinic in England—34% declined any treatment, 25% attended one session, and 41% attended more than one session of treatment (Jackson, Booth, McGuire, & Salmon, 2006).

Early engagement in treatment is associated with participation in treatment sessions and the establishment of a therapeutic relationship, both of which are necessary for treatment completion and positive outcomes (Simpson & Joe, 2004). Engagement has been defined and measured in various ways, including patient ratings of interest in upcoming treatment sessions (Wild, Cunningham, & Ryan, 2006) and objective and subjective measures of patient participation in treatment (Joe, Simpson, & Broome, 1999). Objective measures include compliance with treatment activities and contributions to the session, while subjective measures include patients' experience of cognitive involvement, satisfaction with the program, increase in self-confidence, and experience of a strong therapeutic alliance with the therapist (Joe et al., 1999). The past 15 years has seen a growth of research and interventions designed to improve patient engagement and retention. Miller and Rollnick argue that motivation (to change behavior) is a dynamic construct that is influenced by the interpersonal and environmental context (Miller & Rollnick, 2002). Similarly, engagement may be influenced by the therapeutic context and the dynamics of the relationships between patients and therapist and in the case of group therapy, interpersonal dynamics among members of the therapy group. It is vital therefore that engagement is supported actively throughout the treatment process to ensure that clients feel comfortable and motivated to continue treatment and to achieve positive longer-term outcomes.

Another treatment factor that is highly relevant to addiction treatment is the tendency for addiction to take a chronic relapsing course (Koob, 2000). Clients who have successfully completed detoxification and treatment, and sometimes many months or years of abstinence, may still relapse. The top three triggers for relapse into addictive behavior are negative emotional states, interpersonal conflict, and cues/cravings for the substance (Hodgkins, el Guebaly, & Armstrong, 1995; Witkiewitz & Wu, 2010; Zywiak et al., 2006). This means that treatments must examine and prepare clients to manage successfully both the external triggers for substance use (such as venues where they typically use the substance or the sight, smell, or taste of the substance) and the internal triggers for substance use—in particular, negative emotional states, cravings, and withdrawal sensations.

Unfortunately, treatments that have included a component of exposure to negative emotional states have not been very successful to date—at least partly due to the high rate of dropout from such interventions (Kavanagh et al., 2006). This is because the very clients who need exposure to negative emotional states to learn to tolerate and manage them without using substances are the clients most driven to avoid such experiences. Experiential avoidance is part and parcel of the addictive behavior. This brings us to the potential uses of music as a means of evoking emotions in treatment in a way that is engaging and meaningful to clients.

Music, Drugs, and Emotions

Substance abuse is almost always accompanied by emotional pain (Kassel, 2010, p. 7) and there are several theories to explain the link between substance abuse and emotion. For example, on the one hand, positive reinforcement theories emphasize the connection between addictive behavior and the positive reinforcement given by the euphoric sensations the drugs produce. On the other hand, negative reinforcement theories explain addictive behavior in terms of the escape or release that substances provide from negative emotional states or pain (McCarthy, Curtin, Piper, & Baker, 2010). There is abundant evidence from laboratory studies and survey-based research that music listening and music making produces an emotional response (Sloboda, 2005). The type and intensity of emotional response is a function of features of the music (such as tempo, mode, musical structure), features of the listener/player (such as level of experience and musical preference), and features of the context (such as whether the individual is alone or in a social setting) (Dibben, 2004; Juslin, 2009; Krumhansl, 1997). Substance use and music therefore share one similarity: they both alter or produce an emotion or mood.

Drawing on the above findings, we developed a survey to research the music listening behaviors of people with SUD. We found that people with SUD spend large periods of their day listening to music; up to 45% listen to at least 2 hours per day (*manuscript under review*). Similar to the effects of drugs, we hypothesized that music was functioning to stimulate the "reward" centers in the brain consistent with findings of brain imaging studies that show the mesolimbic structures of the brain activated when participants are listening to music (Menon & Levitin, 2005; Salimpoor et al., 2009). Our study found that more than 50% of participants reported a relationship between music having an impact on their experience of drug-taking and vice versa, and points to the notion that the need for sensation seeking typical of people with SUD may be partly satisfied through these vast amounts of music listening (Kelley & Berridge, 2002). We conjectured that if music was strategically applied to address the need for sensation more fully, there is a potential for drug use to decrease.

Our study found that for people with SUD, music listening tended to be a private experience rather than shared with peers or family. Strong correlations were identified with the meaningfulness of favorite pieces of music with notions of being moved by the music, considering the selection as important or valuable, and the music stimulating thoughts, associations, and memories. Weaker correlations were found for the music reflecting personality/identity. This may be due in part to the fact that when people with SUD enter rehabilitation programs, they leave behind a way of life in which they were familiar in how to interact in the world and view themselves. This life change can leave people feeling vulnerable and questioning their purpose and identity.

Musical Features of Rap Appropriate for a Client with No Prior Formal Musical Training

Most forms of music making require resources such as lessons, instruments, and an ability to read music and stay in tune. In contrast, rap music can be made despite limited access to such resources, suggesting an accessible medium for use within the SUD setting for clients who may not be very comfortable or confident musically. In rap, the pitch content is secondary to rhythmic content (Adams, 2008), so clients may feel more comfortable to verbalize the words in a rhythmic manner over a supportive musical accompaniment. Further, because flexibility of meter is a feature of rap, precision in rhythmic ability is also less important in achieving a solid musical outcome for clients with no formal musical training.

Rapping is a vocal style in which the music artist speaks lyrically, in rhyme and verse, generally to an instrumental or synthesized beat. Beats, usually in 4/4 time, can be created by looping portions of other songs. Typically, rap music can be described as a "flow" where the rhythmical and articulative features of a rapper's delivery of the lyrics involves multiple rhymes in the same rhyme complex, internal rhymes, offbeat rhymes, multiple syncopations, and flexibility of meter and metrical subdivisions of the beat (Adams, 2009). In rap music, there's a lot of "breaking the form" (Sylvan 2002), which may be appealing to people with substance use disorder who often belong to a culture of not wanting to be "mainstream." Such breaking of the form may reflect the identity of the person with substance use disorder. Professional rappers report that they experience power from the "flow" of rap music (Sylvan, 2002).

Rap music developed out of the African American oral tradition and characteristically draws on the call-and-response structure (Rose, 1994; Waterman, 1999). Here the rapper offers a lyric and the audience responds either vocally or physically (e.g., "everybody say wo," and "put your hands in the air"). So the music is participatory (Sylvan, 2002). Such call-and-response features are typical of many music therapy approaches.

Rap Music Is Storytelling

The style of rap music is "hard"—lyrics typically focus on drug taking and violence and contain frequent explicit language, and vocal line is sung at a fast tempo with an almost monotonal melody with the singer singing with a timbre that gives a sense that he is angry (a melodic yell). This style of music may reflect their life, which is hard. Sylvan (2002) suggests that rap music is like a template for the worldviews of people identifying with that culture, thereby reflecting their identity. One of the main reasons why rap music is so popular, particularly among disenfranchised youth, is that it tells stories and describes situations that many can relate to (Diamond et al., 2006). "Gangsta rap" in particular has grown in popularity and audiences and the rappers themselves view it as an expression of real-life experiences (Diamond et al., 2006). It allows them to momentarily transcend their historical circumstances (Sylvan, 2002) and help build identity (Clay, 2003). Truth-telling, "keepin' it real," and being authentic (Sylvan, 2002) are values the rappers hold strongly (McLeod, 1999; Sylvan, 2002). Telling the truth, telling their stories, and being authentic are challenging for those in drug and alcohol rehabilitation. Hence, rap music provides an appropriate medium to achieve this as the clients may try to tell their story in the medium of their favorite rappers. Rap music is also a vehicle for expressing emotion, including anger (Sylvan, 2002), which may be an important emotion to experience and not avoid for people with substance use disorder (Baker et al., 2007). As rap music traditionally presents a commentary on life that many people can connect with, it lends itself to expressing social critique, love, cultural life, and other themes within the context of a therapeutic setting.

Rap Music and Drugs

Illicit drug use is highly visible in contemporary rap music songs and Hip-Hop culture (Herd, 2008) and a number of studies suggest a link between drug use and preference for rap music. For example, rap music was associated with (but not suggested to "cause") crack use in a group of U.S. adolescents (Dent et al., 1992), and Lim et al. (2008) found that those with a preference for dance/house or rap were more likely to report recent use of illicit drugs (55% and 70%, respectively), particularly amphetamines, ecstasy, and cannabis. While studies have identified the high prevalence of lyrics with references to drugs (e.g., Herd, 2008), a recent lyric analysis of rap songs by Diamond et al. (2006) looked more qualitatively at the data and grouped references to drugs (specifically ecstasy) according to (a) messages "glamorizing" it, (b) mixed or ambiguous messages, and (c) messages that directly or indirectly discourage use. While more than twice as many rap songs presented messages glamorizing drug use as opposed to messages discouraging its use, the authors argued that rap music can provide antidrug messages (Diamond et al., 2006).

Clinical Vignette: The Rehab Rap

We offer the example of a rap that was produced by the members of a substance abuse treatment group located at a metropolitan hospital in which the third author, Libby, was the music therapist. Participants attended one music therapy (MT) session per week with activities and themes chosen by the music therapist to reflect the broader content of their group cognitive behavior therapy (CBT) program. The focus of the group CBT sessions throughout the week of this music therapy case study was *Understanding Anxiety, Depression, and Anger.* CBT sessions on these themes explored with group participants the theoretical underpinnings of these emotions, as well as personal experiences and exploration of how these emotions affected the individual in terms of cognitions, behavior, and physiological states. The five participants who attended the MT session included three females and two males. Both males and one female were in their early 20s, all experiencing withdrawal from amphetamine (intravenous and oral) abuse. The other two female participants were middle-aged, both withdrawing from alcohol abuse. Despite a primary diagnosis of substance abuse, co-morbidity was present for all participants, including anxiety, depression, and personality disorders. The following is a reflection by Libby of what happened before, during, and after the session:

On the day of the music therapy session, the group had attended psychoeducation classes (*Understanding Anxiety, Depression, and Anger*) in the morning with the psychologist. Although all the group members were present, keeping the clients engaged in the session appeared difficult at times as their attention span was limited. Furthermore, the dynamics of the group were challenging to contain, with many group members displaying "adolescent" behavior. During a morning tea break, a number of clients were outside the therapy room having a cigarette when a staff member reprimanded them on smoking in a nonsmoking area. Although not an extraordinary encounter, this event caused an exaggerated negative emotional reaction; tears, tantrums, and threats ensued as has been commonly observed with SUD clients.

Based on observations from the morning sessions, I aimed to explore current feeling states through the medium of songwriting. Once this concept was introduced to the group, a unanimous decision was quickly made by all group members to write a rap song. At this point, one of the male group members who was a fan of rap music offered to play the group a rap song from a CD in his collection to "get the feel." As the therapist, on the one hand, I was pleased to see this young male become engaged and active in a session as he offered to share something close to him with his peers; on the other hand, I was concerned with him playing a piece of music I was unfamiliar with: How would the other group members respond? How graphic would the words be? For the next few minutes, gangsta rap blared in the room, as graphic tales of drugs, violence, and ganglands were rapped. I watched the CD's owner become animated, group members' bodies and heads tapping and nodding, and finally a sense of agitation set in across the group. I faded the music.

The songwriting process thus began, and a sense of teenage rebellion was present as boundaries began to be tested by group members. By the second line of the song, a number of group members began singing,

"I wanna be high, so high," and then breaking into laughter, before staring at me. I recognized their behavior as a test to see if I would assume a dominant enforcer role. However, as a therapist in this setting, I strongly believed in accountability and ownership. Hence, limited rules were enforced. Rather, my objective was to encourage the group members to engage in the process of questioning and reasoning with each other. With this in mind, I nodded my head and repeated back to the group, "OK, so I wanna be high, so high?" At this point, some other group members stepped in and started questioning whether that is what they really wanted, as they began to point out the negatives "being high" had led them to. Although just one line of a song, this line led to a lengthy process of group problem solving and personal reflection and reevaluation. A consensus was reached: "I wanna be high, on life."

The process continued for the next hour with the group clearly engaged, as they declined to take the smoke break they usually pleaded for. The challenging behaviors had ceased as the group honestly dealt with and expressed their emotions. The lyrics in the first verse show evidence of the performers' desire to feel good ("I wanna look and feel fine all the time") and to escape difficulties ("Don't want no strife in my life .... It makes me happy when things ain't crappy"), which is consistent with the positive and negative reinforcement theories of substance abuse. At one point, one of the female clients began to mock the song "Am I Not Pretty Enough" by Kasey Chambers. Due to the flexibility of form in rap music, a bridge section was added in which the reference was included. Although initially used mockingly, when pressed as to whether to repeat the same line, she became serious and admitted that what she was really asking was "Am I not good enough?" This becomes a pertinent example of semantics in songwriting and how the ambiguity of words can provide a safe shelter for clients to express themselves behind, until they are ready to be authentic and honest with themselves.

Subsequent lyrics expressed anger and frustration about the performers' current life situation ("I'm in a lot of mess") and their hospital treatment ("[hospital name] got me down ... . They put me on meds (medication), and it's fuckin' with ma head"). Although the prohibition of expletive language is a common group therapy rule, when songwriting, the stylistic qualities of the music must also be kept in mind. In this instance, the group unanimously voted that this choice of words best described how they were feeling, as well as suggesting that it was "in style" with the rap genre. It should be noted, however, that at other points throughout the lyric writing when more expletives were suggested for use, other group members stepped in and questioned the motive behind their inclusion and what their use would offer the song.

Verse 5 expresses anger at a "Smoke Nazi" (nurse) who stopped a patient from smoking, with the argument that if s/he wasn't "pullin a bong" (smoking cannabis), then s/he should be allowed to continue. As discussed earlier, this morning-tea incident created strong emotional reactions from the clients. They struggled with the negative emotions the conflict had brought up. By addressing the incident in the rap song, the group was able to find a safe and positive medium in which to relay the story, ventilate emotions, and find a resolution.

The Rehab Rap

I wanna be fine, so fine,
I wanna be high, on life.
Don't want no strife in my life,
I wanna look and feel fine, all the time.

It makes me happy,
When things ain't crappy.
It's all about balls,
If you've got 'em at all.

I'm feeling kinda stressed,
Cause I'm in a lot of mess.
(*hospital name withheld*) got me down,
Feet ain't on the ground.
They put me on meds,
And it's fuckin with ma head

I'm wonderin …
Am I not pretty enough,
Am I not good enough.

Wanna detox today,
Wanna fly away.
(*hospital name withheld*) got to stay,
I'm smoking my lungs away.

Smoke nazi came along,
Weren't pullin a bong.
It was just a ciggie,
Why's that a biggie?

I wanna be fine, so fine,
I wanna be high on life.
Don't want no strife in my life,
I wanna look and feel fine, all the time.

The session ended in a robust group recording of the rap song, as clients laughed and high-fived each other as they left the room. As they left, the man who offered to play the group a rap song remained behind in the room with me. He approached me and then said quietly, "I've, ah, written my own rap song about being in here. Did you wanna see it?" I replied, "I'd love to, but I don't suppose you'd like to rap it for me?" We sat there in the late afternoon, and I wondered what it was that drove him to open up to me like this, and he, behind the tinny beat of my keyboard, truth-telling, being authentic, and keepin' it real, rapped his story.

Issues for Consideration

While the use of rap music in drug and alcohol rehabilitation is of therapeutic value, there are a number of potential contraindications and issues requiring consideration prior to its inclusion in a therapy program. Our survey found that music is a private experience. Clients may prefer to listen to *their* music in their own time and space. Therefore, when introducing rap within a group therapy context, some clients may respond negatively to the rap music rather than it being a positive aspect of the program purely because it violates what is normally a private activity.

Rap is about "breakin the form," not being mainstream, this matching the behaviors of those with SUD. It is possible that using rap music may reinforce their need to be nonconformist/antisocial, thereby contradicting the rehabilitation goals. Further, the lyrics of many rap songs glamorize drug taking. The use of these songs may lead to some reflecting upon/recalling the positive feelings they experienced when high, and possibly stimulating cravings that lead to relapse. Similarly, our survey found substantial numbers of people with SUD partner music and drug taking. Again, perhaps the use of rap music may be an association that leads to cravings.

Rap music is a form of music that is most utilized by younger generations. People of older generations can have difficulty enjoying and relating to rap music, some finding it offensive and irritating, an opinion which when openly expressed within the group context can create a rift in the group and cause the group to split. This scenario is not uncommon in music therapy group settings like the one we discussed in this chapter. The groups are open to all adult psychiatric patients aged 18 to 80.

Conclusion

The value of writing and performing "The Rehab Rap" within the context of the therapy group is that the performers were able to express such negative emotions as anger and frustration in an effective way that was supported and even caused some humor. Group members were able to share their own feelings of frustration with being in rehabilitation and their difficulties around some of the aspects of hospital treatment. This release of negative emotions was helpful at the time but also gave the participants an experience in which the expression of their emotions was tolerable and helpful and did not result in the abuse of substances. It is hoped that a series of such experiences during hospital treatment would generalize to their ongoing emotional management after discharge from hospital.

The ideas that we have presented here in this clinical example strongly support the inclusion of rap music in the group music therapy context for those being treated for drug and alcohol use disorder. The appropriateness of rap music relates to several factors. First, rap music is often the music of choice of people with substance use disorder and therefore more likely to engage them in music therapy than other types of music. They relate to these songs because they typically express many of the issues affecting people with SUD. Engagement is key to successful therapy and is the most difficult facet to achieve. Second, the dichotomy of rap songs' lyrics, which may feature pro- or antidrug use themes, is an apt vehicle for exploring and reframing within the therapy context. Songs provide messages that explore the life outcomes of both views. Reflecting on these within the group context can open clients to alternative ways of thinking and being without "disconnecting" from their music of choice. Most importantly, by writing their own lyrics, they can tell their story and express difficult emotions within a drug-free context. Music therapy programs that include the use of rap music in a planned and carefully considered way bring possibilities for engagement in drug and alcohol rehabilitation in ways perhaps not possible through the use of other music genres.

Rap music has several advantages over other musical genres for use in therapy with people affected by SUD. First, the "keepin it real" feature of rap music offers clients the possibility of sharing "what is," providing them with opportunities to face and explore "reality." Rap music often tells a story, so through the creation of original rap songs, people affected by SUD can explore their "story" and then compose lyrics to represent it. The monotonal nature of the melodies characteristic of rap (but not other genres) is effective when clients' therapy processes are deepened through their singing and/or recording of the song. The chances of a good musical outcome are increased when there is less dependence on a musically pleasant melody. The "angry" nature of the way rap music is sung can be a vehicle for these people to release their own anger in a way that is acceptable for this musical genre and contained within the context of a piece of music shared with a small supportive group.

References

Adams, K. (2008). Aspects of the music/text relationship in rap. *Music Theory Online, 14*(2). Retrieved from http://mto.societymusictheory.org/issues/mto.08.14.2/mto.08.14.2.adams.html

Australian Institute of Health and Welfare. (2008). *2007 National Drug Strategy Household Survey: Detailed findings.* Drug statistics series No. 22. Cat no. PHE 107. Canberra: AIHW.

Baekeland, F., & Lundwall, L. (1975). Dropping out of treatment: A critical review. *Psychological Bulletin, 82*, 738–783.

Baker, F., Dingle, G. A., & Gleadhill, L. (manuscript under review). Music preferences and music listening experiences of people with substance use disorders.

Baker, F., Gleadhill, L., & Dingle, G. A. (2007). Music therapy and emotional exploration: Exposing substance abuse clients to the experiences of non-drug induced emotions. *Arts in Psychotherapy, 34*, 321–330.

Burns, L., & Teesson, M. (2002). Alcohol use disorders comorbid with anxiety, depression and drug use disorders. Findings from the Australian National Survey of Mental Health and Wellbeing. *Drug and Alcohol Dependence, 68,* 299–307.

Cevasco, A. M., Kennedy, R., & Generally, N. R. (2005). Comparison of movement-to-music, rhythm activities, and competitive games on depression, stress, anxiety, and anger of females in substance abuse rehabilitation. *Journal of Music Therapy, 42*(1), 64–81.

Clay, A. (2003). Keepin' it real: Black youth, hip-hop culture, and black identity. *The American Behavioral Scientist, 46*(10), 1346–1358.

De l'Etoile, S. K. (2002). The effectiveness of music therapy in group psychotherapy for adults with mental illness. *The Arts in Psychotherapy, 29,* 69–78.

de Wit, H., & Phan, L. (2010). Positive reinforcement theories of drug use. In J. Kassel (Ed.), *Substance abuse and emotion* (pp. 43–60). Washington, DC: American Psychological Association.

Dent, C. W., Galaif, J., Sussman, S., Stacy, A. W., Burton, D., & Flay, B. R. (1992). Music preference as a diagnostic indicator of adolescent drug use. *American Journal of Public Health, 82*(1), 124.

Diamond, S., & Schensul, J. (2006). What's the rap about ecstasy? Popular music lyrics and drug trends among American youth. *Journal of Adolescent Research, 21*(3), 269–298.

Dibben, N. (2004). The role of peripheral feedback in emotional experience with music. *Music Perception, 22*(1), 79–115.

Dingle, G. A., Gleadhill, L, & Baker, F. A. (2008). Can music therapy engage patients in group cognitive behaviour therapy for substance abuse treatment? *Drug and Alcohol Review, 27,* 190–196.

Doughtery, K. (1984). Music therapy in the treatment of the alcoholic client. *Music Therapy, 1,* 47–54.

Gallagher, L. M., & Steele, A. L. (2002). Music therapy with offenders in a substance abuse/mental illness treatment program. *Music Therapy Perspectives, 20,* 117–122.

Ghetti, C. M. (2004). Incorporating music therapy into the harm reduction approach to managing substance use problems. *Music Therapy Perspectives, 22,* 84–90.

Hammer, S. E. (1996). The effects of guided imagery through music on state and trait anxiety. *Journal of Music Therapy, 33*(1), 47–70.

Herd, D. (2008). Changes in drug use prevalence in rap music songs, 1979–1997. *Addiction Research and Theory, 16*(2), 167–180.

Hodgkins, D. C., el Guebaly, N., & Armstrong, S. (1995). Prospective and retrospective reports of mood states before relapse to substance use. *Journal of Consulting and Clinical Psychology, 63,* 400–407.

Jackson, K. R., Booth, P. G., McGuire, J., & Salmon, P. (2006). Predictors of starting and remaining in treatment at a specialist alcohol clinic. *Journal of Substance Use, 11*(2), 89–100.

Joe, G. W., Simpson, D. D., & Broome, K. M. (1999). Retention and patient engagement models for different treatment modalities in DATOS. *Drug and Alcohol Dependence, 57,* 113–125.

Jones, J. D. (2005). A comparison of songwriting and lyric analysis techniques to evoke emotional change in a single session with people who are chemically dependent. *Journal of Music Therapy, 42*(2), 94–111.

Juslin, P. N. (2009). Emotional responses to music. In S. Hallam, I. Cross, & M. Thaut (Eds.), *The Oxford handbook of music psychology* (pp. 131–140). Oxford: Oxford University Press.

Kavanagh, D. J., Sitharthan, G., Young, R. M., Sitharthan, T., Saunders, J. B., Shockley, N., & Giannopoulos, V. (2006). Addition of cue exposure to cognitive-behavior therapy for alcohol misuse: A randomized trial with dysphoric drinkers. *Addiction, 101,* 1106–1116.

Kelley, A. E., & Berridge, K. C. (2002). The neuroscience of natural rewards: Relevance to addictive drugs. *Journal of Neuroscience, 22*(9), 3306–3311.

Koob, G. F. (2000). Neurobiology of addiction: Toward the development of new therapies. In S. D. Glick & I. M. Maisonneuve (Eds.), *New medications for drug abuse* (Vol. 909, pp. 170–185). New York: New York Academy of Sciences.

Krumhansl, C. L. (1997). An exploratory study of musical emotions and psychophysiology. *Canadian Journal of Experimental Psychology, 51,* 336–352.

Lim, M. S. C., Hellard, M. E., Hocking, J. S., & Aitken, C. K. (2008). A cross-sectional survey of young people attending a music festival: Associations between drug use and musical preference. *Drug and Alcohol Review, 27*(4), 439–441.

McCarthy, D. E., Curtin, J. J., Piper, M. E., & Baker, T. B. (2010). Negative reinforcement: Possible clinical implications of an integrative model. In J. Kassel (Ed.), *Substance abuse and emotion* (pp. 15–42). Washington, DC: American Psychological Association.

McLeod, K. (1999, Autumn). Authenticity within Hip-Hop culture and other cultures threatened with assimilation. *Journal of Communication,* 134–150.

Menon, V., & Levitin, D. J. (2005). The rewards of music listening: Response and physiological connectivity of the mesolimbic system. *NeuroImage, 28*, 175–184.

Miller, W. R., & Rollnick, S. (2002). *Motivational interviewing: Preparing people for change* (2nd ed.). New York: Guilford.

Rose, T. (1994). *Rap music and Black culture in contemporary America.* Middletown: Wesleyan University Press.

Salimpoor, V. N., Benovoy, M., Longo, G., Cooperstock, J. R., & Zatorre, R. J. (2009). The rewarding aspects of music listening are related to degree of emotional arousal. *PLoS ONE, 4*(10), e7487. doi:10.1371/journal.pone.0007487.

Silverman, M. (2003). Music therapy and clients who are chemically dependent: A review of literature and pilot study. *Arts in Psychotherapy, 30*, 273–281.

Silverman, M. J. (2009). The effect of lyric analysis on treatment eagerness and working alliance in consumers who are in detoxification: A randomised clinical effectiveness study. *Music Therapy Perspectives, 27*(2), 115–121.

Simpson, D. D., & Joe, G. W. (2004). A longitudinal evaluation of treatment engagement and recovery stages. *Journal of Substance Abuse Treatment, 27*, 89–97.

Sloboda, J. A. (2005). Emotional response to music: A review. In *Exploring the musical mind* (pp. 215–223). Oxford: Oxford University Press.

Soshensky, R. (2001). Music therapy and addiction. *Music Therapy Perspectives, 19*, 45–52.

Sylvan, R. (2002). *Traces of the Spirit: The religious dimensions of popular music.* New York: New York University Press.

Teesson, M., Hall, W., Lynskey, M., & Degenhardt, L. (2000). Alcohol- and drug-use disorders in Australia: Implications of the National Survey of Mental Health and Wellbeing. *Australian and New Zealand Journal of Psychiatry, 34*, 206–213.

Teesson, M. A., Ross, J. A., Darke, S., Lynskey, M. B., Alic, R., Ritter, A. D., & Cooke, R. C. (2006). One year outcomes for heroin dependence: Findings from the Australian Treatment Outcome Study (ATOS). *Drug and Alcohol Dependence, 83*, 174–180.

Treder-Wolff, J. (1990). Affecting attitudes: Music therapy in addictions treatment. *Music Therapy Perspectives, 8*, 67–71.

Waterman, R. A. (1999). African influence on the music of Americas. In S. C. Tracy (Ed.), *Write me a few of your lines: A blues reader* (pp. 17–27). Amherst, MA: University of Massachusetts Press.

Wild, T. C., Cunningham, J. A., & Ryan, R. M. (2006). Social pressure, coercion, and client engagement at treatment entry: A self-determination theory perspective. *Addictive Behaviors, 31*, 1858–1872.

Witkiewitz, K., & Wu, J. (2010). Emotions and relapse in substance use: Evidence for a complex interaction among psychological, social and biological processes. In J. D. Kassel (Ed.), *Substance abuse and emotion* (pp. 171–188). Washington, DC: American Psychological Association.

Zywiak, W. H., Stout, R. L., Longabaugh, R., Dyck, I., Connors, G. J., & Maisto, S. A. (2006). Relapse-onset factors in Project MATCH: The Relapse Questionnaire. *Journal of Substance Abuse Treatment, 31*, 341–345.

Chapter 18

"Morphine Mamma"

Creating Original Songs Using Rap with Women with Cancer

Emma O'Brien

This chapter presents two different case examples of songwriting in music therapy using rap as a music landscape. Both cases are with women with cancer and they highlight the diversity of the medium across demographics of age and experience. The first case example is with an individual and the second is with a group. The case examples explore the use of rap as an appropriate musical landscape in a specialized songwriting method, its value in stimulating further creation of lyrics, and its role in performance. The second case example challenges our preconceived ideas of who are consumers of rap music and who will relate easily to the genre. I will begin by briefly laying out the medical and psychosocial background on cancer and its treatment and the role of songwriting in music therapy with this population. A detailed explanation of the specialized songwriting method I use follows and then the two cases are presented.

Cancer is a life-threatening illness that impacts the whole spectrum of human existence and does not discriminate based on demographics. The diagnosis of cancer has been identified as a devastating experience impacting the individual and her/his carers (Holland, 1996). The individual is faced with a crisis of mortality (O'Connor, Wicker, & Germino, 1990), the physical symptoms of the disease, the prospect and consequence of ongoing treatment (Todres & Wojtiuk, 1979), and the possibility of relapse (Vetesse,

1976). Both cancer and its treatment significantly impact on a person's quality of life.

Treatments for cancers differ according to the nature and etiology of the illness and the individual's presentation. Some cancers are treated with surgery, others with chemotherapy regimes and radiation therapy. At times patients experience all treatment modalities including bone marrow transplants and peripheral stem cell transplants. All treatments have moderate to severe side effects. Most cancer patients receive several cycles of treatment and are often hospitalized for extended periods of time.

Songwriting in Music Therapy with People with Cancer

Music therapy (MT) with cancer patients has been documented in qualitative research, mostly in case studies and phenomenologically based enquiries, as a valuable intervention that meets patients' complex psychosocial, emotional, physical, spiritual needs with a positive influence on patients' and carers' ongoing coping strategies (Aldridge, 1996; Bailey, 1984; Bunt, 1994; Bunt et al. 2000; Lane, 1992; Nolan, 1992; O'Brien 1999, 2003, 2006; O'Callaghan, 2001; Rykov, 2008; Vickers et al., 2001; Waldon, 2006). Songwriting in MT with cancer patients has been documented in qualitative research as a positive and empowering therapeutic intervention that offers patients opportunities for self-expression and creativity (O'Brien, 2003, 2004, 2005, 2006; O'Callaghan, 1990, 1996; Robb & Ebberts, 2003). Although songwriting is classified as a singular method, there are many different applications of songwriting in MT. These different applications are influenced by the patients' presentation and the music therapist's training and music skills. Maranto (1993) described some of the varying techniques of songwriting and classified them as follows: word substitution, setting preexisting lyrics to new melodies, writing songs for patients, and the creation of original lyrics and music by the patient with the therapist. The different techniques of songwriting applied in MT offer different opportunities for patient participation in the process of completing a song. While many styles of music have been used in songwriting with cancer patients, there has been little written on the writing of rap music with cancer patients.

Guided Original Lyrics and Music Songwriting Protocol

The songwriting method used in both of the case examples in this chapter is a published protocol that I have developed called GOLM (Guided Original Lyrics and Music; O'Brien, 2007). GOLM is a specialized music therapy songwriting protocol that follows a series of stages. The method aims to create a wholly original song with the therapist acting as a guide through the process. The method is underpinned by therapeutic intent, which is evident in each stage of the GOLM process being validated by the patient/participant. A qualified music therapist administers GOLM because it requires specific training. GOLM was formulated by extensive study into writing songs with cancer patients, and to date I have written over 300 songs with cancer patients using this method. This method requires the therapist to be skilled in an extensive range of song styles. This is necessary to connect with the patient's individual musical expression and song genre choice.

The therapist uses techniques of exploration, reframing, detailed observation, interpretation, and musical reflection of the patient's verbal and nonverbal interactions, and incorporates these elements into the song. The patients are involved in every stage of the method (O'Brien, 2004). There are four basic stages of GOLM:

1. *Brainstorming song ideas and lyrics.* The music therapist's role is to encourage the patient to speak freely about any topic that interests him/her, letting the patient know that it is not expected for him/her to speak in poetic or lyrical lines, or rhyming couplets either. The responsibility of the therapist is to accurately transcribe the patient's words while remaining as true and as accurate as possible to what the patient says. Toward the end of the free brainstorming section, the music therapist draws upon salient comments or remarks made by the patient that can be appropriated into the developing song. Depending on the amount of input from the patient, further exploration, reflection, and confirmation of material may be required.

2. *Structural reframing—Refining lyrics for verse and chorus.* Most songs have verses and a chorus. Some songs will only have verses and a refrain. Other songs will incorporate verse, chorus, bridge, and refrain. The chorus represents the major theme that has been decided for the song. The music therapist gathers the text that expresses or supports the patient's chosen song theme, ensuring consistent reference back to the patient for validation and confirmation. The chorus of a song often has lyric lines repeated. The verses represent further explorations of the theme and may also aid in storytelling. Validation and confirmation must also be sought from the patient when refining the lyrics for the verses, as per the chorus. In some cases word strings or lyrics may not fit into either the verse or chorus, yet still be related to the theme of the song. These word strings or lyric lines may be placed in the bridge or

refrain of the song. The bridge of a song usually is set to a different melody than the chorus or verses.

3. *Determining the style of the song—Setting the lyrics to music.* It is important to confer with the patient regarding his/her preferred musical style. At this point the music therapist offers some musical examples representing the style of music for which the patient has indicated preference. If the patient suggests no specific style of music, the music therapist demonstrates different styles and tonalities on the guitar with verbal explanations of the examples. It is important to describe the music in nontechnical terms (avoiding saying "major" or "minor") and in so doing it neutralizes the "mystique" of music composition and makes it more approachable for the patient. In the event that the patient has musical training and knowledge, it may be more appropriate to use musical terminology. During this stage it is important to offer the patients opportunities to contribute musically to the process regardless of their musical history or experience and to encourage the patient to be directive when selecting from the music that is offered to them.

4. *Recording the completed song.* This can be completed at the end of the session or outside the session depending on the patient's wishes. The patient chooses whether he/she sings on the song or whether the therapist sings alone. The CD is then given to the patient to keep for his/her private use. Some patients may choose not to have their song recorded, but in my practice this has occurred only once. In our program, we have released several public available CD collections (Living Soul, 2003).

GOLM can be completed in a single MT session depending on the presentation of the patient. In a qualitative research study that I conducted that examined the experiences of GOLM with six cancer patients (O'Brien, 2004), I found that seven themes were salient:

1. Songwriting in music therapy was a pleasurable experience.
2. Songwriting functioned as a record of a significant time in a patient's life.
3. Songwriting was helpful to clarify patients' thoughts.
4. Songwriting was a unique experience not usually expected in the hospital environment.
5. Songwriting facilitated a positive experience of self-expression.
6. Songwriting was a calming experience.
7. Songwriting was an easy process, despite illness.

Song Styles Used in GOLM

Through the therapist's facilitation, GOLM enables patients to create music in any genre that they desire. This method has been used to write opera, jazz, folk, country, funk, pop, classical, gospel, rock, cabaret, hybrid music styles, and rap music.

Rap in GOLM

As a musical landscape, rap encompasses a strong beat as a basis, either looped in repetition or with varied sub-rhythms, over which words are spoken or chanted. Rap can be performed without rhythmic backing as well. The delivery of the lyrics in rap encompasses various pitch ranges, rhymes, and rhythms. The variations of the rhythms and rhymes are called the "flow." The flow offers a flexible rhythmic landscape that can accommodate extended prose, rhyming couplets, and poetry, either as regular meters or as variable ones.

The precise origin of rap is debated, though the general view is that rap began in the South Bronx of New York City in the early 1970s (Stephens & Wright, 2000). It was initially a specialized form of cultural expression of male African Americans with political and social commentary (Rose, 1994), but certainly since the 1980s with Blondie's release of "Rapture," which was a synthesis of pop and rap, rap music has become very widespread. It has crossed over into many other music genres, into feminism, and into other countries' cultures. Rap can present a socially conscious message—as first pioneered by Gil Scott-Heron, and then Grandmaster Flash and The Furious Five, in the 1970s and 1980s (Stephens & Wright, 2000)—as the bold stylistic verbal delivery enables the "rapper" to get across a clear narrative.

In GOLM songwriting in MT, I offer rap as a musical landscape for original songs as it appeals to our adult patients. Rap is entrenched in pop culture, and its qualities often lend themselves easily to setting through-composed lyrics with a powerful message. In some cases I also find that the spoken delivery gives our patients more "confidence" when performing, as they don't feel like they are "singing." They seem to be able to relate quickly to the "flow" of rap and also I find that once the rap has begun it often stimulates further lyric production in the session. Rap also has a certain "attitude" about it that can stylistically fit some lyrics, particularly if they are delivering a social or political message, or in some cases a humorous one.

Case Example 1—Individual Songwriting Using GOLM

Kim, a 24-year-old woman of White Anglo Saxon origin, was a long-term inpatient undergoing treatment for cancer, which was complicated by treatment-related issues and by her past history of mild recreational drug use. Kim had undergone a bone marrow transplant for acute leukemia and as a side effect of treatment she had severe graft-versus-host disease (GVHD). GVHD complications can be long term and often require extensive inpatient stays to stabilize the immune response and reduce the effects of the graft cells attacking the patient's immune system. In Kim's case, the GVHD had attacked her skin and bowels, causing her to have mottled skin mostly on her face and neck and extreme pain in her stomach, and she was underweight. Kim was on a regime of high doses of morphine to reduce her pain. During ward rounds with medical and allied health staff, it was noted that Kim was requesting more and more breakthrough doses of morphine. These breakthrough doses were on top of her standard prescribed doses. There was also concern regarding her past history of regular cannabis use and some implications that she had been using cannabis as an inpatient (eating it in cookies) and that this may be compounding the effects of her breakthroughs. Some members of the treatment team felt that Kim lacked insight into the amount of medication she was requesting and may be in fact becoming emotionally dependent on the sedation. This type of dependency can be driven by fear or distress, and it is not uncommon for patients to request more breakthrough doses when their carers leave the room, or when they are fearful of other treatment. Often the team will assist by educating the patient and providing increased psychosocial support while the breakthrough doses are reduced, but the concern was that Kim lacked the insight to grasp what was in her best interest, medically speaking. The treatment team acknowledged that Kim was experiencing pain but believed it was in her best interest for recovery that the level and regularity of the doses be reduced.

Prior to her diagnosis, Kim had played guitar and sang. During this admission, when she first came in contact with MT, she had her guitar with her and despite experiencing extreme fatigue she was often sitting up in bed strumming a blues progression and humming to herself. Kim was very open to MT sessions and rapport was established very quickly as we jammed/improvised on a blues progression on our guitars and sang some of her favorite tunes together. She mentioned that she was always thinking of writing a song and had toyed with a funky blues idea. Over subsequent visits, Kim and I continued to share songs and she also participated in group relaxation sessions. Often when I visited Kim we had to reschedule as she was under high doses of morphine and she was very, very drowsy and incomprehensible. Sometimes, however, I would gently play to her as she drifted off to sleep. When she was more lucid, Kim began to talk to me about the hallucinations that she had while under the medication, some of which she found quite disturbing. I informed the treatment team that Kim had discussed her distress regarding the hallucinations she was experiencing and perhaps we could use songwriting to explore the issues further and get a better sense of her level of insight.

Brainstorming Song Ideas and Lyrics

I approached songwriting in the next session with Kim when she was more lucid. I referred to her earlier discussion with me about her hallucinations and asked whether she felt this would be a good topic about which to write a song. Kim at first found the concept amusing, but as she spoke she became more focused and serious. During this stage of the songwriting, I was taking extensive notes. She spoke of "living in a daze," "her eyes weighing a ton," that it was frustrating and debilitating, and that she wanted her "clarity back." Her more humorous outlook was that she had become "Morphine Mamma." After the brainstorming, Kim began to tire so I suggested we continue the songwriting the following day. She asked if I could leave the rough notes with her, just in case she thought of some more ideas.

Refining Lyrics for Verse and Chorus

When I returned for the next session, Kim had been working extensively on her lyrics. She had begun to formulate prose using long sentences, mixed in with more fragmented thoughts, and she presented them to me in paragraph form. She had started to group her ideas in a narrative format that began with her feeling very much under the influence of morphine, representing her disorientation, and moving through to her desire to have her "clarity back." My role in this phase was to assist her in any word-finding difficulties and help refine the structure, but overall Kim had formulated a through-composed narrative that felt very natural and it didn't seem to fit into any verse and chorus format. Kim suggested that we should set it to a pop or rock style. I asked her to read the lyrics to me to get a sense of where she felt the stress of the words lay, as per the GOLM protocol. However, as she read them it became clear to us both that the flowing prose didn't seem to fit into a traditional pop/rock song style. She read the words quickly and with extended phrasing and in a monotone.

> Living in a world of haze, always a daze, foggy misty cloudy, undefined lines and times. Stay awake, I'm trying but my eyes weigh a ton. The hole is getting bigger its swallowing me whole. Nod, nod, nod, I'm asleep

again. Too many words. I don't know why I said that, weren't you talking to me? I could have sworn I was talking to someone, but I can't remember anyone being here. Get me out of this black hole. Get me out of this haze. I'd rather take all the pain. Turned into a junkie, nine months of stolen clarity of mind. Clarity of mind, I want that back.

Setting the Lyrics to Music

As per the GOLM protocol in which the therapist offers various styles to the patients for setting the song, I asked how Kim would feel about setting it as a rap and whether she would like to try to rap the words. The idea appealed to her, so I began a rhythm on the back of my guitar in 4/4.

Music Ex. 1

Kim began again to read her lyrics. With the steady beat behind her, she seemed to find more freedom in her delivery, using variable rhythmic parameters between prose lines and working on cross rhythms against the beat I was providing. The flow of rap provided the ideal musical landscape to set the initial lyric ideas. Kim also began to repeat some of her lyrics spontaneously and break the through-composed prose into smaller units. Her tone of voice had greater variance. The end of each line demonstrates the new places where Kim was pausing. Note the spontaneous repetition of some of the phrases.

Living in a world of haze, always a daze, foggy misty cloudy, undefined lines and times.
Stay awake, I'm trying but my eyes weigh a ton. Stay awake, I'm trying but my eyes weigh a ton.
The hole is getting bigger its swallowing me whole.
Nod, nod, nod, I'm asleep again Nod, nod, nod. I'm a sleep again. Nod, nod, nod, I'm asleep again.
Too many words.
I don't know why I said that, weren't you talking to me?
I could have sworn I was talking to someone, but I can't remember anyone being here.
Get me out of this black hole.
Get me out of this haze.
I'd rather take all the pain.
Turned into a junkie, nine months of stolen clarity of mind.

Clarity of mind, I want that back.
Clarity of mind, I want that back.
The hole is getting bigger its swallowing me whole.
Nod, nod, nod, I'm asleep again Nod, nod, nod. I'm a sleep again. Nod, nod, nod, I'm asleep again.
Too many words.

After her first attempt at rapping it through, Kim laughed out loud and exclaimed that we forgot to mention morphine. She decided to insert it in between what seemed to be the natural narrative turning points, following "too many words," "I'd rather take all the pain," and after the repetition of "too many words" in the third section. Kim asked me to half sing it, and to sound like I was on morphine, like I was "in a daze." I sang a slurred descending sequenced motif.

Music Ex. 2—The morphine motif

She seemed to find this amusing. We then made a rough recording of the song, during which the rap developed further. Kim began to break up her phrases even more and to add in more stylistic pauses. The repetition of "Nod, nod, nod, I'm asleep again" began to create a secondary motif in the song, developing the structure further. She also kept pointing at me during the song to add in more of the "morphine" motif.

The following is an example of how Kim developed the rhythmic placing of the first line over the process of the rap.

Music Ex. 3—Text set to rhythm

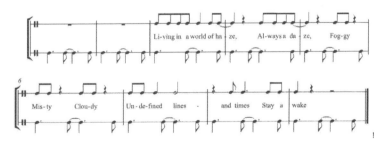

Recording the Original Song—Process and Consequence

When we were finished, I asked Kim what she would like to call it. "Morphine Mamma," of course. At the end of the session, Kim was animated and energized and asked when I could bring in some sort of electronic loop to put underneath the rap. I sourced a grunge loop track through the studio engineer from the current music therapy CD we were working on (which Kim later became a part of). I brought the loop back in to Kim and she validated the choice. We recorded the piece again over the loop track. I asked whether Kim would give permission for her song to be included in the CD project and whether she would be happy for other members of the treatment team to hear her rap at the next ward round meeting. Kim agreed to both requests.

I took the recording to the next ward round meeting. The team was very receptive to listening to the song and hearing Kim's point of view. After the piece was finished there was a thoughtful silence. The lead hematologist on Kim's case broke the silence, stating that it was clear that Kim had insight into her levels of medication and that an overall perspective shift needed to happen within the team to work actively toward reducing her morphine breakthroughs. He added that he was confident that Kim would be a positive participant in this process as it was clear that she had insight. Kim's sedation and pain relief levels were slowly reduced and she was cooperative and active in the process.

We continued MT sessions for Kim as an inpatient and an outpatient and she regained a consistent "clarity of mind." She later came to the studio and recorded three of her songs for the CD project, including "Morphine Mamma," which she requested that I also rap on, and that her treating hematologist record a quote as part of "Morphine Mamma" from Viktor Frankl (1946/1984), "The last of human freedoms, to choose one's attitude in any given set of circumstance, to choose one's own way" (p. 86).

Reflection on the Use of Rap in This Case Example

In this rap piece, we explored issues surrounding Kim's frequent inpatient medication regime of high doses of morphine and challenged the current preconceptions of the treatment team that she lacked insight into the high levels of sedation. Rap was the ideal musical landscape to which to set Kim's words, providing the maximum impact of her message. Rap's rhythmic flexibility as a musical landscape assisted in the creative process toward a sophisticated and successful piece.

Case Example 2—Group Songwriting Using GOLM

These sessions were held in a public inner-city community-based support service for breast and gynecological cancers. The women in this group all had breast cancer and had successfully completed their treatment. There is a general understanding that when women complete their treatment for breast cancer, there is a period of readjustment which can cause stress as the women return to their life before treatment. The support service was interested in providing women with a creative outlet for their experiences and contacted me to facilitate songwriting sessions. There were 15 women in the group and we had a 3-hour weekly program that was held over 4 weeks. The group was advertised as a creative program that would explore the women's voices and also offer songwriting as a group and/or as individuals. One of the end points of the creative workshops was to record the original songs, created in the sessions, and then perform them at a small family-and-friends CD launch. The women in this group had various music skills in terms of a past history of piano lessons and singing in choirs; however, none of them had created an original song before. The women were aged between 38 and 60 years old. They were of mixed origin, first generation Asian and European immigrants, and Anglo Saxon Australians.

Session 1—Completing a Group Song

In our first session, I facilitated a vocal warm-up and some vocal improvisation, and then we commenced writing our first group song. Using the stages of GOLM we workshopped ideas on a large presentation whiteboard and I guided the group toward formulating verse chorus format, seeking validation from all the group members. This group writing process using GOLM can at times take longer than individual GOLM songwriting, as all the group members must come to an agreement with any choice, be it lyrical or musical. Using GOLM, I offered various setting of the lyrics. The group was very accommodating of each member's input and presented a united front. Consequently, lyrical and musical choices were agreed on quite quickly and the women as a group validated individual choices easily. By the end of the session, the song was complete. All the women were then given notebooks to take home and write any reflections on the session or any individual song ideas for the next brainstorming stage of GOLM.

Sessions 2 and 3—Completing Individual Songs

For the next two sessions we continued singing and several members of the group brought in original song lyric ideas. I used stages 2 and 3 of GOLM to complete the songs with individuals. At times the individual's song would be opened up to group input, with the permission of the woman presenting her journal ideas. Song styles chosen included pop, folk, jazz, and a slow blues. One woman, despite being very energetic and vocal in the group, felt she couldn't think of anything and was happy to listen to others' songs and sing, but overall she couldn't decide on a song subject. As there was no prerequisite for the women to create an original song, I didn't feel it was necessary to push her to create lyric ideas outside the space.

Session 4—A Rap

In the final session, we were scheduled to record the songs, the final stage of GOLM. The woman who had previously not wished to write an original song turned up to the session and announced, "I want to write something about mammograms, but not a folksy song. How can I write something like that, with words about boobs?" The group and I found her announcement very amusing and I asked what she had tried out during the week. She read the lyrics to her piece that she had written, instantly chanting on the repetition of the word "mammogram," becoming freer rhythmically and more naturally spoken with the other lyrics.

Music Ex. 4

Mam-mo-gram, mam-mo-gram, This is the way. They squeeze you and pull you. It hurts but it's okay.

Setting the Lyrics to Music

The group spontaneously laughed and they started to chant "mammogram mammogram." To underpin the chant I provided a basic rhythm on the guitar muting the strings with my left hand with a soft full bar across the middle of the neck and with a 1, 2 & -& 4&.

Music Ex. 5

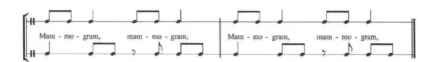

Mam - mo - gram, mam - mo - gram, Mam - mo - gram, mam - mo - gram,

The women continued to chant "mammogram mammogram" to a 1 & 2 beat, over and over again, and the original lyricist was clapping and laughing. Eventually all the women began to laugh and then the lyricist said, "Wouldn't it be a shock to everyone if we wrote a rap? The younger people would be really surprised. We could show them, couldn't we?" All the women agreed and I validated the choice, reiterating that they were around when rap began to get popular, to actually "hear original rap," so it was their music too. The women were eager to use rap, and there was an element of playful rebellion in it, as if they were stepping outside their expected roles, and they seemed to find it exhilarating. I began to offer various rhythmic settings of the lines in between the group chant and the women quickly joined in. As a group they spontaneously started to whisper and repeat the words "takes your breath away, it takes your breath away." This demonstrated great group cohesiveness.

The original lyricist then offered new lyrics in rhythm. These lyrics scanned differently and she spontaneously spoke them in a juxtaposing rhythm to the "mammogram" verses.

Music Ex. 6

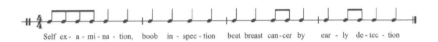

Self ex - a - mi - na - tion, boob in - spec - tion   beat breast can-cer by   ear - ly de - tec - tion

The women then wanted to return to verse 1, and we used a repetition of "mammogram," descending into a whisper similar to the motif of "it takes your breath away."

> Mammogram Mammogram
> This is the way
> They squeeze and pull you
> It hurts but it's okay
> Mammogram Mammogram
> This is the way
> They squash and twist you,
> it takes your breath away
> it takes your breath away
> it takes your breath away
> Mammogram Mammogram
> Self-examination, boob inspection—beat breast cancer by early detection
> Self-examination, boob inspection—beat breast cancer by early detection
> Mammogram mammogram mammogram mammogram mammogram
> mammogram mammogram mammogram

Mammogram Mammogram
This is the way
They squeeze and pull you
It hurts but it's okay!

Recording the Song and Subsequently Performing the Song

The piece was composed very quickly, it had the highest level of spontaneous participation by all the members of the group of all the songs we had created, and we quickly recorded it as a group rap. The women then practiced all their songs for a small public performance, and when we came to rehearsing the rap the women said they felt relieved as they didn't have to worry about how they sounded when they sang. All the songs and the CD were received with great enthusiasm and the audience clapped along to the live performance of "Mammogram."

Reflection on the Use of Rap in This Case Example

For this group of women in posttreatment for their breast cancer, rap was used as it supported the original lyric ideas and underpinned the spontaneous chant-like reading of the lyrics. The concept of rap's rebellious reputation offered the women a different experience that was both fun and liberating. The flow in rap's musical landscape helped to stimulate further lyric production and spontaneous rhythmic phrasing in the session. Rap offered an approachable means of performance for all members of the group. Many women in the group felt more confident rapping in public than singing, despite their demographic.

Conclusion

Both of these case examples illustrate the approachable and flexible nature of rap when writing songs using GOLM with cancer patients in MT. There seems to be two aspects of rap that appealed in both cases—the musical landscape and also the social/historical landscape.

The musical landscape and in particular the flow was ideal for Kim's variable rhythmic prose, and the chant aspect of flow provided the setting for the group song. The flow also helped to stimulate lyric production and spontaneous input. The steady backing rhythm in both cases laid a firm and safe foundation for the exploration of the flow. In both examples, the women felt free to rap and the group of women in particular found it less confronting than singing.

The women in the group reflected on the social/historical landscape of rap, and its attitude appealed to them. They found it fun to write and perform the rap. The lyricist in the group also found that the social/historical landscape could support her lyrics more so than a straight folk or pop genre. In Kim's case, the social/historical landscape of rap embraced her very personal message and it was successful in supporting a change in attitude from her treatment team. It is interesting that Kim chose the Viktor Frankl quote to be in her rap song. It resonated with Kim and her own personal battle with her reduced quality of life and her subsequent choice to improve it, to choose her own way, to be free.

References

Australian Institute of Health and Welfare. (2000). Cancer in Australia.

Bunt, L., Burns, S., & Turton, P. (2000). Variations on a theme: The evolution of a music therapy research programme at the Bristol Cancer Help Centre. *British Journal of Music Therapy, 14*(2), 62–69.

Cassileth, B. R., Vickers, A. J., & Magill, L. A. (2003). Music therapy for mood disturbance during hospitalisation for autologous stem cell transplantation. *Cancer, 98*(12), 2723–2729.

Dileo, C. (2005). *Medical music therapy: A meta-analysis & agenda for future research*. Cherry Hill, NJ: Jeffrey.

Frankl, V. E. (1946/1984). *Man's search for meaning*. New York: Washington Square Press.

Hogan, B. (1999). The experience of music therapy for terminally ill patients: A phenomenological research project. In R. R. Pratt & D. E. Grocke (Eds.), *MusicMedicine 3: MusicMedicine and music therapy: Expanding horizons* (pp. 242–254). Victoria, Australia: University of Melbourne.

Lane, D. (1992). Music therapy: A gift beyond measure. *Oncology Nursing Forum, 19*(6), 863–867.

Maranto, C. D. (1993). Music therapy clinical practice: A global perspective and classification system. In C. D. Maranto (Ed.) *Music therapy: International perspectives*. Pipersville, PA: Jeffrey.

Nolan, P. (1992). Music therapy with bone marrow transplant patients: Reaching beyond the symptoms. In R. Spintge & R. Droh (Eds.), *MusicMedicine* (pp. 209–212). St. Louis: MMB Music.

O'Brien, E. (1999). Cancer patients' evaluation of a music therapy program in a public adult hospital. In R. R. Pratt & D. E. Grocke (Eds.), *MusicMedicine 3: MusicMedicine and music therapy: Expanding horizons* (pp. 242–254). Victoria, Australia: University of Melbourne.

O'Brien, E. (2003). *The nature of the interactions between patient and therapist when writing a song on a bone marrow transplant ward.* Master's thesis: University of Melbourne.

O'Brien, E. (2004). The language of guided song writing with a bone marrow transplant patient. *Voices: A World Forum for Music Therapy.* Retrieved from http://www.voices.no/mainissues/mi40004000139.htmlVoices

O'Brien, E. (2005). Songwriting with adult patients in oncology and clinical haematology. In F. Baker & T. Wigram (Eds.), *Songwriting methods, techniques and clinical applications for music therapy clinicians, educators and students.* United Kingdom: JKP.

O'Brien, E. (2006). Opera therapy—Creating a new work with cancer patients. *Nordic Journal of Music Therapy, 15*(1), 89–103.

O'Callaghan, C. (1990*).* Music therapy skills used in song writing within a palliative care setting. *The Australian Journal of Music Therapy, 1*, 15–22.

O'Callaghan, C. (1996). Lyrical themes in songs written by palliative care patients. *Journal of Music Therapy, 33*(2), 74–92.

O'Callaghan, C. (2001). *Music therapy's relevance in a cancer hospital researched through a constructivists lens.* PhD thesis, Faculty of Music, University of Melbourne.

O'Connor, A.P., Wicker, C.A., & Germino, B. B. (1990). Understanding the cancer patient's search for meaning. *Cancer Nursing, 33*(3), 167–175.

Post-White, J., Ceronsky, C., Kreitzer, M. J., Nickelson, K., Drew, D., Mackey, K. W., Koopmeiners, L., & Gutknecht, S. (1996). Hope, spirituality, sense of coherence, and quality of life in patients with cancer. *Oncology Nurses Forum, 23*(10), 1571–1579.

Robb, S. L., & Ebberts, A. G. (2003). Song writing and digital video production interventions for pediatric patients undergoing bone marrow transplantation, part II: An analysis of patient generated songs and patient perceptions regarding intervention efficacy. *Journal of Pediatric Oncology Nursing, 20*(1), 16–25.

Rykov, M. H. (2008). Experiencing music therapy cancer support. *Journal of Health Psychology, 13*(2).

Stephens, R. J., & Wright, E. (2000). Beyond bitches, niggers, and ho's: Some suggestions for including rap music as a qualitative data source. *Race & Society, 3*, 23–40.

Todres, R. & Wojtiuk, R. (1979). The cancer patient's view of chemotherapy. *Cancer Nursing, 2*(4), 283–286.

Vettese, J. M. (1976). Problems of the patient confronting the diagnosis of cancer. In J. W. Cullen, B. H. Fox, & R. N. Isom (Eds.), *Cancer: The behavioral dimensions.* New York: Raven Press, 275–282.

Vickers, A. J., & Cassileth, B. R. (2001). Unconventional therapies for cancer and cancer-related symptoms. *The Lancet Oncology, 2*, 226–232.

Waldon, E. G. (2006). The effects of group music therapy on mood states and cohesiveness in adult oncology patients. *Journal of Music Therapy, 38*(3), 212–238.

Chapter 19

Rapping Round the System

A Young Black Man's Journey through a High-Security Hospital*

Stella Compton Dickinson and Pauline Souflas

Introduction

Shadee† is a British-born, 18-year-old Black Caribbean man who entered a high-security hospital after having committed an offense of assault occasioning actual bodily harm. Despite Shadee initially being deemed not to fulfill the criteria for admission to high-security treatment, the court nevertheless

* With special thanks to Dr. Pauline Souflas, Consultant Psychiatrist, for her contribution to this chapter and to the patient and his multidisciplinary team for agreeing to informed consent to publish this case study.

My thanks for collaborations with the following: group coworker Darren Woods and the patient escort staff team for ensuring safety; Joan Kenyon, Head of Therapies and Education, for funding and supporting the group-work project; the League of Friends and Glenys Herbert in particular for funding the purchase of the recording equipment; my clinical supervisors; and the Arts Council of Great Britain, Eastern England, for funding attendance and presentation of the clinical work and rap songs at the World Congress of Music Therapy 2005.
† Informed consent has been granted by both the patient and his multidisciplinary team for publication of case material. The patient's identity has been concealed and his real name has not been used.

ordered the decision. Shadee had been rejected by numerous medium-secure units, because he did not fulfill their admission criteria either.

At his assessment, Shadee exhibited aggression and sexualized behavior as a result of a severe episode of encephalitis lethargica at the age of 16. Encephalitis lethargica is thought to be caused by viral infection, and it affects the brain stem and central gray structures including the midbrain and hypothalamus. The symptoms of this syndrome include high fever, headache, double vision, oculargyric crisis (abnormal eye movements), delayed mental and physical response, irritability, dizziness, fatigue, lethargy, and catatonia. In some cases, patients may enter a coma-like state. Patients may experience Parkinsonism, choreiform movements, behavioral disorder, or behavioral changes including psychosis. Encephalitis lethargica can result in the destruction of brain nerve fibers, increased cerebrospinal fluid pressure, and other complex brain alterations.

Shadee had been admitted to neurological units with excessive sleepiness, headache, double vision, and lethargy. He was diagnosed as having a form of encephalitis lethargica of unknown origin, possibly viral, but the medical investigations failed to identify the exact cause. As suggested by the name, the main feature of this type of inflammation of the brain is excessive sleepiness and lethargy.

Shadee presented with impulsive aggressive and sexualized behavior: He made inappropriate comments to nursing staff and was unable to think rationally about his situation or his behavior. As a result, he was transferred to a series of neuropsychiatric units, each of which had difficulty coping with him. He was finally transferred to the prison following two relatively minor but unpredictable assaults. He was placed in seclusion as he was regarded as very dangerous.

Shadee's case preceded the government's drive for equal opportunities in terms of race. Also, at this time, covert racism was still recognized as a specific problem in secure hospital settings. Having a large stature and being a Black male, perceived as dangerous, being poor in class status, having underdeveloped social and communication skills as well as self-care skills, Shadee presented the multidisciplinary team with many challenges. Some of Shadee's presentation, while appropriate for a young adolescent, while not viewed as biologically based, was seen as incongruous and immature in an adult setting. His prognosis did not look good and there were significant legal/ethical issues to address.

The Context of Treatment

There are three high-security hospitals in the United Kingdom for which the admission criterion is that the patient must be a "grave and immediate risk to the public." Because Shadee was regarded as very dangerous, and he did not have a conventional diagnosis of a mental illness, lower-secure units had turned him down. Learning disability units had also rejected him as he was not classically learning disabled. He was finally referred to high security. At that time, there were no medium-secure units specifically for brain-injured patients.

Shadee was charged with two counts of assault occasioning actual bodily harm (AOABH) and he was regarded as so dangerous that the judge cleared the court before he appeared. His barrister admitted to feeling terrified of him. It is important to note that at this point in time Shadee had no previous convictions and no significant history of substance misuse. Illness was the only cause for his serious change in behavior.

Prior to his illness, Shadee had suffered significant losses. These included the death of his grandmother to whom he was close and a lack of contact with his father. Both relationships are important for an adolescent boy in terms of providing positive role modeling. After his illness, which had caused a regression to a more immature stage of development and therefore impairment to his normal adolescent development, Shadee, who had not yet reached the age of 18 years old, had been separated from his family and treated as a serious criminal. He had no opportunity to develop the cognitive and social strategies to deal with this stressful and intimidating situation, and little ability or opportunity to express his distress in constructive ways.

Following admission to the high-security hospital, Shadee went through the usual assessment process and an individual treatment plan was formulated for him. His treatment plan included psychology treatment to address offending behaviors, the development of problem-solving and social skills, treatment and support about adult sexuality, general education, occupational therapy, and fitness activities. Following a creative arts assessment, he chose music therapy as his ongoing primary psychological treatment of choice.

While contact with the family is essential in the rehabilitation of young offenders, it was difficult for Shadee's mother to attend because she lived a long way away and was the sole supporter of her family. She too was grappling with the grief of having her only child in this predicament.

Shadee completed 4 years of music therapy treatment: 2 years in individual therapy followed by 2 years in a cognitive analytic music therapy group (Compton Dickinson, 2006). The latter was tailored to meet the musical needs of the young Black Caribbean male hospital population. Finally, prior to discharge from the hospital, Shadee completed eight sessions of individual therapy. These sessions enabled an effective closure to the therapeutic relationships formed and were part of his preparation to leave the hospital, which had been his home for the past few years. All of this work with Shadee enabled him to move directly from the hospital into the community.

Meeting the Patient

The consultant psychiatrist first met the patient in prison to assess him for suitability for secure hospital treatment. Shadee was very friendly and pleased to have a visitor. The consultant did not have any sense of being at risk in the cell. Some of Shadee's cognitive difficulties were apparent—he suggested to her that she "looked nice, like Jennifer Lopez." This comment raised her curiosity because Shadee had identified the rotund middle-aged psychiatrist with the slim Jennifer Lopez. She also noticed that as he rummaged in a drawer to show her a picture, he dropped his cigarette on the floor and left it, apparently unaware either of the risk of fire or the waste of a cigarette. This raised her curiosity with regard to his neurological functioning and awareness.

The first ward round following admission addressed issues of self-care, self-awareness, musical interests (rapping), problems of concrete thinking, how to create a meaningful and structured day care program, physical health issues, including the treatment of eczema, and a focus on interpersonal responses.

Shadee's First Meeting with the Music Therapist

At Shadee's first meeting with me following his referral, he presented as rather gauche, untidy, and quite childlike. He was very quietly spoken, had a slight squint, and had a skin condition that gave him considerable irritation. He asked if he could show me his rapping ability. I considered this request as Shadee's way of testing out whether or not he and I might be able to relate through music. I also thought that this was his way of being seen in a way that was comfortable to him. It was probably also his way of discovering whether his particular mode of musical expression would be accepted or dismissed. Shadee had a disarming manner and the assembled clinicians agreed to his request. Shadee made up an impromptu song. He stumbled in places, singing very quietly, but he continued unabashed. His use of words within an uneven rhythm was impressively fast and poetic. I was moved by the gentleness of his voice.

I wondered how I would be able to develop any interaction within what seemed like a self-to-self dialogue in Shadee's own music making. Yet clearly Shadee had found a way of expressing himself whether on his own or with others. The rap medium reinforced his sense of self-identity. This may be understood within his treatment context because he would not have anyone to talk to, other than himself, while in seclusion. It is, therefore, not surprising that Shadee enjoyed the captive audience response. I noted that his softly spoken voice had a very limited vocal range of a minor third. The minor third is the musical interval of the universal children's song. This motif is sung across all cultures in children's games with their peers. It is the musical interval of the first infant babbling sounds and therefore the point from which preverbal communication moves toward verbal communication. Hence, Shadee's presentation suggested an early stage of developmental communication.

There were none of the usual messages conveyed through angry or offensive lyrics which characterize some forms of rap. I wondered where Shadee's anger had gone. Earlier reports showed that there were symptoms of depression, which indicated that these emotions had turned inward toward suicidal ideation. Indeed, his depression was so serious earlier in his treatment that at one hospital the reports recorded that Shadee, in desperation, had threatened suicide by finding a high place from which to jump.

After giving him a sense of what music therapy involves, Shadee agreed that he would like to find out more. I planned to start a small group for young offenders. However, we soon discovered that group work was not going to work for Shadee at this early stage of treatment, so this remained a future aim. Initially, Shadee required individual therapy.

The Dark Years

Shadee's presentation led to divided views within the multidisciplinary team. Such divisions caused anxiety and splitting as therapists and nursing staff had polarized perceptions. Shadee was vulnerable to bullying by older hardened patients who knew the system, and there was little compassion for this clumsy young man. He was perceived as dangerous because he displayed some sexual disinhibition in how he dressed and in his difficulties as manifested through impulsive responses to staff. He was also perceived over-simplistically by some: They assumed that if he was not simply "mad," then he must be "bad." As a result, he was referred to the hospital's personality disorders directorate. At the time, this move suggested that he was deemed as almost untreatable. This move led to more feelings of despair and hopelessness.

There were also culture clashes. These may in part have been due to a higher incidence of Black men being admitted to hospital through the criminal justice system at that point in time, that is, relative to the percentage of the non-Black general population (Keating et al., 2002). In fact, there were only a few Black Caribbean male patients in this hospital in comparison with the overall White and Asian patient population and staff in this northern part of the country.

Shadee was considered "different" for several reasons. He was a young Black adolescent. He was from the urban south of the country and he did not have a diagnosis of any mental illness, which was unusual for admission to a high-secure treatment.

His choice in music as a rapper was different from the predominantly White patient norm. The latter norm in music choice consisted of heavy metal, rock'n'roll, or, in music therapy, relatively freely improvised unstructured music in atonal or jazz mediums.

Shadee did not have a criminal history outside of the hospital setting or prior to his illness, suggesting that his behavioral problems were a result of the untreated effects of the viral assault on his brain of encephalitis lethargica.

The paradoxes within Shadee's presentation were that his intrusiveness toward others could be perceived as either playful or perverse. His sexuality might be understood as either immature or dangerous. His narcissistic need for recognition of whom he felt he was, was usually perceived by others as "showing off," viewed negatively as "attention-seeking" or as an irreparable result of his impairment in adolescent development.

Some staff viewed his condition as a permanent organic personality disorder as a result of the brain injury. This may partly be as a result of the stories passed down in the tradition and history of this hospital. In 1918, for example, after the great flu epidemic, special "villas" were built for the children who developed encephalitis lethargica, which was at that time untreatable. They lived out their lives, nursed in the hospital until old age and death. Many of them were buried in the local village churchyard. Of course, treatment has developed immensely since that time.

Initial Musical Presentation

Shadee was one of my first referrals. I was newly appointed to this post, having previously worked in a different treatment context in low-secure forensic and community services. On entering the new music therapy room with one other young patient with whom it was hoped some shared experience and bonding would be created, Shadee remembered that his last visit to this room had been when it had a different use. What then followed demonstrated the value of establishing an identified room for a specific therapeutic purpose, thus providing a safe emotional containment without other previous negative associations.

Shadee explained that on that previous occasion, the chaplain had attended and offered prayers for him because Shadee was upset that his grandmother had recently died. The room brought back memories of this sad event and Shadee began to cry. He sought individual comfort from me and shared memories of his "Nan," who had been kind and loving to him and who had often cooked him meals. He remembered the way she would nurture him, cooking particular cultural dishes that he enjoyed. The things that she did for him and her love were no longer available to him. His feelings of abandonment by his father were also awakened. He said he felt alone and desperate for females to show him maternal care.

Shadee's ability to tolerate any sort of frustration was very low. Perhaps because of his emotional distress and need, he could not bear it when the focus moved to others. So he dominated this small group. My male co-therapist shared that he experienced enormous inner animosity toward Shadee. This response may also have been mirrored in the problems that Shadee encountered with male nursing staff. On reflection, perhaps this situation also demonstrated Shadee's projections and the impact in the counter-transference toward another male. Shadee felt hostile but was unable to understand or express his hostility fully, as the man toward whom it was directed, his father, had not been present for him. Shadee's experience of significant males was primarily that of being abandoned. Fear of further abandonment may have suppressed the appropriate expression of anger about the original loss. Shadee's way of relating to women, however, which mirrored his relationship with his mother, was to seek acceptance.

When Shadee was not the center of attention, he somatized illness with numerous aches, pains, and sicknesses. He would ask for a glass of milk, a comfort drink indicative of regression. He requested to be taken back to the ward. Shadee could not engage with others in improvisation unless everyone else followed *him*. Chaos ensued, nothing musically creative could happen, and this small group was disbanded.

I recall that my on-site supervision was sensitively pitched, so as not to puncture my own narcissistic insecurities at this early stage in a new and responsible post as head of the department. We reflected on the psychoanalytic and cognitive views of narcissism and I continued to develop my practice, underpinning it with theories learned in ongoing cognitive analytic psychotherapy training.

The complexity and depth of Kohut's (1971) psychoanalytic theories fascinated me and I began to understand how the archaic patterns learned in adolescence, including omnipotence and grandiosity, can only be worked through by receiving appropriate narcissistic recognition from others. These are often played out in games such as "I am the king of the castle, and you are the dirty rascal," which, of course, can be antisocial or confrontational. These concepts were central in understanding how to think outside the box and to do something called *music therapy* with this young man, who would not or could not use the assembled choice of music therapy instruments. Shadee only wanted to write rap and to be seen and admired within his own cultural framework. It was therefore vital that

Shadee should receive recognition of who he really was through his own form of music making.

The potential contraindication and indeed assumption, in any young offender, was that antisocial tendencies and aggression would prevail in the rap too. This aspect in forensic treatment is of course undesirable. It amounts to offense paralleling behavior as opposed to correcting behavior. Therapeutic skill and observation is therefore required in assessing the meaning of the patient's communications and behaviors. There is a fine line between recognizing the real person and enabling him to grieve his losses in an authentic manner or unwittingly allowing him to indulge in fantasies that may be perverse and could include sexualized advances toward the therapist.

I also considered Kernberg's (1974) writing on narcissism: the need for boundaries and the psychopathological implications of unhealthy narcissistic gratification. This had to be kept in mind with this frustrated young man. My clinical thinking moved toward an integrative theoretical underpinning of clinical practice, one in which a musical process could remain central. The key point in this case was how Shadee could feel recognized for who he was through this culture-specific form of music making, that is, rap. Grandiose fantasies of fame were not encouraged but they were acknowledged. Shadee had to learn not to steal all the space in his need for gratification because this did not take into account the needs of others.

Individual Therapy and Underlying Theoretical Considerations

Individual therapy lasted for 2 years. As previously described, Shadee was at this time unable to engage in any group work programs. He could not, or would not, use instruments; he only wanted to rap.

His raps were fast and spontaneous with very limited vocal range and had a quirky, uneven rhythmic meter. This may have been due to brain impairment following the encephalitis. His lyrics were about an escape from reality. The confined nature of Shadee's reality and his losses of both function and people were intolerable at the time. Progress was very slow. When an interpretation was made, Shadee would disengage from the emotional pain and the therapy process. Initially, he could not stay in the room for more than 10 minutes. The duration of sessions, however, gradually extended to 50 minutes.

I considered whether we were both culturally bound: myself in the Western musical tradition and Shadee in his rap culture. However, having a broad taste in music, I viewed the main problem as a lack of dialogical exchange within our interactions, whether verbal or musical. At this stage,

Shadee's rap was a personal narrative. As I learned more about the rap medium, I discovered that it could be both narrative and dialogical.

In cognitive analytic theory (Ryle & Kerr, 2002), a dialogue is explained as occurring within reciprocal relating from self to other, from other to self, and within an internal self-to-self dialogue.

Extended narrative is not encouraged in time-limited treatment, but it may be viewed as important in the art of rapping. Extended narrative in treatment, however, can exclude authentic relating if, as is common, words alone become a defense against emotional expression. Thus assessing and encouraging emotional attunement is of value in making music. Extended narrative can also be unconsciously or consciously excluding of other people. It neither encourages the same degree of active listening nor does it create space for responses from the other; thus others may disengage.

However, a dilemma is created by prompting a narrative into becoming a dialogue with pauses for responses. One risks the patient being cut off in telling his/her story. The advantage nevertheless is that one gains structure, containment, and mindful acknowledgment of the full content of each verbal communication without missing vital aspects that may otherwise be swept over.

One can also observe facial and other physical responses and encourage a higher degree of relatedness through the more frequent exchanges. These points are of value in forensic treatment when risk and safety are the priority in treating dangerous offenders who can respond impulsively.

Dialogue between rappers, at least in the hospital treatment context for people with antisocial tendencies, was a challenging medium in which to develop a therapeutic and inclusive form of interpersonal relating. The potential was that it could lead to a fight over hierarchical, cultural, or geographical differences and alliances. Thus, ground rules had to be established.

During the 2 years in which Shadee came for weekly, individual sessions, he brought his own poems. Initially, these did not quite rhyme evenly and they never seemed to get finished. This inability to complete tasks, as yet unconscious, had implications for treatment. Endings for Shadee represented death, whether in reality, as in his grandmother's case or within his internal world with the lack of a father's presence. He had survived a viral brain injury that used to kill people, and after which, part of one dies, because one is no longer quite the same person. Subjectively, therefore, perhaps all that Shadee felt that he had left in his life was his passion for rap. This culturally specific musical genre, I suggest, had a life-sustaining form of musical expression for Shadee. Rap, for him at this time, may perhaps be compared to the role of the African American spirituals during slavery. Indeed, the legacy of slavery remains in the consciousness of many Black Caribbean patients who have offended (Compton Dickinson, 2003, 2004).

Shadee continued to write about his desire for rescue by a beautiful woman and of his fantasies of fame. He would then suddenly plummet for no apparent reason into the desperate depths of contemptible hopelessness. This is typical of the sudden self-state shifts (Ryle & Kerr, 2002) that are common in personality disorders. The treatment challenge was whether Shadee's responses were an unresolved narcissistic aspect of his personality that could be responsive to therapeutic treatment, albeit slowly. Alternatively, his presentation might at this stage prove to be unresponsive to treatment as a result of organic personality disorder and brain impairment brought on by encephalitis lethargica.

The cognitive analytic model of the treatment of narcissistic personality provided an explanation of the situation with the split between two contrasting self-states: one of contemptuous, grandiose fantasies and the other of contemptible hopelessness. The individual can either be in an omnipotent, superior state or otherwise plummet to a hopeless, contemptible, rejected state.

I realized that my psychotherapeutic technique required extreme sensitivity to mediate these sudden switches between self-states, and that the music could play a vital part in Shadee's emotional regulation between the two. If Shadee was to tolerate and sustain the therapy, I would have to contain and help to moderate the emotional levels between the superior and inferior states. The aim was to inhabit a central position between the upper and lower states. This can be diagrammatically explained to the patient as the place of a good enough ordinary/real world (Ryle & Kerr, 2002).

Through closer observation and sensitivity, I became more able to make the links to the tiny triggers that preceded the shifts in self-states, whether it was a word, a sound, or a negative thought either made explicit verbally or perceived in the counter-transference. Shadee, at this point, needed his fantasy world to feel better because of the intolerable impingement into his consciousness of the ghastly reality of his incarcerated situation at this early stage in his adult life. At these times, Shadee presented as desperately trapped.

By remaining sensitive and empathically observant to these tiniest of changes in Shadee's presentation, I considered that my role was akin to that of the attentive mother observing her baby. Shadee gradually became able to stay in the room for longer. Enactment of his old behavior of withdrawal, acting out and retreating to his room, became less frequent. His isolated, withdrawn state represented the solitude that he had grown used to prior to coming to this hospital. Hence, the aim was to gradually provide a more social procedure of relating, one that could become the norm and therefore become internalized.

There were times when both of us felt stuck and I questioned whether there was any value in continuing. I discussed this with the consultant psychiatrist in the ward round. She recognized the value of the positive therapeutic relationship and requested that I should simply "go on being" as supported by Winnicott's (1971) theories.

This was encouraging and may have relieved my internal sense of pressure, as well as that from the organization, for change to happen within this patient. Shadee's sessions began to take on a more peaceful, spacious quality in which he shared his pain, his hopes, and his ignorance about the facts of life.

The transference at this stage was maternal and he began to ask in an innocent way about adult issues of relationship building. He also clearly enjoyed and appreciated the contributions that I made with regard to the content and meaning of his songs. My interventions were very much reality orientated, aimed at promoting self-reflection and empowered decision making within Shadee's own creative process. In this way, we began to think together and Shadee recognized that he was not alone. We sat at a small table in a corner of the music therapy room away from the instruments. This felt safe for Shadee because all my previous invitations to add drums or other sounds had been spurned.

Gradually, my verbal suggestions were accepted regarding how he might choose to make his words rhyme more evenly. In this way, he found a more functional inner rhythm for each line of rap or chorus. His rhythm gradually ceased to limp unevenly and began to have a steady meter. Our dialogue developed into shared reciprocity. The newly accessed, more organized inner sense of rhythm suggested that something more organized was occurring neurologically.

This technique of lyric writing had also helped Shadee to develop a wider verbal vocabulary through my own wider vocabulary. This process demonstrated a fundamental underlying principle of cognitive analytic therapy, which is derived from Vygotsky's (1978) activity theory as follows: "What the child does with a more experienced other today, he or she will do on his or her own tomorrow." This form of structured learning is dialogical rather than didactic in form.

Shadee's growing ability to self-reflect rather than to respond impulsively enabled his rapping to develop a deeper meaning; thus the content of his songs gradually changed. His ability to concentrate developed in parallel.

Shadee was not an exciting patient or one in whom any sudden changes occurred. He was a much misunderstood but interesting patient, who in my view required a developmental approach in his therapy process. This enabled him to mature from delayed boyhood into being and feeling like a young man.

He nevertheless remained the victim of unconscious racism within a wider context. Such racism, in my view, largely manifested itself through a lack of understanding of his emotional needs and sometimes an indifference to, and a general lack of identification with, his musical taste. There was an assumption that because Shadee was big and looked tough, and perhaps even frightening to some, he was also tough on the inside. Yet Shadee had a vulnerable side; he could and did cry within the privacy of sessions and probably also in the solitude of his own bedroom. Yet, he presented a brave face to the wider world and hospital community, rather than his vulnerability. His intention, like most adolescents, was to be cool, but the coolness was a false self (Winnicott, 1960) that concealed his anxieties. Therefore, he was often experienced as frustrated and aggressive. This in turn caused reciprocally frustrating and hostile responses.

Shadee elicited irritation and envy from other men when he "showed off" his songs on the ward. This made it more difficult to address the narcissistic aspects of his personality because he did not feel that he was allowed to be vulnerable anywhere other than in the therapy room. I shared with his consultant psychiatrist that I had a theory that his impairment was that of adolescent delay rather than the organic personality disorder that was a current label on the ward.

A turning point came when Shadee looked at me as he finished writing the lyrics of a verse and recognized something useful. In the manner of a contented and actively engaged child, and as he continued with his task, he said, "You know, Stella, I find it easier when you are here." After such a long period of what felt like little or no change, this felt like an enormous gesture and a significant recognition in the therapeutic relationship and in Shadee's new value in relating to others. It was positive because Shadee was finding value in another person; he was accepting his vulnerability. He was able to recognize some of his inner need rather than presenting a narcissistic lack of regard for others or a self-centered attitude.

This example demonstrated how once again I had applied, and tested out, the central principle that underlies cognitive analytic therapy through the use of Vygotsky's (1978) activity theory. Vygotsky describes how certain provisions by a more experienced other of scaffolded learning (or therapy) "tools" are like building blocks. These are like artifacts that represent the culture of the therapy. The rap, when recorded onto CD, was a tangible and meaningful therapy "tool" and much, much more besides.

The next stage of the therapeutic project was to begin composition of a long rap song about how in real life Shadee might meet a girl. He reflected on the difficulties he would have and how he would develop his social skills to get to know her. The "bling" and the stretch limousines of his fantasy world were gradually replaced by his old familiar regular bus routes and journeys of real life. He sung of his desire to run after the bus that he had glimpsed her catching, just to give her a gift of a single red rose. Within his songs, Shadee's feelings of receiving and giving loving warmth were developing.

This piece of work went on over several weeks. I then had a 2-week break and I asked if he would try to finish the final verse while I was away. The consultant psychiatrist negotiated with staff for Shadee to have access to recording equipment on the ward. Upon my return, he came in for his session and calmly announced, "Stella, I've finished that song." He had written the third verse and for the first time completed the story entirely on his own. From this came the first sense of achievement and a significant sense of empowerment and improvement in self-worth. Shadee had done on his own what we had previously been doing together, and it was a positive completion over which he had ownership.

Shadee gained further recognition of his development in rap song writing in working through his losses. We worked periodically on developing a song about, and for, his father. At times Shadee could not engage with the pain of this subject. At other times he accepted reassurance and became able to persevere and stay with some of the more difficult feelings. After shared thinking, he was able to express his disappointments. He also began to start to see things from his father's point of view. He was able to say how he would like to do things differently if ever he himself became a father. The rap included his feelings of sadness and all he had ever wanted to say to his dad. Thus, Shadee began to mourn his loss and move on. We acknowledged what emotional hard work this had been, with fallow periods of struggling creatively until the emotions became more bearable, at which point there was a return of creativity. Eventually, the multidisciplinary team was able to arrange a phone conversation between Shadee and his father, and this went very well. Shadee told me about this in a nonchalant way. He had taken this reunion maturely in his stride and no doubt with additional support from his nursing team.

I was then invited to present this work at the Canadian Association of Music Therapy annual conference. The opportunity for his rap to be heard outside the walls of the hospital gave Shadee much needed recognition of his skills and development. Consent was approved and we both experienced a sense of achievement. The next step was to enable Shadee to develop his skills and passion in music through an increased ability to work musically with other patients.

Group Therapy: Cognitive Analytic Principles in Action

The individual therapy and Shadee's overall multidisciplinary program had achieved sufficient interpersonal and personality development to suggest that more social integration may now be possible. The first early attempt at group work and individual therapy had demonstrated how young patients require sufficient psychological development and narcissistic recognition to be able to tolerate a group situation. A group specifically for Black Caribbean patients was therefore formed as a specific project, which was supported by the management as a therapeutic initiative to meet the needs of the Black and ethnic minority population. All members had received some individual therapy and all of them wanted to use the medium of rap therapeutically.

The group was carefully planned. The hospital charity, "The League of Friends," provided funding to buy a mixing desk and other recording equipment. A nursing assistant was released from his usual duties for one afternoon a week, during which time he fulfilled his passion by taking on the role of sound engineer as well as participating in the group. This group demonstrated how it is possible to work with staff who have no previous music therapy experience, but who have a passion for music and an interest and commitment to learn.

The aims of the group, all of which were agreed upon by the group, were as follows:

- To promote the ability to self-reflect through recording and listening to their rap and receiving group feedback
- To develop the personal meaning of the verbal content of rap to their real life rather than to fantasy
- To learn from and share reciprocally with each other
- To promote respect and mutual understanding of the different ways that individuals use music creatively
- To discover how to make music with other people
- To provide a therapeutic space where self-expression is not censored

The session would start with discussion and planning of each session. The aim was to use the messages contained in individual raps as a way of reflecting and processing their experiences of life. By safely recognizing and discussing the emotions expressed in the rap within the therapy sessions, and through active self-reflection on their recordings and process, impulsive actions diminished. In this way, group members and Shadee in particular became more tolerant of criticism. We considered through the content of the rap where each of them was in the present, where they aspire to be within their own self-development, and pragmatic aspects of the tasks required to move forward through the hospital system.

Developing Improvisational Skills

Central to my thinking was the use of free improvisation in whatever the group's chosen form may be, but this had to take into account our cultural differences, my lack of rapping ability, and how to develop group cohesion. We would often begin by sitting in a circle, using diverse and culturally specific instruments. For example, to connect and create a group consciousness, we engaged in a djembe drum improvisation. This was a different musical medium for Shadee. In this medium, Shadee was outside his comfort zone, yet he was not exposed. Through the group process he discovered how to extend his abilities of self-expression beyond those of rap. In cognitive analytic therapy we call this the zone of proximal development.

Group rules involved planned negotiation in how to start each piece. This was often difficult, but the group learned how to negotiate. The group would decide who would lead by setting an emotionally based aspect of a practical theme. This was usually focused on a current issue—for example, how to prepare for an annual care program approach or review meeting. The other members of the group could usually follow and support these themes. Thus there was a sense of ownership of each improvisation and a developing ability to share the space and engage with other people's issues.

After individual introductions on one's own choice of instrument and in sharing news (or often sharing the lack of news in how slowly time moved and thus hopes faded), we would then develop the group improvisation. The djembe drum improvisations developed group consciousness and cohesiveness as well as raising energy levels and a sense of embodiment through the use of the hands rather than beaters on the drums.

Individual members then negotiated how to take turns to record a rap over a prerecorded loop of their choice. They would then reflect on the result with the group. This was done not as a performance, but more like an open rehearsal in which mistakes are part of the process and other group members are audience members to whoever was recording their own song.

This structure provided sufficient emotional containment based on the fundamental principle in Black Caribbean culture of "respect." This ensured that the music did not become a chaotic battlefield in which destructive impulses were enacted, or in contrast an uncreative place in which the use of rigid and unchanging rap structures became boring and repetitive for other members. In this way, turn taking, flexibility of responses, and much humor developed.

Once Shadee discovered that he could improvise to some extent with instruments as well as with his voice, he learned how to be more spontaneous by watching and learning from the others. Each member was also supported by my own musical input.

I trained my coworker, a nonmusician, in how to do simple and effective musical techniques that provided a holding quality and a sense of consistency through sustaining an underlying slow beat. I would meanwhile aim to weave the various musical motifs from each individual into an integrated piece of music, for which the group could take ownership.

Shadee gradually overcame his resistance and discovered how to listen and join in with the pervading beat. He also had to learn how to wait if he chose to stop and disengage prior to others choosing to finish. His initial efforts to try to control the ending of the music amounted to ruining the musical creativity of others and the group. He thus risked facing the criticism of his peers. However, the benefit for Shadee was that on subtle, inner levels he became less fearful of endings.

Shadee also discovered how to experiment in music without having developed prior improvisational skills and without the risk of being judged. All the members developed an ability to give constructive feedback to others. In this way, each member received group responses, which were a form of reality testing. The group's carefully mediated responses to each other were accepted and valued, particularly when self-esteem was low and an individual's subjective self-appraisal was negative.

There was always shared time after the group improvisation for each of the four members to record the rap that they were writing and to receive feedback from the rest of the group. The result was the development of both self-identity and group cultural identity.

The underlying theoretical principles of both the analytic and cognitive approaches to narcissism once again came into action in this group-work model. The analytic (Kohut, 1978) involves recognition and resolution of archaic patterns. These archaic patterns often manifested in dominant solo singing and the need to be seen and heard, the emotional qualities of which gradually changed. The cognitive principles of Kernberg (1974) were to promote recognition of the real-life situation rather than defensive or unrealistic fantasies of fame or rescue. This involved reminders that this was a creative form of treatment in a hospital and not a recording studio. These principles enabled nonjudgmental, supportive feedback, acceptance of vulnerability, and the ability to self-evaluate and to listen to oneself.

Group Work Use of Rap

Periods of quiet individual lyric writing sitting round a table often followed from group discussion and sharing. Words were not censored in this group, because they had feeling. Strong words were used to express anger, resentment, and bitterness. These were contained as confidential within the group boundaries. This group rule was unlike the social norm that is necessary in all other aspects of hospital life.

Shadee's predominant theme for lyrics was initially, "If only I had a girlfriend, everything would be all right." This continued to suggest both a sense of helplessness and his need to be rescued by another person as a fantasy, rather than in taking personal responsibility. The lyrics continued, "I am going to keep all my feelings inside myself." This belief required retrospective thought in order for Shadee to reason out why this repressive strategy would not enable him to have his needs met.

Shadee became technically proficient with the recording equipment, which I also learned how to operate when my assistant was no longer able to attend. Shadee would prepare loop tapes to which we could record separate tracks in a self-to-self dialogue. After this, a self-to-other dialogue developed within his rap: "Tell me how do I feel? Tell her how I feel, when the girl I love loves somebody else."

Shadee's lyrics were becoming less egocentric as he began to look outward. Yet he was expressing real and painful feelings that permeated his whole life, namely those of rejection.

The cognitive analytic approach includes the making of meaningful artifacts within the therapy. The music recorded and produced on a CD became an object as well as a symbolic musical expression. As such it was a symbol of the culture of this group.

An important event was that of informed consent in which the group carefully considered whether they wanted to record their songs to be presented at the World Congress of Music Therapy. In their own time, and in consideration with their multidisciplinary teams, they decided that while they themselves could not yet leave the secure confines of the hospital, their creative work and their message could be heard and recognized.

Shadee had recently been deeply affected by the street murder of a school friend and he began to sing about this real-life tragedy. Therefore, the following rap song was one of experience and loss:

Chorus and Title: "Things have got to change, make it a better place for you and me."

Rap: "Street life has got to change there's too much hurt and pain…"

This rap was followed by another one showing his development as a young man who was learning some pickup lines.

Title: KGM 2005.

"Yeah 'scuse me Miss, let me introduce myself. Let me tell you my status. Baby I am a KGM a Kool Gentleman, that's who I am. I don't want no one night stands…… etc."

Shadee's sense of maturity and ability to build relationships was increasing. His commitment to the group process led to increased self-esteem and an ability to learn from the experiences of his peers. Shadee's ability to sustain attention in a group setting had overall developed from a maximum of 20 minutes to 1 hour and 30 minutes. He would be amusing, funny, and entertaining as he made gestures and acted as he used the microphone. He could perform all the movements of a rap artist, with posturing, mimicking, and arm gestures, just like a pop video. He would also tease and he had to learn to accept some reciprocal teasing. Shadee discovered he could join in, learn, and share with peers and contribute verbally as well as on real instruments in group improvisations.

He became more self-reflective. This was demonstrated in one of his later songs, which he called "Wondering": "I'm going to tell her how I feel. I've got all these feelings inside and I'm going to show them."

Shadee continued to choose and record prerecorded loops. The one selected for the above song was more reflective. It had a slower beat, a wistful, serious, almost traditionally religious mood, which started with chords in four-part harmony.

Finally, Shadee teamed up with another group member to write and record collaboratively. In this rap he commented on his peer's rap and they both developed their own narrative to include "freestyle" improvised rap. In this way, they competed as young men in dialogue about what they had to say to each other and about the world. This spontaneously evolved freestyle rap had an entirely new feel to it. As such, it suggested a much less fixed mental state, a form of improvisation which had developed within this cognitive analytic form of music therapy. Initially, such spontaneity had not been possible early in treatment because at that point, neither of these two young men had developed the social skills to have discovered how to collaborate.

This process highlights the necessary patience required in helping an individual to truly develop and integrate effective social skills. Ongoing negotiations within the group process, along with some bargaining and cognitive explanations on my part in terms of the social purposes of connecting within a group improvisation process, were necessary. Perhaps it felt to the group members at times as if the reward was the rapping itself. There were plenty of occasions when the forming, storming, and norming group processes manifested, but respect and harmony would eventually prevail. A significant point for me was that there was no color barrier to my White skin. My attitude, as a mentor of their music, was what they said mattered to them. The respect was mutual and reciprocal.

A contraindication to effective treatment in this group might have been to plunge in at the beginning of group treatment with rap that was not reflective or considerate of others. At such times, hate and denigration of authority or of others or of the self might have prevailed and possibly even become destructive. There would have been no opportunity for social cohesiveness to develop or for these young men to be supported and validated in the process of mourning. Their medium for mourning was their rapping about their hardships, losses, loves, and anger. My role had to be bold enough to challenge any antisocial tendencies and to contain and empathize with their feelings.

Shadee often worked for weeks on his lyrics, which demonstrated acceptance rather than frustration and rejection. He developed tenacity and respect as he discovered how to share the therapy space with others. He could now wait; he gained status and recognition as his views, skills, and opinions were taken seriously.

Conclusion

The active ingredients of rap are complex. They include structured rhythm, poetry, lyrics, and spontaneity. The form develops with both structured choruses and fluid freestyle rap with the use of sound technology in creating prerecorded loops and sound effects that both underpin and enhance the overall creativity. It is a personal form of musical expression that can be both emotionally significant and aesthetically pleasing not only for Black Caribbean patients but also across cultures. Most of all, rap can encapsulate and externalize anger and loss and it can incorporate the fundamental therapeutic process of mourning. As such it merits a serious place in future therapeutic treatment and research.

Changes in presentation of the Black Caribbean males in the group were motivated through rap coupled with the need to feel accepted by others. I too felt accepted by the whole group, albeit as a White middle-aged woman. My skin color appeared not to matter, but none of us were blind to this aspect. My musical knowledge and openness and my acceptance of their musical language was what mattered to them.

Shadee came to recognize the need for others, which led to increased development of social skills and collaboration. He recognized and expressed in his songs his loss of love, experiences of discrimination, social exclusion, and hardship.

He began to accept his own vulnerability and mistakes through self-reflection in recording and listening to his raps. The role of the musical metaphor to life prevailed throughout treatment and in the exploration of underlying bigger issues that were raised through the use of metaphor. The value of hope and being able to change sustained Shadee and replaced his initial hopelessness. The need for tenacity and self-respect in a tough environment developed as well as recognition of the need to develop self-reflection and insight through feedback from others.

Justice or Revenge

Tselis and Booss (2003) conclude that personality and behavioral changes can be prominent in infections of the brain. Antisocial behavior, poor memory, and an inability to organize behavior can lead to dependence on others, or isolation. These aspects were all apparent in Shadee. Tselis and Booss conclude that society's response to such compromised individuals should be therapeutic, not punitive. Attempts at rehabilitation, rather than incarceration, appear to be the most just and humane response. This case study supports their view.

Outcomes

Shadee did not receive a diagnosis of personality disorder; he continued to make good progress with very significant and meaningful input from psychologists, speech and language therapists, and other therapists concurrent with his music therapy. While his progress was a team effort, his passion was rap, and hence rap was central to his therapeutic process.

Shadee was transferred to a lower-secure "villa" ward, where more freedom of movement is permitted. He was subsequently conditionally discharged by a mental health review tribunal to hostel accommodation near his mother's home. At his 3-month review, now living in the community, he was making good progress and attending college part time. His subjects included music technology. Shadee performed rap in some local clubs, also performing as a DJ. His therapy using rap was developed with a view to helping him find out who he really was, improving his self esteem, and validating his sense of self in relation to others and in how he communicates and sees himself in the world. Rap played a central role in helping him to be in the real world rather than in fantasy.

Shadee was also able to hold down a part-time job at a supermarket so that he could support his musical interests in a real way. When the consultant psychiatrist asked him what he said when people asked him what he had been doing previously, Shadee laughed and said that he would say that he'd been doing "a little bit of this, and a little bit of that." This was a very appropriate and discreet way to cover the difficult years of incarceration!

Postscript

Several weeks before the writing of this chapter, as I was walking in the woodlands, my mobile phone rang. A tentative voice said, "This is Shadee."

He asked whether I minded that he had found my number and whether I remembered him. I assured him that of course I remembered him and as he was rehabilitated, I hoped that our mutual trust and respect may still be alive. He said that he just wanted to tell me that he was working in a recording studio and living independently.

References

Compton Dickinson, S. J. (2003). *Community culture and conflict: The role of creativity.* London: BSMT.

Compton Dickinson, S. J. (2004). *Community culture and conflict. Part 2: Changes.* London: BSMT.

Compton Dickinson, S. (2006, December 22). Beyond body, beyond words: Cognitive analytic music therapy in forensic psychiatry—New approaches in the treatment of personality disordered offenders. *Music Therapy Today, VII*(4), 839–875. Retrieved from http://www.musictherapyworld.net

Keating, F., Robertson, D., McCullogh, A., & Francis, E. (2002). *Breaking the circles of fear. A review of the relationship between mental health services and African and Caribbean communities.* London: Sainsbury Centre for Mental Health.

Kernberg, O. F. (1974). Contrasting views on the nature and treatment of narcissistic personalities. *Journal of the American Psychoanalytic Association, 222,* 255–267.

Kohut, H. (1971). *The analysis of the self.* Madison, CT: International Universities Press.

McGuire, P. (2004, June 15). *An overview of structural and functional brain imaging studies in schizophrenia.* Institute of Psychiatry, 1-day seminar, Neurobiological Developments in Schizophrenia.

Ryle, A., & Kerr, I. (2002). *Introducing cognitive analytic therapy.* Chichester, UK: John Wiley and Sons.

Souflas, P. (2005). Young people in high secure hospitals. Poster presentation at Royal College of Psychiatrists Forensic Psychiatry Conference, Dublin.

Tselis, T., & Booss, J. (2003). Behavioural consequences of infections of the central nervous system: With emphasis on viral infections. *Journal of the American Academy of Psychiatry and the Law, 321,* 289–298.

Vygotsky, L. S. (1978). *Mind in society: The development of higher psychological processes.* Cambridge, MA: Harvard University Press.

Winnicott, D. (1971). *Playing and reality.* London: Tavistock.

Winnicott, D. (1960). Ego distortion in terms of true and false self. In *The maturational process and the facilitating environment: Studies in the theory of emotional development.* New York: International Universities Press, 1965, pp. 140–152.

Index

Printed in Great Britain
by Amazon.co.uk, Ltd.,
Marston Gate.